INVISIBLE HANDS, INVISIBLE OBJECTIVES

Invisible Hands, Invisible Objectives

Bringing Workplace Law and Public Policy into Focus

STEPHEN F. BEFORT
and JOHN W. BUDD

STANFORD ECONOMICS AND FINANCE
An Imprint of Stanford University Press
Stanford, California

Stanford University Press
Stanford, California

Printed in the United States of America on acid-free, archival-quality paper

Library of Congress Cataloging-in-Publication Data
Befort, Stephen F., 1948-
Invisible hands, invisible objectives : bringing workplace law and public policy into focus / Stephen F. Befort and John W. Budd.
p. cm.
Includes bibliographical references and index.
ISBN 978-0-8047-6153-6 (cloth : alk. paper)—ISBN 978-0-8047-6154-3 (pbk. : alk. paper)
1. Labor laws and legislation—United States. 2. Industrial relations—United States. I. Budd, John W. II. Title.
KF3319. B44 2009
344.7301—dc22
2008036650

Typeset by Bruce Lundquist in 10/12.5 Palatino

The world has been rushing on with such fiery animation to get work and ever more work done, it has had no time to think of dividing the wages; and has merely left them to be scrambled for by the law of the stronger, law of supply and demand, law of laissez-faire, and other idle laws and unlaws—saying, in its dire haste to get the work done, that is well enough.

—Thomas Carlyle, 1843

Contents

Detailed Table of Contents

Tables

Figures

Preface

THIS BOOK IS THE CULMINATION of a multidisciplinary partnership between an industrial relations scholar and a legal scholar. In 2004, one of us (Budd) published *Employment with a Human Face: Balancing Efficiency, Equity, and Voice*. That book rejects the all-too-frequent focus of employment-related scholarship on processes and rules and argues that discourse on the employment relationship should be grounded in the objectives of the employment relationship. Statutory rights and obligations established by employment and labor laws, for example, are not ends in themselves; they are means of achieving one or more fundamental objectives. Moreover, work-related processes and laws are ultimately rooted in specific models of how one thinks the employment relationship works. But to the detriment of productive discourse and understanding, these models are often left unstated. In the meantime, the other one of us (Befort) was hard at work publishing law review articles criticizing the current state of U.S. employment and labor law and proposing specific reforms. *Invisible Objectives, Invisible Hands* blends our work to present an evaluation of the U.S. system of public policies on work and a comprehensive portfolio of reform proposals that are explicitly rooted in three objectives of the employment relationship—efficiency, equity, and voice—and a pluralist view of how this relationship works.

It should be noted that while reform proposals are an important derivative of this framework, the need for reform is not our central motivation. We see the central contribution of *Invisible Hands, Invisible Objectives* as explicitly rather than implicitly defining concrete objectives and models for workplace law and public policy. We therefore see a broad audience for this book. First, whether or not they are interested in specific reforms, workplace scholars within and outside of legal circles should be concerned with explicitly rooting analyses in the objectives and models of the employment relationship. We therefore hope that our analytical framework will be viewed as intellectually important and will spur our academic colleagues to debate objectives and models, independent from the need for reform. Second, this book can be used by students to develop a deeper understanding of workplace law and public policy than is otherwise possible. Third, we hope that this book proves useful for public policymakers, worker advocates, and others who are interested in reforming workplace law and public policy and seek a meaningful intellectual foundation for this important enterprise.

This is an ambitious project. Numerous books have been written on each element of employment and labor law that we bring together here in a holistic framework. We hope that readers accustomed to rich details on specific policies will excuse our omission of some details in the interest of providing a much-needed comprehensive or "big picture" approach. We do not intend to suggest that details are not important, and we are indebted to too many authors to name for helping us understand the nuances of many policies. We also have strived to make this book accessible to anyone with an interest in work, whether they are students, activists, policymakers, or individuals who simply work for a living. It is our hope that this accessibility will foster local, national, and international dialogues on the nature of work generally, and on work-related public policies specifically.

We are grateful to our editor, Margo Beth Crouppen, for her enthusiasm and encouragement, to two reviewers for their helpful comments, and to Judith Hibbard and the Stanford University Press team for making the production process go so smoothly. We also thank Rafael Gomez, Stefan Zagelmeyer, workshop attendees at the University of Toronto and York University, and conference attendees at the Labor and Employment Relations annual meetings and the European Congress of the International Industrial Relations Association for their insights. Former law students Kimberly Fuhrman, Sarah Link Schultz, Jessica Clay, and Amy York provided invaluable research assistance. Last, this project would not have been possible without the generous research and intellectual support of the University of Minnesota's Carlson School of Management and Law School, and without the support and patience of our families.

Minneapolis, Minnesota
May 2008

Abbreviations

ADA	Americans with Disabilities Act
ADEA	Age Discrimination in Employment Act
AFL	American Federation of Labor
CEO	chief executive officer
COBRA	Consolidated Omnibus Budget Reconciliation Act
EITC	Earned Income Tax Credit
ERISA	Employee Retirement Income Security Act
EU	European Union
FAA	Federal Arbitration Act
FDI	Foreign Direct Investment
FLSA	Fair Labor Standards Act
FMCS	Federal Mediation and Conciliation Service
FMLA	Family and Medical Leave Act
GDP	gross domestic product
HIPAA	Health Insurance Portability and Accountability Act
HMO	health maintenance organization
ILO	International Labor Organization
IRA	Individual Retirement Account
JTPA	Job Training Partnership Act

META	Model Employment Termination Act
NAFTA	North American Free Trade Agreement
NLRA	National Labor Relations Act
NLRB	National Labor Relations Board
OASDHI	Old Age, Survivors, Disability, and Health Insurance
OECD	Organization for Economic Cooperation and Development
OSHA	Occupational Safety and Health Administration
PBGC	Pension Benefit Guaranty Corporation
PPA	Pension Protection Act
WIA	Workforce Investment Act
WRPS	Worker Representation and Participation Survey
WTO	World Trade Organization

INVISIBLE HANDS, INVISIBLE OBJECTIVES

PART ONE

Workplace Law and Public Policy

The world is suffering, today, from an industrial yellow fever, not less fatal, but I am certain, as preventable. Search for the mosquito! That ought to be a slogan with investigators on both sides of the labor question.

—Mother Jones, 1913

CHAPTER 1

The Goals and Assumptions of Workplace Law and Public Policy

The Need for Explicitness

THE HEADLINES ARE FAMILIAR: "Survey Finds 43.6 Million Uninsured in U.S." "Wal-Mart Looms over Two Bills to Improve Worker Health Care." "After Years of Growth, What about Workers' Share?" "Thousands Are Laid Off. What's New?" "Job Discrimination Complaints on the Rise." "Suits Allege Pay Violations at Restaurants." "As Demands on Workers Grow, Groups Push for Paid Family and Sick Leave."[1]

It is therefore not surprising that calls to reform the U.S. legal regulations and public policies pertaining to work and the employment relationship are reaching a crescendo.[2] And there are signs that the political landscape might finally be ripe for significant policy reform—the increase in the federal minimum wage in 2007, for example, was the first such increase in a decade. Missing from all of the arguments and proposals, however, is a conceptual basis for understanding alternative perspectives on government regulation of the employment relationship and for designing effective laws and public policies.

The principal objective of this book is to provide such a conceptual basis. We start with what we believe is a simple yet powerful and overlooked principle: the rationale for government regulation of any market-based activity is rooted in the intersection of the objectives of that activity and its operation. Introductory economics courses, for example, typically teach that government regulation is desirable only when regulation is able to fix a market failure. Underlying this result are assumptions about specific objectives (the efficient allocation of resources) and operational features (rational agents pursuing economic self-interest in markets that ideally are perfectly competitive). Assuming different objectives (such as a fair allocation of resources) or operating features (such as individuals seeking psychological fulfillment) can yield very different prescriptions for government regulation. Workplace law and public policy, therefore, must be understood, analyzed, studied, and reformed within a framework of (1) *explicit objectives* of the employment relationship, and (2) *explicit models* of how the employment relationship works.

Unfortunately, this is usually not how workplace law and public policy is approached. Although scholars and policymakers may seek various ends and objectives in workplace law and public policy (and many are possible), they often fail to articulate them explicitly. Too often, law students are trained in the letter of the law and human resources students are trained in its application, but neither group is educated about the fundamental *purposes* of workplace law and public policy. A deeper understanding of either field requires the recognition of foundational objectives. Otherwise, administration of a policy is reduced to a myopic satisfaction of rules at the expense of a deeper fulfillment of critical objectives. The failure to identify fundamental objectives similarly causes policy debates to focus narrowly on incomplete or misguided objectives. For example, the failure to recognize that the ultimate purpose of a strike replacement ban is to achieve goals that we term "equity" and "voice" has reduced the debates over such bans to technical squabbles over whether a replaced striker has been fired or not, and to narrow disputes over whether such bans cause longer strikes and reduce investment. Although such questions are important, they ignore the fundamental questions of whether a strike replacement ban would promote equity and voice.

Compounding the problem of obscured objectives is the problem of unstated models of how the employment relationship works. As we show later in this chapter, one can believe that the employment relationship works in very different ways: labor markets may or may not be perfectly competitive; employees can be seen as seeking only economic rewards or as also wanting psychological and democratic fulfillment; and employers' interests might align or sharply clash with their employees' interests. These different conceptualizations underlie dramatically different visions of workplace law and public policy, but these visions too often lack explicitness. As a result, students and the public fail to fully understand workplace law and public policy while scholars, policymakers, and advocates from different perspectives talk past each other in their academic analyses and policy debates.

By emphasizing the pursuit of efficiency through the invisible hand of free markets, the neoliberal market thinking that currently dominates public discourse further stifles explicit discussions of employment relationship objectives while also obscuring alternative perspectives on how the employment relationship works. In other words, the area of workplace law and public policy has been reduced to an arena of invisible hands, invisible objectives. Bringing workplace law and public policy into focus requires recognizing that workplace law and public policy is rooted in the intersection of the objectives and the operation of the employment relationship. The central thesis of this book, therefore, is that understanding, analyzing, studying, and reforming workplace law and public policy requires recognizing *explicit* objectives and *explicit* models.

Explicit Objectives

Workplace law and public policy need to have an overarching purpose tied to the fundamental objectives of the employment relationship. These objectives provide the anchor for discourse and analyses of public policies on work. Without this anchor, there is little basis for evaluating whether current employment and labor laws need reform, and there is no foundation on which to build new policies. The long-standing emphasis in scholarship and policy debates on how processes work must therefore be replaced by a deeper discussion of what employment should achieve in a democratic society.

Analyses, debates, and reform proposals pertaining to employment-related public policies should purposefully revolve around the objectives of the employment relationship. But what are these objectives? We follow the framework developed in an earlier book and structure our analyses around a triad of fundamental objectives (see Figure 1.1):

- *Efficiency*: effective, profit-maximizing use of labor and other scarce resources;
- *Equity*: fairness in the distribution of economic rewards, the administration of employment policies, and the provision of employee security;
- *Voice*: meaningful participation in workplace decision-making.[3]

Efficiency is a standard of economic or business performance; equity is a standard of justice; voice is a standard of employee involvement in shaping their lives. Note that voice is independent of distributional issues; it is an activity in which workers engage. Equity and voice can be pursued together (as in labor unions) or through different mechanisms

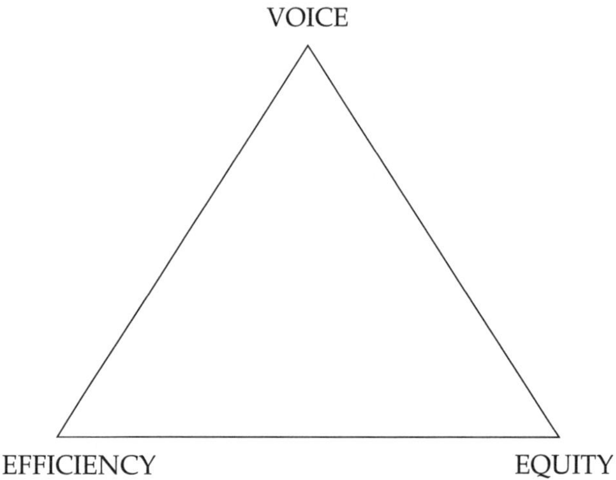

FIGURE 1.1 The objectives of the employment relationship. Source: John W. Budd, *Employment with a Human Face: Balancing Efficiency, Equity, and Voice* (Ithaca, N.Y.: Cornell University Press, 2004).

(as in minimum wage standards for equity and employee free speech protections for voice).

The framework of efficiency, equity, and voice is a powerful one. Collectively, these three dimensions succinctly capture the key objectives of the employment relationship; individually, they allow for a wide range of underlying components. This framework can therefore be used to compare employment systems in different countries, analyze different labor union strategies, evaluate options for workplace dispute resolution, analyze international initiatives for improving labor standards on a global basis, and teach courses on labor relations.[4] In this book, we apply this powerful framework to employment-related public policies. We assert that workplace law and public policy can be fully understood only by analyzing the effects on competitiveness and productivity (that is, efficiency), on the fairness of the distribution and security of economic rewards (equity), and on opportunities for workers to shape their working lives (voice). In effect, efficiency, equity, and voice provide an explicit scorecard for work-related public policies. Part Two of this book applies this scorecard to the contemporary U.S. system of workplace law and public policy; additional details on the dimensions of efficiency, equity, and voice are developed and discussed at that time.

Admittedly, we are not the first to call for a more purposeful approach to analyzing workplace law and public policy. More than twenty years ago, noted Harvard law professor Charles Fried wrote that "the time has come for a review of the premises, and not just the details, of our employment-law system" and that "we should consider afresh what goals such a system should seek to attain." The goals Fried noted specifically are "freedom of association; the provision of a social minimum of resources; the redistribution of proprietary rights in the products of labor; job security; freedom from harassing, demeaning, and arbitrary treatment; industrial democracy; efficiency; and industrial peace." In effect, these goals reduce to considerations of efficiency, equity, and voice. Another noted Harvard law professor, Paul Weiler, has argued that employment and labor law reform needs to be based squarely on the objectives of workers. Paul Osterman has identified efficiency, equity, opportunity, voice, and security as the labor market objectives that public policies should shape. A distinguished team of MIT researchers has argued that "it is time to revisit and recommit to the core values regarding the role of work and its place in society" and that policy reforms must be "constantly [tested] against these values." Ellen Dannin also has forcefully advocated for a values-based approach to reforming U.S. labor law.[5] We applaud these efforts, but they are exceptional rather than the norm. As such, we believe that there remains a void that can be filled by the framework we develop here.

Some might disagree with our specific employment relationship objectives. Marxist and other critical scholars might criticize the omission of power in our employment relationship objectives. To this we respond that power is not an objective in its own right. This is not to say that power issues are not important. Each country's system of workplace law and public policy is shaped by power dynamics in the political process, and employee power is critical for delivering equity and voice—just as free markets underlie efficiency. But power and free markets are not ends in themselves, and they are therefore not explicit objectives. More generally, regardless of the specific objectives used, it is essential that scholars, activists, and policymakers explicitly identify the desired objectives and ground their research, proposals, and policies in them. Otherwise, there is little basis for analysis, understanding, and debate. Note further that efficiency, equity, and voice (or other objectives) can be used analytically to understand the employment relationship without normatively judging the relative importance of each dimension. In Part Three, we apply this analytical framework to the normative challenge of assessing how workplace law and public policy should work. There we argue that efficiency, equity, and voice should be balanced. While some might disagree with our normative recommendations in Part Three, the analytical power of focusing on these explicit objectives of the employment relationship is not weakened by such disagreements.

Explicit Models

Public policies on work and the employment relationship consist of laws and regulations establishing labor standards with which employers and employees must comply. But embedded in these public policies is a deeper issue—what are the rules for making the web of workplace rules that define each person's employment? How are the literal rules of behavior as well as broader written and unwritten policies regarding compensation, benefits, advancement opportunities, and other "rules" determined? Are they mandated by government laws? Are they dictated by the marketplace? Are they established unilaterally by managers and human resources professionals, or by workers themselves? Or do they result from negotiations between employers and labor unions or other employee associations? Each of these possibilities represents a different form of workplace governance.[6]

Public policies critically affect the nature of workplace governance not only by specifying standards for some workplace "rules"—such as those requiring minimum wages and nondiscriminatory hiring and firing—but also by establishing the broader parameters of workplace governance. A general lack of work-related public policies leaves workplace governance in the invisible hand of the marketplace and the visible hands of human resource managers and common-law judges. Extensive government-mandated standards insert lawmakers into workplace rule-making. And the legal protection or promotion of labor unions or other employee associations can create a shared model of workplace governance, such as through collective bargaining or mandatory employee consultation.

The different forms of workplace governance are rooted intellectually and analytically in four visions or models of work—the egoist, unitarist, pluralist, and critical employment relationships. As summarized in Table 1.1, these four frames of reference differ along three dimensions: (1) the extent to which markets are seen as perfectly competitive, (2) whether labor is seen as just an economic commodity, and (3) the nature of conflict (or lack thereof) assumed to characterize the employment relationship. Understanding these fundamental perspectives is essential for understanding the employment relationship generally, and workplace law and public policy specifically.[7]

The egoist model of the employment relationship is derived from mainstream economics and is driven by rational, individual self-interest,

TABLE 1.1
Four Explicit Models of the Employment Relationship

Model	Key Assumptions	Workplace Law and Public Policy Applications
The Egoist Employment Relationship / *Neoclassical Economics*	Markets are perfectly competitive, so employers and employees are equals and must abide by the market Labor is just an economic commodity; employment is an economic transaction Voluntary, self-interested, mutually beneficial transactions, not conflict, define the employment relationship	Pre-1930s "old deal" and current global era with emphasis on free markets, individual liberty, and personal responsibility
The Unitarist Employment Relationship / *Human Resource Management*	Markets are imperfectly competitive, so employers and employees have choices Labor is not just a commodity; workers also have feelings and aspirations Employer and employee interests can always be aligned with well-designed managerial policies	Postwar employment law era with primacy of nonunion human resource management practices
The Pluralist Employment Relationship / *Industrial Relations*	Markets are imperfectly competitive, so employers have greater bargaining power than employees Labor is not just a commodity; workers also have moral worth and democratic rights Employers and employees have some conflicts of interest that are confined to the employment relationship	New Deal era with emphasis on labor unions, social insurance, and mandated labor standards to balance the employment relationship
The Critical Employment Relationship / *Critical Industrial Relations*	Segmented labor markets perpetuate inequality and employer control Labor is not just a commodity; workers also have moral worth and democratic rights Employment relationship conflict is embedded in a broader system of social relations among persistently dominant and subordinate groups or classes	An understanding of workplace law and public policy rooted in power and class dynamics; proposals for fundamental structural reforms

especially as pursued through market-based economic transactions. Labor is conceptualized as a commodity like any other useful resource, and work is conceptualized as a lousy activity that individuals endure only to earn income. As such, there is not a conflict between employers and employees; rather, they simply engage in voluntary, mutually beneficial transactions buying and selling units of labor as in any other free-market transaction. In short, economics sees itself as "a science of exchange rather than production" or conflict, and assumes that "both parties must benefit from voluntary exchange; otherwise that exchange would never have occurred in the first place."[8] Our egoist label is therefore not intended as a pejorative term with negative connotations; rather, it is intended to highlight the centrality of self-interest rather than benevolence or conflict. In the famous words of Adam Smith, "It is not from the benevolence of the butcher, the brewer, or the baker that we expect our dinner, but from their regard to their own interest."[9]

If markets are assumed to be *perfectly* competitive, then employers and employees are economic equals. If employers and employees are also equal in their political influence and legal expertise, then neoclassical economic theory shows that abuses and exploitation are prevented by perfect competition in the labor market. Wages are never seen as too low or too high; they simply reflect each worker's productive contributions. Moreover, with these assumptions, unregulated free markets optimize the use of scarce resources in the best interests of all concerned—shareholders, workers, consumers, and others.[10] This is admittedly a stylized portrayal of what is now a very sophisticated body of economic theory, but a lengthier, more nuanced description would not alter the implications for public policy or the contrasts with alternative models. When expanded from the employment relationship to the economic system more generally, the neoclassical economic premises of the egoist model give rise to a neoliberal market ideology. In other words, as used in this book, neoliberal market ideology is defined as a belief that economic outcomes are of primary importance, and are best-served by laissez-faire public policies that support property rights, free markets, and free trade.[11]

If markets do not fulfill the neoclassical economist's assumption of *perfect* competition, or if there are political or legal imbalances between employees and employers, then the egoist employment relationship's emphasis on unrestrained individual self-interest is harder to embrace, both morally and as a means of maximizing economic welfare. Three other models of the employment relationship reject the assumptions that markets are completely deterministic and that labor is simply an economic commodity. In these alternative visions, markets are seen as important, especially for allocating scarce resources to productive uses, but are believed to fall short of the ideal of perfect competition because of information problems, unequal access to financial and legal resources, behavioral elements of decision-making such as fairness or social pressure, cognitive limitations that undermine coldly rational decision-making, and other real-world complications. Employers and employees cannot get too far out of line from what the market will bear, but labor markets are not seen as perfectly deterministic—employers and employees can make choices about how much to pay, how hard to work, and the like; neither are they seen as perfectly equalizing—employers often have power advantages over employees. The primacy of markets is also weakened in these three models by the belief that labor is not just an economic commodity. Workers are seen as human beings with psychological and physical needs and aspirations, and perhaps even moral worth and democratic rights.[12] As Henry Ford is reported to have once complained, "Why is it that when I hire a pair of hands, I get a human being as well?"

The fundamental distinction between the remaining three models lies in their assumptions about conflicts between employers and employees. The unitarist model of the employment relationship assumes that labor and management have the same interests.[13] If there is employer-employee conflict in a specific workplace, it is assumed to stem from poor employment-related managerial practices, not from something inherent in the employment relationship. Scholarship in this area is frequently rooted in industrial/organizational psychology, and therefore emphasizes behavioral influences on decision-making, such as fairness, social pressure, and cognitive limitations, rather than economic self-interest.[14] The combination of unitarist interests and behavioral decision-making forms the foundation for the human resource management school of thought, which believes that fair employment policies and practices will align the interests of employers and employees. The practice of human resource management therefore focuses on creating human resources policies that benefit employers and employees simultaneously.

The model of the pluralist employment relationship, in contrast, assumes that there are multiple parties (e.g., employers and employees) with legitimate but sometimes conflicting interests—employers might want lower labor costs, flexibility, and an intense pace of work while employees might want higher wages, employment security, and a safe workplace—as well as shared interests such as quality products, productive workers, and profitable companies.[15] The key distinction with the unitarist model is that the pluralist model does not assume that all employer and employee interests are shared. Higher wages mean that less of a firm's net income can be paid to shareholders; higher dividend payments reduce a firm's ability to pay higher wages or bonuses. To wit, in a week that Microsoft publicly announced that it was cutting employee benefits by $1 billion, its stock significantly outperformed other technology stocks because stock analysts saw these benefits as "fat."[16] This reflects a pluralist rather than unitarist perspective.

The pluralist belief that some employer-employee interests conflict magnifies the importance of the assumption that labor markets are imperfectly competitive. Taken together, these assumptions imply that the employment relationship is a bargained relationship between employers and employees with differing levels of bargaining power. Institutions and customs shape these interactions and are therefore essential determinants of employment outcomes. This analytical perspective is embraced most strongly by the industrial relations school of thought and in institutionalist labor economics.[17] In industrial relations scholarship, labor unions are seen as a productive counterweight to corporate bargaining power, while public policies such as social insurance programs and mandated minimum standards also help protect all workers against the vagaries of the business cycle and corporate power.[18] Unlike in the egoist and unitarist models, employees' interests are not always well served by competitive markets or corporate goodwill and self-interest. Instead, labor market interventions are needed to help overcome market imperfections while also serving noneconomic goals such as equity and voice.

Last, the model of the critical employment relationship sees employer-employee conflict as embedded in a deeper system of social relations between competing groups—not confined to the workplace—in largely economic terms as in the pluralist model. This assumption underlies the critical industrial relations school that encompasses Marxist, feminist, and other sociological perspectives that are rooted in analytical foundations that emphasize antagonistic interests, power, control, and resources. With antagonistic interests, competing social groups vie for superiority, and the more powerful group uses its access to resources to structure relationships to serve its own interests. But again because of antagonistic interests, the members of subordinate groups resist, and struggles for control become an important element of intergroup dynamics. In orthodox Marxist thought, the competing groups are the capitalist and working classes, and the former's ownership of the means of production underlies class conflict and capitalist power. Numerous contemporary theories deviate from the orthodox Marxist paradigm, but similarly highlight the importance of conflicting interests, power dynamics, control, and resistance in the modern employment relationship.[19]

The critical perspective forces us to take questions of class seriously—not "class" defined purely by income levels, but in terms of "relative power over the terms and conditions of employment."[20] In doing so, issues of inequality are brought to the fore. In critical scholarship, inequality is not a natural and just by-product of market exchange as in neoclassical economic scholarship; rather inequality is socially constructed through institutions that reproduce existing differences in resources and opportunities. Labor markets are not seen as neutral forums for matching employees and employers, but as segmented or balkanized social creations in which social norms, networks, and credentials perpetuate the existing advantages of certain workers, such as educated white men, while limiting the opportunities of others. Corporate-controlled internal labor markets and human resource management practices are similarly seen as intentionally designed to control a workforce prone to resistance and as enforced by inequalities in property rights over productive assets. In a similar vein, government-sponsored training programs can be seen as controlling rather than benefiting employees.[21] Moving beyond concepts of class, the critical perspective's emphasis on power and inequality raises important issues pertaining to gender, race, and other social strata, such as the undervaluing of "women's work."[22]

One cannot understand workplace law and public policy without explicitly appreciating these four alternative models of the employment relationship. In the egoist model, workplace laws and public policies are essentially seen as bad because they distort free markets and benefit special interests at the expense of others. State intervention is narrowly limited to cases where a clear market failure can be improved, not worsened, by regulation. In the unitarist perspective, work-related public policies are largely seen as unnecessary. Well-designed and properly executed human resource management policies are the preferred mechanisms for fulfilling the needs of employers and employees, though perhaps some mandated minimal standards are useful for preventing unenlightened employers from undermining a desired baseline of good human resource management practice.

The pluralist model, in contrast, views workplace laws and public policies as important because they are necessary to counter corporate bargaining power advantages and to balance efficiency, equity, and voice in democratic, capitalist societies. Again, this is not to say that free markets are bad; rather, it is to say that institutional interventions can help markets work even better. In the critical model, work-related public policies reflect antagonistic interests based on social strata and are insufficient by themselves to fully protect workers' interests. They can perhaps soften the harshest aspects of capitalism for workers, but because the employment relationship is seen as embedded in systemic sociopolitical inequalities, more systemic changes than minimum wage laws or family leave policies are needed for true reform. From this perspective, workplace law and public policy is seen as manipulative—dominant interest groups enact limited public policies to mollify those who would press for deeper reform, or use their power to limit the effectiveness of existing public policies. Overall, then, because of the dramatically different implications of the four models of the employment relationship for government regulation, they must be made explicit.

Explicit Reform

Many argue that the U.S. system of public policies for governing the workplace is broken.[23] This partly reflects the failure of labor and employment law to keep pace with societal and economic change. Since the 1930s, the proportion of the population with four or more years of high school has gone from less than 20 to over 80 percent, blue-collar workers have declined from being fully half of the nonagricultural labor force to less than one quarter today, and life expectancy has increased from less than sixty years to more than seventy-five years. So perhaps the labor laws and public policies on social insurance crafted for a 1930s workforce no longer fit the contemporary workplace. Similarly, modern U.S. employment law began to emerge in the 1960s, but since that time the percentage of women who work outside the home has jumped from 35 to 60 percent, the percentage of households headed by a married couple has fallen from 75 to 50 percent, and the percentage of workers represented by a union has declined from around 30 percent to less than 15 percent.[24]

Since 1960, imports of goods and services into the United States have increased by more than 7,000 percent, while computers have gone from nonexistent to ubiquitous. Monopolistic smokestack industries have given way to a hypercompetitive digital economy. Standardization, stability, security, and bureaucracy have been replaced in today's workplace by customization, flexibility, insecurity, and teamwork. Ideals of lifetime employment (even if only imagined for some) have been pushed aside by the realities of contingent employment and outsourcing. As such, today's worker, family, and workplace could hardly have been imagined by the policymakers of yesteryear who crafted most of the public policies that continue to govern today's U.S. employment relationship. The U.S. system of labor and employment law is largely built on the assumptions that workers are male breadwinners in traditional families working for large companies that dominate the world economy through mass production of standardized products with stable jobs and clear distinctions between managers and workers. It therefore can be argued that, as these assumptions have become increasingly inaccurate over the past half-century, so too has our system of labor and employment law become outdated.[25]

Others argue that public policies for governing the U.S. workplace are broken because of technical inconsistencies. First, many workers are omitted from the coverage of various laws. More than 20 percent of all private sector workers lack the protections of the National Labor Relations Act (NLRA) because they are supervisors or independent contractors, they work for companies that are too small to be covered, or they work in agriculture.[26] Some laws provide benefits only to employees who work a certain number of hours for an employer and therefore exclude many temporary or contingent employees. Independent contractors are legally not employees and are therefore not covered by U.S. labor and employment laws; some companies strategically designate workers as independent contractors in an attempt to deny workers coverage and benefits under various statutes. Second, exclusions vary from law to law. "Small" employers are usually excluded, but the definition of small can be $500,000 in annual sales (Fair Labor Standards Act), $50,000 in annual sales (nonretail establishments under the NLRA), fifteen employees (Title VII of the Civil Rights Act), or fifty employees within a seventy-five-mile radius (Family and Medical Leave Act). And judges do not always consistently determine whether specific employees are excluded because they are supervisors or independent contractors. While different legal definitions might sensibly stem from the unique needs of each policy, critics have attacked the inefficiencies and inequities of this aspect of U.S. workplace law and public policy.[27]

Our framework reveals a more fundamental yet overlooked problem that goes beyond the changing nature of work and technical inconsistencies: the U.S. system of workplace law and public policy has conflicting intellectual foundations. As we explain in the next chapter, the collective rights of the NLRA (rooted in the pluralist model of the employment relationship), the individual rights of the post–World War II employment law era (loosely consistent with the unitarist model), and the continued importance of employment-at-will (consistent with the egoist model) emphasize different fundamental objectives and are rooted in different visions of how the employment relationship works.

Beyond providing the necessary intellectual foundation for understanding workplace law and public policy, an explicit recognition of alternative objectives and models of the employment relationship has important practical implications. While the patchwork system of workplace law and public policy undoubtedly reflects the changing power dynamics of various interest groups in different eras, we submit that a failure to explicitly recognize these objectives and models as policies are developed and as legal doctrines evolve has contributed to the creation of a confusing and incoherent system with contradictory intellectual foundations. This, in turn, has created doctrinal inconsistencies and outright conflicts between various laws and public policies, as well as a maze of multiple forums for pursuing claims. In fact, in the United States the law of the workplace is typically seen as having distinct areas, such as common-law doctrine pertaining to employment-at-will, antidiscrimination employment law, and labor law. Richard Fischl has documented the increase in doctrinal integration across these areas and the resulting need for a more holistic understanding of workplace law.[28] Being explicit about the objectives and models of the employment relationship takes this further by revealing why these areas developed distinctly and by illuminating the problems of layering them onto the modern employment relationship without recognizing the different assumptions that underlie each approach.

So how should the matter of reforming U.S. employment and labor law be tackled? Public policies are usually considered on an issue-by-issue basis—an academic journal article might focus on strike replacement policies, a union or employer policy briefing might be limited to paid family leave, or a legislative proposal might deal only with pension reform. Because of the complexity of work-related policy issues, this focused approach is important, but it is easy to lose sight of the big picture. More than a century of piecemeal development has created an urgent need to take a broader view and reconcile the largely separate domains of employment law, labor law, and other work-related public policies into one coherent, updated body of workplace law and public policy.

Moreover, debates over reforming work-related public policies—in the United States and around the globe—have largely been unproductive to date, at least partly because such debates are frequently divorced from their intellectual underpinnings. When this happens, and reform proposals are therefore seen as naive or irrational, or as serving special interests, debates are acrimonious and polarizing rather than constructive and consensus-building. But each model of workplace governance should not be seen as a way to benefit some special interest—such as corporations in a free-market model, or labor unions in a model of shared governance. Rather, supporters of each model differ in their beliefs about the extent to which markets are competitive, whether labor is just an economic commodity, and the nature of conflict in the employment relationship. Thus we must explicitly confront the underlying objectives and models of the employment relationship to appreciate alternative reform strategies, and choose the preferred one. Whether we rely on markets and managers or policy and institutional intervention crucially depends on what we want to achieve and how the employment relationship works in practice.

We therefore need to move beyond the usual narrow operational focus of laws and institutions to instead ground our analyses in the fundamental objectives of work-related public policies and explicit models of the employment relationship. Contrary to the dominant approach to analyzing work-related public policies and the institutions that they support, we do not find it productive to assume that these things are self-evidently good or bad and to treat them as ends in themselves. Rather, such policies and institutions are means of achieving more fundamental objectives and are good or bad only to the extent that they promote or obstruct these objectives. In fact, there is no basis for evaluating public policies and institutions without a clear understanding of what they are intended to achieve and how the employment relationship works—an understanding that unfortunately is rarely articulated in scholarly and popular discourse. Our premise is therefore that reforming public policies on work must be rooted in a principled framework that puts front and center the objectives of the employment relationship and models of how we think the world of work operates. The explicit objectives of efficiency, equity, and voice paired with the egoist, unitarist, pluralist, and critical models provide the foundational principles for evaluating today's work-related public policies and crafting a coherent body of workplace law and public policy for the 21st-century workplace.

Workplace and Public Policy XXX

The fundamental objective of *Invisible Hands, Invisible Objectives* is to demonstrate the need to embrace explicit objectives and models of the employment relationship in order to understand, analyze, study, and reform workplace law and public policy. A critic might counter that the objectives and four models of the employment relationship used here are already implicitly recognized in research and practice. That is perhaps partially true, but there is still a need to make these objectives and models explicit. A deep understanding of workplace law and public policy will come only from this explicitness, and such explicitness is needed as the basis for productive dialogue across scholars, policymakers, and advocates from differing perspectives. The emphasis on discourse in recent postmodern scholarship reinforces the importance of explicitly recognizing the power of language in work-related issues.[29] By rooting analyses and debates on workplace law and public policy in explicit objectives and models, we can see how clashes in discourse and practice between different camps stem from different values and assumptions regarding the modern employment relationship. As such, what is needed is "Workplace Law and Public Policy XXX"—a richer approach in which, as in XXX-rated movies, everything is explicit. In "Workplace Law and Public Policy XXX," ends (objectives) and models are fully revealed for all to see.

Invisible Hands, Invisible Objectives therefore proceeds in three parts. Part One emphasizes the need for explicitness. This part includes this chapter and continues in Chapter 2, in which a review of major developments in U.S. employment and labor law from the birth of the modern employment relationship in the 1800s to the present reveals the inconsistent intellectual foundations of U.S. workplace law and public policy. Chapter 2 also provides the essential institutional background for readers not familiar with U.S. workplace law and public policy. Part Two presents an explicit scorecard for U.S. workplace law and public policy using the dimensions of efficiency, equity, and voice. More specifically, Chapter 3 reviews the current state of efficiency in the U.S. employment relationship while Chapters 4 and 5 do the same for equity and voice, respectively. Parts One and Two, therefore, develop an analytical framework for understanding and studying workplace law and public policy. Note carefully that this framework is not motivated solely by a need to reform the U.S. employment system. Rather, the use of explicit objectives and models stems from the need for a holistic approach to understanding workplace law and public policy that complements the more focused analyses that dominate today's scholarship, and that recognizes the increasing doctrinal and functional integration across different areas of workplace law that is occurring in the contemporary employment relationship.[30]

A major implication of our Workplace Law and Public Policy XXX framework is that any platform of reforms must be coherently rooted in an explicit model and the explicit objectives of the employment relationship. Part Three demonstrates this approach by using a pluralist model of the employment relationship paired with the objective of balancing efficiency, equity, and voice. Chapter 6 discusses the reasons for grounding reform proposals in the intersection of the pluralist model and a balancing of efficiency, equity, and voice. Chapter 7 proposes reforms targeted toward efficiency, such as streamlined regulatory enforcement, portable employee benefits, and improved training programs. Chapter 8 discusses policy reforms that promote equity with respect to living wages, workplace safety and health, work-family balance, security and social safety nets, nondiscrimination, just cause discipline and dismissal, and balanced income distributions. Chapter 9 focuses on voice, and our proposed reforms include free speech protections for employees, policies to promote both individual and collective decision-making, and enhanced mechanisms for allowing workers to form unions if they so desire. A final chapter sums up and looks to the future by discussing how these proposals might become reality.

While it is beyond the scope of this book to analyze comprehensively the diverse public policies embodied in the labor and employment laws of other countries—or what is frequently called individual and collective labor law outside of the United States—our analytical framework is globally applicable. The complex challenges of the employment relationship are worldwide concerns.[31] There are contemporary debates in Great Britain over adhering to European Union employment directives, in numerous European countries over labor market flexibility, in Brazil over labor contracts, in China over free labor unions and widening income disparities, in Costa Rica over sweatshops, and in Africa over creating decent jobs with basic social protections in the face of extreme poverty. The keys to understanding these debates as well as to designing appropriate reforms can be found in the use of explicit objectives and models of the employment relationship to guide analysis and reform. The specific policies considered in this book might be U.S.-specific, but the broader analytical framework is not.

Academic writings, advocacy pieces, and legislative debates on work almost always take an issue-by-issue approach. A typical book on the changing 21st-century employment relationship, for example, might have a chapter on contingent workers, another on health insurance, and yet another on declining unionization. Our approach is very different. One of our goals is to re-ground policy discussions in the fundamental objectives of the employment relationship—efficiency, equity, and voice. As such, our discussions are structured around these objectives. Unlike the conventional approach, a single issue might be discussed in multiple places. The subject of contingent workers, for example, is discussed in the efficiency chapters because it pertains to the flexibility aspect of efficiency; it is raised again in the equity chapters because equity concerns in the U.S. workplace are particularly severe for contingent workers; and it is again confronted in the voice chapters because U.S. labor law has special implications for contingent workers in the context of unionization. This repetition demonstrates the multiple aspects of important issues in the modern employment relationship. Our comprehensive approach to the broad span of work-related public polices also prevents us from exploring each policy in exhaustive detail. The interested reader is referred to the cited references for additional consideration of each policy.

There has been a recent spate of provocative books, policy briefs, and think tank projects on economic and employment policies.[32] These works bring many contemporary employment problems to life and reinforce the vast importance of workplace law and public policy for the health of the U.S. economy and populace. But *Invisible Hands, Invisible Objectives* is unique in providing an explicit intellectual foundation for thinking about employment policy specifically, and economic policy more generally. Our reform proposals in Part Three are uniquely and importantly structured around explicit objectives and carefully rooted in the assumptions of the pluralist employment relationship, but our aspirations are as much analytical as normative. Even if one disagrees with our choice of the specific model of how the employment relationship works and with our evaluations of the three objectives of the employment relationship that serve as foundations for our reform proposals, we believe that *Invisible Hands, Invisible Objectives* first and foremost illustrates the necessity of using specific models and objectives not only for reforming workplace law and public policy, but for improved analyses and understandings. As such, if our analyses and proposals foster long-overdue considerations of U.S. and international employment policies explicitly grounded in the workings and objectives of the employment relationship, then we will have succeeded.

CHAPTER 2

The Evolution of U.S. Workplace Law and Public Policy

A Tapestry of Hidden Assumptions

THIS CHAPTER REVIEWS the historical evolution of U.S. workplace law and public policy. This review serves not only to describe the range of important public policies currently governing the U.S. workplace, but also to reveal alternative approaches and to reinforce the need for explicitly identifying the objectives and models of the employment relationship.

The modern U.S. workplace has experienced four eras—an initial period up to the 1930s that we label the "old deal," in which free markets were paramount; the New Deal era beginning in the 1930s that featured government promotion of labor unions, social insurance programs, and minimum labor standards; the mid-century period marked by the rise of nonunion human resource management policies and employment law focused on individual rights; and an emerging global era with a renewed focus on free markets and free trade (see Table 2.1). Each era is rooted in one of the models of the employment relationship presented in Chapter 1, but these analytical foundations are frequently overlooked. As such, U.S. workplace law and public policy embodies an important set of hidden assumptions that need to be explicitly recognized.

The Old Deal: Free Markets and Contracts Between Equals

Although work is millions of years old, the modern U.S. employment relationship is a 19th-century development. At the end of the 1700s, most free men were self-employed as farmers, millers, blacksmiths, shoemakers, carpenters, and coopers, and in other artisan and building

TABLE 2.1

Regulating the Modern U.S. Employment Relationship

Old Deal		1880s	Emergence of the employment-at-will doctrine
		1895	Labor injunctions are constitutional (*In re Debs*)
		1905	State law limiting working hours is unconstitutional (*Lochner v. New York*)
		1908	Sherman Antitrust Act (1890) applied to labor unions (*Danbury Hatters*)
		1910	Emergence of workers' compensation policies
		1917	Yellow-dog contracts are legal (*Hitchman Coal and Coke*)
	New Deal	1932	Norris-LaGuardia Act restricts federal injunctions and ends enforceability of yellow-dog contracts
		1935	National Labor Relations Act (NLRA) encourages and protects union activity
		1935	Social Security Act creates federal retirement program and state unemployment insurance programs
		1938	Fair Labor Standards Act establishes minimum wages and overtime premium
		1947	Taft-Hartley Act amends the NLRA
Employment Law Era		1954	Corporate payments for employee health insurance benefits made tax exempt
		1959	Welfare and Pension Plans Disclosure Act requires employers to disclose details about employee benefits plans
		1959	Landrum-Griffin Act creates standards for internal union democracy
		1963	Equal Pay Act prohibits sex discrimination for equal work
		1964	Civil Rights Act prohibits employment discrimination on the basis of race and sex
		1967	Age Discrimination in Employment Act outlaws discrimination against employees over the age of 40
		1970	Occupational Safety and Health Act establishes standards for safe workplaces
		1973	Comprehensive Employment and Training Act provides federal government funds for many local worker training programs as well as subsidized public service jobs
		1974	Employee Retirement Income Security Act creates minimum requirements for employee benefit plans
	Global Era	1982	Job Training Partnership Act ends subsidized public service employment and further decentralizes training programs and adds business involvement
		1985	Consolidated Omnibus Budget Reconciliation Act allows terminated employees to continue their health insurance at their own expense
		1989	Worker Adjustment and Retraining Act requires employers to provide advance notice of mass layoffs.
		1990	Americans with Disabilities Act (ADA) prohibits discrimination against individuals with disabilities
		1992	North American Free Trade Agreement creates a free-trade area among the United States, Canada, and Mexico
		1993	Family and Medical Leave Act provides twelve weeks of family and medical leave
		1995	The World Trade Organization is created to promote and administer global free trade
		1998	Workforce Investment Act consolidates federal training programs and creates individual training accounts
		2002	Sarbanes-Oxley Act reinforces primacy of shareholders in corporate governance
		2006	Pension Protection Act changes funding rules and disclosure requirements for traditional pension plans while also encouraging personal retirement savings
		2008	ADA Amendments Act restores ADA protections by reversing unfavorable Supreme Court decisions

occupations; unfree labor consisted of slaves and indentured servants. In urban areas, a few skilled workers were employed by master craftsmen whose businesses were small and local—a "large" business at the time was an iron foundry that employed perhaps twenty-five workers. The development of textile mills in the 1820s marks the start of big business as we know it today—large-scale operations using the latest technologies, centralized management control of large pools of wage labor, and significant investment capital. The rise of the railroads in the 1850s further expanded and perfected this model.[1] By the end of the 19th century, wage work was widespread and the era of self-employment was over.

Early wage work followed the centuries-old traditions of late medieval and early modern England pertaining to "servants"—that is, anyone "in the service of" and residing with a single master, including agricultural laborers and unskilled craft workers. These early wage workers were employed with a contract for a specific duration, often one year. Disputes over these contracts flared up as employers and employees sought to define the legal boundaries of the emerging modern employment relationship. By the middle of the 1800s, U.S. judges had extended and adapted the English master-servant doctrine to most wage workers—"anyone who served another for wages was, in legal contemplation, a servant." As a result, U.S. workers who quit working before the end of their contract might forfeit several months or more of back wages for failing to live up to the complete contract. But contracts were equally binding on employers, who could terminate a worker before the end of the contract only with good cause—that is, if the worker failed to perform adequately.[2]

For reasons that are still debated (but that likely include workers' push for freedom to quit at any time, employers' push for freedom to terminate troublesome employees such as union supporters, and employers' desire for shorter contracts to avoid employment rigidities), by the start of the 20th century the employment-at-will doctrine had replaced the earlier hierarchical employment relationship of the master-servant doctrine.[3] Under the employment-at-will doctrine, in the absence of legal limitations or contractual restrictions, employees can be fired at any time for any reason. In the oft-repeated words of an 1884 Tennessee court, "all may dismiss their employees at will, be they many or few, for good cause, for no cause or even for cause morally wrong, without being thereby guilty of legal wrong." Employees can similarly quit at any time for any reason—in the Tennessee court's words, "it is a right which an employee may exercise in the same way, to the same extent, for the same cause or want of cause as the employer."[4]

Employment-at-will is a centerpiece of the pre-1930s U.S. model of workplace governance that emphasized free markets and contracts between equals. Under this approach, employers and employees should be able to enter into any explicit or implicit agreement—that is, a contract—involving any mutually agreeable terms and conditions of employment, including compensation, hours, duration of employment, job duties, and the like. In the interests of both economic optimization and individual freedom, employers and employees likewise should be able to end these arrangements when conditions or preferences change, or if a better deal comes along.

In this vision of the employment relationship, property rights and freedom to contract are of primary importance. Legal interferences with these principles were seen as violations of substantive or economic due process. From the 1880s to the 1920s, many laws specifying labor standards were rendered unconstitutional because they were seen as violating the 14th Amendment's prohibition against "any state [depriving] any person of life, liberty, or property, without due process of law." As specific examples, courts invalidated state laws limiting working hours in bakeries to ten hours per day, specifying minimum wages, outlawing yellow-dog contracts (in which workers promise not to join or form a union), and prohibiting wages paid in company scrip redeemable only at the company store because they violated economic due process by interfering with property rights and the freedom to contract.[5] In short, if employers and employees were willing to voluntarily agree to long hours, low wages, yellow-dog contracts, or payment in company scrip, for example, then the government had no business forbidding such terms and conditions of employment.

This approach depends critically on workers and employers having equal economic power, legal expertise, and political influence. As long as workers and employers are equals—that is, neither party has an economic, legal, or political advantage—then it is reasonable to assume that the terms and conditions of employment are voluntary rather than coerced. As it was put as early as 1853:

> In a free government like ours, employment is simply a contract between parties having equal rights. The operative agrees to perform a certain amount of work in consideration of receiving a certain amount of money. The work to be performed is, by the contract, an equivalent for the money to be paid. The relation, when properly entered into, is one of mutual benefit. The employed

is under no greater obligation to the employer than the employer is to the employed.[6]

With contracts between equals in free markets, individual freedom—of workers as well as employers—and economic efficiency are well served. Both libertarian moral philosophy and neoclassical economic theory are fulfilled.[7] This is a model of workplace governance rooted in free markets and voluntary contracts between employers and employees as equals—the egoist model of the employment relationship presented in Chapter 1.

One notable exception to this pre-1930s model of workplace governance was the enactment of workers' compensation laws by many states between 1910 and 1920. In return for not being able to sue their employers in court to collect damages if they were injured on the job, employees were guaranteed a set schedule of disability benefits. That workers' compensation laws persisted while other labor standards often did not is perhaps explained by the fact that *employers* benefit substantially from workers' compensation programs by being protected from litigation expenses and the possibility of very large damage awards. Some business leaders and reformers also were concerned with creating broader labor-management cooperation, especially in the wake of strikes and radicalism at the end of World War I. These business-led efforts focused on internally driven, private systems of welfare capitalism—the forerunner of today's human resource management, which is discussed below.[8] Although as a result workers were perhaps treated more humanely, these efforts nevertheless focused on serving the overarching goals of economic efficiency and profit while also emphasizing corporate freedom to develop and change personnel policies at will. Innovations such as scientific management—the "scientific" determination of the one best way to structure jobs by breaking them into simple, repetitive tasks championed by Frederick Winslow Taylor—further emphasized efficiency as the sole goal of the employment relationship and enhanced managerial control over the workplace.[9]

In spite of the theoretical equality implicit in the pre-1930s era of workplace governance, workers often felt that they were not the economic and legal equals of the 19th century's growing businesses and the early 20th century's huge modern corporations. Consequently, workers increasingly began to turn to collective action—especially labor unions—starting in the early 1800s to increase their power and establish minimum labor standards. The country's first unions focused on single occupations like shoemakers or printers, and as business organizations became national in the middle of the 19th century, so too did unions. For example, in 1860 the National [iron] Molders Union had forty-four locals stretching from St. Louis to Toronto and a national strike fund to support its emphasis on collective bargaining. In 1886 the National Molders Union joined with twenty-four other national unions to form the American Federation of Labor (AFL) to help coordinate the labor movement's economic and political activities.

The fortunes of U.S. labor unions between 1800 and 1930 waxed and waned with the business cycle, and were punctuated by numerous major conflicts with employers. Depressions in 1819 and 1837 severely weakened the early labor movement, but in 1860 a shoemakers' strike involved 20,000 workers across several states. The Great Uprising of 1877 grew out of a railroad strike and mushroomed into labor protests across the country involving thousands of workers and millions of dollars of property damage. A successful railroad strike by the Knights of Labor against the Southwest System in 1885 proved to be a short-lived victory as Pinkerton spies helped to crush a violent strike the next year. The 1890s witnessed violent strikes in Chicago, New Orleans, Homestead, Pennsylvania, and Coeur d'Alene, Idaho, while the following decade saw a failed national AFL boycott of a nonunion hat maker. The radical Industrial Workers of the World won a textile strike in 1912 that was remarkable for the solidarity demonstrated by diverse ethnic groups. A strike by numerous AFL-affiliated craft unions to unionize the steel industry failed in 1919. Many of these conflicts involved strikebreaking through the use of federal or local troops, armed Pinkerton guards, and the manipulation of racial and ethnic prejudices.[10]

All of this labor activity raised important legal issues and further helped define the early model of U.S. workplace governance. As was the case for the employment relationship more generally, in the 19th century there were not any laws specifically pertaining to unions. Consequently, workers who tried to influence their wages and working conditions by forming unions, striking, and leading boycotts were regularly repressed by a legal system that subjected these workers to common-law prohibitions on conspiracy, property rights infringements, and breach of contract. Starting with the Philadelphia shoemakers who struck in 1804 and 1805 for higher wages, unions were prosecuted as illegal conspiracies because they harmed the community and violated notions of individual liberty. Individual efforts to influence wages and working conditions were part of the early-19th-century vision of liberty, but the collective aspect of union activity was viewed as particularly harmful—so harmful as to be viewed as an illegal criminal conspiracy. In 1842, however, the Massachusetts Supreme Court in *Commonwealth v. Hunt* determined that while some union actions might be conspiratorial, labor unions were not per se unlawful conspiracies. This decision granted unions some element of legal legitimacy, and ultimately marked the beginning of the end for the conspiracy doctrine in U.S. labor relations. It also marked a shift to a pragmatic legal evaluation of the effects of specific actions on the market economy.[11]

Labor unions also were repressed through injunctions to stop or severely limit picketing during strikes, or even in some cases to prohibit employees from unionizing at all. Such injunctions were justified through common-law protections against irreparable harm to an employer's property. Because "property" in the U.S. common-law tradition includes both physical assets (factories, machines, railroad cars) and intangible assets (the right to do business, to hire and fire employees, and interact with customers), any strike or boycott that threatened to interfere with an employer's business could potentially be challenged by an injunction. By one estimate, at least 4,300 injunctions were issued between 1880 and 1930. These were powerful anti-union devices that turned public opinion away from strikers, drained unions' financial and human resources, and demoralized strikers through fear and confusion.[12]

At this same time, corporations increased dramatically in size and power. As the 20th century started, the Standard Oil Company was refining nearly 25 million barrels of oil per year and controlled 85 percent of the market, U.S. Steel controlled 60 percent of the steel industry with its 150,000 employees and 200 mills, and International Harvester dominated the harvesting machinery industry by annually producing more than 500,000 harvesters, which constituted 85 percent of the market.[13] To prohibit such monopolies and prevent the accompanying negative economic and social effects, Congress passed the Sherman Antitrust Act in 1890. Whether this act also applied to labor unions was a matter of interpretation. The hat boycott noted above became the test case, and in a 1908 ruling the Supreme Court found that the union-led boycott violated the Sherman Antitrust Act; a later ruling held individual union members responsible for over $200,000 in damages.[14] The subsequent Clayton Act enacted by Congress in 1914 sought to exempt labor unions from antitrust prohibitions, but court rulings narrowed the reach of that exemption and continued to subject unions to significant restraints, such as limiting picketing to single individuals.[15]

The legal treatment of labor unions during this period further reveals the elements of this early U.S. model of workplace governance. Unions were viewed as illegal conspiracies that interfered with individual liberty, injunctions were used to restrain strikes and other union activity because of the harm to private property, and antitrust law was used to make sure that unions did not undermine free-market competition. These rulings are all consistent with a belief in the benefits of free markets and contracts between equals. These central tenets are similarly reflected in the rhetoric of the "open shop" movement in the early 1900s in which employers pushed for union-free workplaces (open shops) by portraying unions as violating individual liberties by denying workers the ability to choose where to work and on what terms. To further this rhetorical attack, the open shop movement was renamed the American Plan in the 1920s.[16] Free markets and voluntary contracts between employers and employees as equals were portrayed as the American way—and legally, until the 1930s, they were.

The New Deal: Balancing Power Through Labor Unions and Fair Labor Standards

In spite of the conceptual appeal of free markets and contracts between equals, the plight of many workers in the decades before the 1930s raised significant concerns. While railroad tycoon Jay Gould earned $10 million a year in the early 1900s, the average unskilled worker who earned $10 a week could barely afford a run-down, two-room apartment without running water. By one count, industrial accidents resulted in 25,000 deaths, 25,000 permanent disability cases, and 2 million temporary disability cases per year. If these numbers are accurate, then there were more U.S. casualties in the workplace than on the battlefield during World War I. A 1909 government survey revealed that 85 percent of wage earners typically worked at least fifty-four hours per week; in some regions, over 20 percent had standard workweeks of more than sixty hours. One of the major issues of the time therefore was the "labor problem": low wages, long hours, monotonous work in dangerous conditions, abusive supervision, and frequent periods of unemployment and insecurity; in short, an oppressive and exploitative employment relationship.[17]

Social critics, reformers, policymakers, academics, and revolutionaries were concerned by the vagaries of modern capitalism as it was developing. Karl Marx saw capitalism as a way for the capitalist class to dominate and control the working class. From this perspective, individual freedom was a pretext for judges from the capitalist class to overturn minimum wage laws or restrain labor unions in order to perpetuate the dominance of employers over laborers. A less radical vision developed in the United States—as described in Chapter 1, the pluralist industrial relations school of thought accepted the modern corporation as being an efficient organization of mass production (as did Marx), but rejected the tenet of neoclassical economics that markets were perfectly competitive. Rather, the industrial relations school believes that market imperfections such as persistent unemployment, company towns dominated by a single employer, and a lack of worker savings and other safety nets give large, monopolistic employers undue influence in the labor market and in the political arena. Even Adam Smith, the founder of modern economics and champion of the market's invisible hand, recognized this imbalance:

> Many workmen could not subsist a week, few could subsist a month, and scarce any a year without employment. In the long-run the workman may be as necessary to his master as his master is to him, but the necessity is not so immediate.[18]

In other words, employers and employees are not labor market equals; rather, employers have greater bargaining power than individual employees, which allows employers to pay low wages for working long hours under dangerous working conditions with autocratic supervisors. These problems are compounded by business cycles, which create additional insecurities for workers and their families.[19]

In addition to this belief in the inequality of bargaining power, a key tenet of the pluralist school is that labor is more than a commodity. In the laissez-faire/neoclassical economics model of workplace governance, labor is a commodity, and like other productive inputs—steel, oil, investment capital—its price is determined by supply and demand; efficiency is the sole metric of the employment relationship. In industrial relations thought, labor is seen as human beings with rights in a democratic society. Poor working conditions—even if efficient and produced by the forces of supply and demand—are not consistent with modern standards of human dignity; authoritarian supervision, even when efficient, undermines human autonomy and freedom. The human aspect of labor makes employment a moral issue. Additional standards beyond efficiency, such as equity and voice, are therefore needed to evaluate and guide the employment relationship.[20] Note carefully that these hidden assumptions are significantly different from the assumptions of the egoist model that underlies the old deal era.

The beliefs of the industrial relations school of thought are reflected in some pre-1930s developments. The aforementioned Clayton Act in 1914 included the pronouncement that "the labor of a human being is not a commodity or article of commerce." On an international level, the International Labor Organization (ILO) was founded as part of the peace process ending World War I in 1919 with the goal of promoting peace based on justice for workers by solving the inequities of the labor problem. Enshrined in its founding principles is the statement that "labor should not be regarded as a commodity or article of commerce." The ILO continues today as the chief international authority on international labor standards and human rights for workers in pursuit of economic prosperity and security as well as freedom and dignity. But in the United States, the biggest impact of the industrial relations vision would occur during the Great Depression in the 1930s.[21]

The U.S. stock market unexpectedly crashed on October 24, 1929. Consumer purchases slowed, unemployment increased, weak farm prices bankrupted farmers, panics wiped out savings accounts, and banks closed. By 1933, wage and salary income had fallen 40 percent, and the unemployment rate was an astounding 25 percent—nearly 50 percent in some industrial cities—with millions of those lucky enough to work being able to work only part-time. Bread lines, evictions, and cardboard Hoovervilles of homeless families were common; thousands roamed the country looking for work. Poverty relief and unemployment assistance were nearly nonexistent. The Great Depression's severity upset the intellectual foundations of the U.S. economy. Faith in the invisible hand of free markets and in the nation's elite—especially big business and its unilaterally imposed welfare capitalism or human resource management policies—to achieve widespread economic prosperity crumbled.

As a result, legislation to limit the use of injunctions against unions was finally passed in the form of the Norris-LaGuardia Act in 1932. This act rests on a rejection of the free-market model of workplace governance through the finding that, relative to corporations, "the individual unorganized worker is commonly helpless to exercise actual liberty of contract and to protect his freedom of labor, and thereby to obtain acceptable terms and condition of employment." In addition to severely limiting the conditions under which injunctions can be issued, the Norris-LaGuardia Act made yellow-dog contracts unenforceable, ended the criminal conspiracy doctrine, and effectively exempted labor unions from the Sherman Antitrust Act.[22]

Later in 1932, Franklin Delano Roosevelt was elected president and by pledging "a new deal for the American people" began a more activist approach to regulating the modern workplace and providing broad economic security. Following after a number of relief and jobs programs, such as the Works Progress Administration, as well as a failed attempt to stabilize industry competition through the National Industrial Recovery Act, the primary and lasting elements of the New Deal pertaining to the employment relationship were enacted in 1935 and 1938—the National Labor Relations Act (NLRA or Wagner Act, 1935), the Social Security Act (1935), and the Fair Labor Standards Act (FLSA, 1938). Other work-related legislation includes significant amendments to the Railway Labor Act (1934), the Walsh-Healy Public Contracts Act (1936), and the National Apprenticeship Act (1937). The New Deal reflects the pluralist beliefs that both unionization and government regulation of the employment relationship are necessary for balancing efficiency, equity, and voice, and also reflects a changing power dynamic in which the threat of economic and political instability caused legislation and judicial rulings to be more responsive to the interests of workers.[23]

Unions are critically important in the New Deal model of workplace governance because of the premise of bargaining power inequality: if individual workers have inadequate bargaining power relative to corporate employers, then unions are the key mechanism for equalizing bargaining power between employees and employers. In fact, corporations are essentially groups of unionized shareholders; in the words of the 1898 annual report of the Ohio State Board of Arbitration,

> Stockholders unite their accumulations of capital and knowledge in a particular line of business and create a simple agency called a corporation. The agency secures the best skill and ability money will command to conduct its affairs. Thus, supplied with a sagacious and powerful representative, they stand back and say to their laborers through this representative: "No representative from you will be heard. You each must speak and act for yourself."[24]

Letting workers unite and use representatives to advocate their collective interests is seen as putting workers on par with what corporations already do.

Giving workers equal bargaining power with employers in turn protects workers against low wages, dangerous working conditions, and other forms of exploitation. An equal playing field for labor and management also boosts economic growth through two avenues: increased consumer purchasing power that stems from higher wages and greater economic stability that stems from reduced strike activity.[25] Last, unions are also seen as critical vehicles for employee voice and industrial democracy. As Senator Wagner, the champion and prime mover of the NLRA, put it,

> there can no more be democratic self-government in industry without workers participating therein, than there could be democratic government in politics without workers having the right to vote. . . . That is why the right to bargain collectively is at the bottom of social justice for the worker, as well as the sensible conduct of business affairs. The denial or observance of this right means the difference between despotism and democracy.[26]

The NLRA therefore protects employees' rights to form unions and engage in other forms of concerted activity that can help equalize bargaining power. More specifically, the NLRA prohibits employer interference, restraint, or coercion of employees who are pursuing their rights to engage in concerted activity, specifies a certification procedure for establishing whether a majority of workers wants union representation, grants a certified, majority-status union the right to be the exclusive representative of the relevant employees, and obligates the employer to bargain with that union. The NLRA was amended in 1947 by the Taft-Hartley Act and again in 1959 by the Landrum-Griffin Act and still governs most U.S. private sector labor relations today.[27]

The second pillar of the New Deal model of workplace governance is a social safety net consisting of social insurance programs and mandated minimum labor standards. Social insurance programs were created by the Social Security Act, especially through the establishment of what has grown into Old Age, Survivors, Disability, and Health Insurance (OASDHI), which provides varying combinations of monetary assistance and health care coverage to retirees, the disabled, and their dependents. The Social Security Act also created today's state unemployment insurance benefits programs. Mandated labor standards were created by the FLSA—notably a national minimum wage, a mandatory overtime premium for covered workers for hours worked in excess of a weekly standard (now forty hours), and restrictions on child labor.[28]

The idea that freedom stems from a balance of power in society as well as from minimum living standards was articulated more ambitiously in 1944 with President Roosevelt's call for a second bill of rights—an economic bill of rights to supplement the civil and political rights protected in the original Bill of Rights to the U.S. Constitution. This economic bill of rights was proposed to include the right to "a useful and remunerative job," a decent home, adequate medical care, "protection from the economic fears of old age and sickness and accident and unemployment," and the opportunity "to earn enough to provide adequate food and clothing and recreation."[29]

This second bill of rights was not enacted, but at the conclusion of World War II the United Nations was founded to, as stated in its charter, "reaffirm faith in fundamental human rights, in the dignity and worth of the human person, in the equal rights of men and women of nations large and small." As a result, the Universal Declaration of Human Rights was adopted and proclaimed by the United Nations General Assembly on December 10, 1948. Along with many civil, political, economic, and social rights, article 23 of the Universal Declaration proclaims that "Everyone has the right . . . to just and favorable conditions of work and to protection against unemployment," nondiscrimination in employment, "just and favorable remuneration ensuring for himself and his family an existence worthy of human dignity, and supplemented, if necessary, by other means of social protection," and "the right to form and to join trade unions for the protection of his interests." Complementing this human rights perspective are arguments for industrial citizenship that assert that workers are entitled to these types of rights by virtue of being free and equal members of a community. Creating models of workplace governance—typically through a combination of labor unions and fair labor standards—to make these rights, whether seen as human or citizenship rights, a reality continues to be a significant challenge for the ILO and other advocates of the industrial relations school of thought and the pluralist model of the employment relationship.[30]

The Employment Law Era: Human Resource Management and Individual Rights

Even before the New Deal, some nonunion employers used what was then called "welfare capitalism" and is now called "human resource management" to provide varying degrees of decent working conditions and supervision, better pay and benefits, and employee voice through various forms of nonunion representation plans. The unilateral abandonment or manipulation of many of these policies during the Great Depression, as well as the activist government philosophy of the New Deal, temporarily pushed welfare capitalism into the shadows. But after World War II employers regained the economic and political power to assert their control over the terms and conditions of employment and to keep unions and government regulation in check. Employers therefore created personnel policies and internal labor markets to promote a unitarist model of the employment relationship through stability and security because the postwar mass manufacturing system relied on economies of scale and predictability (in contrast with today's emphasis on specialization and flexibility) and because the New Deal created a lasting desire among workers for security. The threat of unionization and/or government regulation, however, required that these nonunion policies be more generous, lasting, and legitimate than in the first three decades of the 1900s. In fact, it is common to see this postwar era as characterized by a strong social contract in which employee loyalty was rewarded with job security and opportunities for promotions, and even lifetime employment.[31]

As the percentage of U.S. private sector belonging to unions declined from around 35 percent in the mid-1950s to less than half that amount thirty years later, the unitarist, nonunion human resource management model came to dominate the U.S. employment relationship during the second half of the 20th century. This transformation resulted from the growth of nonunion companies as well as from the opening of new nonunion plants in the southern United States by heavily unionized companies.[32] By 1980 (and much earlier in many cases), the human resource management model emphasizing job and organizational design, employee selection and development, performance management, compensation and benefits, and employee relations was well established. Standard human resource management policies include valid and reliable selection measures for hiring and promoting employees; training and development opportunities; respectful methods of supervision; compensation that provides more than a living wage while also rewarding performance; benefits that foster personal growth, security, and work-life balance; and informal or formal dispute resolution procedures. A strong theme of distributive and procedural justice—that is, fairness in both outcomes and processes—runs through the application and administration of all of these policies.[33] Though typically not explicitly recognized, all of these human resource management strategies flow from the assumptions of the unitarist vision of the employment relationship presented in Chapter 1.

Government regulation of the U.S. employment relationship in the postwar period is consistent with the dominance of the human resource management approach to workplace governance and the unitarist model of the employment relationship. Before 1950, U.S. public policies on work largely consisted of a combination of private sector labor law (protecting and regulating workers' rights to form unions and collectively bargain with their employers), social insurance (workers' compensation, unemployment insurance, Social Security), and protective employment standards (minimum wages, maximum hours, and child labor restrictions). Since that time, labor unions and other worker advocates have not had enough power to strengthen labor law and social insurance programs to further enhance workers' independence from their employers. Rather, postwar public policies concede employees' dependence on corporations and essentially seek to ensure that human resource management policies treat workers with minimum levels of fairness.

Congressional proposals to provide for national or universal health insurance, ranging from the Wagner-Murray-Dingell bill in the 1940s to the Clinton plan in the 1990s, were sharply opposed by business and conservative groups and therefore were not enacted. Employers preferred to have employees dependent on them for health insurance and pension benefits; public policy reflected this preference by making employers' payments for employee health insurance tax exempt beginning in 1954. Instead of expanding the generosity of Social Security retirement benefits, the Welfare and Pension Plans Disclosure Act (1959) simply required those employers who chose to offer health insurance and pension benefits to file annual reports about these plans so that employees could monitor their plans. This reporting requirement was expanded in 1974 with the passage of the Employee Retirement Income Security Act (ERISA). Employers are not required to provide benefits such as health insurance or pensions (and many do not), but if they do, ERISA seeks to prevent abuse by establishing standards such as minimum vesting requirements. ERISA also created the Pension Benefit Guaranty Corporation (PBGC) to insure against a complete loss of vested pension benefits (for example, when a company goes bankrupt).[34] Concerns over the solvency of the PBGC led to the Pension Protection Act in 2006 that tightened up funding and disclosure rules for pension plans.

The importance of management-determined working conditions is also reflected in the passage of the Occupational Safety and Health Act in 1970, which requires employers to provide a safe workplace. Under this act, the Occupational Safety and Health Administration is empowered to establish specific safety standards and to inspect workplaces to monitor compliance by employers. There have also been some public policy initiatives to provide training—such as the Manpower Development and Training Act (1962), the Comprehensive Employment and Training Act (1973), and the Job Training Partnership Act (1982)—but training is primarily a company-provided human resources activity. Vacation and other leave policies are also unregulated, though the Family and Medical Leave Act (1993) guarantees employees twelve weeks of unpaid leave to care for themselves, their parents, or their children. Employers are free to lay off employees, close plants, and make other hiring and firing decisions, but public policies outline some minimum standards for these decisions: state legislatures and courts have developed a patchwork of limited exceptions to the employment-at-will doctrine, and the Worker Adjustment and Retraining Notification Act (1989) requires employers to provide advance notice of mass layoffs. The most visible standards, however, pertain to nondiscrimination.

President Roosevelt prohibited racial discrimination in government agencies and contractors in 1941; other state and local "fair employment" laws date back to the 1940s; and the Equal Pay Act of 1963 amended the Fair Labor Standards Act to require equal pay for men and women doing equal work. But the civil rights movement in the 1960s prompted the most important U.S. employment law—the Civil Rights Act of 1964.[35] Title VII of this act prohibits employment discrimination by employers and unions on the basis of race, color, religion, sex, or national origin. This act thereby establishes the principle of equal employment opportunity on a nationwide basis. The Age Discrimination in Employment Act (1967) further outlawed discrimination against employees over the age of 40, and the Americans with Disabilities Act (1990) added disabled individuals to the list of protected classes, a class that was significantly expanded by amendments adopted in 2008. Initially, these acts allowed victims of employment discrimination to collect back pay only for lost wages, but the Civil Rights Act of 1991 strengthened the remedies by allowing for compensatory and punitive damages. Some state and local laws include additional protected categories, such as sexual orientation and marital status.

With respect to public policies on work, then, the postwar era is the employment law era. These employment laws are an important element of the postwar human resource management model of workplace governance in that they largely eschew the provision of specific benefits in favor of nondiscrimination and disclosure requirements for employer-controlled terms and conditions of employment. These employment laws also focus on individual rather than collective rights, and are notable for their omission of a number of measures adopted in other industrialized countries, such as universal health insurance, comprehensive pension benefits beyond Social Security, a minimum number of vacation days, paid family leave, and unjust dismissal protections. By the 1980s, most U.S. workplaces were governed largely by corporate human resources policies. While markets establish the broad parameters for employment policies, and while employment laws provide some important standards of individual rights, the prime movers of employment conditions in this era are human resource managers.

The premise of this human resource management model of workplace governance is that employers and employees have a shared interest in profitability and decent working conditions. Employees who are treated with respect via the right human resources policies will work hard for their employers, and their employers will be profitable. In other words, human resource management is predicated on the assumptions of the unitarist model of the employment relationship. On the other hand, critics of human resource management note the lack of checks and balances—a company can unilaterally reduce pay and benefits, for example, if it thinks that doing so will improve profitability. Similarly, the fairness of nonunion dispute resolution procedures relies almost entirely on managerial goodwill. Moreover, human resources policies are often used to prevent unionization or the implementation of stronger government standards. As such, some question whether the human resource management focus on employee well-being is more rhetoric than reality.[36]

The Global Era: Free Trade and Personal Responsibility

By many accounts, the employment relationship at the start of the 21st century is again changing significantly. The collapse of state socialism and communism in the former Soviet Union and Eastern Europe, along with China's push for foreign investment and trade, have allowed capitalism, international financial flows, and multinational corporations to reach nearly every corner of the globe.[37] While bringing many benefits, globalization places great competitive pressures on companies, workers, and communities. Mass manufacturing is being replaced by production methods that emphasize specialization and quality, and employee teams are replacing narrowly defined jobs. Technology can replace jobs of many types, and information technology allows numerous white-collar and service jobs to be outsourced to low-wage countries around the globe. Globalization and technology have apparently furthered the decline in union bargaining power and membership; unions now represent only 12 percent of manufacturing workers, and 8 percent of private sector workers overall. With little threat of unionization or new employment laws in the United States, the corporate finance function has trumped the human resources function; and the concerns of shareholders have overwhelmed the concerns of employees and other stakeholders in the economic and political arenas. Employment systems are becoming more decentralized, with more decisions made locally by operations managers than centrally by human resource managers.[38]

All of these trends elevate the importance of external over internal labor markets, and of flexibility over standardization in employment practices. Employees now face more uncertainty and bear more risk than in the postwar period. Compensation is increasingly driven by the global labor market's going rate plus individual and organizational performance, not by internal equity and predictable salary schedules. Expectations of stable employment and careers with a single company are being replaced by short-term employment episodes. Increasing numbers of individuals can be classified as contingent workers—independent contractors, temps, and part-time workers. Corporate reorganizations, outsourcing, and global production decisions resulting from an obsession with short-term financial performance and the threat of low-wage international competition causes jobs to be frequently restructured or eliminated. Responsibilities for career development are shifting from employers to individuals. In short, the social contract of the employment law era has been broken, and we are witnessing a return to the pre-1930s model in which workplaces are governed by the egoist model of market forces and unilateral employer control.[39]

As in the other eras of the U.S. employment relationship, public policy initiatives and omissions significantly contribute to the nature of workplace governance in the global era. Globalization, in particular, is shaped and fostered by U.S. public policy. In 1930 the average tariff rate on imports to the United States was more than 50 percent. Since that time, U.S. laws, treaties, and free-trade agreements have significantly reduced or completely removed tariff levels and other barriers to free trade. The North American Free Trade Agreement (NAFTA) has now eliminated tariff and nontariff trade barriers between the United States, Canada, and Mexico, protected intellectual property rights, and permitted companies of any of the three countries to invest, sell services, and bid on government contracts in all three countries. On a much broader scale, the World Trade Organization (WTO) negotiates and administers global trade agreements covering over 150 countries. While some trade barriers remain in agriculture and services, the WTO is responsible for the average tariff rate in manufacturing dropping to less than 4 percent.[40]

Free-trade public policy initiatives like NAFTA and the WTO affect the workplace in many ways. Free-trade agreements sharpen global competition and place downward pressure on wages, benefits, and working conditions. Increased capital mobility threatens U.S. jobs and weakens unions. And although free-trade agreements contain strong protections for intellectual property rights, they set few labor standards. The NAFTA labor side agreement—the North American Agreement on Labor Cooperation—includes eleven guiding principles (such as nondiscrimination and workplace safety), but limits enforcement to public consultations on whether existing domestic laws are being fulfilled. The WTO's record on labor standards is even weaker. There are no explicit labor standards in the WTO's free-trade agreements, and there is strong evidence that any national attempt to link labor standards with trade would be determined by the WTO to constitute an illegal trade barrier. Weak U.S. trade adjustment policies that fail to provide meaningful assistance to workers displaced by globalization further place workers at the mercy of the free-trade forces of globalization.[41] U.S. and international public policies on globalization therefore have increased the role of market forces in today's model of workplace governance.

In this global era, consumption, not production, has become the central economic activity, which means that individuals are increasingly seen as consumers rather than workers.[42] Thus there is an emerging ethos of personal responsibility in domestic-level policy discussions related to work. The universal health insurance initiative proposed by the Clinton administration in 1993 failed, and most proposals to reform health insurance now focus on individual health savings accounts or tax credits to help individuals purchase their own insurance. Individual retirement accounts have also been central in the debates over reforming and privatizing Social Security. Neither employers nor the government typically provides health insurance for the unemployed, but under the Consolidated Omnibus Budget Reconciliation Act (COBRA, 1985), individuals are allowed to continue their employer-provided health insurance at their own expense. The Pension Protection Act in 2006 included several reforms to encourage individual savings for both retirement and personal care. In short, individuals are increasingly personally responsible for managing their own security.

Individuals are also seen as personally responsible for managing their own careers. The Job Training Partnership Act (JTPA) reflected an ideology in which a lack of personal skills rather than a lack of decent jobs underlies poverty and unemployment.[43] Similarly, proposals to raise the minimum wage are usually countered by calls for low-wage individuals to increase their marketable skills. In fact, the major reform legislation that essentially replaced welfare with workfare in 1996, the Personal Responsibility and Work Opportunity Reconciliation Act, even includes "personal responsibility" in its title. Similarly, when the Workforce Investment Act replaced the JTPA in 1998, individual training accounts were created for eligible individuals to use to purchase training through approved programs. The George W. Bush administration praised this new system's attempt to "promote individual empowerment and market principles."[44]

The United States is again becoming a "free agent nation" or a "winner-take-all society."[45] While couched in language of global free trade and personal responsibility rather than domestic free markets and individual liberty, the early-21st-century model of workplace governance is conceptually the same as the late-19th-century model. Both rest on the egoist model's faith that voluntary contracts between equals with strong property rights interacting in free markets produce socially optimal outcomes. The benefits (such as efficiency, freedom, and mobility) and challenges (such as insecurity, inequality, and social divides) are the same today as they were a hundred years ago. Technology and transportation changed the marketplace in the late 1800s and early 1900s from regional to national and created a growing imbalance between capital and labor not that dissimilar to what we have today, and the public policies and judicial rulings of both eras reflect this power imbalance.[46]

Hidden Assumptions, Conflicting Assumptions

Whether in the form of common-law rulings, federal and state statutes, government-mandated social insurance programs, or international free-trade agreements, government regulation has been a central feature of the U.S. employment relationship since its modern development in the 1800s. A sampling of the most important rulings and federal laws that apply to U.S. private sector workers are summarized in Table 2.1; numerous state and local laws and judicial decisions magnify these trends, as do various policies pertaining to public sector employees (though perhaps to a lesser extent). And legislative and judicial choices to refrain from enacting universal health insurance, paid family leave, unjust dismissal standards, or other policies also critically shape the U.S. employment relationship.

These inclusions and omissions of U.S. public policies on work reflect four different periods of workplace governance since the mid-1800s: an initial era emphasizing free markets and contracts between equals (the "old deal"); the New Deal era focused on labor unions, social insurance, and minimum labor standards to balance power between employers and employees; the employment law era, which marks the rise of human resource management and individually focused employment laws; and the global era in which an emphasis on free trade and personal responsibility harkens back to the old deal philosophy of free markets and individual liberty. From these four periods one can clearly see the importance of each model of the employment relationship described in Chapter 1, and the shifting power dynamics that shape how public policies embody these models. These four eras also provide a greater understanding of the contemporary state of U.S. public policies on work as well as ideas for alternative approaches to governing the workplace.

At the same time, it is crucial to recognize that these four periods overlap—today's employment relationship includes the employment-at-will doctrine from the old deal, the National Labor Relations Act and social insurance programs from the New Deal, numerous laws from the employment law era, and the pressures of free trade from the global era. In fact, the historical record of U.S. workplace governance is one of piecemeal development, and today's system is the product of a complex mixture of ever-changing economic, political, social, and legal forces that determined the relative power structure of various interest groups with competing intellectual visions of the employment relationship over the past hundred and fifty years.

The four visions or models of the employment relationship presented in Chapter 1 are essential for considering work-related public policies because each model supports a significantly different approach to such public policies. Employment regulation is harmful in the egoist model, largely unnecessary in the unitarist model, welfare improving in the pluralist model, and inadequate or manipulative in the critical model. We can now see, however, that the U.S. workplace is in reality governed by an amalgamation of approaches that are rooted in these frames of reference. The egoist model of the employment relationship underlies the old deal and global eras of U.S. workplace governance with their emphasis on unregulated free markets, domestically and now internationally. The unitarist perspective is reflected in the employment law era in U.S. workplace governance to the extent that U.S. employment law largely leaves the determination of the terms and conditions of employment in the hands of employers, albeit subject to some minimal standards of good human resources practice such as nondiscrimination. The pluralist model is clearly enshrined in the New Deal era. And the critical model helps reveal the dynamics of power and the tensions between employer control and employee resistance that explain how far advocates of a particular school of thought can push their regulatory agenda at any given time. As such, U.S. labor and employment laws reflect a tapestry of not only hidden, but also largely inconsistent, intellectual foundations. An effective understanding of workplace law and public policy requires making these hidden assumptions explicit.

PART TWO

An Explicit Scorecard for Workplace Law and Public Policy

It is no easy matter to define the relative rights and mutual duties of the rich and of the poor, of capital and of labor.

—Pope Leo XIII, 1891

CHAPTER 3

Efficiency

"WASTE NOT, WANT NOT." "A penny saved is a penny earned." "A stitch in time saves nine." There are many popular proverbs emphasizing the sensible use of scarce resources. When money, time, energy, and our other most precious commodities are limited, it is important to use them effectively. In fact, the entire field of economics is largely about the optimal pricing and allocation of scarce resources. In the employment relationship, the effective use of scarce resources is critical for promoting economic development, prosperity, and job creation, and is rooted in the pursuit of productivity and competitiveness. All of these important concerns fall under the broad heading of "efficiency." An efficient employment relationship is productive and maximizes the use of scarce resources; an inefficient employment relationship is wasteful and unable to compete in the global economy.

Of the three objectives underlying the employment relationship, the efficiency objective is currently ascendant in the American workplace. This ascendancy reflects the dominance of the neoliberal market ethos in local, national, and international policy discourse and its emphasis on unregulated markets, profits, shareholder returns, and consumerism. Moreover, while markets are becoming increasingly global in nature, legal rules continue to be mostly local or national in their reach. For the United States in particular, laissez-faire employment rules combined with increasingly global economic pressures have strengthened the clout of corporate interests in efficiency, profits, and property rights relative to labor's interests in equity and voice.

The neoliberal market ethos is rooted in the neoclassical economics school of thought and embraces the egoist model of the employment relationship described in Chapter 1. Self-interested actors with well-defined freedoms and property rights are seen as interacting in perfectly competitive markets; the invisible hand of these markets is seen as guiding the actors toward efficient, optimal outcomes. Beyond protecting physical, intellectual, and intangible property rights and shielding competitive markets from monopoly power, fraud, and coercion, mainstream economic thought asserts that an absence of legal rules promotes efficiency. Additional legal regulation of the workplace, the argument goes, distorts market forces, constrains the use of private property, and inhibits flexible employment practices; accordingly, the most efficient employment regime is the one with the fewest legal constraints. By this measure, the U.S. workplace should rank as highly efficient. U.S. labor and employment law evolved from a strong laissez-faire tradition. Historically, common-law doctrines protecting property rights and constitutional interpretations of economic due process largely minimized the roles of federal and state governments as legislative regulators of the employment relationship.

Although the government's role has grown dramatically since the 1930s, the contemporary American workplace is affected by far less governmental "interference" than workplaces in the rest of the industrialized world. To wit, the United States is the only industrialized nation without a broad limitation on an employer's right to terminate the employment relationship. Nearly all western European countries also mandate minimum annual vacation periods of between four and six weeks; U.S. law contains no statutory mandate whatsoever. Most industrialized nations require paid parental leave upon the birth or adoption of an employee's child; the parental leave mandate in the United States is unpaid and tends to be significantly shorter in duration. American employers, accordingly, compete with a comparative advantage by virtue of operating subject to less cumbersome rules than their foreign competitors. In other words, a paucity of legal constraints is a boon to American employers.[1]

Efficiency is nevertheless a critical dimension of our consideration of public policies for the 21st-century workplace for at least two reasons. One, efficiency promotes economic prosperity, which is a frequent concern of policymakers. Two, while the best public policies for promoting efficiency might often be limited to common-law supports for property rights and contracts, there are some areas in which public policies on work can offset market imperfections and enhance efficiency. The consideration of these areas is particularly important today as globalization, technology, and other 21st-century pressures are leading employers and economies to achieve efficiencies in new and different ways.

The Efficiency Scorecard

In the aggregate, the U.S. economy rates high in efficiency. From the end of World War II to the start of the 21st century, the median annual family income grew from $20,000 to over $50,000 in real terms (in other words, after adjusting for inflationary increases). Between 1960 and 2000, real gross domestic product (GDP) increased by nearly 300 percent, real personal consumption expenditures increased by more than 300 percent, and real investment increased by over 500 percent. The values of imports and exports have jumped by over 1,000 percent. In this same period, corporate profits rose by more than 150 percent and the index of New York Stock Exchange stock prices climbed by more than 2,000 percent. Productivity (output per hour) has increased by nearly 125 percent, and compensation is up nearly 250 percent. Since the 1980s, over 40 million new jobs have been created, and GDP growth has outpaced that in the other six major industrialized democracies (Canada, France, Germany, Italy, Japan, and the United Kingdom). In that time period, unit labor costs in U.S. manufacturing increased by less than 10 percent, compared to more than 30 percent in competitor countries. Since 1995, the unemployment rate in the European Union has ranged between 7 and 10 percent, while the U.S. unemployment rate has ranged between 4 and 7 percent. Finally, the United States continues to have the highest per capita GDP among major industrialized democracies.[2]

Average living standards, productivity growth, corporate profits, and other measures of economic prosperity are therefore quite robust in the United States, even if occasionally tempered by cyclical downturns such as the credit crisis of 2008. As such, from the aggregate perspective of consumers and corporations—that is, along the efficiency dimension—the United States scores quite highly and is perhaps the envy of the world. Setting aside important questions about the distribution of this economic wealth—that is, the equity dimension—which we address in later chapters, there are nevertheless important competitive pressures that are necessary to examine in order to understand the efficiency dimension of public policy discussions about the workplace of the 21st century. These pressures can be broadly categorized under the headings globalization, technology and skills, flexibility, employee benefits, and administrative burdens of the U.S. legal system.

Globalization

As recently as the 1970s, most economies were principally national in scale. In that climate, internal labor markets and stable industrial relations systems generally prevailed. Advances in trade and technology during the second half of the 20th century, however, altered the climate and spawned a global economy in which firms around the globe now compete internationally. Free-trade policies have mushroomed since the end of World War II, first with several rounds of the General Agreement on Tariffs and Trade and then with the creation of the World Trade Organization in 1995. As a result, average U.S. tariff rates on manufactured goods that exceeded 50 percent in 1930 have fallen to less than 4 percent. On the technology front, advances in information and communication technologies now enable firms to produce and sell goods wherever costs and markets are most attractive.[3]

Four dimensions of globalization illustrate the profound impact of these phenomena. The first dimension is international trade—the cross-border flow of goods and services as imports and exports. The total value of international trade in 2006 was $11.8 trillion and has been growing steadily. In the United States, exports have jumped from 10 percent of the merchandise produced in 1960 to 40 percent today. A second dimension of globalization is foreign direct investment (FDI), which consists of corporate investments that establish an interest in or control over an enterprise in another country. Global FDI exceeds $1 trillion annually, or about five times more than in 1990. International financial markets represent a third component of globalization. In April 2007, for example, more than $3.2 trillion worth of foreign exchange transactions occurred daily. The fourth dimension of globalization is immigration, especially the flow of people from poorer to richer countries. In fact, nearly 200 million people currently live outside their country of birth.[4]

Globalization presents both opportunities and challenges for employers everywhere. The expanded global economy serves employer interests by opening up new sources of production and new markets for the sale of goods and services. Globalization, accordingly, enhances efficiency by enabling both production and sales to seek out new equilibriums. But globalization also means that U.S. firms must compete on a grander scale. Some foreign competitors operate with a significant advantage in terms of low-cost resources, including labor. As but one example, garment workers in the Dominican Republic earn an average of 57¢ an hour. The competitive pressures on U.S. firms can therefore be severe.[5]

While globalization is often seen as enhancing the efficiency of individual firms—at least those that are able to survive intense global competition—the efficiency of the entire nation is also important. Globalization creates winners and, at least in the short run, losers. Thousands of well-paying jobs disappeared with the decline of the U.S. steel industry and individual cities experienced sharp increases in unemployment, small business failures, and crime. For example, in the Youngstown, Ohio area, the loss of 40,000 manufacturing jobs caused 400 local businesses to close, reduced personal income by $414 million, and decreased tax revenues for public schools by as much as 75 percent. In the textbook economic model, globalization creates new opportunities that offset these costs, but in reality the adjustment process is not painless. Policymakers need to be concerned with these efficiency losses created by intense global competition.[6]

Technology and Skills

Up until the 18th century, most work related to agriculture and natural resources. With the Industrial Revolution, manufacturing began to displace agriculture as the primary economic sector and, for much of the 20th century, dominated the economies of the United States and other industrialized countries. Today, however, the United States is considered a service-based or postindustrial rather than a manufacturing economy. Some take it a step further and argue that the United States is a knowledge-based economy. These sectoral changes—what Barry Jones describes as the shift from digging things up to making things, doing things, and finally processing symbolic things—were all facilitated by technological advances. Developments in machinery allowed sufficient food to be grown by fewer people. Advances in transportation first created regional, then national, and now international markets for goods and services. Automation allows manufacturing and routine service jobs to be replaced by machines. And advances in information and computing technology, of course, underlie today's information or knowledge economy.[7]

Technological change affects work in various ways. Technology alters an economy's relative mix of jobs and occupations—19th-century lamplighters, ice delivery drivers, and locomotive firemen are no longer needed; automobile assemblers, airline pilots, and computer programmers are 20th-century creations. Technological change also affects how work is done within specific occupations. Designing a building, making and repairing a car, and checking out groceries all are done differently today than they were fifty years ago. Rising and falling demand for different occupations, as well as changes within occupations, in turn, affect the relative wages of workers and the skills needed to prosper. Deskilling technological change reduces the skills needed for a specific job—and therefore wages too, while skill-biased technological change increases the skills required to do a job—and therefore the monetary rewards. Finally, technology also affects employee-employer relationships. The advent of the assembly line reduced employee autonomy and increased managerial control over the pace of work. More recently, computer-based systems are used to monitor customer service representatives, truck drivers, and even doctors.[8]

When people speak of "technology" in the 21st century they almost always are referring to information technology. Like earlier generations of technological innovation, information technology has significantly changed work, the labor market, and the employment relationship. More than half of Americans use a computer at work, while many others use scanners and other information technology devices. In some instances, information technology is deskilling and can cause incomes to stagnate; in other instances, information technology is skill-biased and pushes incomes up. In previous eras, technological advancements usually caused machines to replace *physical* aspects of work; today's information technology allows computers to replace some *cognitive* aspects of work. Technology in the 21st century, therefore, has the greatest likelihood of replacing workers who do routine information processing—occupations in which actions can be programmed to follow well-defined rules—while boosting the demand for occupations involving complex information processing tasks.[9]

The constant evolution of information technology places great pressure on efficiency through at least two channels. First, by allowing work to be replaced by computers while also facilitating the movement of work around the globe in search of the lowest labor costs, information technology creates a powerful competitive dynamic for employers. Employers who fail to fully harness the power of information technology may find themselves uncompetitive in the global marketplace. Second, by changing the nature of work, the use of information technology frequently creates a demand for new technical skills. To the extent that these new skills are not widespread, information technology creates a skills gap.

When technology and business practices change, it is fashionable to predict an end to employment as we know it. Jeremy Rifkin, for example, argues that

> millions of new entrants into the workforce find themselves without jobs, many victims of a technology revolution that is fast replacing human beings with machines in virtually every sector and industry of the global economy. . . . In the years ahead, new, more sophisticated software technologies are going to bring civilization ever closer to a near-workerless world.[10]

Fears of mass unemployment accompanied earlier technological advances as well. In the early 1800s, for example, Luddites destroyed weaving frames to protest the use of these new labor-saving machines; today, the term "Luddite" still refers to someone who opposes technological change. Often, though, new technologies bring with them new opportunities. Workers displaced from the agricultural sector by advances in machinery in the early 20th century were absorbed by the manufacturing sector as mass production exploded. Currently, many workers who are being displaced by the decline in U.S. manufacturing employment are being absorbed by the rise in the service sector—albeit not painlessly, since many workers are unemployed during the transition and earn less in their new service sector jobs.[11]

While new technology has therefore not yet created a workerless world, efficiency requires that advances in technology and business practices be matched by changes in workers' skills. When technological change is deskilling, no new skills are required (other than for those displaced who need to learn new skills for a new job), but at least some of today's innovations result in skill-biased technological change. In such cases, new skills are often required on a broad scale. Moreover, when bureaucratic work structures are replaced by flexible, team-oriented arrangements, new problem-solving, communication, and teamwork skills are needed. Many observers of the employment relationship therefore assert that the U.S. and other economies face a skills gap or a skills shortage—both technical and interpersonal skills are in great demand, but in short supply.[12]

Evaluating the skills gap is not easy. One analyst forecasts "significant labor shortages of at least 20 million workers [by 2020], especially in jobs that require the most skill and provide the greatest economic value."[13] Moreover, income differences between those with and without a college degree have widened, and this might stem from a shortage of more highly educated workers. On the other hand, this widening income gap might instead reflect a weakening of the institutions (such as unions) and public policies (such as minimum wages) that have traditionally boosted unskilled wages, while the policies that protect skilled workers (such as requirements for professional licenses and educational credentials) have remained strong. The true extent of a skills gap can therefore be debated, but the overall distribution of education and skills in a country's workforce is undeniably an important determinant of efficiency. In a global economy with technological change and flexible work practices, the issue of worker skills cannot be ignored.[14]

Flexibility

The postwar economy rested on mass production methods in which narrowly defined jobs fit together as standardized cogs in a vast bureaucratic machine. Efficiency and profitability were achieved through the economies of scale made possible by the large volume and quantity of identical goods produced or services delivered. But in the 1970s the economic instability created by the oil crisis ended the era of mass markets for standardized products. Profitability now depends on producing high-quality goods and services that can be developed and tailored in response to quickly changing consumer tastes. Information and communication technology is increasingly a major component of this endeavor, and knowledge management has become a key determinant of success or failure.[15]

Pressures to achieve efficiency in this new competitive dynamic—which have continued to increase into the 21st century with the hypercompetition of the global economy—are causing many employers to adopt practices designed to increase their ability to quickly respond to changes in market forces. In addition, foreign competitors such as Japanese and European automakers have provided examples of alternative methods of organizing work and deploying workers. The result is a significant reordering of the "who" and "how" of work in the United States to achieve greater flexibility and therefore efficiency. The extent to which these changes are possible is rooted in the flexibility of a country's labor market. The following discussion, therefore, first considers labor market flexibility and then turns to the changes in the "who" and "how" of work.

Labor Market Flexibility

Commentators frequently contrast the degree of labor market flexibility in Europe with that in the United States. In Germany, for example, most employment arrangements are legally considered to be permanent, which means that employees can be dismissed only for valid economic reasons (such as an economic downturn or poor performance) with at least four weeks' notice (often more); collective dismissals such as large-scale layoffs also require consultation with the employees' works council (a legally protected representative body of employees) and the negotiation of a social plan for compensating laid-off workers. Unemployment insurance pays workers about two-thirds of their regular pay for up to thirty-two months, depending on age and work history; afterward, there is the possibility of receiving paid unemployment assistance indefinitely. German employers must also provide their workers with at least twenty days of paid vacation annually; new mothers are entitled to fourteen weeks of paid maternity leave. Last, collective bargaining is very centralized, and in many cases the resulting agreement is binding on an entire industry. As a result, over 90 percent of German workers are covered by a collective bargaining agreement.[16]

While the details differ, this picture is broadly representative of labor markets throughout western Europe, excepting Great Britain. Consider how the United States sharply differs from this picture. Except for the small number of workers covered by collective bargaining agreements, U.S. employees can be dismissed at-will at any time for nearly any reason except discrimination; large-scale layoffs require only advance notification. Unemployment benefits replace approximately half of a laid-off worker's usual earnings for up to six months. Employees are entitled to twelve weeks of unpaid family leave, but there is no requirement for paid vacation days or paid maternity leave.

These comparisons between the U.S. and western European labor markets are frequently raised in policy discussions in both regions because, while the United States has been a job creation machine over the past two decades, the opposite has been true in western Europe, where job creation has been weak and the unemployment rate has been stubbornly high. Putting two and two together then, critics blame this "Eurosclerosis" on inflexible labor markets created by institutional rigidities. The logic is simple—as globalization, technology, and other factors "shock" economic systems, flexible labor markets allow companies and workers to adjust to new realities; inflexible labor markets prevent adjustment and are unable to combat the unemployment that results from these shocks.[17]

Reality, however, appears to be more complex. First, Eurosclerosis may be the result of factors other than labor market rigidities. For example, tight European monetary policy may have limited job growth while increased immigration into Europe kept unemployment rates high. Second, adjustment to shocks can occur in various ways. Employers in western Europe, for example, seem to adjust hours rather than staffing levels in response to changes in demand. Third, the cross-country statistical evidence on labor market flexibility and unemployment is not as strong as initially claimed. The results are very sensitive to the time period analyzed and the measurement of key labor market policies. Fourth, even taking the statistical results at face value, not all European labor policies negatively affect unemployment rates; for example, unemployment benefits with fixed rather than indefinite durations that are accompanied by interventions such as retraining to help the unemployed find work are not associated with higher unemployment rates. Fifth, case study analyses comparing individual countries do not always make a compelling link between labor market rigidities and unemployment. And last, U.S. labor market flexibility does not come without a price—low-skilled workers, in particular, have borne the heavy burden of stagnating incomes.[18]

It is therefore simplistic to say that labor market rigidity causes high unemployment and that labor market flexibility is unambiguously desirable. Nevertheless, labor market flexibility is an important consideration for work-related public policies in that one needs to guard against excessive labor standards. A balance between flexibility's promotion of efficiency on the one hand, and security and other dimensions of equity and voice on the other should be the goal. In fact, balancing flexibility and security is so important that European scholars and policymakers have coined a specific term for it: "flexicurity."[19]

Who: The Contingent Workforce

For much of the 20th century, the predominant employment model in the United States could be described as that of a "core worker system" characterized by long-term employment relationships. Rather than periodically bidding for workers in external markets, employers looked within their organizations for a dependable supply of labor. The prevalent internal labor market model of this period was designed to encourage career rather than casual employment. Toward this end, employers adopted personnel policies that included such features as competitive wage rates, training and development plans, and internal lines of progression and promotion. The most important of these policies was managerial commitment to long-term job security.[20]

Today, in contrast, a large and growing group of workers provide labor or services based on a variety of arrangements that deviate from the traditional core worker model. This contingent workforce encompasses a diverse group of non-core workers who provide work other than on a long-term, full-time basis. Contingent workers can be grouped into two broad categories. One group, consisting of independent contractors, contracted workers, and leased employees, are not legally classified as employees of the entity for whom they provide services. The second group, consisting of part-time and temporary employees, have the legal status of employees, but with less attachment to the workplace than full-time "core" employees. Both groups of contingent workers are not typically considered to be part of the corporate family and have lesser expectations of stable, long-term employment with a single employing entity. Although it is difficult to determine the exact number of contingent workers, reliable estimates range between 20 and 30 percent of all American workers. In fact, the country's largest private sector employer is not Wal-Mart or General Motors; it is Manpower, Inc., a provider of temporary and contingent workers. It is also difficult to determine how many contingent workers have voluntarily chosen this type of arrangement. Some studies indicate that as many as 60 percent of temporary employees and 25 percent of part-time employees would prefer more traditional full-time jobs.[21]

Many firms see contingent work arrangements as a means of increasing their labor market flexibility by adjusting personnel and staffing levels without the expense of hiring and laying off regular employees. Contingent workers therefore act as a flexible cushion in the external labor market that supports the core workers in each firm's internal labor market. Firms expand their workforce by hiring contingent workers in boom times, and then let the contingent workers go when demand turns downward. Similarly, pressures to "restructure" or "downsize," and even to avoid unionization, have led corporations to increase their use of contingent employees. Further, employers have an incentive to hire contingent workers because they typically work for less pay and fewer benefits, and, by virtue of not being "employees" in a legal sense, are exempt from most employment regulation. In short, an increase in contingent work facilitates a flexible labor market and significant perceived, and in some cases real, cost savings for American firms.[22]

How: New Ways of Organizing Work

In addition to creating flexibility through contingent and nontraditional staffing arrangements, U.S. employers have sought greater flexibility by adopting new ways of organizing work. In a nutshell, U.S. employers have transformed a regime characterized by a highly bureaucratic work structure into one that is increasingly lean and team-oriented. The prevailing methodology of organizing work for most of the 20th century was based on principles known as scientific management (or "Taylorism" after Frederick Winslow Taylor and his highly influential 1911 treatise *The Principles of Scientific Management*). Taylor and others maintained that employers could maximize efficiency by carefully studying work tasks and scientifically determining the one best way of completing a task. The Taylorist model creates a hierarchical work structure in which employees are assigned to highly specialized, standardized, and routine job tasks (picture an assembly line worker repeating the same limited tasks hundreds of times a day). A corollary teaching of scientific management is that employers should organize employment by means of hierarchical job ladders and long-term tenure. Scientific management principles and internal labor markets dominated corporate America into the 1970s.[23]

The bureaucratic structure of scientific management was well suited to the mass production of standardized goods in a stable economy, but this economic system broke down in the 1970s. By 2000, flexibility had replaced standardization as a key management objective. With the superior performance of the Japanese economy (at least until the 1990s)—and the quality of Japanese cars—team-based Japanese work structures provided an intriguing model for reform. In response, numerous U.S. employers replaced hierarchical production systems with various forms of flatter and sometimes team-oriented work structures that serve flexible specialization rather than mass manufacturing. The tedium and rigidity of narrowly defined jobs are being replaced by the challenge and variety of job rotation, job enrichment, and cross-training. Employee suggestions are encouraged, and in the most ambitious examples, self-directed work teams exercise significant decision-making authority.[24] These new forms of work organization promote functional flexibility by enabling employers to shift workers to different tasks and functions in response to changing market opportunities and production needs.

All told, these various forms of flexibility—labor market flexibility, contingent workers, and new forms of work organization—are perceived to promote efficient employment relationships and benefit employers. The implications for employees, however, are more equivocal, and are decidedly negative for labor unions. We revisit these effects on equity and voice in later chapters.

Employee Benefits

A major source of inefficiency in the contemporary American workplace is the predominantly employment-sponsored system of employee benefits, especially retirement (beyond Social Security) and health insurance coverage. Approximately 50 percent of workers are covered by employer-provided pensions. Approximately 60 percent of all individuals in the United States obtain health insurance through an employer-provided plan. Put another way, approximately 80 percent of all Americans with health insurance under the age of 65 obtain that coverage through a plan sponsored by their own employer or the employer of another family member. With health care and employment so closely intertwined, problems in health care delivery translate into problems with employment policy as well.[25]

The biggest problem areas of health care policy concern cost and access. The United States currently leads the world in health care spending per capita. In 2006 the annual health insurance benefit cost for a full-time insured American worker was $11,480 for family coverage—an enormous 87 percent increase since 2000 and a rate of increase four times faster than wage growth. Total health care expenditures now consume approximately 15 percent of U.S. gross domestic product (GDP) and are expected to rise to more than 20 percent of GDP by 2015. These spiraling costs have a direct and significant effect on the employment relationship. Faced with an ever-increasing health insurance cost burden, employers have responded with a variety of efforts to cut or at least curtail costs. These efforts include reducing benefits, limiting coverage, and curtailing wage increases. Perhaps the most common strategy adopted by employers has been to require employees to bear a higher individual financial responsibility in the form of premium contributions, co-payments, and deductibles. Rising health insurance costs also have become a contentious issue in labor-management relations. Several high-profile labor disputes, such as the work stoppage involving tens of thousands of Southern California grocery workers in 2003, centered on health insurance cost concerns. All too often, these labor-management disputes focus on how to split the burden of escalating costs, rather than on how to share the bounty of increasing profits.[26]

Rising costs in a regime of employer-sponsored health insurance also cause inefficiencies on a broader societal scale. First, these costs can reduce employment. Health insurance constitutes approximately one-fourth of all benefit costs, and both overall benefit costs and health care costs continue to grow as a proportion of total compensation. Even though a number of economic studies show that about 75 percent of employer-paid health insurance costs are passed back to employees in the form of lower wages, employers tend not to believe such claims and work hard to curb rising benefit costs. Since the cost of health insurance is usually fixed per employee, firms can reduce compensation outlays by hiring fewer employees and asking them to work longer hours.[27]

Second, employer-provided health insurance contributes to the phenomenon of "job lock." A number of studies show that the availability of health insurance plays an important role in job mobility decisions. In particular, evidence suggests that employees with health insurance coverage through their job are less likely to accept a new job or to retire before age 65 if the change in job status is accompanied by a loss of health insurance coverage. The resulting decrease in job mobility constitutes a market failure that decreases the efficiency of the U.S. economy.[28]

Third, U.S. firms that finance employee health insurance incur costs that are not borne by their competitors in the global economy. In virtually all other industrialized nations, including twenty-eight out of thirty OECD countries, public health insurance programs provide essentially universal coverage. Accordingly, those U.S. employers that subsidize employee health insurance coverage, a category that includes most large employers, operate at a competitive disadvantage to foreign firms that do not have the same responsibility. As a report issued by the Employment Policy Foundation has concluded:

> As health insurance costs continue to rise, they create challenges to U.S. employers' ability to attract and retain employees and remain competitive in the global economy. The U.S. system of employer-paid health insurance benefits for individual employees and their families places a unique cost burden on American producers of goods and services that is not incurred by their foreign competitors.[29]

Similar conclusions apply to pensions, paid family leave, and other employer-provided benefits that are granted universally in other countries. In fact, employee benefit costs currently account for 30 percent of employer costs of total employee compensation in the United States.[30] And as these costs continue to rise, this system of employer-provided benefits will increasingly reduce efficiency in the U.S. employment relationship.

Administrative Burdens of the Litigation Enforcement Model

Disputes over employee discrimination and other elements of employment law are typically adjudicated in the U.S. court system. The same is true for accusations of unjust discharges that allegedly violate a state's exceptions to the employment-at-will doctrine. In other words, U.S. employment law relies on a litigation enforcement model. The regulatory boom over the past forty years (recall Table 2.1) has caused an explosion of employment litigation, with employment cases now constituting approximately 10 percent of the total federal court docket. To a considerable extent, turning an old phrase, we have made a federal case out of routine employment disputes.

This litigation enforcement model has considerable drawbacks. Disputants, particularly in the context of employment termination, face a maze of potential laws and forums. The parties involved in an employment termination lawsuit, as well as the judiciary, must devote considerable time and attention to navigating this maze. A fired worker, for example, might assert a host of claims challenging his or her former employer's termination decision. It is not uncommon for employee discharge complaints today to plead claims numbering in the double digits. Table 3.1 lists just some of those claims that may be asserted under existing federal and state employment law. This maze is further complicated by the multiple forums in which a claim can be made. Discharge-related claims can be heard by a federal court, a state court, an administrative agency, or a private arbitrator, often with different trial mechanisms (juries or judges) and remedies (punitive damages, lawyers' fees, reinstatement).[31]

Other inefficiencies result from the fact that many U.S. public policies on work operate in isolation, and even sometimes in conflict. Different statutes and policies have different definitions of "employee" and "supervisor." Someone with a serious health condition might also be considered disabled and therefore covered under the Family and Medical Leave Act, the Americans with Disabilities Act, and the relevant state workers' compensation statute. Exceptions to the at-will doctrine can vary widely from state to state. Retaliation for filing a

TABLE 3.1
The Maze of Laws and Forums for Claiming Wrongful Discharge

Federal Claims	State Claims
Antidiscrimination Statutes	*Statutes*
Title VII of the Civil Rights Act	Antidiscrimination statutes
Age Discrimination in Employment Act	Whistleblower statutes
Americans with Disabilities Act	
	Common-Law Claims
Other Statutes (Claims)	Public policy tort
National Labor Relations Act (unfair labor practices)	Contract
Family and Medical Leave Act; Employee Retirement Income Security Act; Occupational Health and Safety Act (retaliation)	Covenant of Good Faith and Fair Dealing
	Defamation
	Intentional infliction of emotional distress
Constitutional Claims	*Collective Bargaining Agreements*
First Amendment	Public sector grievance arbitration
Due process	
Equal protection	
Collective Bargaining Agreements	
Private sector grievance arbitration	

workers' compensation claim is often seen as contrary to public policy and therefore impermissible, but curiously, retaliation for filing an unemployment insurance claim is rarely seen as a similar enforceable exception to the at-will doctrine. A maze of multiple forums might be justified if each forum involved specific expertise on the nature of a focused employment issue, but this is rarely the case. Rather, the maze also includes courts and agencies with overlapping jurisdictions and uneven expertise. Employers and employees alike suffer from the inefficiencies of this piecemeal system.

Much of today's employment litigation entails the sorting and accommodation of these multiple claims and forums. Some federal statutes, such the Employee Retirement Income Security Act (ERISA), broadly preempt state law claims relating to employee benefit plans, while others, such as Title VII of the Civil Rights Act of 1964, preempt very few state law claims. In between are no fewer than three different strands of federal labor law preemption, each with its own complicated standard for ousting state law claims. At the state level, courts sometimes find that certain statutory claims are exclusive and preclude common-law claims based on the same set of facts. Other courts, however, view common-law claims as supplementary and permit both statutory and parallel common-law claims to proceed at the same time. Still other jurisdictions chart something of a middle course by permitting multiple claims to proceed simultaneously, but limiting the amount of damages to a single claim where the harm asserted in the multiple counts is essentially identical.[32]

Civil litigation also is a relatively slow method of dispute resolution. The median time plaintiffs must wait until a civil trial is two years. While waiting for a trial date, parties typically engage in discovery, pre-trial motions, and settlement discussions. The litigation time line may be extended further with post-trial proceedings and subsequent appeals. Litigation also is an expensive mechanism for resolving employment disputes. The cost of taking a case from complaint to trial typically reaches or exceeds $300,000. Attorneys' fees paid by defendant employers make up the vast bulk of this amount. In addition, parties to an employment suit incur indirect expenses due to the necessary diversion of time and resources from productive activity to litigation preparation activity. Many employers also hire lawyers and consultants to assist them in avoiding litigation, such as by auditing corporate practices, creating policies, and generating favorable evidence.[33]

Finally, the litigation model fails to interject the views of an expert body into the decision-making process. In contrast to the labor law arena in which an expert National Labor Relations Board oversees individual decisions and the development of controlling legal principles, employment law disputes are usually heard in courts of general jurisdiction. These courts hear employment cases with a mix of criminal cases, contract disputes, and other matters. Given the increasing complexity of American employment law, this is not the most efficient means of guiding and coordinating future doctrinal developments.[34]

Beyond these systemic problems, the litigation model also results in some unique problems for employees and employers. For terminated employees, the problem is one of access to the justice system. The high cost of attorneys' fees, out-of-pocket expenses, and the considerable amount of time it takes to litigate a claim all make it difficult for employees to use the courts. These obstacles disproportionately affect lower-paid employees. It is more difficult for this group to afford the combined cost and delay of litigation than for more highly compensated workers. Although some attorneys are willing to handle employment discharge cases on a contingency-fee basis, they are less likely to do so on behalf of lower-income workers. In part this is because workers who earn modest wages before discharge are less likely to receive large monetary jury verdicts even if they win the lawsuit. For many low-income employees, the lawyer's cost of litigating such a claim could exceed the likely amount of recovery.[35]

Many employers experience a similar problem at the opposite end of the spectrum. Employers have a strong incentive to settle employment claims in order to avoid the costs associated with litigation. Given that defense costs through trial hover at around $300,000 in a typical employment termination case, settling even a nonmeritorious claim may make financial sense. This incentive is heightened by the potential for a sizable jury verdict if a case is taken to trial. A study by the Employer's Resource Group revealed an average award of $733,000 in employment termination cases tried before a jury. Moreover, while employers prevail in most employment suits, this same study indicated that plaintiffs won in 64 percent of those cases that ended with a jury verdict. Not surprisingly, the vast majority of employment lawsuits result in voluntary settlements.[36]

What we have, in effect, is a uniquely American employment law lottery. Most employees work on an at-will basis and have no viable legal claim in the event of a job termination. Many of those workers who may have a legitimate claim are unable to pursue it because of the high entry cost of our justice system. Employers, nonetheless, fear employment termination suits and spend considerable sums deterring and settling lawsuits. The only real winners in this system are the handful of plaintiffs who strike it big before a jury.

Conclusion

Efficiency is important because it promotes economic prosperity. In the neoliberal market paradigm, efficiency is achieved by consumers, workers, investors, and managers pursuing their selfish interests in competitive markets. In the neoliberal market model, the role of public policy is to protect freedom, property rights, and competition in the name of liberty and efficiency. If these forces are working correctly, economic prosperity, quality jobs, and rising living standards will follow. However, globalization, information technology, and other changes are dramatically altering the competitive dynamic of the 21st century. Worker skills, employee benefits, the U.S. litigation enforcement system, and the multiple dimensions of flexibility therefore represent major challenges for the efficiency of the U.S. employment relationship.

Compared to many other countries, the U.S. employment relationship is more flexible and less regulated. But this does not necessarily mean that the system of workplace regulation currently in place operates in an efficient manner. Indeed, two aspects of the present-day U.S. regime fall particularly low on the overall efficiency scale. First, the U.S. regulatory scheme that governs the individual employer-employee relationship is a confusing, overlapping maze that imposes undesirable transaction costs. Second, the prevalent employer-sponsored system of employee benefits in the United States, particularly with respect to health care, unfairly taxes employers, under-provides benefits, and dampens employment.

In response to competitive pressures, the adoption of flexible business practices by U.S. employers has dramatically altered the "who" and "how" of work. By garnering more flexibility in assigning and structuring work, U.S. employers have been able to compete more successfully in the global economy. The accompanying weakening of unions and regulatory labor standards also serves the efficiency objective of the employment relationship. In fact, while imperfect, the U.S. workplace is perhaps the model of efficiency for many other countries. But this rise of flexible business practices and decline in institutional protections has shifted the loci of risk assumption in the global economy away from firms and toward individual workers.[37] In other words, U.S. efficiency gains are not without human costs. Public policies on the employment relationship should therefore consider not only efficiency, but also the effects on equity and voice. It is to the current status of these two objectives of the employment relationship that we now turn.

CHAPTER 4

Equity

EVERYONE WANTS TO BE TREATED FAIRLY. In all walks of life—as children, parents, students, employees, citizens, consumers—we chafe at favoritism that seems to unfairly benefit others. In spite of the popular contention that "life is unfair," human beings seek fairness and justice. As applied to the employment relationship, fairness and justice are frequently labeled equity. Employment relationship equity can be defined in various ways. To some, whatever is produced by free-market exchange is seen as equitable because it reflects what the market will bear. To provide a richer exploration, however, we here define employment relationship equity more broadly: it is a set of fair employment standards that encompass wages and benefits to support a family, safe working conditions, security, and nondiscriminatory treatment. This broader definition is consistent with religious teachings on the sanctity of human life, ethical theories on basic human rights, and democratic principles of citizenship, freedom, and equality that support minimum labor standards for all workers regardless of their market power.[1]

The equity dimension of an explicit scorecard for workplace law and public policy consists of seven components: balancing work and nonwork needs; a living wage; balanced income distributions; income, retirement, health, and physical security; nondiscrimination and fairness; good-cause dismissal; and nonstandard work arrangements.

The trends discussed in the previous chapter, however, have placed significant pressure on these seven issues over the past two decades. Although globalization and technology are arguably positive developments for workers in terms of fostering high-skilled job growth, thus far they have also had very negative effects on some workers, especially the lower-skilled. After adjusting for inflation, average weekly earnings for the production and nonsupervisory workers that make up 80 percent of the U.S. labor force fell more than 12 percent from 1973 to 1995; increases since 1995 have still not returned average weekly earnings to 1970s levels.[2]

Corporations around the world face intense pressure to cut costs in order to be competitive in the new global economy. American businesses, particularly beginning in the 1980s, have turned to reorganizations, downsizings, and contingent work arrangements as cost-cutting measures. Trade and technology have made capital considerably more mobile than labor, and enable employers to produce goods wherever labor costs are the most attractive. American employers, accordingly, have shifted production first to the U.S. Sunbelt and more recently to developing nations as means of escaping unions and lowering labor costs. Outsourcing and offshoring are also starting to threaten a wide range of white-collar occupations. Even the saying of special intentions (requests by individuals for a priest to pray for a family member or friend) has been outsourced by the Catholic Church to India. As a result, workers, especially unionized ones, are frequently on the defensive trying to prevent wage and benefit cuts and protecting jobs from moving overseas.[3]

In short, the forces of global trade and technology have dramatically altered the relative power of labor and capital in the economic marketplace, with negative consequences for equity in the U.S. employment relationship. Compared to thirty years ago, Americans with regular, full-time jobs are working longer hours with fewer benefits and face much greater insecurity; meanwhile, the rolls of contingent workers are growing. In fact, the share of U.S. national income paid out as wages and salaries is at its lowest point since statistics started being collected in 1947. In contrast, the share accounted for by corporate profits is the highest in more than fifty years. It is perhaps not surprising then, that one-third of U.S. workers feel chronically overworked.[4]

These are critical issues for public policies on work. In fact, the deterioration of equity in the U.S. employment relationship has been exacerbated by the inability of local and national legal systems to regulate internationally mobile employers. As aptly summarized by Kenneth Dau-Schmidt:

> If a country regulates the employment relationship in such a way as to impose costs on capital, this gives the employer incentive to move his operations to a

country that does not impose such costs. As a result countries have incentive to minimize their regulations of employers, a result known as "the race to the bottom."[5]

The erosion of fair employment outcomes has also been magnified by the exclusion of contingent workers from social insurance programs and employment laws. Against this backdrop, a careful assessment of the state of equity in the contemporary U.S. employment relationship is necessary in order to assess the contemporary state of workplace law and public policy.

Balancing Work and Non-Work Needs

America is hard at work. While American employees traditionally have exhibited a strong work ethic, the past few decades have seen a remarkable increase in the overall amount of work effort in the United States. Two parallel forces have led this surge. First, many individuals, primarily middle-class women, who were full-time caregivers in the past, now divide their time between family care and paid work. Second, this larger cadre of workers is putting in significantly more time at work per person.

These trends are driven by at least two factors. First, families need to work harder to maintain their living standards. Since the 1970s, real hourly wages have been relatively stagnant. Male workers have been particularly hard hit, experiencing an overall drop in real wages during the 1980s and the early 1990s. Even though real wages rebounded in the second half of the 1990s, the median real wage for male workers in 2000 and 2005 was still below the 1979 level. To maintain household income levels, many employees have taken on additional hours and many households have added a second wage earner. In fact, during the 1980s, middle-income families would have experienced net losses in income if not for the added contributions of working spouses.[6]

Second, employers have financial incentives to squeeze more working time out of their employees. Salaried employees who perform executive, administrative, or professional duties receive a fixed salary regardless of the number of hours worked and are exempt from the overtime requirements of the Fair Labor Standards Act (FLSA).[7] Thus employers do not pay more if they require salaried employees to work additional hours; and the proportion of employees working in exempt, salaried positions has virtually doubled since the FLSA was enacted in 1938. Similarly, dramatic increases in the cost of employee benefits have encouraged employers to require longer workweeks. Since benefit costs are usually independent of how many hours an employee actually works, the hourly cost of employee benefits declines as the employee puts in more hours. As benefits become more expensive, employers have greater economic incentives to meet labor needs by increasing the number of hours rather than the number of employees.[8]

As a result of these pressures, the average full-time American employee now works nearly 200 more hours each year than he or she worked thirty years ago. The total work hours of husbands and wives have increased even more. In fact, while it is questionable whether the stereotypical family of the 1950s—a breadwinning father, a stay-at-home mom, and several children—was ever the norm among nonwhite or low-income households, it is no longer the norm even in the white middle class because the participation rate of women in the American labor force has doubled since 1950. In fact, increases in female labor force participation rates have been particularly sharp for married women and those with young children. In 1950, 23 percent of married women and only 12 percent of women with children under the age of 6 participated in the labor force. Today, the labor force participation rate for both of these categories is around 60 percent. As a result, just 15 percent of American households today consist of a married couple with only a male earner. Over 60 percent of married couples with children are dual-earner households. Single parents now head more than 10 million families.[9]

The stereotypical family arrangement of the 21st century is therefore one that lacks a stay-at-home caregiver. The problems of balancing work and family obligations in this new reality are well known. Commonly overlooked, however, is that the problem of balancing work and non-work time demands is not limited to caregivers. American workers generally are experiencing a significant and growing time crunch problem. This observation is not meant to denigrate the particularly heavy time demands on working caregivers, especially women. It is meant, instead, to reinforce the pervasiveness of the time crunch for all American workers. The United States now leads the industrialized world in hours worked, and only trails New Zealand and Japan in the high fraction of employees working more than 49 hours per week. The average American employee works approximately 200–400 more hours per year than his or her European counterpart. It is not surprising, then, that surveys conducted by the Families and Work Institute show that 70 percent of American workers sometimes feel overwhelmed by work and that 63 percent would prefer to work fewer hours.[10]

The realities of the American worker time crunch must be juxtaposed with the requirements of an equitable employment relationship that should allow workers to balance their work and non-work responsibilities. This desired balance is important for several reasons. As employees spend more time at work, they spend less time caring for and interacting with family members. In particular, the amount of time parents spend with their children has declined dramatically over the past thirty years, with negative consequences for children's emotional and intellectual development. Similar issues arise with respect to extended family members, as one out of four U.S. families is responsible for the care of an elderly relative. Research shows that paid leave to care for a newborn reduces infant mortality and that infants of mothers who return to work less than twelve weeks after giving birth are less likely to receive regular medical checkups and to have all of their immunizations. Family obligations also interfere with workplace productivity. With so many working caregivers, family emergencies readily become workplace disruptions. The worker time crunch also translates into less leisure time and lower participation rates in community clubs and activities. And overworked employees report less successful relationships with spouses, family, and friends.[11]

The U.S. federal government's principal attempt to ease the worker time crunch is the Family and Medical Leave Act (FMLA) of 1993.[12] The FMLA entitles eligible employees to a total of twelve weeks of leave per twelve-month period to care for a newborn or newly adopted child, a child, parent, or spouse with a serious health condition, or the employee's own serious health condition. Employers are required to maintain the employee's health insurance coverage during the leave period and to return the employee to his or her previous position or a comparable one. Note, however, that the FMLA does not require employers to offer paid leave. A Department of Labor survey revealed that nearly 20 percent of employees covered by the FMLA took a leave under the act in an eighteen-month period ending in 2000. Because of gaps in coverage, this translates to less than 2 percent of all U.S. employees. During this same time period, 2.4 percent of the survey respondents—which translates to 3.5 million workers when applied to the entire labor force—reported that they needed family or medical leave, but were unable to take it. Nearly 80 percent of these leave-needers indicated that they did not take a leave because they could not afford it.[13]

With only three exceptions (California, New Jersey, and Washington),[14] state-level leave policies are not any stronger. In fact, it is estimated that

59 million U.S. workers lack paid sick leave to care for themselves, and 86 million do not have any paid sick leave that they can use to care for a sick child. But what about personal time to pursue one's interests when not sick? There is no required minimum vacation time for U.S. workers. Employers are free to offer as much or as little vacation time as they choose. Roughly three-quarters of private sector employees are given paid vacations, but the average worker must work for an employer for ten years before earning three weeks of paid annual vacation; the average after twenty-five years of service is still less than four weeks of vacation. In contrast, nearly all western European countries statutorily mandate a minimum of four to five weeks of paid annual vacation. Many U.S. employees also have little influence over their work schedules; and there are no legal restrictions on an employer's use of mandatory overtime, even if an employee has work-family conflicts or other commitments. Equity in the employment relationship requires that employees be able to balance their work and non-work responsibilities and interests in a healthy manner. This is largely an issue of time—the amount of work time, control over work time, and the affordability of non-work time. For many American workers, it is time for an improvement.[15]

A Living Wage

Against this backdrop of American workers hard at work, the United Nations Universal Declaration of Human Rights declares that "Everyone who works has the right to just and favorable remuneration ensuring for himself and his family an existence worthy of human dignity, and supplemented, if necessary, by other means of social protection" (article 23). Other international human rights instruments similarly proclaim the right to fair wages that allow workers and their families a decent living. In other words, it is widely accepted that workers should earn at least a living wage. A living wage provides for more than bare subsistence; a living wage is a wage high enough to provide for a decent standard of living with some reasonable level of comfort. One can cite theologians and moral philosophers from diverse camps on this issue, but the intuition is quite straightforward: human beings deserve the means to live a decent life simply because they are human. It also can be argued that a living wage is an essential element of a democracy because individuals who lack basic material resources are not autonomous, free citizens and cannot be the political equals of those who have basic material resources.[16]

The United States has had a national minimum wage since 1938, when the FLSA established 25¢ per hour as the legal minimum. But the value of the minimum wage peaked in the 1960s. From 1968 to 2006, the minimum wage's real (inflation-adjusted) value fell by more than 30 percent, and at the end of 2006 stood at its lowest real value in fifty years, before federal legislation in 2007 enacted a three-step increase from $5.15 per hour to $5.85 in July 2007, to $6.55 in July 2008, and to $7.25 in July 2009. Before the increase in 2007, a full-time minimum wage earner did not earn enough to live above the official poverty line for a family of four; after the minimum wage reaches $7.25 in 2009, the annual wages of such an earner will be slightly higher than the poverty line.[17]

But many believe that the official poverty line understates the threshold needed for true self-sufficiency. There are over 9 million working families with household incomes less than one and a half times the official poverty level and over 5 million of these families have at least one member working full-time on a year-round basis; these figures increase to 14 and 9 million families, respectively, for working families with household incomes less than twice the official poverty level. Barbara Ehrenreich poignantly brought these statistics to life in her description of her own efforts to survive as a waitress, hotel maid, house cleaner, nursing home aide, and Wal-Mart salesperson. Even without a family to support, she was able to make ends meet only by working two jobs or seven days a week, as long as she did not get sick and her car did not break down. The statistics reveal that these troubling experiences are widespread across the U.S. labor market. The living wage component of equity is tenuous at best for millions of workers and their families.[18]

Balanced Income Distributions

The third component of equity goes beyond the dignified minimum income level of a living wage to consider the fairness of the overall distribution of economic rewards throughout society. A capitalist economy will naturally produce income differences, since such differences reflect the diversity of skill, effort, responsibility, and working conditions of individuals and jobs. Reasonable income differences are normal in a healthy economy, but the empirical record leaves no doubt that the United States has experienced a dramatic increase in income disparities over the past thirty years. There is a broad consensus that since the 1970s, wage inequality and family income inequality have sharply increased. In fact, in the early 2000s the income shares of the top income groups are at their highest levels since World War II.[19]

Disparities between the average worker's income and that of CEOs graphically illustrate this inequality: in 2000, the average CEO earned 300 times more than the average worker; in other words, the average CEO earned more in one working day than the average worker earned in an entire year. The year 2000 was a peak year for this disparity, but the ratio of CEO to average worker pay almost a decade later is still more than five times what it was in the 1970s, and is much greater than in other countries. These trends are not limited to the excesses of CEO pay. From the end of World War II to the oil crisis of the early 1970s, families of all income levels saw their income nearly double. But between the oil crisis and the end of the century, income growth among low-income families was 12 percent; in comparison, it was 27 percent for families in the middle of the income distribution and 67 percent for high-income families. The poorest 20 percent of all U.S. households now earn less than 5 percent of U.S. total income; the richest 20 percent enjoy nearly half of the country's total income. The United States also is a leader among industrialized countries in the level of income inequality, with a 50 percent higher earnings gap between high- and low-earning households than the average of other OECD countries. Unfortunately, increases in U.S. income inequality have not been accompanied by an increase in economic mobility; if anything, it is getting more difficult to climb the economic ladder.[20]

The statistics on income inequality are even more dramatic when one considers the impacts of productivity and taxation. Between 1973 and 2001, the productivity of the U.S. workforce grew by 55 percent. This figure exceeded the real income growth of the bottom 20 percent of households by more than five times, and was more than double the median growth of household income over this period. Individual earners fared even worse. The median male wage in 2000 was still below its 1979 level in spite of a 44 percent jump in productivity during that period. Clearly, capital rather than labor disproportionately enjoyed the fruits of this increased productivity. Meanwhile, U.S. income tax rates have become considerably less progressive. For example, the tax cuts enacted by the Bush administration starting in 2001 have disproportionately reduced the tax burden of the wealthy, providing for greater tax rate reductions at higher income levels. A reduction in progressive tax rates exacerbates income inequality by leaving low-income earners with less take-home pay, both absolutely and proportionately, than those in the highest earning brackets.[21]

Multiple factors appear responsible for the growing income inequality in the United States—globalization, technology, and increases in contingent work (as described in Chapter 3), the erosion of legislated labor standards (as documented in this chapter), and the decline in union density (as discussed in Chapter 5). Whatever the cause, the spiraling increase in income inequality is a matter for great concern. As Barbara Ehrenreich wrote of her experience as a low-wage worker, the tragic cycle of ever-deepening inequality has created for many an unsustainable lifestyle of acute stress. This cycle not only represents a fundamental lack of equity for those who can no longer succeed through hard work; it also contains the seeds for societal instability. Economic inequality exacerbates social inequalities in schooling, health, housing, and political participation. Excessive economic inequality erodes political equality and therefore undermines democratic institutions. High rates of income inequality correlate with a high incidence of violent crime and other undesirable social conditions.[22] An empirical study of two international surveys shows that individuals in countries with high income inequality are more likely to support radical societal changes through "revolutionary action" than individuals in countries with lower levels of inequality.[23] In the end, the diminution of the American dream through significant inequality is a problem for all of us, and should therefore be a significant public policy concern.

Security and Social Safety Nets

The widening income gap between rich and poor discussed in the previous section has received a lot of attention. Less well known is that income insecurity has increased even more than income inequality. In other words, families today experience much greater year-to-year income swings than in previous eras. This is not surprising: the volatility of corporate profits has increased, so pay raises have become less certain, worries about job loss more pervasive, and temporary work more prevalent. These trends tie directly into another critical dimension of equity—namely, security. As proclaimed in article 25 of the United Nations Universal Declaration of Human Rights, everyone has "the right to security in the event of unemployment, sickness, disability, widowhood, old age or other lack of livelihood in circumstances beyond his control." Conceptually, security does not need to be an employment issue; public assistance programs such as food stamps and housing subsidies provide a measure of security unrelated to one's employment. Nevertheless, security is closely intertwined with work, especially in the United States, and therefore is a key element of equity in the American employment relationship.[24]

A culture of laissez faire and personal responsibility leaves the provision of security to the private market such that the ability to purchase security is tightly linked to wage and salary income. One hundred years ago, the famous union leader Samuel Gompers avidly championed higher wages as the means to afford health care and meet other individual needs; this thinking continues to be popular today in conservative and business circles. Moreover, during much of the 20th century, American employers developed extensive employee benefit packages to strengthen employees' dependence on and therefore loyalty to their employers. A strong societal work ethic also creates an ethos in which only workers are deserving of public support. For over seventy years, the U.S. unemployment insurance system has focused on covering short-term interruptions in one's regular employment; more recently, the Personal Responsibility and Work Opportunity Reconciliation Act in 1996 tightly links welfare payments to working.[25] So in the United States, the critical elements of security—income, retirement, and health security—are, for better or worse, employment issues, and therefore demand our attention.

Income Security

Recent research documents the uncertainty of year-to-year income changes that confront U.S. families. After adjusting for inflation, approximately half of all U.S. households see their income fall in any given two-year period, and the average decline has increased from around 25 percent in the early 1970s to around 40 percent thirty years later. The probability that an American household will suffer an income loss of more than 50 percent in any given two-year period has doubled since 1970. After adjusting for inflation, a household earning $50,000 in its best year could, on average, expect to earn at least $21,000 in its worst year of the 1970s, but only $12,500 in its worst year of the 1990s. Income volatility has increased the greatest for low-income families, but one striking feature of this rise in insecurity is its effect on both blue-collar and white-collar families. Moreover, unlike investors who can demand a higher average return to compensate for higher levels of risk, workers and their families are caught by a perversion of the risk-reward trade-off: household risk and uncertainty have increased while income growth has slowed and stalled.[26]

In an ideal world, families can borrow in lean years and repay debt in good years to smooth their consumption and living standards in the face of income fluctuations. This requires what economists call complete insurance markets, but research has shown that insurance markets are incomplete and individuals are unable to borrow enough to completely smooth their consumption.[27] The resulting inefficiencies as well as personal and social ills lead governments to create social safety nets. The most important social safety net for income insecurity is unemployment insurance, which pays temporary benefits to partially replace lost earnings when a worker loses a job through no fault of his own. Though specific benefit levels and eligibility criteria vary from state to state, unemployment insurance benefits typically replace one-third to one-half of an unemployed worker's previous earnings for up to twenty-six weeks as long as the individual is actively seeking a new job. These benefits are intended to help families maintain their living standards during a spell of unemployment and to provide workers with the financial ability to look for another job that matches their skills rather than having to take the first low-paying job that comes along. Partial rather than full income replacement is intended to provide an incentive to find work. The Social Security system and state-level workers' compensation programs also provide an element of social insurance against income insecurity stemming from work-related disabilities.[28]

But public policy has not kept pace with the dramatic rise in income insecurity. Only one-third of unemployed workers collect unemployment benefits—less than half the proportion in 1947. This is partly because some workers choose not to apply for benefits, but it also reflects the fact that large numbers are ineligible for benefits. To be eligible, a worker must typically have earned $2,500–3,500 in a previous quarter, which puts part-time, temporary, and low-wage workers on the margins of eligibility. Of those who do receive benefits, over 40 percent exhaust their benefits before finding a job.[29] And, income loss stemming from reduced hours or wage cuts are not covered by unemployment insurance. Putting all of these factors together, then, it has been estimated that of all of the earnings lost in a recession, only 8–15 percent is replaced by unemployment insurance.[30] Disability-related social insurance programs, meanwhile, are a confusing maze with high administrative costs, low income replacement levels, and strong disincentives to work. That both unemployment insurance and workers' compensation are state-level programs further means that states sometimes compete with one another for jobs by weakening these programs in order to make their states more attractive to employers.[31]

Increasingly, therefore, the social safety net for income insecurity is being replaced by a "plastic" safety net in which workers use credit cards to pay for rent, groceries, and medical expenses. Although, as economists argue, consumer credit can be a desirable means of consumption smoothing, the explosion of consumer debt is alarming. The value of consumer debt tripled between 1990 and 2005, while credit card debt for the average family increased by 50 percent, with even larger increases among low-income families. For many years, lower- and middle-income families borrowed money against their home equity through refinancing to keep pace with credit card debt and basic necessities. But this cushion has evaporated for many in the housing market downturn, with the result that household debt levels are again soaring. In the end, it is dangerous to fill the holes in the social safety net with plastic, especially at rates of interest that create perpetual indebtedness.[32]

Retirement Security

The ingredients for a financially secure retirement are often equated with a three-legged stool. If any one leg becomes unstable, the whole thing risks collapse. The financial platform of the retirement stool is supported by three sources of retirement income: (1) Social Security, (2) employer-provided retirement plans, and (3) individual savings and assets. With projected shortfalls looming for all three legs of this stool, the financial prospects for future retirees are looking more shaky than secure.

Social Security. Analysts project that, beginning in 2017, total Social Security benefit outlays will exceed tax revenues, with the consequence that the Social Security Trust Fund will be fully exhausted by 2041. Much of the projected shortfall necessary to maintain current benefit levels is rooted in two demographic factors. The first is longer life spans. When the government set the retirement age at 65 in the 1930s, the average American life expectancy was only 63 years; life expectancy in the United States today is 77 years. The second factor is that the large post–World War II baby boom population will retire at the same time that the growth rate of number of future wage earners slows down because of a relative decline in both fertility and immigration rates.[33]

The combined effect of these demographic factors is startling. While the number of retirees is projected to grow by 90 percent between now and 2030, the number of wage-earning taxpayers is projected to grow by only 15 percent. As a result, the number of workers per beneficiary will drop from the current 3.3 to 2.2 in 2030. If nothing is done and the Social Security Trust Fund is depleted, Social Security benefits will have to be financed out of current tax revenues and retirees will receive less than three-quarters of their scheduled benefits. This benefit shortfall would have a severe impact on the many Americans who depend on Social Security benefits as their principal or only source of retirement income. At present, the Social Security program provides more than half of all income for 65 percent of retirees, more than 90 percent for one-third of retirees, and it constitutes the sole source of income for 21 percent of current beneficiaries.[34]

Pension Plans. Problems also abound in the highly technical realm of pension plans. These problems include: serious underfunding (by approximately $450 billion) of defined benefit plan assets by plan sponsors, the freezing or "wearaway" of benefit accrual for older workers in the termination or conversion of defined benefit plans, and an overconcentration of company stock in the asset holdings of many defined contribution plan participants. Fortunately, the Pension Protection Act of 2006 addressed each of these issues by setting a new 100 percent funding target for defined benefit plans over a seven-year period, banning the "wearaway" practice in the conversion of a defined benefit plan to a cash balance format, and giving investors more leeway to diversify their holdings in defined contribution plans. These reforms are far from perfect, but they are largely beneficial and demonstrate that meaningful legislative reform is possible.[35]

The most significant remaining problem with the current pension regime in the United States is the inadequacy of private retirement plans. Although estimates vary by methodology, research shows that no more than half of all U.S. workers participate in an employer-sponsored retirement plan. The noncovered group includes a disproportionately large number of women, Hispanic, and low-wage workers. Those who are covered by a retirement plan are now more likely to participate in a defined contribution plan such as a 401(k) than in a traditional defined benefit pension plan that pays a specific benefit to retirees from retirement to death. This well-known and pronounced trend raises three important concerns. First, even when an employer does sponsor a 401(k) plan, more than one-fourth of all employees choose not to participate, perhaps because of inertia, an inability to contribute, or a conscious choice to prefer current disposable income over deferred retirement benefits, even when enhanced by an employer's promise of a matching contribution. Second, participants in 401(k) plans might not be saving enough for retirement because 401(k) contributions have not increased in the face of the decline in traditional pension plans. Third, workers bear all of the risks of 401(k) plans, including managing their money wisely in a complex and risky environment—risks that were dramatically hammered home in October 2008 as the stock market lost $2.4 trillion in value in one week during the credit crisis. As a result, millions of American workers face the prospect of retirement with no pension leg or a weak and uncertain pension leg on their already shaky retirement stool.[36]

Personal Savings. The personal savings rate has fallen precipitously over the past twenty-five years, from 11 percent in 1984 to 5 percent in 1994 to −0.5 percent in 2005. The last time there was a negative savings rate was during the worst years of the Great Depression. Admittedly, these rates omit capital gains—gains that were sizable in recent years before the housing bubble burst and the stock market declined in 2008—but those gains only partially offset the decline in personal savings, and also primarily accrue to high-income households. As a result, less than half of U.S. households have saved more than $25,000 for retirement; this figure is only slightly higher for those close to retirement. Low levels of personal savings, then, exacerbate the impact of looming shortfalls in Social Security and the questionable adequacy of employer-sponsored retirement programs.[37]

In sum, measuring the adequacy of retirement benefits—including Social Security payments, income from employer-sponsored defined benefit and contribution plans, and personal savings—is quite complex. It is therefore difficult to calculate specific statistics regarding the severity of retirement insecurity. Nevertheless, numerous studies show that the trends described here are a cause for significant concern. The combination of greater longevity and larger asset shortfalls will create lower and even inadequate living standards for people during their retirement years if ameliorating steps are not taken.[38] All of this was exacerbated by the 2008 credit crisis and stock market plunge, which depleted trillions of dollars in potential retirement assets. Thus the retirement stool is an increasingly wobbly platform that threatens too many American workers with an insecure post-work financial future.

Health Security

Health security includes two closely related individual and household needs—the ability to access quality health care and the protection against catastrophic financial loss because of the expenses of a serious health condition. Except for the United States, all affluent democratic countries meet both of these needs through publicly financed systems of universal health care. Only when one includes Mexico and Turkey among the world's thirty leading industrialized, market-based democracies (OECD countries) does the United States not stand alone in lacking universal health care; all others extend health care coverage to more than 98 percent of their populations.[39] Michael Graetz and Jerry Mashaw mince few words in this regard: "No domain of American social insurance rivals the incompetence of American health insurance. While spending nearly twice the average for OECD member nations . . . we manage to leave 43 million Americans without insurance."[40] The number of uninsured Americans has now grown to more than 47 million, including 8.7 million children.[41]

The U.S. health insurance system is a voluntary one dominated by employer-based coverage that, since the 1950s, has been encouraged by tax breaks to employers for their provision of employee health insurance. This system is supplemented by Medicare (for the elderly) and Medicaid (for the poor and disabled), programs constructed by Congress in the 1960s as a health care safety net for the most vulnerable Americans. These and related public insurance programs now provide coverage for more than one-quarter of the American population, including nearly 18 percent of those under the age of 65. But lacking a mandate for coverage beyond these specific groups, the U.S. health care system remains a predominantly private regime characterized by employer-sponsored plans. In 2006, 62 percent of nonelderly (under age 65) Americans were covered by employment-based health insurance plans. Another 6.8 percent purchased private insurance plans, but 17.9 percent of the nonelderly population were without any type of health insurance. In other words, there are nearly 47 million noninsured individuals under the age of 65. Moreover, since some individuals move in and out of coverage, more than one-third of all nonelderly Americans—nearly 90 million people—are without health insurance at some time during a two-year period.[42]

The proportion without insurance has grown since 2000 as health care costs have skyrocketed and some employers have stopped providing coverage. More than 60 percent of the nonelderly uninsured are in families in which the head of the household is a full-time worker. Most of these workers are self-employed or work for an employer that does not offer health insurance coverage. A lack of health insurance correlates with a number of negative outcomes, including difficult access to health care and adverse health consequences. Seventy-one percent of the uninsured report postponing needed care, while 34 percent report a failure to get needed care at all over a one-year span. Some studies have found that the mortality rate is as much as 25 percent higher among the uninsured than it is among the insured. A lack of insurance also correlates with higher financial risk, and lower educational achievement and earning capacity.[43]

It must be emphasized that the lack of health security is not just a problem for the uninsured. The insured bear the costs of the uninsured. The uninsured who go without preventive care frequently require more invasive, and expensive, treatment in the emergency room. The resulting financial burden on emergency and catastrophic health care resources is ultimately borne by the insured and by taxpayers. In addition, when the health of the uninsured declines, economic productivity suffers and the costs of social and income maintenance programs go up. Moreover, even the insured are increasingly affected by a lack of personal health security. For those fortunate enough to have employment-based insurance, out-of-pocket expenses have significantly increased. In addition to larger deductibles and co-pays, increases in employee contributions for employer-provided health insurance premiums have grown much faster than wages and now average around $300 per month for family coverage. According to Families USA, more than 10 million individuals spent more than 25 percent of their income on health care even though they had insurance, and 75 percent of individuals filing for personal bankruptcy because of an illness had medical insurance when they got sick.[44]

The U.S. employment system also fails to protect against catastrophic financial loss that results from bad decisions made by managed care health plans about what is medically necessary. The major piece of federal legislation pertaining to employee benefits, the Employee Retirement Income Security Act (ERISA), provides very little regulation of the substantive content of health insurance and other welfare benefit plans and also broadly preempts state regulation.[45] This combination results in a significant regulatory vacuum. Take, for example, the case of a patient whose treating physician recommends an organ transplant, but whose health care plan denies coverage for the procedure based on the negligent pre-utilization opinion of another, non-treating health care professional. If the patient dies a month later, what remedies are available to his estate? The answer is virtually none. The estate cannot successfully maintain a state law claim against the plan for the erroneous eligibility decision because that is viewed as a claim for benefits and is pre-empted by ERISA.[46] Meanwhile, ERISA authorizes a plan beneficiary to recover only benefits or to seek injunctive relief. Monetary damages are not available. Thus our hypothetical employee/patient could have sought injunctive relief to compel the plan to provide the transplant, but the emergency timeframe makes this option practically unavailable. Alternatively, the patient could pay for the procedure and then sue for reimbursement. For most individuals, this option is financially unfeasible. In the end, the patient and his estate are left with no real remedy, because the substance and administration of these plans, which are so critical for the health of the American populace, are unchecked by either federal or state law. We all pay the price for these failings.[47]

Physical Security: Workplace Safety and Health

Another security-related issue is workplace safety and health. There are roughly 350,000 workplace fatalities and 264 million occupational accidents per year worldwide; perhaps an additional 1.5 million people die each year from work-related diseases, such as those caused by exposure to asbestos and other harmful substances. In the United States, there were 5,702 fatal work injuries in 2005, and an additional 4.2 million work-related nonfatal injuries and illnesses in the private sector. While today's American workplace is significantly safer than it was a hundred years ago, workplace safety requires continuous vigilance. To wit, research has linked contemporary work practices such as quality circles, work teams, and job rotation to higher levels of cumulative trauma disorders such as carpal tunnel injuries.[48]

There is little public disagreement with the principle that workplaces should be safe; rather, the debates are over how to achieve workplace safety. Like other employment-related issues, these debates are rooted in the different models of the employment relationship outlined in Chapter 1. Some see workplace safety as an individual responsibility with unregulated competitive markets placing a check on abuses (consistent with the egoist model); others prefer to rely on corporate self-interest (the unitarist model); and another group favors explicit government intervention (the pluralist model). The unregulated model, however, produced inhumane levels of workplace accidents and disease in the late 1800s and early 1900s. A journalist's investigation of a Chicago steel mill in 1907 led him to estimate that 12 percent of the mill's workforce was killed or seriously injured every year. Other investigations showed that workers and their families suffered financially because of these dangerous working conditions, even when employers were at fault. As a result, workers' compensation programs were started in the 1910s to pay employer-funded no-fault insurance benefits to injured workers or their survivors. These programs have a unitarist element: by making employers financially responsible for the costs of unsafe workplaces, they align the interests of both employers and employees in seeking a safe workplace.[49]

State-level workers' compensation programs are now an ingrained part of the employment-related public policy landscape. Although they have succeeded in providing benefits for injured workers and their families, their record on improving workplace safety is less clear. Employers' workers' compensation costs are only imperfectly related to their injury experience, so if companies see workers' compensation as a fixed expense, they have little incentive to improve safety. Moreover, no-fault benefits can create a "moral hazard" problem in which workers are not as careful as they might otherwise be. These deficiencies led to a more explicit approach to setting safety standards that culminated in the passage of the Occupational Safety and Health Act in 1970.[50] The act created the Occupational Safety and Health Administration (OSHA), which sets safety and health standards for American workplaces and also inspects those workplaces to promote compliance.

Whether OSHA is effective is controversial. Aggregate safety trends appear unaffected by the law's adoption in 1970. Business says this is because OSHA regulations are too bureaucratic, adversarial, inflexible, and costly and argues that business self-interest is the key to safety. Workers' rights groups, in contrast, point to the continuing deaths and injuries in the contemporary American workplace and argue that OSHA would be more effective if it had a reasonable number of inspectors. Under Republican administrations, the business lobby has weakened OSHA from an active enforcement agency to one with reduced resources and power that is limited to guidance and compliance assistance. The ergonomic standards developed during the Clinton administration, for example, were quickly repealed by the Bush administration and replaced by voluntary ergonomic guidelines that have been issued for only a few industries. At this writing in 2008 there is only one federal and state safety inspector for every 60,000 workers, which is far short of the International Labor Organization's standard of one inspector per 10,000 workers, and is on par with the level of inspection in Thailand and Zambia.[51]

OSHA focuses on physical safety standards such as specifications for safety equipment, noise limits, and chemical exposure to prevent occupational injuries and illness. But another very important issue deserves attention as a safety and health issue: excessive work hours. As discussed earlier in this chapter, someone who works an excessive number of hours has difficulty achieving a work-family balance and puts his own safety and health at risk. Research shows that long work shifts increase not only the likelihood of accidents and injuries, but also the risk of serious health conditions that result from stress. The Japanese even have a specific word for death from overwork—*karoshi*. With the long hours that Americans are famous for, overwork is a serious issue that undermines equity in the U.S. employment relationship.[52]

Nondiscrimination and Fairness

Equity in the employment relationship also includes standards of fair interpersonal treatment. It is well accepted that discrimination on the basis of race, sex, and other personal qualities unrelated to work performance should be unacceptable in a democratic society. U.S. employers universally claim to be "equal opportunity employers." Statements of equal opportunity and nondiscrimination with respect to race, color, religion, sex, age, national origin, disability, and veteran status appear on employers' websites, in job announcements and applications, and in employee handbooks and annual reports. As Nelson Lichtenstein reminds us, however, racial and gender equality was a radical idea only fifty years ago, and the ubiquitous equal opportunity affirmations are the direct result of employment laws banning discrimination dating back to the Equal Pay Act of 1963 and Title VII of the Civil Rights Act of 1964.[53] These statutes were subsequently expanded and reinforced by the federal Age Discrimination in Employment Act (ADEA, 1967) and the Americans with Disabilities Act (ADA, 1990), as well as by state and local laws.[54]

Title VII prohibits employers and labor unions from discriminating on the basis of race, color, religion, sex, or national origin. Intentional discrimination with respect to hiring, discharge, compensation, and other terms and conditions of employment is explicitly prohibited. Starting with *Griggs v. Duke Power Co.* in 1971, the Supreme Court has interpreted Title VII as also prohibiting facially neutral employment practices that have a disproportionate, negative impact on a protected class. An employer may avoid liability for such disparate impact claims only by showing that the employment practice in question is compelled by business necessity.[55] Under the ADEA, employees over the age of 40 are protected from discrimination in hiring, discharge, and mandatory retirement. The ADA prohibits employers from discriminating against an otherwise qualified disabled person who, with or without a reasonable accommodation, is capable of performing the essential functions of the job in question. An employer need not provide an accommodation, however, if doing so would impose an undue hardship on the employer.[56]

Thanks to these federal statutes and related state and local laws, the widespread acceptance of "equal employment opportunity" is arguably the U.S. employment relationship's greatest success in the equity dimension. There are nevertheless at least two shortfalls that should be noted. First, the concerns we described in Chapter 3 pertaining to the litigation model of antidiscrimination enforcement are also relevant here. At the federal level, for example, allegations of employment discrimination are resolved through the Equal Employment Opportunity Commission and the federal court system. Even after one successfully navigates the maze of multiple forums, the process is slow and expensive. Attorneys' fees and out-of-pocket costs combined with the lengthy time required to litigate a claim are real barriers for employees seeking justice. That these barriers are proportionately steeper for low-wage employees further magnifies the inequitable aspects of the enforcement scheme.[57]

The second principal shortfall of equity in the employment discrimination field has been the unpredictable and shrinking class of employees with a qualifying "disability" as defined by the ADA. Under the ADA's statutory formula, a plaintiff may assert a claim of discrimination only if he or she has a disability—that is, "a physical or mental impairment that substantially limits one or more of the major life activities of such individual." This vague definition spawned a deluge of litigation, and, in several decisions beginning in 1999, the Supreme Court significantly narrowed the class of protected "disabled" employees. The most important of these decisions was *Sutton v. United Air Lines, Inc.* in which the Court rejected a contrary Equal Employment Opportunity Commission guideline and ruled that mitigating measures, such as medication and prosthetic devices, should be taken into account in determining whether a person is disabled for purposes of the ADA.[58] The Court also ruled that a plaintiff is not protected by virtue of being "regarded as" disabled in the major life activity of working unless the employer perceives the plaintiff as unable to perform a class or broad range of jobs.

These narrow rulings excessively raise the bar for ADA plaintiffs and undermine equitable employment relationships by making it lawful for employers to base employment decisions on stereotypical assumptions about physical and mental impairments. Not surprisingly, employees lose more than 90 percent of the time in reported federal court decisions interpreting the ADA.[59]

Congress enacted the ADA Amendments Act of 2008 for the express purpose of overturning these restrictive decisions and "reinstating a broad scope of protection to be available under the ADA." The amendments expand the reach of the disability definition through three principal provisions. First, the amendments provide that the determination of whether an impairment substantially limits a major life activity must be made without regard to the use of mitigating measures (other than ordinary eyeglasses and contact lenses). Second, the amendments state that an individual meets the "regarded as" prong of the disability definition if she has been subjected to discrimination because of an actual or perceived impairment, whether or not the impairment limits or is perceived to limit a major life activity. This expansion is tempered, however, by a provision that relieves employers of any duty to accommodate individuals who are only regarded as disabled. Third, the act retains the current definition of disability, but directs the EEOC to revise its regulations to provide a lower standard for the determination of what the term "substantially limits" means.[60]

The 2008 act takes a significant step toward redressing the Supreme Court's overly restrictive interpretation of the ADA's disability definition. The act's directive to disregard the effect of mitigating measures, for example, will extend protection to several million individuals with physical or mental impairments. The act's new take on the "regarded as" prong offers a similar potential, although it remains to be seen how the courts will interpret this language, and the unavailability of reasonable accommodations likely will pose serious obstacles for many ADA claimants. The biggest shortcoming of the 2008 act, however, lies in the retention of the existing disability definition coupled with Congressional reliance on a hoped-for fix through revised EEOC regulations. The Supreme Court easily circumvented this same formula in the original version of the ADA in narrowing the scope of ADA protection. This imprecise reform measure will certainly spawn considerable litigation, and the courts are likely to find new and creative interpretations to limit the act's expansive intent. The 2008 act takes an important step in the right direction, but additional reform is needed to improve this aspect of equity in the American workplace.

Good-Cause Dismissal

You work in a grocery store for twenty-six years and are then fired because your police officer spouse arrested your boss's wife for drunk driving.[61] You are a pharmacist fired by Wal-Mart for refusing to obey an order to stop filling low-profit prescriptions.[62] You are a sales person fired so that your employer can avoid paying you the commission you have earned.[63] Unfair? Yes. Unethical? Yes. Contrary to the public interest? Yes. Illegal? No, not in the United States. Each of these discharges was upheld as legal by a state court. The rulings—and many more like them—reflect the dominance of the employment-at-will doctrine in governing the U.S. employment relationship. Under the employment-at-will rule, employers "may dismiss their employees at will, be they many or few, for good cause, for no cause or even for a cause morally wrong, without being thereby guilty of legal wrong."[64]

The employment-at-will doctrine was developed by American judges in the 18th century and is consistent with the belief that individuals should be able to use their property and labor as they see fit; so employers can fire workers at any time and employees can quit at any time. When labor markets are not perfectly competitive, having the power to fire employees at any time for any reason—including a bad reason, or no reason at all—creates opportunities for abuse. In fact, lawmakers and judges have recognized these abuses. In 1935, Congress limited the employment-at-will doctrine when the National Labor Relations Act made it illegal for employers to fire workers because they support a union. Starting with Title VII of the Civil Rights Act in 1964, federal and state antidiscrimination statutes further made it illegal to terminate employees because of their race, gender, and other protected characteristics. Judges, too, have reacted to abuses and carved out three judicial exceptions to the employment-at-will doctrine for terminations that violate (1) another public policy, (2) an implied employment contract, and (3) an implied covenant of good faith.[65]

The growth of these judicial exceptions led some commentators to conclude that employment-at-will is dead, but this simply is not true. For the most part, American employers still retain unilateral authority to structure employment, including the discretion to terminate employees without cause. The judiciary typically follows a very narrow construction of any exceptions.[66] Pennsylvania, for example, is considered a state with a public policy exception, and yet that state's Supreme Court refused to uphold a wrongful termination finding when the public policy in question was a federal rather than a state law.[67] Judges also make it very difficult for agreements to be considered a binding contract under the implied contract exception. For example, a Pennsylvania court did not believe that an explicit statement in an employee handbook that read "You may only be discharged for just cause" created an implied contract.[68] There are also inconsistencies from state to state: for example, Wisconsin recognizes a public policy exception, but not an implied covenant of good faith exception; New York does the opposite.[69] As Joseph Slater has summarized, "perhaps the best description of the at-will rule today is that it embodies the worst of both worlds, with exceptions so numerous and unclear as to frustrate employers but too small and narrow to protect employees in the vast majority of circumstances."[70]

In contrast, a standard of good or just cause for being terminated is nearly universal in union contracts in the United States and is also frequently found in the civil service policies that apply to many government employees. U.S. CEOs also routinely negotiate good-cause dismissal policies into their employment contracts. Further, the at-will rule is at odds with the prevailing standards in the rest of the industrialized world. Canadian law provides that employees must be discharged with cause or given a wrongful termination severance payment. Similarly, virtually all European countries have enacted statutory limitations on wrongful dismissal. As such, the almost universal recognition of statutes in other countries limiting an employer's right to terminate employment establish a global norm of fundamental fairness with respect to this aspect of employment relationship equity. As Jack Stieber argued more than twenty years ago:

> In principle there is widespread agreement that the employment-at-will doctrine has no economic or moral justification in a modern industrialized Nation. The idea that there is equity in a rule under which the individual employee and the employer have the same right to terminate an employment relationship is obviously fictional in a society in which most workers are dependent upon employers for their livelihood.[71]

Our American exceptionalism falls far short of the global normative standard.[72]

Several factors heighten the problems of this shortfall. First, the risk of job loss for U.S. workers has become decidedly more precarious in the 21st century. For much of the preceding century, U.S. employers were committed to internal labor markets and personnel policies that encouraged career rather than casual employment tenure. An implied social contract perpetuated the understanding that employees could expect continued employment so long as they performed their job duties in an adequate fashion. In recent years, the pressures of globalization and the drive for flexibility have prompted many employers to shift the risk of market insecurity to their employees and abandon the earlier commitment to long-term employment.[73] The end of the postwar social contract means that the need for some type of protection against unjust dismissal is greater than ever.

Second, the decline of the labor movement also makes the at-will rule harsher on U.S. employees. A shrinking union sector means that there are fewer workers covered by just-cause discharge protections, a lack of a viable alternative for nonunion employees frustrated by their at-will employer, and less need for nonunion employers to emulate the union sector to either claim the moral high ground or prevent unionization.

Third, the employment-at-will doctrine undermines the effectiveness of antidiscrimination and labor laws by making it more difficult for employees to prove violations of these laws. To demonstrate the illegal basis of her termination, an employee fired because of discrimination or union activity effectively needs to disprove any number of possible at-will reasons suggested by the employer.[74]

Fourth, surveys show that most U.S. workers *think* that they can be fired only for good reasons. In their responses to the Worker Representation and Participation Survey in 1995, for example, more than 80 percent incorrectly thought it was illegal to fire someone for no reason. This is particularly troubling because the laissez-faire model that underlies the employment-at-will doctrine assumes that employees are fully informed and choose to work under employment-at-will terms. If it is ignorance, not liberty or freedom, that is at work here, both the desirability and the legal basis for at-will employment are severely questioned. As Ellen Dannin notes, "judges say that at-will employment is based on contract law, but the at-will doctrine makes no sense when contract law is applied." If employees believe they can only be fired for good reasons, it can hardly be said that they thought they had consented to an at-will contract.[75]

Nonstandard Work Arrangements

Equity along many dimensions is even more difficult to achieve among part-time workers, temporary employees, and other contingent workers. Contingent workers often (though not always) receive less in pay and benefits than do traditional, full-time employees. The benefit shortfall is particularly notable with respect to health insurance. In fact, one of the key motivating factors for companies using contingent workers is to reduce the cost of wages and benefits. Contingent workers also generally receive less training and more frequently experience periods of unemployment than their core employee counterparts. Not surprisingly, contingent workers are disproportionately female and African American. Also, because of their weak affiliation with their employers, contingent workers are difficult to organize into unions. Employers are well aware that contingent work and unions do not typically go hand-in-hand, and some employers hire contingent workers as a tool for union avoidance.[76]

Of particular relevance for public policy is the fact that many contingent workers fall outside of the regulatory safety net constructed for the employment relationship.[77] This occurs primarily for two reasons. First, some employment statutes apply only to employees who have attained a certain level of workplace attachment with a particular employer. The FMLA, for example, guarantees leave time only to employees who have worked for the same employer for at least one year and for at least 1,250 hours during the previous twelve-month period. Similarly, most state unemployment compensation statutes require an employee to work twenty weeks per year in order to qualify for unemployment insurance benefits. Many part-time and temporary employees fail to meet these threshold jurisdictional requirements.

Second, American employment and labor regulations invariably extend only to "employees." Given the restrictive tests currently used to determine employee status, many contingent workers fall outside the zone of statutory coverage; this critical issue is discussed further in Chapter 8. Note further that several statutes apply only to employers with a minimum number of "employees." The FMLA, for example, does not apply to employers with fewer than fifty employees. Both Title VII of the Civil Rights Act and the ADA require a minimum of fifteen employees for coverage to occur. These exclusions enable employers to avoid the applicability of such laws to a considerable body of dependent workers. Reforms are needed to close these loopholes and bring contingent workers squarely within the coverage of work-related public polices in the United States.[78]

Conclusion

Since the modern employment relationship is a socially created institution, society needs to ensure that employment serves human needs, not vice versa. The U.S. economy employs 145 million people and creates $10 trillion in income annually. Many employees have good jobs and are treated fairly, and their families enjoy a standard of living that is the envy of the world. But there are also many U.S. workers with lousy jobs—poverty-level wages, excessive hours, little physical and economic security, and discriminatory and abusive supervision—whose families do not have a decent standard of living. By failing to provide an equitable employment relationship, the U.S. economy is not working fairly for all. The "gloves-off economy," in which some employers evade established labor standards and undercut more responsible employers, is growing.[79] This not only offends the humanity of individuals caught in a poverty trap or lousy jobs, but also imposes costs on society that range from additional burdens on taxpayers and a weakened educational system to crime and social instability.

Many workers face working lives full of contingencies that an inequitable employment relationship leaves them ill-prepared to weather. Dan Zuberi has described the plight of Seattle hotel workers struggling to make ends meet by working long hours at multiple jobs with only a minimal safety net for support when they have a sick child, a broken car, a death in the family, a personal injury, or a layoff. All of the dimensions of (in)equity come together for these workers: low wages, a lack of paid leave and affordable child care, minimal unemployment insurance and retirement benefits, patchy health insurance coverage, discrimination, and the threat of dismissal for making minor mistakes or complaining. Institutional failings and perhaps bad luck, not some mythical personal irresponsibility, make it exceedingly difficult for these workers to get ahead.[80]

Thus equity is a key issue for work-related public policies. But equity is not just an issue for the working poor or for low-wage workers. There are many justifications for arguing that all employees are entitled to a living wage and to just levels of physical, economic, social, and health security. Work-family balance and discrimination are challenges for high-paid as well as low-paid workers. Workers from all occupations are harmed by the lack of good-cause discharge requirements. Equity is a universal concern of the modern employment relationship and a key part of an explicit scorecard for workplace law and public policy.

CHAPTER 5

Voice

FROM SIX YEAR-OLD RUTHIE in the comic strip "One Big Happy" who laments, "Nobody listens to me, and I don't like it! I'm never the boss of anything! It's my life, and I think I should have a say in it!" to the Sons of Liberty who famously demanded "no taxation without representation," voice is deeply ingrained in American culture. Americans want a voice in the political arena, in civic organizations, and in their social lives. And it is also true in the workplace. Consider how you want your job conditions determined—your work schedule established, your tasks prioritized, your methods for best accomplishing your responsibilities, and the like. Individuals we talk to uniformly respond that they want to talk with their managers and have input into these decisions. Numerous formal surveys—many from the United States, but from all over the world, as well—document this same preference. No matter how the questions are worded, the result is the same: employees want a voice in the workplace.[1]

Academics and practitioners define voice in many ways. Albert Hirschman essentially defined voice as a complaint mechanism, while some employers see suggestion boxes as providing voice. Advocates of high-performance human resources practices narrowly see voice as employee involvement in improving business efficiency through problem-solving teams and other methods. Free-market advocates see voice as expressed by one's feet in the form of quitting. Labor movements around the world equate legitimate employee voice with collective bargaining and other activities pursued by labor unions. In this book, we adopt an inclusive perspective and define voice as expressing opinions and having meaningful input into work-related decision-making. This includes both individual and collective voice, and covers job conditions, employment terms, and business issues.[2]

Voice is the third objective of the employment relationship and the third critical dimension for work-related public policies because a variety of theories indicate that employees should be entitled to express opinions and have meaningful input into decision-making. Employee voice can improve economic performance (efficiency), as advocated by human resource management scholars and practitioners, and can also improve the distribution of economic rewards (equity), as emphasized by industrial relations scholars and practitioners. But the importance of voice goes beyond the promotion of efficiency and the achievement of equity. In particular, the ability to speak freely and participate in decision-making can be seen as ends in themselves for rational human beings in free, democratic societies. In this view, in a democratic society there should not be an arbitrary distinction between having a voice in political decisions and (not) having a voice in economic decisions, especially since the latter often affects our lives more directly. Moreover, religious social teachings, Kantian ethics, humanistic psychology, the stakeholder theory of the firm, and various political theories all support the centrality of employee voice in the modern employment relationship.[3] In short, employees are entitled to voice because they are human beings and because they are citizens in democratic societies: "working with dignity ultimately requires the right to participate actively in all aspects of work life, through both formal and informal means. Dignity rests on the opportunity to exercise agency—to operate purposively and effectively in one's environment."[4]

To be inclusive, we analyze four dimensions of employee voice. The first dimension is free speech rights. Such rights are well established in the political arena. Employee voice includes the translation of these political rights into the modern workplace. The second dimension of employee voice is individual participation in decision-making and control over day-to-day work tasks that stems from the importance of self-determination for fulfilling psychological needs and human dignity. The third dimension of employee voice is consultation, codetermination, and social dialogue rooted in political theories of self-determination. This dimension is related to the previous one, but occurs at a work group, organizational, or societal rather than an individual level and is therefore focused on collective voice. The fourth dimension of employee voice is countervailing collective voice. Because democratic principles and equitable economic outcomes are undermined by power imbalances, this dimension focuses on collective voice in which formal groups of workers—such as labor unions—participate in the creation and administration of workplace policies to prevent power disparities between individual employees and corporate and governmental employers.

Employee Free Speech

The first element of voice in the workplace is freedom of speech for employees. Freedom of speech means the right to freely express opinions and views. It is not limited to literally voicing opinions; also included under the freedom of speech / freedom of expression umbrella is expressive conduct, such as tearing up a memo in front of co-workers, putting up a poster on your office door, or picketing an employer. The 1st Amendment to the U.S. Constitution protects freedom of expression by restricting government limitations on freedom of speech, and article 19 of the United Nations Universal Declaration of Human Rights proclaims that "everyone has the right to freedom of opinion and expression." But freedom of speech rights are strikingly weak for employees in U.S. private sector (that is, nongovernmental) workplaces, and are only slightly stronger in public sector workplaces. In fact, by holding employers accountable for the offensive speech of its employees, laws banning sexual and other forms of workplace harassment affirmatively encourage private employers to limit employee free speech.[5]

There are two closely related reasons why free speech rights rarely extend to employees. First, the employment relationship is traditionally viewed as a voluntary private relationship in which companies can direct and control their private property and employees as they see fit. Even in the public sector, governments as employers are given significant rights to direct and control employees in the name of organizational efficiency. In other words, neither the private nor the public sector workplace is seen as a democracy. If employees don't like it, they can quit. Second, freedom of speech is popularly associated with the political arena, where free speech is valued because it spreads ideas, creates an informed electorate, and helps ensure that governmental decision-making reflects the will of the people. Thus it would seem there is little need to intrude on the private employer-employee relationship and inject freedom of expression into the workplace.

These arguments do not stand up to scrutiny. First, even if freedom of speech finds its greatest support in the realm of political discourse, the workplace's role in political discourse is too important for free speech to be limited:

> The average American does not go to public demonstrations, or burn flags outside the Republican party convention, or write books, or go to political discussion groups. A great part, maybe even the majority, of most Americans' political speech happens in the workplace, where people spend more of their waking hours than anywhere else except (possibly) their homes.[6]

A democratic society requires that individuals be exposed to diverse viewpoints while also sharing common experiences. For many Americans today, the workplace is the primary location for these two activities, especially as working hours increase and as shopping malls, housing developments, and other once-public forums increasingly hide behind a shield of property rights to limit demonstrations, leafleting, and other forms of information dissemination. The connections between the workplace and political discourse are further magnified by the fact that many workplace issues cannot be divorced from the political arena—equal opportunity, pay equity, safety standards, living wages, union organizing, outsourcing, and low-wage import competition, to name just a few. Limiting freedom of expression in the workplace, accordingly, is harmful to democracy.[7]

Second, the importance of freedom of speech is not tied simply to political discourse, but is more deeply rooted in individual self-determination and the ability to make decisions about *all* aspects of one's life. To see this, contrast a decision in the political arena (for example, whether to raise taxes) with a private decision (for example, where to buy a house). For decisions in the political arena, individuals in a representative democracy typically have only indirect input; for private decisions, individuals typically have full control. We now have a striking paradox: if free speech rights protect the exchange of ideas only in the political arena, then individuals have much greater rights to information and opinions about decisions in which they have only indirect input than about decisions that they fully control! If the exchange of ideas is important for decision-making—as the conventional wisdom regarding freedom of speech emphasizes—then this exchange should be at least as important for decisions over which individuals exercise significant control. Freedom of speech, therefore, should underlie all forms of decision-making because it serves the fundamental goal of individual self-determination.[8] As such, freedom of speech should be important in all aspects of life, including the employment relationship.

In practice, however, U.S. public policy fails to protect workplace freedom of speech. Consider the following true story. Gluteraldehyde is used as a disinfectant in medical clinics treating gastrointestinal ailments. It is a highly noxious chemical and, according to federal safety regulations, must be used in open, well-ventilated areas. At one clinic in Pennsylvania, however, the chemical was stored in a small closet that lacked ventilation. Whenever the closet was opened, toxic vapors escaped. Shortly after joining this clinic as the office manager, Mary experienced migraine headaches, nausea, fatigue, shortness of breath, and dizziness. After learning that her co-workers were experiencing these same maladies, she complained to the clinic's manager that gluteraldehyde was being stored without proper ventilation, but nothing was done. Mary then tested the toxicity level of the room that housed the storage closet. When the test revealed a toxicity level more than twice the federal maximum exposure limit, she complained again, and as a result was fired shortly afterward. The Pennsylvania courts upheld the legality of Mary's termination.[9]

This case is not unusual. After complaining several times about faulty brakes, a truck driver was fired for reporting the unsafe brakes—which by that time had caused an accident—to the state's public service commission.[10] An employee at a major insurance company was fired after she wrote a memo to an executive challenging the substance of the company's highly publicized family-friendly policies.[11] Another employee was fired for publicly opposing a co-worker's sexual harassment of another co-worker,[12] and another was fired for saying "blacks have rights too" in response to perceived racial discrimination.[13] Expressive speech also is not protected. A group of supervisors was fired for refusing to wear buttons urging workers to vote against a union.[14] In another case, an employee was fired for questioning why the employer was making everyone display an American flag at their work stations and for refusing to comply.[15] Though largely untested, some legal experts believe that off-duty expressive activities are unprotected in most states, so workers can be fired for blogging and other forms of speech outside of the workplace.[16]

The current range of protected employee speech in the workplace is quite narrow and, for the most part, exists only in the public sector. The 1st Amendment protects freedom of speech from government interference ("state action" in legal jargon) but not from the actions of private entities. But even the free speech rights of public employees are highly circumscribed. To be protected, the speech must relate to a matter of public concern, which encompasses political, social, or other community issues, but not matters primarily related to the functioning of the workplace. Even then, the employee's right to comment on matters of public concern must be balanced against the employer's interest in the effective and efficient fulfillment of its responsibilities. Under this standard, government employers have been granted wide latitude to manage their operations as if they were private employers, and public employee speech is protected only if uttered in the role of a citizen as opposed to that of a worker.[17] In 2006 the Supreme Court underscored the narrowness of this protected zone in ruling that an employee speaking in furtherance of his "official duties" loses all protection regardless of the importance of the comments uttered. Somewhat perversely, the court also implied that speech is more likely to be protected if the speaker broadcasts a complaint publicly rather than doing so internally.[18]

Even this narrow band of protection for employee speech, however, does not exist in private employment. The only speech-related protection that private sector employees currently enjoy comes from statutes, such as the federal Sarbanes-Oxley Act, that protect employees who "blow the whistle" on illegal corporate acts,[19] and from the National Labor Relations Act, which protects employees engaged in "concerted activity" for mutual aid or protection, such as when talking with other employees about wages and working conditions.[20] Although these safeguards are important, the protection afforded is quite narrow.

It would be tempting to accept the lack of employee free speech if the workplace were neutral, apolitical terrain. But this is not the case. The Supreme Court, in fact, has extended the 1st Amendment's freedom of speech protections to employers. As such, the workplace is not devoid of speech-related issues; rather, corporations control what speech is allowed and what is not. A New Hampshire mall allowed Republican presidential candidates to campaign, but did not allow a group to pass out leaflets criticizing the sweatshop conditions that produce sneakers sold at the mall. The Milwaukee Brewers baseball team does not allow fans to display their own political messages, but distributed signs to fans to pressure lawmakers to subsidize a new stadium. During the 2004 presidential election, with help from the Republican Party, businesses used their e-mail systems to urge employees to vote and directed them to pro-business websites that rated the candidates. During the same election, the pro-Bush Sinclair Broadcast Group required its sixty-two television stations to preempt their regular programming to show an anti-Kerry documentary and fired its Washington bureau chief for criticizing the company's characterization of the documentary as "news" rather than "commentary." Other employees have been forced to attend on-site political speeches. A regional manager was fired after he failed to follow the CEO's "suggestion" that he purchase tickets to a specific candidate's fundraiser. During union organizing drives, employers routinely force employees to listen to anti-union captive-audience speeches but do not allow similar opportunities for pro-union messages. In short, property rights allow corporations to freely express their views while simultaneously limiting their employees' speech. Such biased control over workplace speech by employers reinforces the need for statutory protections for employees.[21]

In sum, employees deserve free speech rights in their workplaces. The denial of these rights to employees is hard to justify when corporations enjoy freedom of speech protections. This protection for corporations is justified by the importance of political discourse in the workplace and by the recognition that the free exchange of ideas is an essential part of being human and is beneficial for all decision-making; either justification applies equally well to employees, so they too should be entitled to free speech rights. At the same time, the extension of freedom of expression to workers does not imply unlimited rights to undermine an employer's business or harass co-workers. As in other areas of the employment relationship, a balance is required. Specific policy proposals to achieve a balance through employee free speech rights are discussed in Chapter 9. In the meantime, free speech is sorely lacking in the U.S. employment relationship. The chilling effect on issues of importance to both workers and the public is revealed by the statement of a state forester in a newspaper story on a controversial plan to allow off-road truck trails in state forests: "I think it would be inappropriate to give my real opinion. We're good employees, we do what we're told."[22] Such is the poor state of individual voice in the U.S. employment relationship.

Individual Self-Determination

One key characteristic of any job is the extent of autonomy the employee enjoys in performing the job. In this context, autonomy is frequently defined as "the degree to which the job provides substantial freedom, independence, and discretion to the individual in scheduling the work and in determining the procedures to be used in carrying it out." Employees with high levels of autonomy are characterized by psychologists as having a high internal locus of control and are characterized by management scholars as being able to participate in workplace decision-making. More generally, actions and choices made autonomously are by definition self-determined. A tremendous amount of research demonstrates that employees with higher levels of autonomy / locus of control / participation / self-determination are more satisfied with their jobs and, to a lesser extent, have higher levels of job performance.[23]

More important, self-determination can be argued to be a basic or fundamental human need. In other words, being controlled contradicts what it means to be a healthy adult by undermining our psychological well-being and interfering with our development.[24] Studies have shown that workers with low levels of job control are more likely to experience ailments relating to both mental health (such as stress and anxiety) and physical health (such as heart disease). Workers with low levels of autonomy are also more likely to experience sickness-related absences from work.[25] These findings are reinforced by prominent sociologists, from the founders of the field such as Karl Marx, Emile Durkheim, and Max Weber to contemporary scholars such as Randy Hodson, who stress the loss of human dignity (and accompanying alienation) caused by too much authoritarianism in the modern employment relationship, and are similarly echoed by contemporary Kantian ethicists such as Norm Bowie.[26] While the employment relationship undoubtedly involves sacrificing some autonomy in return for pay, the effects of excessive subservience on individuals and society are too corrosive to allow all autonomy to be sacrificed.

Our second dimension of voice—individual self-determination—is rooted in this psychological conception of autonomy that is so critical to individual well-being. Employee voice, therefore, includes an important element of "choice." Workers should have opportunities for self-determination in which they can make choices consistent with those of a healthy, autonomous individual. In other words, a job *should* provide "substantial freedom, independence, and discretion to the individual in scheduling the work and determining the procedures to be used in carrying it out," to again use the standard definition of job autonomy.[27] This would include, where appropriate, the ability to prioritize tasks, select solutions for problems, and have input into scheduling one's work time. There are obviously constraints on job autonomy and individual self-determination—for example, bus drivers need to follow their routes and assembly line workers need to follow the pace of the assembly line.

But even these kinds of workers can be given opportunities to control parts of their job, such as by involving them in the allocation of assignments and tasks, by allowing them to evaluate the quality of their own work, and by giving them the authority to troubleshoot problems and refuse unsafe work.

Designing jobs with significant amounts of employee self-determination, however, runs counter to the traditional management mindset. Frederick Winslow Taylor and others developed scientific management in the early 20th century in which time and motion studies are used by managers to find the one best way of doing each job. There is no self-determination in this approach; rather, instruction cards tell each worker specifically what to do, sometimes down to the fraction of a second. Though not always followed to this extreme, scientific management nevertheless shaped the dominant management paradigm of the 20th century: managers, not workers, provided the brains, determined job content, and made other decisions while labor provided the brawn. The competitive environment of the 21st century has undermined the scientific management mindset, but it is reasonable to question how much self-determination is provided in new forms of work organization. By definition, self-directed work teams involve significant worker autonomy, but the more widespread lean production methods emphasize standardized processes and the tight control of teams by supervisors.[28]

U.S. public policies also are not very supportive of the individual self-determination dimension of employee voice. The employment-at-will doctrine reduces self-determination to the right to quit. The recourse for workers who do not like the way their employer structures their jobs is not to try to negotiate greater autonomy, but to look for another job. Although the freedom to quit should be an important element of self-determination, it is insufficient by itself to give workers true autonomy. The lack of free speech protections discussed in the previous section also undermines self-determination to the extent that employees are fearful of speaking out to gain more control over their jobs. In fact, research shows that employees in Sweden are reluctant to voice criticisms of their working conditions even though Swedish law protects such complaints. U.S. employers also have free rein to force workers to cede control over their work schedules, including forcing employees to work mandatory overtime, and to aggressively monitor workers using electronic surveillance methods. Even employee protections for refusing unsafe work are fairly weak.[29]

Against this backdrop, it is our assessment that while some workers have autonomy in their jobs, there is significant room for improvement. In the 2002 General Social Survey (a nationally representative survey of U.S. adults), only 43 percent of those interviewed indicated that they often "take part with others in making decisions" that affect them in their jobs, while 25 percent disagreed or strongly disagreed with the statement, "I have a lot of say about what happens on my job."[30] In the Worker Representation and Participation Survey conducted in 1995, 76 percent of the workers surveyed indicated that it was very important to them to have a lot of influence in "deciding how to do your job and organize the work," but only 57 percent responded that they currently have a lot of influence and involvement in this regard; only 30 percent said that they have a lot of influence in setting work schedules.[31] According to the U.S. Department of Labor, only 30 percent of U.S. workers can vary the starting and ending times of their workday.[32] A lack of autonomy is not limited to the American workplace, as demonstrated by the European Survey on Working Conditions (a representative survey of workers across the countries of the European Union conducted in 2000); 35 percent of those surveyed said that they were not able to choose or change the order of tasks in their jobs, and 40 percent did not have control over break times.[33] Other research shows that levels of employee self-determination continue to be linked to hierarchical workplace structures—in other words, managers and professionals have the highest levels of autonomy while blue-collar workers have the least.[34]

Self-determination also requires information. Individuals cannot make good decisions when they fail to understand key issues. But a number of empirical studies document widespread employee ignorance. In phone surveys conducted two and seven years after the enactment of the Family and Medical Leave Act in 1993, 40 percent of the respondents had not heard of this important law; among those who had heard of it, 50 percent were unsure whether they were personally eligible to use it.[35] Another study shows that employees are ignorant of the employment-at-will legal doctrine; for example, less than 20 percent of employees surveyed in the late 1990s correctly recognized that they could legally be fired to make room for another employee to do the same job at a lower wage.[36] Other research reveals employee misunderstandings of their compensation systems, health care coverage, retirement plans, and family-friendly benefits.[37] Employee ignorance appears to be another barrier to self-determination in the American workplace.

Consultation, Codetermination, and Social Dialogue

The third dimension of employee voice is consultation, codetermination, and social dialogue. These forms of communication include wide-ranging exchanges of information and views between employers and employees that stop short of formal bargaining. A meeting in which managers debrief employees by providing information about the employer's finances and future plans is one simple example. Consultation may take place in workplace committees that must be allowed to express their views before managerial actions are taken; codetermination exists when committees are empowered to reject or approve these actions. Employee representatives on a corporation's board of directors contribute to collective voice by keeping other workers informed and sharing workers' views with an organization's leaders. All of these examples of voice take place within an organization; extending these activities to a broader industry or an economy-wide level yields what we call "social dialogue."

Social dialogue can mean different things to different people, but we limit it here to refer to exchanges of information and views between representatives of employers and employees from more than one organization, that stop short of formal bargaining. Government representatives and other interested parties might also be included. One example of social dialogue is employers and unions working together in a region to establish a vocational training program. A second example is a government consulting with an employers' association and workers' representatives to establish principles for macroeconomic reform, such as aggregate inflation and wage growth targets. Note that these exchanges help give workers a say in the determination of important decisions that affect them; it is for this reason that we group social dialogue together with consultation and codetermination. Consultation, codetermination, and social dialogue do not require labor unions, though their presence could strengthen these forms of voice. Labor unions as a distinct form of employee voice are discussed in the next section of this chapter.

Consultation, codetermination, and social dialogue are essential elements of employee voice for intrinsic and instrumental reasons. To consider the intrinsic element, ask yourself why Americans strongly support democracy. Democracy is not necessarily efficient, and in fact can be quite messy. But few Americans are likely to trade democracy for another form of governance, even one that has proven to be more efficient. Thus the most compelling reason for supporting democracy is an inherent belief in the value of self-rule because an essential part of being human is being able to control one's own destiny. This reasoning is reminiscent of the self-determination dimension of voice discussed in the previous section, but is rooted in political theory rather than psychology:

> It is a fundamental doctrine of political democracy that one should have some voice in regard to matters that vitally affect him. . . . For unless he has this voice, usually exercised through the vote, then the most important incidents of his life, his wealth, his property, indeed his very life itself are removed from . . . his control. . . . If there is an argument for giving [a worker] a vote, even more is there an argument for giving him a voice in the conditions of shop and factory.[38]

This grounding in political theory is significant because governance is a collective activity. *Collective* forms of employee voice, such as consultation, codetermination, and social dialogue around employment-related issues, are therefore desirable.[39]

On a more practical level, there are instrumental benefits that flow from consultation, codetermination, and social dialogue. These forms of voice serve as training grounds for political democracies by creating citizens who value participation and respect diverse viewpoints. Individual expression may not be representative of broader group preferences and generally does not promote deliberations among employees that cultivate shared preferences. And collective forms of voice can be critical for implementing and enforcing legislated labor standards such as working time regulations, safety standards, and nondiscrimination principles. In fact, transparency and self-regulation are increasingly seen as the preferred methods for enforcing diverse government regulations, but relying on information disclosure and self-monitoring by employers is largely ineffective for enforcing workplace laws without strong supports for employees that are at least partially independent of their employers. Mechanisms for consultation and codetermination can provide these necessary supports.[40]

Because these intrinsic and instrumental rationales ultimately support the health of a country's democracy, they can be referred to as the industrial democracy reasons for consultation, codetermination, and social dialogue. Some argue that industrial democracy can improve efficiency and economic performance, but statistical analyses fail to uncover significant effects in this regard. In other words, it is difficult to conclude that consultation, codetermination, and social dialogue either improve or harm productivity, employee turnover, and the like. But our rationale for these forms of collective voice is not rooted in efficiency; it is rooted in industrial democracy. At the same time, we are not arguing that work needs to be democratic in an absolute sense; rather, collective forms of employee voice are needed so that the workplace supports rather than undermines the health of a modern, democratic society.[41]

The European Union's Charter of Fundamental Rights includes employees' rights to information and consultation within their companies (article 27), but the U.S. employment relationship does not similarly promote industrial democracy. Perhaps one-third of U.S. employees participate in quality circles or other joint committees. But these are established at the discretion of managers, not employees, and their focus is improving efficiency, not industrial democracy. Information sharing is perhaps more widespread, but is again at the discretion of a company's management. One could rightly argue that unionized workers have access to workplace consultation and codetermination, but less than 15 percent of all U.S. workers are represented by labor unions. Some companies have employee representatives on their boards of directors, but these are typically employee-owned companies or those in which labor unions negotiate for board representation when conceding massive wage concessions. With respect to social dialogue, there are some examples of joint business-labor training programs, but otherwise social dialogue is rare in the United States, with business and labor more likely to be hostile than cooperative in the public arena. Moreover, the U.S. political system relies on political lobbying rather than consultation to express views in the political process, and there is also an imbalance in this realm as labor's political influence has declined in recent decades.[42]

On balance, the current U.S. system of employment and labor law is also more hostile than supportive of consultation, codetermination, and social dialogue. Only in the federal sector is there the possibility of legally supported consultation rights. The Civil Service Reform Act provides that a union that represents at least 10 percent but less than a majority of a group of federal employees is entitled to be "informed of any substantive change in conditions of employment proposed by the agency" and to be "permitted reasonable time to present its views and recommendations regarding the changes." The relevant agency must "consider the views or recommendations before taking final action on any matter with respect to which the views or recommendations are presented" and provide "a written statement of the reasons for taking the final action."[43] The U.S. Department of Agriculture has consulted with the American Federation of Government Employees and the National Federation of Federal Employees over issues pertaining to equal employment opportunity procedures, reasonable accommodation procedures, telecommuting, mentoring, childcare, and tuition subsidies. With the limited exception of mandatory joint labor-management health and safety committees in some states, no such consultation rights exist in the private sector. Rather, private sector labor law is frequently interpreted by the National Labor Relations Board (NLRB) and federal courts as not requiring information sharing except in a very limited fashion with respect to some issues being discussed in collective bargaining.[44]

And most notably, consultation and codetermination are negatively affected by section 8(a)(2) of the National Labor Relations Act (NLRA). This provision makes it illegal for employers "to dominate or interfere with the formation or administration of any labor organization or contribute financial or other support to it."[45] Although originally adopted as a means to prohibit the sham company-dominated unions that proliferated in the 1920s and 1930s, the NLRA's broad definition of a covered "labor organization" also serves as a potential bar to many types of employer-sponsored participation plans. The NLRB's landmark decision in *Electromation, Inc.* illustrates the reach of the section 8(a)(2) prohibition. In that case, an employer established five "action committees" in which certain employees and management representatives met to discuss such issues as absenteeism, workplace smoking, and pay progression for premium positions. The NLRB found that the committees constituted labor organizations because the participating employees bilaterally discussed terms and conditions of employment with management representatives. The NLRB further ruled that the employer dominated these organizations by creating the committees and by determining their structure and functions. The NLRB thus concluded that the employer violated section 8(a)(2), despite the lack of any evidence that the employer established the committees for the purpose of deterring union organization efforts.[46]

Employers often are able to work around these restrictions either by avoiding bilateral discussions (and thus perhaps reducing consultation to a suggestion box approach) or by focusing on issues of efficiency and productivity to the exclusion of terms and conditions of employment (thereby limiting the scope of issues for which workers have a voice). Moreover, many employer-sponsored participation programs that are ostensibly within the section 8(a)(2) ban go unchallenged. As such, while section 8(a)(2) does not serve as a fatal barrier to many types of employee participation programs favored by companies, it does provide a deterrent to the growth and development of consultation and codetermination programs that focus on employee interests.[47]

It should therefore not come as a surprise that surveys reveal a large demand among workers for collective voice that goes unfilled by the current U.S. employment system. In the Worker Representation and Participation Survey, 63 percent of those responding expressed a desire for more influence on workplace issues and the responses further show that some type of jointly run workplace committee is the preferred mechanism for addressing this shortfall. In the words of the survey's authors, "the majority of workers . . . want an institutional form that does not effectively exist in the United States: joint employee-management committees that discuss and resolve workplace problems." Moreover, 85 percent of workers responded that a workplace committee is a good idea or a very good idea for enforcing workplace standards, and 73 percent felt that this would be good not only for workers, but for management as well.[48] As we explain in Chapter 9, a reformed system of U.S. workplace law can draw on the experience of health and safety committees from this country, as well as works councils from around the world to redress the current state of affairs.

Countervailing Collective Voice

Chapter 1 outlined four models of work—the egoist, unitarist, pluralist, and critical employment relationships. In the egoist model, there is little role for public policies on voice because voice is largely exercised by one's feet when one expresses dissatisfaction by quitting. The other models allow for a richer conception of employee voice by seeing workers as more than just commodities and as concerned with more than income. The unitarist model furthermore sees employees and employers as having interests that can always be aligned through the correct human resource management policies. In contrast, in the pluralist model, employees and employers are seen as having a mix of shared and conflicting interests—everyone wants their company to be financially healthy, but there can be conflicts, for example, between an employer's push for lower labor costs and flexibility on the one hand, and the employees' desires for higher wages and employment security on the other. These conflicts of interest are why the stock market reacts positively when companies lay off workers or cut benefits. Moreover, with imperfect labor markets, employers can have the upper hand with greater bargaining power than individual employees. In the critical employment relationship, this power imbalance is magnified and seen as embedded throughout the economic and political system rather than limited to the employment relationship as assumed by pluralists.

These models of the employment relationship are very important at this juncture of our analysis because, for adherents of the unitarist view, the three dimensions of voice—employee free speech, individual self-determination, and consultation—are sufficient to provide meaningful voice for employees. But those who subscribe to the pluralist or critical models are skeptical of the unitarist approach because, if there are conflicting employer-employee interests and unequal economic power, there is the potential for employers to ignore or manipulate individual and consultative forms of voice. Further, individual employees may be reluctant to express their candid viewpoints out of a concern for how their employer will react. In fact, some pluralist and critical adherents see this power imbalance as rendering any form of voice except labor unions to be illegitimate. We think this is overly critical, especially if individual voice and consultation are supported by the public policies we propose in Chapter 9. But a full accounting of employee voice must include forms that explicitly grant employees more power than in the three other dimensions.

The fourth and final element of voice is therefore countervailing collective voice—a voice mechanism that has sufficient power to act as a countervailing balance to corporate power. Government standards such as minimum wage laws can provide checks and balances against excessive corporate power in imperfect labor markets, but government standards do not provide employee voice. The key institution of countervailing collective voice is independent labor unions. In the pluralist model of the employment relationship, corporations are seen as unionized shareholders: individual investors leverage their collective resources by pooling them and hiring experts such as executives and lawyers to manage their affairs. Allowing workers to do the same—in other words, to unionize—is the obvious method for balancing the bargaining power of employers and employees. Unions can then protect workers against low wages and abusive working conditions, help workers obtain their fair share of the economic success of their employer, and allow workers to exercise their voice by negotiating mutually agreeable terms and conditions of employment with their employers:

> Unions have given to the average isolated wage earner lost in the struggling crowd of exploited workers a feeling of independence, of dignity, of self-reliance, of self-respect. Without unions he becomes a sort of commodity, bought and sold in the market, dominated by formidable and very impersonal economic

forces, a person of no importance, hardly a person at all. In his group, and through his group, he can do something to impose his will on his surroundings, he can bargain in dignified fashion with his employer. He can make himself felt; and in doing so he has recovered his personality that was being lost in the maze of economic forces.[49]

From a pluralist perspective on the employment relationship, unions can uniquely achieve these elements of equity and voice because they have power independent of employers to a much greater extent than other voice mechanisms: unions have the right to select their own leaders, collect dues, manage their own budgets and internal affairs, negotiate contracts with employers, go on strike, represent workers across numerous organizations, and receive support from other unions.

According to one widely cited statistic, the U.S. employment system seemingly fails to deliver collective voice in the form of labor unions: in 2007, only 13.3 percent of U.S. workers were represented by unions.[50] While 39.8 percent of public sector workers are represented by unions, union density in the private sector is a minuscule 8.2 percent, less than one-fourth what it was in the 1950s. But these statistics only represent a failing of U.S. public policy if there are significant numbers of workers who want to form unions but are unable to do so. The reasons for the long decline in private sector union density, however, are controversial. It is common to point to structural or composition factors: employment in traditionally unionized industries, occupations, demographic groups, or regions has declined while employment in nonunion industries, occupations, demographic groups, or regions has increased. But these explanations are not fully satisfactory because they beg important questions about why certain industries, occupations, demographic groups, or regions are more or less receptive to unionization. An alternative explanation is that demand for union services has declined, perhaps because unions are not sufficiently responsive to workers' changing needs, because employees are increasingly satisfied with their jobs, or because the growth in government regulations has reduced the need for union protections. Globalization is another often-cited reason for the decline in U.S. unions, with greater international capital mobility arguably eroding union strength.[51]

Contingent work arrangements can also contribute to the decline in U.S. labor unions. As noted in Chapter 4, in the eyes of the law, many contingent workers are not employees of the entity for whom they provide work. Consequently, these workers are excluded from coverage under the NLRA and are denied the NLRA's protections against discharge or other retaliatory acts when trying to form a union. The NLRB has also excluded contingent workers from bargaining units with permanent employees on the basis that these two groups do not share a sufficient community of interests. Similarly, the NLRB has clarified recently that workers who are leased from a supplier firm and the regular employees they work with can only be included in a single bargaining unit if both the user and leasing firms consent to this joint unit, even when the leased and regular employees are working side-by-side doing the same work.[52] Beyond these legal obstacles is the reality that contingent workers can be difficult to organize into a union because they do not see the benefits of union representation in an environment of short-term employment. Some employers, therefore, hire contingent workers as part of an affirmative union avoidance strategy.[53]

The most controversial explanation for the decline in U.S. union density is employer resistance or opposition to unions. Relative to managers in other industrialized countries, American managers appear to be exceptionally hostile toward unions. In particular, they have a stronger tradition of using aggressive tactics to fight union organizing drives by firing union supporters, interrogating workers about their support for a union, and making threats and promises relative to union support. Much employer opposition results from the NLRA's adoption of an electoral model for determining representational status. In most other industrialized countries, employers play no overt role in an employee's decision to join a union, and any opposition to union demands typically does not occur until the parties meet at the bargaining table. In the United Sates, in contrast, an employer is not obligated to bargain until after a union first establishes its majority status in a representation election. U.S. employers may participate actively in this election process and generally are free to express their opposition to unionization efforts. Many employers hire professional consultants for the purpose of orchestrating sophisticated anti-union campaigns that not infrequently spill over to include unlawful as well as lawful conduct. Labor unions and their supporters argue that these anti-union tactics often are successful in influencing election outcomes and are therefore the primary reason that U.S. union density is so low.[54]

According to the U.S. General Accounting Office, about 25 percent of the workforce is not covered by laws protecting their rights to engage in collective bargaining because they are supervisors or independent contractors, or because they work for businesses that are too small to be covered or in industries such as agriculture that are excluded. In fact, because increasing numbers of jobs require exercising independent judgment and delegating minor tasks to co-workers, the legal definition of "supervisor" has become a sharp legal controversy as employers have tried increasingly to exclude nurses and others from coverage under U.S. labor law.[55]

But even for workers covered by protective labor laws, managerial oppositional tactics are arguably facilitated by the remedial shortcomings of these laws. Three examples relating to the NLRA are illustrative. First, a common employer tactic in opposing union organizational campaigns is to fire leading employee organizers. A conservative estimate is that such terminations occur in one-quarter of all representation elections, and perhaps as many as one of every five union activists illegally lose their jobs. Survey evidence reveals the fear that has been created—40 percent of nonunion respondents agreed that "it is likely I will lose my job if I tried to form a union," and nearly 80 percent of all respondents said it is "very" or "somewhat" likely that "nonunion workers will get fired if they try to organize a union." While the NLRA makes this conduct unlawful, it does little to deter its occurrence. The usual remedy under the NLRA for the illegal discharge of an employee organizer is a cease and desist order coupled with reinstatement and back pay. The NLRA does not provide for fines, punitive damages, or any other penalty. This "make whole" approach provides little in the way of deterrence for employers who realize that they can chill union organization efforts by immediately firing employee organizers, subject only to a much later order to reinstate them with back pay.[56]

Second, the NLRA's relatively weak remedial scheme also lessens the effectiveness of the act's bargaining mandate. The only remedy recognized under the NLRA for a party's refusal to engage in good-faith bargaining is an order requiring that party to return to the bargaining table. The Supreme Court has ruled that the NLRB is without power to impose substantive contract terms in the event of a violation, even where the NLRB has concluded that an employer has acted in a manner designed to frustrate the bargaining process.[57] Thus an employer may engage in protracted "surface bargaining" with little fear of meaningful legal intervention. The problem of surface bargaining is particularly acute when used by an employer to avoid the consummation of an initial collective bargaining agreement. Approximately one-third of all newly certified union representatives fail to conclude a first contract. At this early stage, a union's inability to obtain a collective bargaining agreement virtually dooms it to eventual decertification.[58]

A third shortcoming of the NLRA scheme flows from an employer's ability to hire permanent replacements to fill the positions of striking employees. An employer lawfully may decline to reinstate a striker at the conclusion of a strike so long as the position continues to be occupied by a replacement worker. For many striking workers, this is tantamount to losing their jobs. This practice also significantly undercuts the power of unions in two respects. First, the threat of being permanently replaced serves to deter strikes and decreases the union's ability to use the threat of a strike as leverage in collective bargaining. Second, the permanent replacements have the right to vote in decertification elections, while the voting rights of displaced strikers typically cease twelve months after the beginning of the strike. These electoral rules permit an employer to rid itself of a union by pushing employees into a strike and then hiring permanent replacements who vote to decertify the union in an election held a little more than twelve months after being hired.[59]

As these examples illustrate, U.S. labor law is not kind to employees who desire union representation. Given management's natural economic leverage in the workplace, the significance of employer opposition activities is not lost on the employee electorate. Many employees who voluntarily would choose union representation lack the practical ability to convert that desire into reality. While polling data reveal that more than 40 percent of American workers desire union representation, labor organizations currently represent less than one-third of this percentage. As such, there is persuasive evidence of a representation gap in the U.S. workplace because U.S. public policy lacks protections and assistance for workers who try to form unions.[60]

Conclusion

Employee voice is a hot topic among employee advocates, human resource managers, and scholars interested in the workplace. And for good reason. Even 2,000 years ago, the Roman farmer Columella made it "a practice to call [his slaves] into consultation on any new work" because "they are more willing to set about a piece of work on which they think that their opinions have been asked and their advice followed."[61] Beyond this potential for employee voice to improve organizational performance, collective voice in the form of labor unions can improve the distribution of economic rewards, and various forms of individual and collective voice support the dignity and freedom of workers as

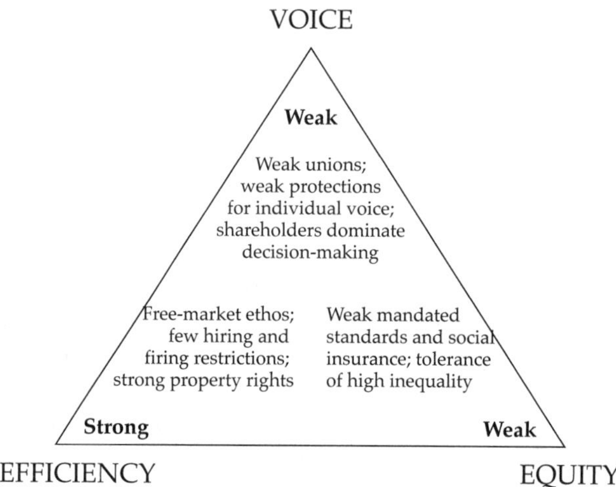

FIGURE 5.1 Efficiency, equity, and voice in the U.S. employment relationship.

human beings and citizens in democratic societies. With respect to work-related public policies, we outline four key dimensions of employee voice: employee free speech; individual self-determination; consultation, codetermination, and social dialogue; and countervailing collective voice. Our analysis of these dimensions uncovers a widespread lack of employee voice, both individually and collectively, for many U.S. workers.

The U.S. employment relationship is also weak with respect to equity and strongest in terms of efficiency (see Figure 5.1). The normative implications of these analyses depend on the relative importance one wants to give the three objectives. Regardless of these weights, however, analyzing the dimensions of efficiency, equity, and voice provides an explicit scorecard for workplace law and public policy, and is an important part of a deeper understanding of any country's employment system. With that said, in the next section of the book we apply the intellectual framework of Parts One and Two to the normative question of what the U.S. system of workplace law and public policy should try to achieve. We ground this application in the pluralist model of the employment relationship and in the objective of balancing efficiency, equity, and voice. Normatively, we see the current weaknesses in equity and voice as problematic, and we therefore develop policy proposals that will create a comprehensive new system of workplace law that better balances efficiency, equity, and voice. The normative application in Part Three is intended to reveal simultaneously the importance of using an explicit framework of employment relationship objectives and models for considering work-related public policy issues, and the feasibility of balancing efficiency, equity, and voice in the U.S. workplace.

PART THREE

Creating Coherent Laws and Public Policies on Work

A man must always live by his work, and his wages must at least be sufficient to maintain him. . . . No society can surely be flourishing and happy, of which the far greater part of the members are poor and miserable. It is but equity, besides, that they who feed, clothe and lodge the whole body of the people, should have such a share of the produce of their own labor as to be themselves tolerably well fed, clothed and lodged.

—Adam Smith, 1776

CHAPTER 6

A Pluralist Manifesto for Workplace Law and Public Policy

THE IMPORTANCE OF WORK for individuals and society demands that the legal regulations and public policies related to work receive our continued scrutiny. In the global economy of the 21st century, employment is increasingly seen as a purely economic transaction, where business is concerned only with competitiveness and workers are focused solely on income to pay for consumption. Social welfare is reduced to economic welfare, and justice is narrowed to "marginal productivity justice"—market-based outcomes are viewed as fair simply because they are produced by market exchange and efficiently allocate scarce resources.[1] In short, a neoliberal market economy ethos has become the baseline for discourse on the employment relationship generally, and on government regulation of the employment relationship specifically. What's good for General Motors, as the old saying went, is now seen as good for the world.

But is it? In recent years, the world's economic output has grown by 4–5 percent annually while employment growth has struggled to keep pace with the less than 2 percent annual growth of the labor force. In other words, each year, $2–4 trillion in additional wealth is created, but this new wealth is not distributed in such a way as to reduce global unemployment.[2] Efficiency has trumped equity and voice. We believe that updated laws and public policies can be developed that deliver the flexibility to promote economic prosperity, but also provide the standards and safeguards to protect human rights and dignity. In other words, the analytical framework we presented in Parts One and Two can be harnessed to craft reformed systems of workplace law and public policy that are rooted in a consistent set of intellectual principles and that aspire to balance efficiency, equity, and voice.

Analytical Insights, Normative Concerns

The central goal of Parts One and Two is to show the importance of rooting our understanding and continued scrutiny of workplace law and public policy in explicit objectives and models of the employment relationship. We can therefore now see that the neoliberal market approach to workplace law and public policy reflects an egoist model of the employment relationship in which efficiency is paramount and equity and voice are seen in narrow, market-based terms. But from some alternative perspectives, the U.S. system of public policies on work is broken. It is common to criticize U.S. workplace law and public policy for failing to keep pace with changes in demographic trends, technology, the nature of work, the intensity of product market competition, and globalization.[3] The explicit scorecard developed in Part Two provides a more fundamental way of assessing the status of workplace law and public policy.

Using our analytical framework as a springboard for normative prescriptions, we contend that employment systems in practice must move beyond today's focus on productivity, competitiveness, and the effective use of scarce resources (concerns that we have grouped together under the shorthand heading of "efficiency"). Workers are not simply commodities or productive human resources; employment provides much more than income for consumption. In earlier agrarian and craft-based societies, one's quality of life was firmly rooted in one's property, such as farmland or a workshop; in today's industrial or post-industrial society, modern workers and their families are often completely dependent on jobs rather than property. Moreover, working adults spend much of their lives at work and "the workplace is the single most important site of cooperative interactivity and sociability among adult citizens outside the family."[4] As a result, workplace law and public policy must promote employment *with a human face*—"a productive and efficient employment relationship that also fulfills the standards of human rights."[5] This echoes the calls for "just work" by the political scientist Russell Muirhead, for "meaningful work" by the ethicist Norm Bowie, and for "decent work" by the International Labor Organization.[6]

Moreover, our "Workplace Law and Public Policy XXX" framework further reveals another fundamental problem—the U.S. system of workplace law and public policy reflects more than 100 years of shifting power dynamics between multiple interest groups and therefore lacks a coherent intellectual foundation. The labor law portion of today's system is premised on putting the pluralist model of the employment relationship into practice by promoting unionization to equalize employee-employer bargaining power. The employment law wing, however, is grounded in the unitarist model. And since this model largely sees government intervention as unnecessary, it is unsurprising that the current body of employment law does not articulate any central foundational legal principles. The closest pretender to that throne probably is the at-will rule, under which U.S. employers lawfully may terminate employees for any or no reason. But the egoist intellectual foundations of the at-will rule are hostile to government regulation. When surveyed, most Americans have indicated that the at-will rule either is not or should not be the prevailing principle governing the employment relationship.[7] So the employment-at-will doctrine is hardly a compelling guiding principle for workplace law.

Appreciating these clashing egoist, unitarist, and pluralist foundations illuminates why there are conflicts in practice between the existing areas of labor and employment law. The egoist emphasis on property rights and employment-at-will undermines both employment and labor law. To wit, the National Labor Relations Act (NLRA) says that the right to strike should not be diminished, but the Supreme Court allows employers to use permanent strike replacements as part of their property rights to manage their business.[8] The employment-at-will doctrine makes it easier for employers to fire union supporters and more difficult for plaintiffs to prove violations of antidiscrimination laws.[9] The unitarist and pluralist approaches also clash. For example, in its 2004 *IBM Corp.* decision, the National Labor Relations Board curtailed nonunion employees' NLRA rights of collective activity in favor of an "employer's right to conduct prompt, efficient, thorough, and confidential workplace investigations" as necessitated by a host of employment laws.[10] Labor law empowers employees to decide what issues are of particular importance in their own workplaces and to collectively work with employers to fashion mutually agreeable resolutions; employment law discards this approach and instead tries to legislate uniform minimum standards across millions of diverse U.S. workplaces, but only for selected issues because the employment-at-will approach favors quitting over regulation or unionization in response to substandard conditions.[11]

By emphasizing individual rights, unitarist employment laws undermine the collective approach of pluralist labor law by weakening the need for labor unions to obtain some workplace protections. But because of the difficulties inherent in educating workers about the numerous employment laws and in enforcing these public policies, unions are often important for improving the effectiveness of work-related public policies. For example, research shows that unionized workplaces are more likely to comply with mandated safety standards and that unionized workers are more likely than comparable nonunion workers to know about the Family and Medical Leave Act and to file for unemployment insurance benefits.[12] In some respects then, employment law contains the seeds of its own weakness. More generally, the prediction of the eminent legal scholar Clyde Summers has come true: the morass of labor and employment law doctrinal inconsistencies "hold out [false] promises to the employee, harass and impoverish the employer, enrich the lawyers, and clog the legal machinery."[13]

The Need for a Principled System of Workplace Law and Public Policy

We think it is clear that U.S. public policies on work need significant reform. Moreover, our analytical framework reveals the need for principled reform that is coherent and purposeful.[14] The guiding principle of coherence demands that a reformed system of workplace law be built on the foundation of one consistent model of the employment relationship. By purposeful, we mean that a reformed system of workplace law and public policy must promote the fundamental objectives of the employment relationship. Workplace regulations and institutions are not ends in themselves; they are only important to the extent that they fulfill these fundamental objectives.

Our proposals for principled reform start with the pluralist model of the employment relationship. We see employees as more than simply commodities—employees are human beings with economic and psychological needs, as well as with citizenship rights in a democratic society. We see markets as important, but as falling short of the idealized assumptions of the textbook economics model of perfect competition. Consequently, employees and employers are not economic, legal, political, and social equals. And we see the employment relationship as characterized by a plurality of legitimate interests; employers and employees have shared as well as conflicting goals. Putting these assumptions together means that workplace law should help balance the power of employers and employees to prevent substandard work outcomes, promote a vibrant, participatory democracy, and create broadly shared prosperity. Contrary to popular beliefs, this pluralist or industrial relations school of thought is not simply about labor unions. Various institutional mechanisms can serve the pluralist needs for balancing power and promoting employee voice.

Progressive human resource management policies and market-based transactions can also have important roles in the pluralist model of the employment relationship. The principle of coherence, however, requires that these diverse approaches work in tandem rather than in conflict. Progressive human resource management policies can benefit employees, but the pluralist model does not rely solely on corporate self-interest to satisfy workers' needs. Similarly, the pluralist model accepts the centrality of market-based transactions, but challenges the sole reliance on unfettered markets to produce fair outcomes and broadly shared prosperity. Public policies need not rule out human resource management policies and markets, but should ensure that such approaches promote the core objectives of the employment relationship. In contrast to today's conflict between the individual approach of employment and the collective approach of labor law, a reformed system of workplace law and public policy needs to integrate individual and collective approaches so that they can support each other.[15]

But what should a coherent system of work-related public policies strive to achieve? This brings us to the second principle, purposefulness. Based on the pluralist conception of employees as human beings with rights in a democratic society, the central purpose of a reformed system of workplace law and public policy should be to balance efficiency, equity, and voice. This framework embraces more than the contemporary neoliberal market paradigm's emphasis on competitive markets. Even if produced by free markets, efficient outcomes that violate principles of human dignity—poverty wages, dangerous working conditions, discriminatory hiring practices, and the like—are unacceptable. Rather, social and human boundaries on efficiency are needed. In our framework, these boundaries for the employment relationship are equity and voice.

Efficiency, equity, and voice can be mutually reinforcing. An efficient organization or country can afford to provide equity and voice; equity and voice can inspire workers to be more productive and create greater efficiencies. In such cases, government regulation of the employment relationship is less necessary. More often, however, efficiency, equity, and voice clash. Standardized overtime payments (equity) can conflict with individual desires to have input into compensation decisions (voice) and with business needs for flexibility (efficiency). How should policymakers approach these conflicts? All too frequently such conflicts are resolved by favoring efficiency over other concerns.

Efficiency is clearly an important consideration because of its implications for competitiveness, economic development, jobs, and economic prosperity. The problem lies with taking the market-based agenda too far. Work in the neoliberal market vision is a coldly rational economic transaction in which outcomes are dictated by the demands of competitive markets that are believed to maximize efficiency. The mainstream media's coverage of work-related issues has similarly elevated the importance of consumers over workers in the American social imagination. Debates over labor unions, minimum wage laws, and paid family or sick leave are reduced to debates over their effects on businesses and consumers through reduced competitiveness and increased costs. In reality, however, employment is given a human face only when efficiency is *balanced* with equity and voice.[16]

The importance of balancing sometimes-competing interests has long been addressed in industrial relations scholarship. Its importance is rooted in two key premises of the pluralist model of the employment relationship—the existence of imperfect labor markets and the view that labor is more than a commodity. First, when markets fail to be perfectly competitive, institutional intervention to balance bargaining power can be welfare-improving. This is a standard market failure result from economic theory. Second, when labor is more than just an economic commodity, employees as human beings are entitled to justice and democratic participation consistent with human dignity. The importance of these human elements is underscored by the wide-ranging yet fundamentally powerful rationales for equity and voice: political theories of liberty, democracy, and citizenship, moral views of human dignity, humanistic psychology theories of human nature, and religious beliefs about the sanctity of human life and self-determination. In fact, important dimensions of equity and voice are increasingly seen as universal human rights. The property rights of business (a common justification for the laissez-faire employment relationship that emphasizes efficiency) cannot be allowed to trump these human rights. That consideration again brings us back to the importance of seeking a balance.[17] Note carefully that the importance of equity and voice, therefore, is not rooted only in market failures. Rather than continue to bow to the neoliberal market ethos that forces everything to be justified as a market fix, it is time to return to the fundamental justification for equity and voice—the fulfillment of human dignity and citizenship.

This argument for a balanced workplace should not be equated with a vision of harmonious mutual gains in which the interests of employers and employees are assumed to always be aligned, as in the unitarist model. A balanced workplace might very well require adversarial unions representing workers' interests in opposition to management's interests. Moreover, the idea of a balance should not be pushed so far as to require strict equality in the importance of efficiency and equity and voice in all situations. The point of a balanced workplace is that neither efficiency nor equity nor voice should consistently dominate.

It is admittedly difficult to know when a balance has been achieved. But this does not obviate the need for guiding principles. Too much employment research and too many policy debates lose sight of the broader objectives of the employment relationship by focusing on the operational details of specific laws and processes. Public policies on the employment relationship need guiding principles, or what philosophers might call a regulative ideal—something to strive for even if it is not always achieved. For example, Russell Muirhead argues that trying to structure work that is responsive to both social fit (what society needs done) and individual fit (what individuals find interesting and rewarding) is a regulative ideal for the nature of work even if a perfect balance between these two constructs is unattainable.[18] Trying to balance efficiency, equity, and voice is a similar regulative ideal.

A Pluralist Manifesto for Regulating the Employment Relationship

Government regulations and public policies are warranted if they serve the public interest. Police and courts serve the public's interest in law and order. The military serves the public's interest in national security. Requiring motor vehicle drivers to have a license serves the public's interest in safety. But with respect to the employment relationship, what is the public interest? If it is competitiveness and the other economic concerns we are labeling efficiency, then the contemporary neoliberal market paradigm would reject the need to regulate markets, corporations, and the employment relationship to promote efficiency. "Free" markets and corporations are supposed to be best for achieving efficiency and economic prosperity. This paradigm is clearly articulated in an *Economic Report of the President* from the George W. Bush administration:

> An important reason for Americans' high standard of living is that they live in a free-market economy in which competition establishes prices and the government enforces property rights and contracts. Typically, free markets allocate resources to their highest-valued uses, avoid waste, prevent shortages, and foster innovation. By providing a legal foundation for transactions, the government makes the market system reliable: it gives people certainty about what they can trade and keep, and it allows people to establish terms of trade that will be honored by both sellers and buyers. The absence of any one of these elements—competition, enforceable property rights, or an ability to form mutually advantageous contracts—can result in inefficiency and lower living standards.[19]

Government-sponsored social safety nets are therefore seen as inhibiting labor market flexibility; proposals to add labor standards to international trade agreements are attacked as harmful barriers to free trade; and policies to give stakeholders a voice in corporate governance are criticized for infringing on shareholders' rights.

The normative prescriptions developed in the remainder of this book are based on four premises that differ significantly from this neoliberal market thinking:

1. Labor markets are imperfect and therefore do not serve everyone equally; in other words, "often the invisible guiding hand of competition is all thumbs."[20]
2. Setting aside questions about market imperfections, efficiency is not the only element comprising the public interest. The public interest is the broad quality of human life; in other words, man does not live by bread alone.
3. We cannot rely on corporate self-interest always to serve the public interest; in other words, what's good for General Motors is not necessarily good for the country.
4. Neither corporations nor the modern employment relationship nor markets are "natural" institutions that are inherently entitled to autonomy or freedom; in other words, only people are entitled to life, liberty, and the pursuit of happiness.

These four premises provide the foundation for work-related government regulation and public policy intervention in the pluralist model of the employment relationship. As such, they constitute a manifesto for a pluralist system of workplace law and public policy.

Imperfect Labor Markets

The neoliberal market ethos is rooted in mainstream economic thought (more specifically, neoclassical economics) in which the invisible hand of competitive markets guides self-interested firms, workers, consumers, investors, and suppliers (all of whom are assumed to possess both perfect information and the ability to contract with each other costlessly) toward optimal outcomes. Aggregate welfare is maximized and scarce resources are allocated to their most productive uses. There is no divergence between public and private welfare: no groups have power advantages over others, and prices (including wages) fully reflect their value. Employers and employees are seen as legal and economic equals; employees are free to choose among jobs while an abusive or exploitative employer will fail to retain employees and will go bankrupt. The invisible hand, therefore, does not need help from policymakers. Employment and labor laws, no matter how well intentioned, inhibit free markets and therefore prevent the maximization of aggregate welfare. The only legal help the invisible hand needs is common-law rulings in support of property rights and contracts.[21]

This neoliberal market thinking, however, contains a major proviso: if markets are not perfectly competitive, then prices do not reflect true social value. If markets are not perfectly competitive, then power imbalances can lead to the exploitation of workers and the environment. Markets, of course, are "competitive" in laypersons' terms, but to truly serve society's interests, the neoliberal market paradigm requires the idealized *perfect* competition of mainstream economic theorizing.

Even though labor markets may look competitive, in reality there are a number of reasons why they are only imperfectly competitive. One market imperfection is the existence of what economists call negative externalities and lawyers call common-law nuisances—spillovers from private behavior that harm someone else. Low wages, dangerous working conditions, and the lack of health insurance can impose negative externalities on the rest of the community because taxpayers foot the bill for welfare, subsidized food purchases, public housing, and public health clinics. One hundred years ago, this was called "industrial parasitism" because companies were living off community subsidies. Today it is often expressed as a concern that Wal-Mart and other low-wage retailers fail to provide affordable health care benefits and are consequently subsidized by taxpayers' contributions to the public assistance health care plans that ultimately cover their workers. Other negative externalities can stem from gross levels of income inequality that prevent workers from getting college degrees or training while also creating social instability that undermines not only economic growth, but also democracy and public safety.[22]

Labor markets are also imperfect because of technical issues such as information asymmetries, mobility costs, liquidity constraints, and transaction costs. For example, employees often have incomplete information about dismissal policies and the risks of workplace accidents. But most important, the resource imbalance between workers and today's global corporations hardly make them legal and economic equals. Internal labor markets, unvested pension benefits, and employer-specific health insurance plans further a firm's advantage over its workers by making it more difficult for employees to find an equivalent job elsewhere. With imperfect labor markets, it is unwise to rely on the invisible hand to produce socially desirable outcomes; public policies are a necessary complement to ensure that markets work effectively.

Efficiency Is Not Enough

In the neoliberal market ethos, efficiency is key: "companies want efficient production processes to maximize profits, consumers want efficient companies to maximize value, and employees want efficient employment opportunities to maximize their earnings and leisure."[23] As just described, there are good reasons for doubting that labor markets can be relied on to generate optimal efficiency. But even if they did, there is still a very powerful reason to regulate markets and the employment relationship—efficiency should not be the sole yardstick for the employment relationship. All of the economic concerns captured by this concept of efficiency—including productivity, competitiveness, economic prosperity, and the effective use of scarce resources—are important, but they are not the only purposes of the employment relationship.

Workers are not simply commodities or productive resources; they are human beings with aspirations, needs, and rights in democratic societies. Work is not simply an economic transaction; it also fulfills important psychological and social needs. Workers therefore have rights to what we have labeled equity and voice. Critics of this perspective will respond that government regulation of the employment relationship to promote equity and voice can harm efficiency. We do not disagree, but it is "better that social relationships distort economic relations than that economic relationships be allowed to distort and destroy social relationships."[24] To wit, ask yourself how you want to be treated in the workplace and have your working conditions determined. Individuals we talk to want respect and fairness (in other words, equity) and input and autonomy (in other words, voice). More important, consider why you want to be treated this way. Is it because it will make you a more productive employee (assumed by the unitarist school), or is it because you have the market power to command such treatment (as assumed by the egoist school)? No. We assert that most people believe they are entitled to fairness and input (equity and voice) because they are human. This is a core pluralist belief. Efficiency is not enough. Employment with a human face requires balancing efficiency, equity, and voice.

Corporate Self-Interest Is Not Enough

Because of market imperfections and the human goals of the employment relationship, we cannot rely on free markets to achieve employment with a human face. What about corporations? In a global economy driven by a neoliberal market ethos, corporations have become the dominant actor on the world's dominant stage, the global economic system. In fact, the annual sales of some of the largest global corporations are larger than the gross domestic product of whole countries (Israel, Norway, Poland, and the Philippines, for example). If corporations serve the public interest—that is, if corporations universally showed a concern for promoting justice, human rights, and democracy—then government regulation of corporate conduct would be unnecessary. But corporations are legally bound to pursue profits for their shareholders. Executives and managers cannot pursue corporate social responsibility and act in the interests of workers, consumers, society, or the environment except to the extent that these interests are aligned with seeking higher profits. When a society's standards include more than aggregate wealth maximization, we cannot rely on corporate self-interest to serve these standards—a corporation is in business to make money, not to promote other things that human beings value, such as democracy, empathy, relationships, justice, and dignity.[25]

This is not to say that corporations or their managers are corrupt. Rather, corporations are simply programmed to pursue profits. Profits trump human concerns like freedom, as demonstrated by the fact that Microsoft, Yahoo!, and Google block their China-based search engines from accepting the words "democracy," "freedom," and "human rights." This preoccupation with profits creates strong incentives to exploit negative externalities in which society rather than business bears the costs of, for example, pollution, training, disability supports, and health care.[26] As a result, when self-interest is a defining feature of corporations, it is naive to rely on self-policing. When in 2005 a Union Pacific railroad car broke loose and rambled unattended through suburban St. Paul, the railroad chose not to tell anyone. That same day it came to light that, a few miles away, Guidant Corp. had kept quiet for three years knowing that heart defibrillators that had been implanted in 24,000 people were defective.[27] In both cases, the corporate response was that it did not think anyone would get hurt (Union Pacific was lucky, and no one did; Guidant was not so lucky, and several deaths have been linked to defective implants). That these two examples represent just one day in the news in one major city clearly illustrates the pitfalls of relying on self-policing of corporate self-interest. Critics might respond that some companies are model corporate citizens and respect their employees, communities, and the environment. We do not disagree, and such companies should be applauded. But contrary to the old saying, what's good for General Motors is not always good for the country. We cannot rely on self-interest to ensure that all corporations are always model citizens.

Natural Institutions Free from Regulation?

The importance of achieving more than efficiency in the employment relationship, paired with imperfect markets and corporate self-interest, creates the need to regulate the employment relationship. But some might still object to regulation on the basis that markets, the employment relationship, and corporations are "natural" institutions. Natural (as opposed to man-made) institutions are entitled to basic rights such as freedom simply by their existence. As highlighted by the rhetoric of the American and French Revolutions, people have natural rights that stem from the basic quality of being human. If markets and the employment relationship are natural institutions, then employment and labor laws interfere with their natural state; if corporations are natural institutions, then government regulations infringe on their freedom and other natural rights.

The neoliberal market ethos sees markets as natural institutions in which their perfect state is a lack of legal regulation. This view is misguided. Without laws pertaining to private property, contracts, fraud, and coercion, today's economic markets could not function and would not exist. In other words, "free markets" are not actually free in the sense of having no regulation. Since markets are social and legal creations that serve society's needs, regulations to promote the public interest are legitimate. Similarly for the modern employment relationship—work of some sort is necessary for survival (and is therefore perhaps "natural"), but wage work in limited-liability corporations mediated by labor markets was created by society to serve human and social ends and should be regulated when necessary to promote those ends. Sometimes the invisible hand needs a helping hand.[28]

There is also a popular tendency to view corporations as natural. But corporations are man-made institutions first created by European spice importers in the 1600s to finance risky Asian voyages. They have risen to prominence over the past two hundred years because England and the United States enacted limited-liability laws to protect individual investors against personal liability for the debts and misdeeds of a corporation.[29] The U.S. legal system treats corporations as people by endowing them with rights to equal protection and due process, but such rights are not natural. Rather, these rights were developed by Supreme Court justices, and even by the court reporter in *Santa Clara County v. Southern Pacific Railroad*, who first wrote that "corporations are persons" in his inaccurate, but frequently relied-upon, summary of this Supreme Court decision.[30] Thus corporations are societal creations granted certain rights and protections to serve society's needs. It is therefore valid to regulate corporations to promote social goals. Employment and labor laws do not violate any inherent corporate right to freedom; there is no "divine right of capital."[31]

Similarly, the contemporary emphasis on maximizing shareholder value is given an unduly elevated importance. In stylized theoretical models where labor markets are perfectly competitive and individuals can easily find new jobs at the same rate of pay, shareholders bear all of the risk of poor corporate performance because they are residual claimants—they are entitled to whatever profits are left over after workers and suppliers are paid. As a result, economic performance is optimized when managers maximize shareholder value. But given the real-world complexities of imperfect labor markets, there is little reason to believe that shareholders face greater risks than employees and that shareholders contribute more to corporate performance than employees do. Shareholders deserve a fair rate of return on their investment, but the ideal of *maximizing* shareholder value without regard for other interests rests on questionable foundations and cannot be used to elevate the importance of corporations over other participants in the economic system.[32]

Balancing Efficiency, Equity, and Voice Through Pluralist Policy Reform

To recap, we assert that neither markets nor the employment relationship nor corporations are natural institutions; rather, it is legitimate to regulate these institutions to serve the public interest. With respect to work, the public interest in the pluralist model is served by employment with a human face that balances efficiency, equity, and voice. The U.S. democratic system is based on a system of checks and balances; so too should our economic system. Some might say that the employment systems in many countries are broken because of too many rigidities in local, state, and federal government laws, in administrative regulations, in international treaties, and in labor unions and works councils. But that does not mean that a regulation-free environment is desirable. Living in an insecure world with no safeguards, safety nets, or checks and balances would also have economic and human costs.

At the same time, the U.S. system is a complex maze of common law doctrines and individual statutes on varied employment and labor law topics from racial discrimination to whistleblowing, from childbirth leave to Social Security benefits, from workplace safety to collective bargaining, from explicit minimum wage standards to tax subsidies for private health insurance. There are multiple forums for resolving disputes, gaps in coverage, inconsistent definitions, and a host of other complexities. For these reasons alone, U.S. laws and public policies on work need reforming.

But there is an even more important reason for reform—U.S. workplace law and public policy fails to achieve employment with a human face in today's global economy. The nature of work, technology, demographic structures, the world economy, and other key elements of the employment relationship have changed enormously over the past seventy-five years. Flexibility, not stability, is now the driving force of corporate employment strategies. With the rise in dual-income families and single working parents, employment issues can no longer be separated from family issues. An individual's employer used to be a single entity, but increases in the prevalence of contingent work have created a confusing maze of interrelated employers and agencies. And to some observers, social identities linked to gender, race, ethnicity, age, disability, and sexual orientation have displaced economic identities linked to class, industry, occupation, and employer for today's workers.[33] U.S. workplace law and public policy lacks a coherent intellectual approach for keeping pace with these fundamental changes and therefore fails to balance efficiency, equity, and voice.

In the remainder of *Invisible Hands, Invisible Objectives* we therefore focus on the needed links between work-related laws and public policies and the key employment relationship objectives in the context of a pluralist vision of the employment relationship. The next three chapters develop policy options for promoting efficiency, achieving equity, and facilitating voice, respectively, with the goal of merging employment law, labor law, and other work-related public policies into one coherent body of workplace law and public policy. The final chapter discusses ways to make these policy reforms a reality. Although many of the individual policy proposals are not new, it is critically important to package them together within a clear and consistent principled framework—a package of visible hands and explicit objectives rather than invisible hands and invisible objectives.

CHAPTER 7

Promoting Efficiency

AN EFFICIENT WORKPLACE is important because it promotes the preservation and creation of jobs in a competitive global economy. To many, the best government policies for promoting economic efficiency are limited to maintaining law and order. In the absence of fraud and coercion, the invisible hand of the marketplace will ensure that rational economic actors use scarce resources efficiently. There is little doubt that real-world economic markets are "competitive" as most people use the term, but to be completely effective, the invisible hand requires *perfectly* competitive markets. Employees often have imperfect information about accident risks and pensions. It is not costless to quit your job and find another. A lack of savings can make it difficult to hold out for the best job. And many economic activities are not completely private—pollution, poverty-level wages, and dangerous working conditions impose costs on society, and they are not borne completely by the company that creates them. Economists call these costs externalities. All of these realities mean that today's markets do not match the perfectly competitive markets found in economics textbooks.[1] As such, public policies that correct market failures can enhance efficiency.

In Chapter 3 we reviewed five key pressures on efficiency in the employment relationship of the 21st century: globalization, technology, flexibility, employee benefits, and a burdensome regulatory approach to employment law. These pressures provide the impetus for the reforms proposed in this chapter: workplace standards that reflect international norms that will accommodate the global marketplace; improved training programs; portable employee benefits that enhance labor market flexibility; health insurance benefits that are divorced from employment; and a coherent, efficient system of workplace law and enforcement mechanisms.

International Labor Standards

Globalization cannot be ignored in any discussion of employment-related public policies. The business lobby frequently cites the need for competitiveness in the global economy to argue against government regulation of the employment relationship. For example, American Axle and Manufacturing, a U.S. auto parts company, told a Senate committee that the Family and Medical Leave Act (FMLA) increases "the already substantial competitiveness gap that domestic manufacturers currently face" and supported this position by comparing its 229 average annual working days with the higher number of working days in Mexico (282), Brazil (264), and India (249).[2]

This type of comparison highlights the need for a level playing field throughout the global economy in order to prevent destructive competition. When markets are not perfectly competitive, a race to the bottom can result. Countries with high labor standards lose jobs to countries with lower standards. Companies with progressive human resources policies and generous benefits are punished by the global marketplace and struggle to remain competitive. Downward pressure is exerted on wages and working conditions, and local communities suffer. International labor standards are therefore needed to promote efficiency gains that come from legitimate sources of competitive advantage—smarter uses of technology, innovative products, effective human resources policies—by preventing competition along illegitimate dimensions—modern forms of slavery, child labor, poverty wages, ethnic and gender exploitation, dangerous working conditions, and the like.[3]

Such standards ultimately need to be established at a global level. Since 1919 the International Labor Organization (ILO) has been promoting workers' rights and labor standards through the adoption of conventions and the provision of technical assistance. Eight of these conventions pertaining to freedom of association and collective bargaining, the abolition of forced labor, equal opportunity and pay, and the elimination of child labor have been declared to be fundamental such that all countries have a moral obligation to promote them. The United Nations Universal Declaration of Human Rights similarly proclaims as human rights the following labor standards: just and favorable conditions of work including pay sufficient for an existence worthy of human dignity; equal pay for equal work; reasonable working hours; periodic paid holidays; unemployment and disability insurance; and the right to form labor unions. In 2003, the United Nations issued a set of corporate norms rooted in these human rights instruments that obligate companies to provide a safe workplace, pay a living wage, and respect freedom of association to form unions and engage in collective bargaining. There is thus increasing consensus on the list of international labor standards.[4]

The controversy is over how to enforce such international labor standards. To date, efforts to incorporate core labor standards into the World Trade Organization's global trading system have failed. And the United States does not have a strong track record of ratifying ILO conventions. On the other hand, labor standards were attached to the North American Free Trade Agreement with Canada and Mexico through a side agreement; more recent free-trade agreements between the United States and Australia (2005), Peru (2007), and Korea (2007) incorporate standards into the body of the treaties. In each of these, the signatory countries pledge to respect the core ILO labor standards through enforcement of their respective domestic labor laws. No changes to the existing labor laws are required, however, even if they appear inadequate.[5]

Through these channels, international labor standards have crept into U.S. public policymaking. Such initiatives are frequently justified on the basis of enhancing equity and voice for workers around the world. This is a very important rationale and is consistent with our overall framework, but such standards can also enhance efficiency by preventing destructive competition in imperfect markets. Building on recent free-trade agreements and enhancing core labor standards at home and abroad is therefore an important element of reforming public policies on work and achieving employment with a human face.

Training Programs

The potential for a persistent skills gap as technological advancements and flexible work practices increase the skill requirements for success in the 21st century workplace means that effective training policies are an important element of promoting efficiency. But employers are frequently reluctant to bear the costs of training for skills that can be used at competing firms for fear that newly trained workers will be poached by these competitors.[6] This is a classic market failure problem that can be addressed by government intervention. U.S. government-sponsored training programs date back to at least the 1930s. Regardless of the era, the impetus is often the same—lawmakers compare the paradoxical existence of both significant unemployment and help-wanted ads and conclude that "the problem [is] one of square pegs in round holes. The people [do] not fit the jobs."[7] Unemployed workers typically "do not fit the jobs" for one of two reasons: they never acquired basic skills to begin with, or their skills have become obsolete because of technological change. As such, government-sponsored training programs typically focus on disadvantaged and dislocated workers and include combinations of training in basic work skills and retraining for specific occupations. While the details vary from program to program, training has arguably become the primary U.S. employment policy over the past two decades because it is the only work-related initiative on which, at least in principle, both Republicans and Democrats can agree.[8]

There are long-standing debates, however, over how to deliver government-sponsored training. Each successive federal act, from the Manpower Development and Training Act (1962) to the Comprehensive Employment and Training Act (1973) to the Job Training Partnership Act (1982) to, most recently, the Workforce Investment Act (WIA, 1998), sought to improve on the apparent and imagined failings of the delivery method utilized by the preceding act. As these programs evolved, funding remained at the federal level, but delivery has become more decentralized, public service employment has been discontinued, and the involvement of employers has increased. Under the current WIA system, federal dollars are distributed to employer-led Local Workforce Investment Boards that are responsible for arranging approved training opportunities. The WIA further seeks to make training services available to all workers—not just dislocated or disadvantaged workers—through local one-stop service centers. Individual training accounts were created to give individuals discretion over where to "purchase" their training. The large body of research on the effectiveness of government-sponsored training programs generally finds that these programs improve workers' post-training income, but that the positive effects of these policies are often modest. In short, they raise incomes, but not by a lot. The WIA therefore needs to be improved.[9]

To positively affect more individuals, the first necessary reform is increased funding. Relative to other countries, the United States spends a minimal amount on training, and since 1998 the number of individuals served has declined significantly. Greater funding needs to be devoted both to local infrastructure and to individual training accounts, Pell grants, and other funding sources for workers and students. More employers need to be involved in the Local Workforce Investment Boards, and worker representation from unions, civil rights groups, churches, and other advocacy groups should also be strengthened. Much of the current training focuses on job search assistance and effective work behaviors like punctuality. Greater attention needs to be devoted to developing concrete skills applicable to an "occupational cluster" (that is, not one narrow occupation, but a range of related occupations). To increase the effectiveness of this initiative, apprenticeship programs with widely recognized skills standards and credentials should be created. Labor-management sectoral councils could oversee these skills standards, as they do in Canada. Unemployment insurance funds could also be used to retrain workers after a corporate restructuring to help prevent job loss and unemployment. And ultimately, job training programs need to be better integrated into the secondary and postsecondary educational systems, as well as into other support systems such as counseling and child care services.[10]

While government-sponsored training programs should be strengthened, it is also important not to overemphasize their significance. It is difficult to design effective skill creation programs when no one knows for certain what skills will be needed in the future, but that sort of uncertainty is inherent in today's dynamic global economy. And yet, in the neoliberal market economy, there is a strong tendency among employers and conservative policymakers to see training programs as the primary solution to all workplace ills. In particular, the favored fix for ending poverty and raising the living standards of low-wage workers is to improve earning power through training. After all, a competitive labor market rewards greater skills. But although government-sponsored training programs appear to raise incomes on a micro level, they fail to raise living standards on a macro level. One reason is that these programs reach only a small fraction of the targeted individuals. But perhaps even more important, there is no evidence that training programs create, or fill, new, high-quality jobs. There are simply not enough good jobs available to lift significant numbers of impoverished families out of poverty. Thirty years ago, Garth Mangum likened the completion of a government-sponsored training program to a hunting license: it allows an individual to search for a high-quality job, but success is at best elusive and uncertain. This characterization remains true today.[11] Training is necessary, but not sufficient, for realizing employment with a human face.

Flexibility

In the 21st-century employment relationship, employers frequently emphasize the need for flexibility—to adjust staffing levels, work hours and assignments, how work is organized, compensation levels, and the like—to achieve efficiency and profitability. This is largely a private issue best left to individual employers, and the U.S. employment relationship is already quite flexible by international standards, so we do not propose any public policies specifically targeted toward improving employers' flexibility. A critic, however, might argue that many of our policy recommendations will *reduce* employers' flexibility. From the neoliberal market perspective, a minimalist approach to public policy is preferred because the best way to promote flexibility is to avoid restrictive or constraining laws and regulations.

We recognize this assertion, but there is little evidence that all public policies on work reduce flexibility to such an extent as to have widespread negative consequences for an economy's efficiency.[12] Neoliberal market proponents typically point to the European experience for confirmation; specifically, they say that European labor market rigidities rooted in generous unemployment benefits and restrictions on employee terminations are responsible for high unemployment rates. As discussed in Chapter 3, however, the empirical support for this link between European labor market rigidities and unemployment is weak. Rather, we interpret the debates over Eurosclerosis as revealing that the right policies can provide security and social insurance as well as the flexibility to adjust to economic shocks and achieve efficiency. In other words, it is possible to work out a balance between flexibility and security to achieve what is now labeled "flexicurity" in Europe.[13]

This thinking underlies the proposals we develop in this book. In the next section, we argue that making employee benefits more portable and decoupling health insurance benefits from employment can benefit employees *and* promote labor market flexibility. In later chapters, we further develop several policies that would allow employers and employees to craft their own solutions rather than being forced to adopt inflexible one-size-fits-all mandates. In sum, flexibility in support of efficiency is a concern in our analyses, but it needs to be balanced with other fundamental objectives of the employment relationship.

Weakening the Ties That Bind: Employee Benefits

One of the factors fueling the growth of employee benefits during the mid-twentieth century was a desire by employers to bind employees to the firm. Employee benefit programs, particularly those that provide health insurance and retirement income, became essential ingredients in the development of internal labor markets. From the 1940s on, business lobbied against national or universal health insurance so that employees would need to rely on employer-provided benefits, and therefore be loyal solely to their employers, not to the government or a labor union. Moreover, when the postwar business model emphasized stability and predictability, employers commonly designed benefit programs to reward long-term employment. Many defined-benefit pension plans, for example, backload pay-out amounts so as to provide greater benefits to long-term employees.[14] Some employers also withhold benefits from employees until they demonstrate a long-term work attachment with that particular employer. Thus an employer might provide health insurance coverage to employees only after they have been on the job for three or six months. Until 2007, for example, new assistant professors at the University of Minnesota were excluded from the retirement plan for their first two years of employment.

A number of employment statutes similarly reserve benefit programs for longer-term employees. The FMLA, for example, guarantees leave time only to employees who have worked for the same employer for at least one year and for at least 1,250 hours during the previous twelve-month period.[15] Under the Employee Retirement Income Security Act (ERISA), employers may establish a threshold employment period of between two and six years before an employee's pension fully vests. In addition, ERISA does not compel an employer to allow participation in a pension plan until an employee works at least 1,000 hours in a twelve-month period.[16] Similarly, most state statutes require an employee to work twenty weeks per year in order to qualify for unemployment insurance benefits.[17]

Employee benefits generally, and these loyalty or length-of-tenure requirements specifically, however, are problematic in an environment characterized by flexibility and short-term employment. Part-time and temporary employees often fail to meet threshold benefit eligibility requirements, whether established by statute or by plan design. Employees who do have benefits can be involuntarily locked into their jobs if changing jobs would require them to forfeit unvested pension accumulations, go without medical coverage, change doctors, or lose health care coverage entirely. In short, benefits that are tied to one's full-time employer are mismatched with a labor market that increasingly favors contingent, part-time, and short-term jobs.[18]

One might be tempted to see the benefits issue as a purely private concern. After all, private business was instrumental in creating the employment-based system of benefits provision. But it is, in fact, an important public policy issue. First, government policies support the current system. For example, Internal Revenue Service regulations make employer payments for employee health insurance tax exempt. Second, reforming how benefits are provided requires coordination across employers, and such coordination is unlikely to occur without government involvement. Third, a common business response to skyrocketing benefits expenses is to stop offering some benefits. Public policies need to ensure that employees receive key benefits. We outline two policy responses that would do so: a decoupling of health care benefits from employment and an increase in the portability of other benefits.

Decoupling Health Care and Employment

The matter of health care reform has long been a front-burner issue in the United States. The Clinton administration fought (but failed) to bring about broad-based health care reform in 1993, Congress has had a long-running debate over a proposed patient's bill of rights, and health insurance was a major campaign issue during the 2008 presidential election. But while almost everyone agrees that the American system of health care needs fixing, no clear consensus for a solution has emerged. The core of the problem is a matter of costs and access. While the United States spends more than twice as much on health care per capita as the average of the other OECD countries, it is the sole Western democracy to permit a large percentage of its population to go without health insurance coverage.[19]

In terms of efficiency, more specifically, the core of the problem is the link between health care and employment. As discussed in Chapter 3, the fact that most health care insurance in the United States is provided through a voluntary system of employer-sponsored coverage has the effect of dampening overall employment, contributing to job lock, and imposing anticompetitive costs on American employers. Instead of reducing costs as proponents claim, the private health insurance system increases both health care and administrative costs by dividing up risk pools. From an efficiency viewpoint, accordingly, any set of reforms ultimately adopted for revamping the American health care system should include decoupling health care and employment. Mandating minimal levels of employer-provided benefits or employer contributions toward a Medicare-type fund would help make health care coverage less dependent on a specific job and lower costs by improving risk sharing. A more complete decoupling would be achieved through some version of a single-payer universal health system such as that utilized in virtually all other industrial democracies. Such a system need not be wholly financed and administered by the federal government. Other countries have adopted public and private partnerships to support their single payer systems, and the United States would be well served to take a good look at some of these models.[20]

This recommendation, of course, does not address the myriad of funding and design issues necessarily involved in crafting a new health care delivery system for the United States. That is a task, however, that is beyond the scope of this book. The point here is to address the employment-related economic inefficiencies inherent in the current health care system. On that score, the solution is clear: the United States should move past its current reliance on voluntary employment-sponsored coverage to mandated or single-payer systems.

Portable Benefits

As a policy matter, employee benefits should be made more portable. This could be accomplished by linking benefits with workers and their careers rather than with a particular employing entity. In fact, a good model for this approach already exists. There are nearly 3,000 multiemployer pension plans covering more than 12 million workers in U.S. private industry in which two or more employers make contributions to a single retirement fund. These plans are almost always jointly run with a union and can be found in a wide range of industries—construction, coal mining, transportation, entertainment, hospitality, and elsewhere. Numerous multiemployer plans have also been established to provide health insurance, legal services, supplemental unemployment benefits, and even housing benefits. These portable benefit plans serve efficiency by leveling the competitive playing field across employers (since most employers make the same contribution per hour worked), preventing job lock because employees can change employers without jeopardizing their benefits, and creating a larger shared risk pool that reduces the cost of providing benefits. Policymakers should learn from these existing multiemployer plans and devise policies to expand them by industry, occupation, or geographic area.[21]

Where such a transformation is not possible, other steps should be explored to enable workers to continue benefit coverage despite a change in employing entity. The Consolidated Omnibus Budget Reconciliation Act of 1985 (COBRA) is an example of an existing federal statute that facilitates the portability of employee benefits. Pursuant to COBRA, employers are required to offer continued group health insurance coverage to terminated employees and their family members at the employee's own expense for up to eighteen months.[22] In 1996, Congress further enhanced the portability of health insurance benefits through the enactment of the Health Insurance Portability and Accountability Act (HIPAA). HIPAA restricts the ability of group health plans to limit or exclude benefits because of a preexisting medical condition.[23] Taken together, these statutes significantly improve the ability of employees to retain health insurance coverage as they move between jobs.

Policies should be adopted to facilitate the portability of other benefits as well. As an example, Congress could amend ERISA to provide that employees who work for more than one employer may accumulate periods of service to meet the minimum vesting period for a defined contribution pension plan. Similarly, state unemployment compensation laws could be altered to permit more employees who work at part-time and temporary positions to qualify for some proportion of unemployment benefits. In both situations, the cost of providing these benefits could be prorated among the employing entities. In sum, "the very logic of organizing benefits around employment is a flawed concept."[24] All parties to the employment relationship would benefit from new methods of providing health, retirement, and other forms of security.

A Coherent Body of Workplace Law

As we have emphasized in several places, U.S. labor and employment law is currently a mess. Employees and employers face a maze of forums for resolving disputes under statutes that are often overlapping and inconsistent. Different laws have different definitions of "employee" and "supervisor" and different exclusion criteria for small employers. Federal employment laws are adjudicated in different ways, but often in forums that lack an expert in employment issues. Exceptions to the at-will doctrine can vary widely from state-to-state.

Large gains in efficiency can be achieved by cleaning up this mess. A coherent body of workplace law should establish consistent definitions of employees, supervisors, and covered employers. The largely separate collective approach of labor law and individual approach of employment law need to be reconciled into a single body of workplace law such that individual and collective approaches complement rather than undermine each other. These improvements will serve not only equity and voice, but also efficiency by adding operational clarity to the system. Crafting a comprehensive definition of employee that includes contingent workers should be a priority because of the legal costs associated with the current definitional morass (efficiency), as well as the gaps in employment protection (equity) and barriers to forming unions (voice) faced by today's contingent workers who are not legally "employees" as defined by U.S. employment and labor law.

Achieving operational consistency, however, is only one piece of the puzzle. As we explore in more detail below, streamlining the regulatory enforcement process would greatly improve efficiency. But any gains in this regard will be minimal if plaintiffs and defendants must operate within the existing maze of forums, so we begin this section by proposing a good-cause standard for employee termination. We focus here on the efficiency benefits that would result from a single standard and forum for resolving termination disputes; the important equity rationales for this good-cause standard are discussed in Chapter 8.

An American Good-Cause Termination Act

Congress should enact a statute that systematically governs the issue of employment termination. As described in the two chapters on equity, this statute should adopt a unitary good- or just-cause standard for termination. In addition, the statute should establish a streamlined administrative structure for determining individual cases coupled with a reasonable cap on monetary damages. This recommendation is not new. Many legal scholars have called for a statutory solution to today's cumbersome employment termination system.[25] Moreover, the nonpartisan National Conference of Commissioners on Uniform State Laws adopted a Model Employment Termination Act (META) in 1991 that embraces a just-cause standard and a streamlined administrative structure.[26] META, however, fails to strike the proper balance between employee and employer interests and has largely been ignored. A reformulated solution is necessary.

META incorporates many of the common attributes of the national employment security acts in other industrialized countries. META would prohibit the discharge of most private sector employees in the absence of "good cause," which is meant to be similar to the "just-cause" standard incorporated in most collective bargaining agreements. META departs from traditional labor arbitration principles, however, in placing the burden on the discharged employee to show an employer's lack of good cause. META would permit an employer and an employee to jointly waive the good-cause limitation on discharge by entering into an agreement whereby the employer promises to "provide severance pay in an amount equal to at least one month's pay for each full year of employment." The drafters of META attempt to balance this significant departure from the traditional at-will rule with three benefits for employers. First, META would extinguish most common-law limitations on an employer's discharge prerogative, including all tort-based actions. Note, however, that META would not bar claims based upon either an express contract or a federal or state statute. Second, META would cap available damages so as to eliminate the costly punitive and compensatory damage awards that not infrequently result from successful tort claims under the current system. Finally, META would route termination claims into a streamlined forum, which presumably would translate into proceedings that are quicker and less costly for all parties concerned.[27] This last element is discussed in the next subsection.

At this point, however, META is a proposal that has not yet borne fruit. Only one state, Montana, has enacted legislation bearing any resemblance to META, and that statute predates META's 1991 birth date.[28] Critics have assailed META's compromise from many angles. Some fault META for failing to adequately protect employee interests.[29] At the opposite end of the spectrum, others criticize META for imposing too many burdens on employers.[30] In spite of these criticisms, META embodies a rational, policy-based attempt to redress a number of the shortcomings of the current employment law regime. The fundamental problem with the current version of META is that it does not provide employers with an adequate trade-off for their loss of the at-will prerogative. We believe that this problem can be rectified by broadening META's preemptive scope.

An American Good-Cause Termination Act would function most efficiently by consolidating the existing bases for challenging an employment termination. As noted above, the current law of employment termination encompasses a multitude of potential claims and forums. This is particularly burdensome to employers who may be forced to defend a single dismissal decision in multiple proceedings. Although a purported goal of META is to simplify the current maze by "extinguish[ing] a variety of subsidiary tort claims," META's current formula tends to do the opposite by adding yet an additional layer without removing much from the current maze.

The good-cause claim should supplant rather than add to the existing host of alternative claims. We therefore propose that all existing termination claims, except for those arising under a collective bargaining agreement, be funneled into a single forum created by our American Good-Cause Termination Act and merged with META's good-cause claim. In this manner, statutes and express contracts would not survive as independent claims, but they would inform the new good-cause substantive standard. Take, for example, the claim of an employee who believes that she was selected by her employer for layoff because of her age. Under our proposal, the employee could not pursue a separate action in court under the Age Discrimination in Employment Act (ADEA). The employee, however, could argue in a good-cause-based proceeding that the employer's layoff action was influenced unlawfully by considerations of age. If the employee succeeds in establishing that the employer's action violated the substantive standards of the ADEA, then she automatically has established a violation of the American Good-Cause Termination Act's good-cause provision. In essence, our proposed good-cause inquiry would subsume the standards established by other statutes and by express contracts. The resulting violation and remedy, however, would flow solely from the American Good-Cause Termination Act. This would significantly enhance the coherence of U.S. employment law because claims based on federal antidiscrimination statutes, state whistleblowing laws, antiretaliation provisions contained in the federal Occupational Safety and Health Act and state-level workers' compensation laws, and other statutes would be consolidated in one forum.[31]

Critics undoubtedly will voice the concern that META's remedies will not adequately deter workplace discrimination. At present, the remedial schemes embodied in federal antidiscrimination laws go beyond simply making whole the victims of employment discrimination. Title VII and the Americans with Disabilities Act authorize awards of compensatory and punitive damages in addition to back pay and reinstatement. The ADEA, similarly, permits an award of liquidated damages in an amount equal to the back-pay award in the event of a willful violation. These remedies reflect the fact that these statutes serve a societal goal of eradicating discrimination in the workplace. The enhanced remedies, accordingly, are designed to deter discriminatory conduct as well as to compensate employees who have been injured by such conduct.[32] Under our proposal, META should be modified to allow double or treble damages awards upon a finding that the lack of good cause for termination was attributable to unlawful discrimination. In sum, the adoption of an American good-cause termination statute that modifies META as outlined here would eliminate the current maze of multiple claims and forums with respect to termination decisions. The fix can be accomplished by transferring all employment termination challenges into a single just-cause claim subject to resolution in a single forum.

Streamlined Regulatory Enforcement

Reforms such as the good-cause termination proposal just outlined will be only partially successful in enhancing efficiency if the expenses of the current regulatory model are not reduced. U.S. employment law is primarily enforced through litigation in general courts of law, and a good-cause termination standard could be similarly adjudicated. The administratively cumbersome nature of this litigation model, however, is underscored by comparisons to alternative systems. Employment termination disputes that arise in the U.S. unionized sector are usually addressed through an interactive grievance process that culminates in arbitration. This process is widely believed to be "faster, cheaper, and simpler than litigation."[33] Most European and Latin American countries test the validity of job termination decisions in proceedings before a specialized labor tribunal of one form or another. Here again, the use of these specialized tribunals is "thought to dispense a cheaper, quicker, more accessible and expert justice."[34]

Data compiled by Federal Mediation and Conciliation Service (FMCS), the federal agency primarily charged with overseeing private sector labor arbitration matters, tend to confirm the "faster, cheaper, and simpler" assertion. In contrast to the typical two-and-a-half-year timetable for litigated employment termination cases to reach trial, FMCS statistics show that the average labor arbitration case in fiscal year 2007 was completed from start to finish in 259 days. In reality, the contrast is greater still because arbitration awards typically are final and subject to a very narrow scope of review. Similarly, the average labor arbitration hearing conducted in 2007 took only 1.10 days to complete, a far cry from the length of a formal jury trial. An additional piece of FMCS data shows that the average fee charged by an arbitrator to handle an arbitration case in fiscal year 2007 was $3,929. These figures certainly suggest that arbitration is both quicker and cheaper than litigation.[35]

A small but growing number of U.S. employers have sought to fashion a private system of arbitration as an alternative to the litigation-based model. These employers typically require employees to sign arbitration agreements by which the parties agree to funnel all workplace-related claims into a single arbitral forum. Although many courts initially tended to view such agreements with skepticism, the Supreme Court, in its 1991 landmark decision in *Gilmer v. Interstate/Johnson Lane Corp.*, ruled that an employment discrimination plaintiff may waive his right to proceed in court by entering into a pre-dispute agreement to submit such claims to arbitration. The Court in *Gilmer* effectively reversed decades of judicial hostility to arbitration and ruled that arbitration agreements are valid under the Federal Arbitration Act (FAA) unless the statute in question expressly evinces a policy proscribing such a waiver.[36] A decade later, the Supreme Court extended the FAA's preference for arbitration to the vast majority of American employees through its ruling in *Circuit City Stores, Inc. v. Adams*.[37] Following *Gilmer* and *Circuit City*, most arbitration agreements are enforceable unless they are procedurally defective or limit the substantive rights or remedies available to the parties.[38] The Supreme Court, accordingly, has opened the door for employers and employees to agree to substitute private arbitration for federal court litigation. However, a *systemic* solution that specifies fair and explicit procedures is preferable to this ad hoc resolution of employment law claims, especially when dictated by employers. The first part of this systemic solution is an American Good-Cause Termination Act as proposed above. The second part is specifying an efficient method for resolving disputes under this good-cause standard.

One possibility is to funnel all good-cause claims into an arbitration system. But many commentators, particularly in the context of individual arbitration agreements, have raised concerns about the lack of basic due process safeguards in the arbitration of statutory employment claims. These concerns involve such hallmarks of fairness as the selection and training of arbitrators, prehearing discovery, and the issuance of a written decision.[39] These have an easy solution: incorporation of the due process guidelines that have been developed by John Dunlop and Arnold Zack, the American Arbitration Association, or other neutral, expert groups into the American Good-Cause Termination Act. These basic procedural requirements can ensure that the arbitration proceedings will be fair as well as expeditious.[40]

Moreover, we could take things one step further and turn the private arbitration system into a publicly funded system of specialized employment tribunals. There are several advantages of adjudicating employment law claims in this specialized forum instead of in the general court system. One, the maze of multiple forums would be replaced by a single forum. Two, the labor tribunal judges would develop expertise in employment-related issues and be better able to manage the complexities of claims. This would help avoid the current situation in which rulings on one part of employment law may have the effect of undermining another part. Labor tribunal systems are frequently used in Europe and are therefore well tested.[41]

Finally, a tribunal system also may be fairer than arbitration because it can lessen any advantages that accrue to employers by virtue of being repeat players in an arbitration system. For one thing, when employers but not individual employees are repeat players, employers have a greater knowledge base for selecting potentially favorable arbitrators. Moreover, arbitrators might unfairly favor employers in order to develop a pro-business reputation so that employers will choose them again in the future to resolve disputes. Since a tribunal is permanent in nature, the repeat-player imbalance inherent in the ad hoc arbitrator selection process simply would not arise. In either case, a private system of labor arbitration or a public system of specialized labor tribunals along with procedural standards for fairness would streamline the current regulatory enforcement process and aid employment relationship efficiency while not sacrificing equity and voice.

Promoting Efficiency

We do not doubt that private economic activity is the primary driver of efficiency in the employment relationship. But this does not mean that efficiency is not an important dimension of public policy. In the presence of market imperfections and failures, there can be a productive role for government involvement to help markets work better and achieve better outcomes. With respect to employment issues, this is particularly true in the areas of training programs, portable benefits, and streamlined regulatory enforcement. Policy issues pertaining to international labor standards and workplace flexibility are also important in the 21st-century employment relationship.

But achieving employment with a human face requires more than just improved efficiency. Our model of streamlined regulatory enforcement builds on a foundation of good-cause dismissal, but this foundation also would greatly enhance the fair treatment of employees. Portable benefits can help mobility and therefore efficiency, but by itself do not necessarily increase coverage rates. Government-sponsored training programs can improve efficiency by closing a skills gap. Yet with a limited supply of good jobs, training is a poor method for achieving equity and voice. Putting all of these concerns together yields one conclusion: work-related public policies must also improve the quality of jobs. We therefore turn in the next two chapters to policy suggestions for achieving equity and facilitating voice.

CHAPTER 8

Achieving Equity

EQUITY CONSISTS OF FAIR EMPLOYMENT STANDARDS that all workers are entitled to, including wages and benefits to support a family, decent working conditions, security, and nondiscriminatory treatment. Some might see equity in laissez-faire terms: market-based transactions are fair because they are voluntary. Economists might take this one step further: market-based transactions are fair because competitive markets ensure that everything commands its economic worth. From that perspective, improving equity is a private rather than a public issue—low-paid workers who want higher incomes should work harder and improve their skills. Our pluralist perspective is different. The complexity of the employment relationship undermines the realism of the ideal competitive model; in many cases, market-determined terms and conditions of employment at least partly reflect bargaining power differentials rather than only economic value. Structural barriers, not just a lack of personal responsibility and individual self-improvement, can prevent workers from bettering their economic position. And as labor is more than just an economic commodity, the metrics for employment-relationship equity must stem from human dignity, not from the marketplace—regardless of how perfectly competitive the market may be. As such, markets and individual initiative cannot be solely relied on to provide equity in the modern employment relationship.

As shown in Chapter 4, the current U.S. employment system—which is heavily focused on markets and individual initiative—fails to provide equity to many employees. Even Adam Smith, who is typically associated with the invisible hand of free markets, recognized that labor markets are imperfect: employers can hold out longer than workers and therefore can "force the other into a compliance with their terms."[1] Credit markets, especially for the poor, can also be imperfect. This means that some individuals cannot afford to invest in education and training that would improve their economic standing and cannot create their own safety nets by borrowing money when they are laid off. Substandard wages and working conditions can result from these market imperfections. These problems are reinforced by negative externalities that spill over into the public arena—or what was called "industrial parasitism" more than a hundred years ago. Private corporations might benefit from low labor costs, but society bears the cost of workers injured on dangerous jobs, families that live in low-wage poverty, and children that are uninsured. Critics of Wal-Mart, for example, point out that the very profitable retailing giant receives millions of dollars in economic development aid from state and local governments, but does not provide health insurance to many of its hourly wage employees; it therefore shifts the cost of health care to these states when Wal-Mart employees have to turn to public health care programs and emergency rooms for treatment. Equity is therefore a public issue, and a significant public policy concern.[2]

In the pluralist approach to the employment relationship, government policymaking can and should play an important role in establishing minimum standards and in crafting other policies to redress bargaining power imbalances and ensure that the employment relationship is not only efficient, but also equitable. It is important to emphasize that job creation is not enough. Globally, more than 40 percent of the world's workers earn less than the $2 per day the International Labor Organization (ILO) has established as the poverty level. There is not a single county in the United States in which a single full-time minimum wage earner can afford to rent a one-bedroom apartment. Moreover, one-quarter of all U.S. workers are in jobs that pay less than a family of four needs to live above the poverty line; and with average year-to-year income swings of 50 percent for low-income households, their economic situation is very volatile and precarious.[3] Equity requires quality jobs and safety nets, which in turn require public policy supports. This chapter therefore outlines public policies that can achieve equity along seven key dimensions: balancing work and non-work needs; a living wage; balanced income distributions; income, retirement, health, and physical security; nondiscrimination and fairness; good-cause dismissal; and nonstandard work arrangements.

Balancing Work and Non-Work Needs

As employees spend more time at work and fewer families operate under the breadwinner/homemaker model, American workers increasingly are caught in a serious time crunch. As discussed in Chapter 4, workers do not have enough time to tend to family responsibilities and other non-work needs. Although this problem is particularly acute for family caregivers of children and elderly relatives, the worker time crunch affects many individuals, and policy reform should not be focused exclusively on work-family conflicts. We thus see the Family and Medical Leave Act (FMLA) as only a first step in addressing the worker time crunch.[4] Workers need more options for time away from work that will not create economic hardship and that are easy to negotiate with their employers.

The most direct and equitable way to address the worker time crunch problem is to expand the options available to employees under the FMLA as follows:

1. Employers must permit employees to take paid personal leave for two weeks of the FMLA's twelve-week period of protected leave.
2. Upon a minimum of seven days' advance notice, an employee may take all or part of the period of paid personal leave without restriction as to the reason or use of such personal leave time.
3. Pay for such leave should be provided in a manner and an amount similar to that provided for unemployment insurance purposes. That is, the pay should be provided from a government fund, payable at one-half of the employee's average weekly wage, subject to a maximum equal to two-thirds of the applicable statewide average weekly wage.
4. The government fund would be financed by equivalent one-third contributions from employees, employers, and general revenue. The employer's contribution would be a percentage payroll tax, rather than an experience-rated contribution. The employee's contribution also would be a percentage payroll tax similar to the current Social Security tax.
5. Employers could opt out of the personal leave mandate by providing a minimum of four weeks of leave per year that may be taken by employees for care, sickness, or personal leave/vacation. Employers that provide a minimum of three weeks of leave per year for such purposes would be obligated to provide and contribute toward only one week of paid personal leave time.[5]

This proposal has a number of strengths. The proposal provides a modest amount of compensation that will make leave for caregiving and other purposes more accessible. It provides a flexible format for leave-taking that requires little government oversight, yet provides employers with advance notice for planning purposes. The proposal builds on the existing FMLA's framework of a twelve-week leave period. Employers are provided with a self-help mechanism to avoid difficulties complying with administrative requirements. Finally, by addressing the American worker time crunch problem systematically, the proposal does not suffer from criticism that it would marginalize either female caregivers or non-caregivers.

Some commentators may object that a paid leave mandate would harm the ability of American employers to compete successfully in the global marketplace. This outcome is unlikely, however, since the amount of paid leave or vacation provided by this proposal is still far less than international norms. A recent study identified 169 countries—not including the United States—that provide paid maternity leave benefits and sixty-six—again not including the United States—that provide paid paternity leave benefits. For example, in the United Kingdom, new mothers are entitled to fifty-two weeks of maternity leave, the first thirty-nine of which are paid at a statutorily defined rate; fathers are entitled to two weeks of paid paternity leave. At least 137 countries also mandate annual paid leave; nearly all western European countries require employers to provide a minimum of four to five weeks of paid annual vacation. The states of California, New Jersey, and Washington have adopted paid parental leave programs, and a number of others have enacted policies to strengthen the FMLA for workers in their states. Although American employers highly value flexibility in today's global economy, America's competitive edge should not depend on substandard labor practices.[6]

Another large part of allowing employees to balance work and non-work needs is giving them greater control over their work schedules. This can be accomplished by giving workers the right to refuse overtime hours and the right to discuss their work schedule with their employer. So, in effect, we propose a three-part solution to the worker time crunch problem: (1) expanding the FMLA to include a paid leave component as described above; (2) banning mandatory overtime; and (3) giving employees the right to request a new work schedule. The last two policies are presented in Chapter 9 because they enhance employee voice and address the worker time crunch problem.

A Living Wage

If a society widely sees work as the primary and preferred method of supporting oneself and one's family, then that society needs to ensure that jobs allow workers to support themselves and their families at a level that does not damage human dignity, citizenship, and liberty. Thus U.S. public policy should guarantee workers a living wage—that is, a wage high enough to provide for a decent standard of living with some reasonable level of comfort. There are two complementary approaches to this policy objective: ensuring a decent level for the minimum wage and expanding the Earned Income Tax Credit (EITC).

The federal minimum wage is scheduled to rise to $7.25 in July 2009. This will relieve some of the pressures faced by the working poor, who saw the minimum wage fall to its lowest real value in fifty years in 2006 before being increased. Policymakers need to be vigilant and guard against a recurrence of this situation. Admittedly, most economists object to increases in the minimum wage on the free-market theory that mandated wage increases will lead to a reduction in the demand for labor. If labor markets are not perfectly competitive, as in the pluralist model of the employment relationship, a minimum wage increase does not necessarily decrease employment. Some research supports the latter view. As just one example, economists David Card and Alan Krueger found that employment in New Jersey fast-food establishments grew more than it did in Pennsylvania after New Jersey increased its minimum wage requirement. Most research finds that the employment effects of minimum wages—whether positive or negative—are small. With such a long period of federal inaction on the minimum wage before 2007, numerous community groups have turned their attention to lobbying for local-level living wage ordinances that apply to municipal contractors. More than 100 cities now have living wage ordinances, and the research on these ordinances echoes that of the minimum wage research: when enforced, such ordinances can enhance living standards for low-wage workers with perhaps, but not necessarily, some small negative employment effects.[7]

Second, a vigilant living wage policy should be supplemented with an expanded Earned Income Tax Credit. The EITC was enacted in the 1970s with the slogan "make work pay" and has been expanded several times since. The EITC provides a refundable tax credit that reduces the income tax liability of low-income workers and creates a cash payment for any amount by which the credit exceeds the worker's tax liability. In 2008, the maximum credit of $4,824 was available to married couples with two or more children with incomes from approximately $12,000 to 16,000. The EITC declined beyond that income level and was not available to married taxpayers with adjusted gross incomes in excess of approximately $38,000 (depending on filing status). A considerably lower credit is available for low-income workers without children.[8]

The EITC has broader support than the minimum wage, including support across the political spectrum. It can more effectively target the working poor than the minimum wage, especially since increases in the minimum wage can benefit, for example, teens from high-income families working in summer jobs. Unlike the minimum wage, the EITC does not interfere with market-based wage rates. Conservatives favor the EITC over welfare-type programs because the EITC includes an incentive to work. Research also shows that the EITC works. For parents working at the minimum wage with two or more children, the EITC can effectively raise hourly earnings by as much as two dollars per hour. In 2002, the EITC is estimated to have lifted 5 million people out of poverty. The EITC should probably be simplified, but it encourages work and raises income among a targeted population and should therefore be expanded. An increase in the minimum wage would further bolster the impact of the EITC.[9]

Balanced Income Distributions

The problem of America's growing income inequality is the result of several intersecting forces. Some of these forces, such as globalization, technological change, and flexible work practices, cannot be legislated away. But this does not mean that there is no role for public policy. Skill-biased technological change is often asserted as the primary cause, which would imply that the best policy response is training. But the evidence indicates that institutional changes such as the decline in the value of the minimum wage and declining rates of unionization should not be overlooked as causes of widening income inequality.[10] In other words, the growing disparity in earned income is at least partly a symptom of the undersupply of equity and voice in the contemporary workplace.

A number of the reforms suggested in this chapter and elsewhere in this book should have a beneficial impact on this problem. Bolstering the bottom end of the income distribution through living wage policies would reduce income inequality. Extending unemployment insurance benefits to low-wage and part-time employees, and increasing the level of benefits for all low-paid workers, would raise income levels at the bottom of the labor market. More equitable access to union representation and health care should also boost the economic prospects of low-wage earners. Income disparities inhibit equality of opportunity, the hallmark of the American dream; making college more affordable and accessible, for example, should improve intergenerational mobility and equality of opportunity.

Two other policies can directly reduce income inequality. First, the United States should revert to a more progressively indexed rate of income taxation. Sizable tax cuts in the 1980s and 2000s disproportionately benefited high-income taxpayers.[11] Contrary to the assertions of some supply-side economists, tax reductions for the rich have not resulted in a rising tide that lifts all boats. Instead, the tax cuts of the 1980s benefited only high-income earners while "swamp[ing] those boats too short on the anchor line."[12] In fact, the more regressive tax climate that has resulted is arguably less efficient. Robert Frank and Phillip Cook contend that the combination of winner-take-all markets and a non-progressive tax structure distorts the supply of labor by inefficiently channeling more participants into high-risk ventures than into tasks where their talents might better contribute to societal welfare.[13] More important, the unfairness of the more regressive tax system is difficult to deny because it exacerbates an already unacceptable level of income inequality. An increasingly progressive income tax system would counter this problem by narrowing the income distribution in two ways: directly by differentially affecting the after-tax income of different portions of the income spectrum, and indirectly by transferring some of the income of high-salary earners to increases in social service programs designed to boost the prospects of the working poor.

Second, the tax code should be amended to limit the size of the deduction that companies can take for compensation paid to high-level executives. One possible model for accomplishing this task is the Income Equity Act proposal that was introduced as H.R. 3260 in 2005. This bill would eliminate the business expense tax deduction for executive compensation to the extent that such compensation exceeds twenty-five times the annual amount paid to the firm's lowest-paid full-time employee. As an example, if the lowest paid full-time employee of a firm earned $20,000 in a year, the bill would cap the available deduction for executive compensation at $500,000. In the words of H.R. 3260's sponsor, this bill "does not tell companies what they are allowed to pay top executives, but it intends to make them think about the top and bottom pay within a company and how they relate to one another."[14] Section 162 of the Internal Revenue Code already limits the deduction for executive compensation at $1 million, but a reform like the Income Equity Act could take this one step further and offer a modest incentive to U.S. firms to raise the wages of low-income workers and curb the growth in executive compensation, thereby helping to improve equity in the U.S. employment relationship.

Security and Social Safety Nets

Enacting public policies to provide a healthier work-life balance, boost minimum living standards, and create a fairer distribution of income would go a long way toward improving equity, but these policies would not address another closely related issue: the rise of insecurity in the U.S. employment relationship. The U.S. approach to income, retirement, and health security largely relies on private rather than public actors to provide this security. Workers are told to save for the rainy day when they lose their job, to regularly contribute to a retirement plan, to find a job that provides health insurance benefits and safe working conditions, and to upgrade their skills if they cannot find a job that is adequate to provide the security they need. But these are not purely private issues. Laid-off workers desperate for work might have to take jobs that do not fully utilize their talents, which creates both human and economic costs. Senior citizens without an adequate pension slip into poverty and become dependent on the government for support. Workers without health insurance are less productive; families without health insurance lack preventive health care, which taxes the health care system in the long run. Unhealthy children are less likely to develop into productive adults; unhealthy adults are unable to fully contribute to society.[15]

It is therefore common for public policies around the world to provide some degree of social safety net through social insurance. Major aspects of the U.S. social safety net for workers include unemployment insurance, workers' compensation and disability programs, and Social Security. There is, however, no broad-based safety net for health care for working-age adults.

Insecurity was a major public policy concern during the Great Depression in the 1930s, but New Deal policies eased this concern through government programs. Now, with what Jacob Hacker has called the "great risk shift," the burdens of health care, retirement, and job loss once again have been pushed onto workers and their families in recent years, and insecurity is again a major concern. Policy reforms are needed to patch these holes in the U.S. social safety net for workers.[16]

Income Security

The primary public program to provide some level of income security for workers is the unemployment insurance system. Unemployment insurance in the United States dates back to the 1930s and began "primarily as a program to support male factory workers who worked to support themselves and their nonworking wives and families during recessionary periods."[17] Based on this fact alone, unemployment insurance merits reform. In fact, in the 1990s the Advisory Council on Unemployment Compensation was created by Congress and produced fifty-two recommendations for reform. Others have called for similar reforms. Expanding eligibility for low-wage and part-time employees by reducing the prior earnings requirements, bolstering benefits to ensure adequate income replacement, and providing greater federal oversight to prevent a race to the bottom as states compete for jobs should be priorities for reform.[18]

The impact of these reforms would be magnified by complementary improvements described elsewhere in this book. Problems of income insecurity can be lessened by improved health insurance coverage, enhanced portability of benefits, and a more progressive income tax structure. Unemployment insurance take-up rates for individuals already eligible for benefits can be improved by stronger collective voice institutions that provide information about how to collect benefits. A more comprehensive approach has been proposed by the Hamilton Project, in which a program of universal insurance would provide income replacement for a limited period of time for families that experience more than, say, a 20 percent drop in income due to unemployment, disability, illness, or death of a spouse.[19] This is another option for using social insurance to improve equity for American workers and their families.

Retirement Security

As described in Chapter 4, it is common to portray employees' financial resources for retirement as a three-legged stool consisting of Social Security benefits, employer-sponsored retirement plans, and personal savings. Improved public policies can help strengthen each leg of this stool.

Social Security. In his 2005 State of the Union address, President George W. Bush proposed a systemic overhaul of the current Social Security system with a centerpiece proposal for the creation of personal retirement accounts. Under this plan, workers under the age of 55 would have the option to divert up to four percentage points of their payroll taxes (approximately one-third of the current combined employer and employee assessment of 12.4 percent) to individual accounts that would pay benefits in addition to a correspondingly reduced amount of traditionally funded Social Security benefits. President Bush suggested that the retirement accounts could be invested in a limited mix of stock and bond funds and be centrally administered in a manner similar to the Thrift Savings Plan currently in place for federal employees. Unfortunately, the president's proposal failed to address the critical problem at hand: the creation of personal accounts would neither increase program revenue nor decrease program costs. Further, if the debatable proposition that equity holdings would generate higher investment returns is accurate, these higher returns could be achieved by investing the combined trust accounts in these same investments without exposing individual retirees to the risks of investment volatility.[20]

A more fundamental problem with the proposal for private retirement accounts is that such accounts would worsen the financial position of the Social Security system. Implementing the president's individual account initiative would require the Social Security system to finance two programs simultaneously for a lengthy transitional period; the trust funds would continue to pay benefits under the present pay-as-you-go retirement system while also pre-funding individual accounts for future benefit payments. While some commentators suggest that up to $2 billion in borrowing would be necessary to fund the private account proposal, even the official summary of the president's plan acknowledges a transition cost of $754 million. Although the trust funds would recoup the overall outflow of funds over a period of seventy-five years or so as account holders retire, the ensuing transitional deficit would hasten the trust fund's exhaustion by about a decade.[21]

There are a wide variety of superior options for correcting Social Security's fiscal imbalance without making radical structural changes. The shortfall in Social Security finances over the next seventy-five years (the usual durational yardstick for measuring program solvency) amounts to 1.7 percent of payroll.[22] That means that a 1.7 percent reduction in benefits, a corresponding increase in payroll taxes (i.e., from 12.4 to

14.1 percent), or any combination of the two would solve the Social Security crisis. Although many solutions are possible, we believe that the gap should be filled by a combination of benefit and tax adjustments. Structuring the solution solely through benefit reductions would undercut Social Security's critical social insurance function at a time when retirement resources are challenged in all directions. On the other hand, a tax-only solution would exacerbate the budgetary burden generated by escalating mandatory social welfare expenditures. With these principles in mind, we recommend three reform proposals.[23]

Our first proposal is to raise the retirement age. Shifting demographic trends have transformed Social Security from a system paying benefits to a minority of former workers for a relatively few years to a system paying benefits to a majority of former workers for a period of one to several decades. Against this backdrop, a modest increase in the retirement age would generate sizable cost savings without undermining Social Security's fundamental retirement insurance objectives. Present law provides for phasing in an increase in the normal retirement age from 65 to 67. A recommendation of the Social Security Advisory Council to speed up that increase so as to be fully effective in 2011 would eliminate 7 percent of the seventy-five-year deficit. The council also recommended indexing both the normal and early retirement ages thereafter to coincide with future increases in life expectancy. These two modifications would eliminate approximately 40 percent of the deficit over the seventy-five-year measuring period.[24] Special accommodations in the disability insurance system could be created for workers who, because they spend their working lives in physically demanding jobs, are unable to work until an older retirement age.

Our second proposal stems from the current practice of "wage-indexing," in which a retiree's level of Social Security benefits is determined by recalculating the worker's past earnings to reflect the value of those past earnings in terms of present wage levels. A relatively painless, yet helpful step would be to index benefit levels to after-tax rather than pre-tax wages. Most economists expect the tax burden on workers to rise in future years as the baby-boom generation retires and budgetary pressures increase. After-tax wage indexing would tie a retiree's Social Security benefits to the after-tax rather than pre-tax living standards of contemporary workers. This should not be confused with more aggressive proposals to replace wage indexing with price indexing, which would create more drastic cuts in Social Security benefits. A shift to after-tax indexing would provide a gentle and fair curb on future benefit growth while eliminating approximately 25 percent of the seventy-five-year trust fund deficit.[25]

Our third Social Security proposal tackles the revenue side of the ledger by raising the payroll tax ceiling. An individual's earnings in excess of the maximum taxable earnings base (e.g., $97,500 in 2007) are not subject to the Social Security payroll tax or considered when calculating benefits. While the maximum taxable earnings base automatically increases each year based on average wage growth, the resulting fraction of national work-related earnings that is taxed continues to decline. This reflects widening income inequality: higher incomes are growing faster than lower incomes, so these higher incomes are also growing faster than the payroll tax cap. Phasing in increases in the cap through 2015 to restore the 1983 level (when 90 percent of national income was taxed) would produce approximately the same amount of revenue as a 0.8 percent across-the-board increase in the payroll tax. We prefer this solution since it avoids an overall increase in the payroll tax and responds to growing income inequality by extending a previously determined contribution arrangement for those taxpayers with the greatest ability to pay.[26]

These three reform proposals would close the 1.7 percent gap and avert Social Security's oncoming fiscal crisis. A striking attribute of these proposals is their relative modesty. They do not entail systemic modification to the structure of the Social Security system, and they require only minor adjustments to existing obligations and benefits. In short, the Social Security financial crisis would not be difficult to remedy if only we could find the political will to accomplish the task.

Pensions and Personal Savings. American workers need to set aside more assets to supplement Social Security benefits in retirement. We suggest two policies that could serve as important incentives toward this end by reversing the default options for plan participation and by encouraging savings by low- and middle-income earners. These policies might not be sufficient by themselves, but they would provide a foundation for further enhancements to the retirement security of U.S. workers.

As the prevalence of defined contribution retirement plans has increased in the United States, so too has the degree of personal responsibility for employees to manage their own retirement resources. But individual financial planning is not a simple task. Many employees, faced with application forms and a dizzying array of investment options, simply procrastinate and do nothing. Since the problem here is essentially a matter of inertia, using employee inertia to their advantage offers an intriguing solution. Rather than putting the onus on individual employees to undertake the steps necessary to opt into an offered 401(k) plan, we join with others in supporting the automatic enrollment of a covered employee unless he or she opts out of the plan. Several studies suggest that automatic enrollment could boost the rate of plan participation by about 25 percent.[27]

The Pension Protection Act of 2006 (PPA) embraces this strategy by encouraging employers to enroll employees automatically in defined contribution plans in exchange for a safe harbor from nondiscrimination and fiduciary requirements.[28] While the PPA removes potential obstacles to default enrollment, it remains to be seen how many employers will voluntarily utilize this option. Some employers that make matching contributions on behalf of participating employees might decide against automatic enrollment because it would add to costs. Ultimately, Congress should monitor employer participation rates to determine whether an automatic enrollment mandate would be preferable.

Congress also should consider the adoption of default options for some other 401(k) decisions as well. Once an employee is enrolled in a 401(k) plan, contribution levels and investment allocations can stagnate if the individual never changes her initial investment level or allocation. Furthermore, when employees with small balances in their 401(k) account change jobs, they frequently cash in their accounts rather than roll them over into other retirement accounts. As in the case of the initial enrollment decision, it is reasonable to believe that this practice could be altered if 401(k) plans automatically provided for periodic increases in contributions, default investment allocations (such as life-cycle funds), and the default rollover of plan funds upon job change. While employees should have the right to override each of these settings, these new default options could harness the powerful force of inertia for greater retirement savings.[29]

A second way to help American workers save more for retirement is to explicitly encourage savings by low- and middle-income earners. The Saver's Credit, enacted in 2001, was a start. This program provides a government matching contribution in the form of a tax credit for voluntary individual contributions to 401(k) plans, IRAs, and similar retirement savings arrangements. The Saver's Credit has a progressive structure in which lower-income households receive a larger tax credit, but this program breaks down for the lowest income group because the Saver's Credit only benefits taxpayers who have a federal income tax liability against which to apply the credit. In order to reach this low-earner group, a monetary payment should be available in lieu of an income tax credit for those individuals who make a matching contribution to a qualifying pension or savings program, but who do not have a sufficient tax liability to make use of the tax credit.[30]

Health Security

The private system of U.S. health care is characterized by high costs and unequal access. The United States spends more on health care per person and a higher fraction of total income than any other country, yet 47 million Americans lack health insurance. As shown by Jacob Hacker, "health care is at the epicenter of economic insecurity in the United States" and is in dire need of comprehensive reform.[31] It is time to move toward a universal health care system. Universal health care can be justified on the basis of efficiency, need, or rights.[32] As noted in the previous chapter, the efficiency reasons are alone sufficient to justify replacing the voluntary system of U.S. health insurance with a universal approach that makes it less of an employment issue. The interest in equity further reinforces the need for major reform.

Proposals for individual health savings accounts do little to solve the fundamental problems and instead increase the coupling of health security and employment by further tying affordability to wages. Other options, such as the Massachusetts Health Care Reform Plan enacted in 2006, can expand federal or state-level Medicare-type programs and require employers to pay to enroll their workers if they don't provide coverage that is at least as good as these expanded programs.[33] Such reforms could be a positive step if they weaken the tight link between health security and employment by providing coverage to everyone, especially if they also increase the portability of benefits so that job-switchers are not caught without coverage. A single-payer universal health system would go the furthest toward decoupling health security from employment.[34] As an additional measure, Congress should enact a "Patients' Bill of Rights" to provide adequate remedies to employees and dependents who are injured as a result of negligent decisions by managed care health maintenance organizations (HMOs).[35]

Physical Security: Workplace Safety and Health

It is rare for someone to publicly deny the importance of safe workplaces. The real debates are over the specific mechanisms for achieving workplace safety and health. Some prefer to rely on the employer self-interest that comes from needing to recruit employees in competitive labor markets and managing workers' compensation expenses. Others argue for a system of government standards backed by inspections and penalties. In fact, such a system has been in place since the passage of the Occupational Safety and Health Act and the creation of the Occupational Safety and Health Administration (OSHA) in 1970.[36] Safety standards therefore exist for a number of physical hazards such as dangerous equipment, excessive noise, and toxic chemicals. These standards are enforced through workplace inspections.[37]

Events like the 2006 Sago Mine tragedy in West Virginia in which twelve coal miners died after an explosion raise questions about the effectiveness of the current workers' compensation–OSHA approach. But the OSHA model can be successful in improving workplace safety and health. Research shows that OSHA inspections can improve compliance with safety standards and reduce injuries. But three factors are important: (1) inspections must actually take place; (2) penalties must be meaningful; and (3) employees must participate. There are only 2,000 federal and state safety inspectors available to monitor 7.2 million workplaces, so only a small fraction of workplaces are inspected each year. Under Republican administrations, enforcement has been weakened and replaced by voluntary guidelines. Where mandatory standards exist, financial penalties for violations are small, and criminal penalties are virtually nonexistent. Measures to promote employee participation in safety and health efforts are similarly weak.[38]

Workplace safety and health can be improved by devoting more resources to enforcement, increasing the number of inspectors to approach the ILO's benchmark of one inspector per 10,000 workers, increasing the penalties for violations, and, as we describe in the next chapter, strengthening employees' voice by protecting their right to refuse to work in unsafe conditions and through worker participation in health and safety committees or labor unions. The Sago Mine tragedy is again instructive: the Sago Mine was cited for more than 270 safety violations in the two years before the explosion, but the most serious violations had a penalty of less than $500 and the workers lacked a union to advocate on their behalf.

As noted in Chapter 4, another major concern for employee safety and health is excessive working hours. As part of improving the employee self-determination dimension of voice, we argue in Chapter 9 that a revised system of U.S. workplace law should ban mandatory overtime. This reform would also help improve workplace safety and health and help prevent what the Japanese call *karoshi* (death from overwork). Such a ban would not prevent workers from choosing to work overtime when they believe that it is safe, but would allow them to refuse overtime—for safety or any other reason—without the fear of discipline or discharge.[39] This is another example of the complementary nature of various aspects of employment and labor law and further underscores the need for comprehensive rather than piecemeal reform.

Nondiscrimination and Fairness

We just noted that there are debates over how to achieve safe workplaces, but not over the desirability of workplace safety. The same is true of nondiscrimination—there is widespread agreement that the employment relationship should be free of discrimination, but there are different perspectives on how to best achieve this. Affirmative action—the use of explicit preferences in hiring employees with specific demographic characteristics—is particularly controversial.[40] In contrast, the nondiscrimination requirements of Title VII of the Civil Rights Act and other pieces of legislation are generally well accepted and have become thoroughly ingrained in the public face of the U.S. employment relationship as the phrase "equal opportunity employer" has become standard business jargon. Some improvements, however, would make this jargon a stronger reality for more American workers.

Enforcement of the existing nondiscrimination statutes needs to be more accessible, especially for lower-paid workers. There are several options in this regard. Strengthening labor unions would provide individuals with a low-cost advocate to represent them in discrimination suits. Providing funding to public-interest legal organizations that could assist low-income workers in discrimination cases is another way of reducing the financial burden on individual workers. As described in the previous chapter, streamlining the current litigation model through the use of alternative dispute resolution methods such as arbitration or through specialized labor courts would similarly improve accessibility for employees by lowering the overall costs of enforcement. Most ambitiously, the enactment of a comprehensive good-cause discipline and discharge requirement (as articulated in the next section) would simplify the maze of legal forums for pursuing claims while also making the enforcement system more accessible financially. This last option would go the furthest toward improving the nondiscrimination dimension of equity in the contemporary U.S. employment relationship.[41]

Another reform is needed to redress the Supreme Court's decisions that excessively narrowed the class of individuals with a "disability" protected by the Americans with Disabilities Act (ADA).[42] The ADA Amendments Act of 2008 took an important step in this direction by directing courts to disregard the effect of mitigating measures and to broaden the reach of the "regarded as" prong of the disability definition. But the 2008 act fell short by retaining the ADA's current definition of disability and betting that revised Equal Employment Opportunity Commission (EEOC) regulations will accomplish the hoped-for expansion in ADA coverage. The courts are likely to seize on this less-than-explicit approach to once again fashion restrictions on the scope of ADA protections.[43]

We believe that the 2008 act should be supplemented by the reform proposed by a group of legal and medical experts spearheaded by Mark Rothstein. They suggest that Congress should direct the EEOC to establish medical standards for determining when most common mental and physical impairments are sufficiently severe so as to constitute a covered disability for ADA purposes. These standards would be based on medical practice guidelines and standard diagnostic and treatment protocols. An individual whose medical condition met a promulgated standard would be covered by the ADA, with opt-in and opt-out mechanisms for special cases. A medical-based list of disabilities would bring much-needed certainty and predictability to the ADA standing issue. This approach can admittedly be seen as a step backward in the realm of disability theory by defining disability in medical terms rather than in a civil rights model of functionality, but it would nevertheless be a strong improvement over the vague and subjective language that has enabled overly restrictive judicial interpretations.[44] The medical standards approach therefore appears to provide the best available vehicle for determining the proper scope of ADA protection. With that needed reform, attention under the ADA finally could be refocused on the truly important issues of individual qualifications and reasonable accommodations, and therefore improve this important aspect of equity in the American workplace.

Good-Cause Dismissal

The United States should enact an American Good-Cause Termination Act in which employees can be fired only if there is "good cause" for such an action. A just-cause standard is nearly universal in U.S. union contracts (and CEO contracts), and decades worth of decisions by labor arbitrators applying this standard have created a reasonably coherent framework for determining if an employer has good cause to discharge an employee.[45]

In particular, at least three broad factors are important: job performance, the appropriateness of the termination remedy, and the nature of the investigation and evidence. First, the notion of good cause encompasses only reasons related to job performance. Violations of company rules, absenteeism, abusive behavior, producing poor-quality work, and the like are presumably related to one's job performance; except in rare circumstances, demographic characteristics such as one's race or gender, conduct and pursuits away from work, engaging in civic and political activities including freedom of association and speech, refusing to break the law, whistleblowing, and pursuing one's legal rights such as trying to form a union or filing a valid workers' compensation claim are not related to job performance, and therefore should not be valid reasons for discipline or termination. Layoffs and other terminations resulting from changes in an employer's staffing needs owing to shifts in the economy or an employer's business strategy are included under the rubric of good cause. Quitting is not considered a termination in this context unless the employer manipulates an employee's terms and conditions of employment so as to force the employee to quit (i.e., a constructive discharge).

Second, good cause requires that the consequences fit the infraction. Any disciplinary action needs to be reasonably related to the worker's record and the severity of the conduct. Minor or first-time offenses should be disciplined with a warning; severe or repeated offenses might warrant a suspension or discharge. The action also must not be discriminatory. If other employees have not been terminated in the past for the same misconduct, an employer will have a more difficult time showing good cause to terminate a specific offender. If employees are not aware of the rules that an employer claims were violated, then good cause might also be lacking.

Third, discharge procedures should fulfill basic standards of due process. Investigations need to be fair and objective and to provide convincing proof of guilt before any disciplinary action is imposed. Investigating an employee after imposing discipline looks like an attempt to find evidence to support a predetermined desire to terminate the employee—this is contrary to the essence of just or good cause.

Clogging the U.S. legal system with suits over employee terminations that lack good cause, however, would be counterproductive. As outlined in the previous chapter, good-cause claims should be adjudicated in a streamlined regulatory process that is accessible to individual employees and not overly burdensome for employers. There are at least two options in this regard: (1) follow the U.S. unionized sector and use neutral, third-party arbitrators; or (2) follow many other countries and use a specialized labor court. In either case, procedural standards of fairness and due process would be necessary. Unionized employees with just-cause discipline and discharge standards in their collective bargaining agreements would be allowed to continue to use their private grievance and arbitration systems, but all other termination disputes would be funneled into the American Good-Cause Termination Act machinery. Employees would not be allowed to bring a separate discrimination suit in federal court, but a finding of discrimination under our proposed statute would automatically be a violation of the good-cause standard.

Numerous commentators have championed a universal good-cause standard for the American workplace, and there are ample precedents for such a standard. Beyond the well-developed system of just cause and labor arbitration in the U.S. unionized sector, Montana's Wrongful Discharge from Employment Act, enacted in 1987, prohibits employee terminations that are: (a) in retaliation for refusing to violate public policy or reporting a public policy violation; (b) not for "good cause" after completing a probationary period; or (c) a violation of explicit provisions in written personnel policies. Good cause is defined as "reasonable job-related grounds for dismissal based on a failure to satisfactorily perform job duties, disruption of the employer's operation, or other legitimate business reason."[46] Employees who are wrongfully discharged under this law can receive up to four years' pay and benefits and the parties are allowed to resolve disputes through arbitration. Also, the nonpartisan National Conference of Commissioners on Uniform State Laws adopted a Model Employment Termination Act in 1991 that focuses on a good-cause standard and a streamlined administrative structure.[47] As discussed in Chapter 7, we believe that the model act provides a good foundation for implementing a good-cause standard, but that it should be modified in a few respects to achieve a proper balance.[48]

The employment-at-will rule is often defended on the grounds that it promotes overall economic efficiency with a minimum of administrative costs.[49] This flexible employment system, the argument goes, enables the United States to compete more efficiently in the global economy than countries with more cumbersome employment security rules. Empirical research, however, fails to uncover unambiguously negative effects of employment protection legislation.[50] Moreover, our proposed universal good-cause standard does not prevent employers from terminating employees because of substandard performance or changes in the direction of the business. It is also difficult to argue that U.S. employers would be at a competitive disadvantage in the global economy because the United States stands virtually alone in failing to a provide broad statutory protection against unjust terminations.[51] The remedies provided by other countries' statutes, however, are considerably less generous and more predictable than the sizable damages that are occasionally awarded in the American legal system. In the United Kingdom, for example, a basic award for those unfairly dismissed is computed using a formula based on an employee's age, years of service, and weekly pay. In Belgium, employees are entitled to a maximum of six months' pay with no possibility of reinstatement. Punitive damage awards usually are not authorized. To balance employer and employee interests, we propose that a U.S. good-cause standard be remedied by a maximum of one year's back pay, except in cases of unlawful discrimination in which case awards of double or treble damages would be allowed.

The benefits of our American Good-Cause Termination Act would be widespread. Equity would be enhanced by outlawing both bad and irrelevant reasons for dismissing employees. Other employment policies would also be enhanced; for example, workers would have greater protections in exercising their rights, such as by filing a valid workers' compensation claim or taking family or medical leave. A universal good-cause standard can also counter the real and perceived differential standards for termination that currently stem from the uneasy coexistence of the at-will presumption and nondiscrimination statutes. The perception—although inaccurate—of special protective rules for women and minorities fuels resentment of those groups, a result most clearly manifested in the sharp debates over affirmative action. The adoption of a unitary standard for discharge would diminish this resentment while still banning dismissals wrongly premised on stereotypical notions of race or gender characteristics.[52]

The benefits of a universal good-cause standard are not limited to the equity dimension. Employee voice would be facilitated because employee free speech, autonomy, and unionization would be protected: terminations in retaliation for pursuing these activities would not possess good cause unless the activities interfered with job performance. Efficiency would be promoted by reducing the regulatory burdens of the current system—including multiple forums and an approach that relies on expensive litigation—with a streamlined system that is quicker and cheaper. For example, in Montana, where employers lobbied for passage of the state's good-cause law, the stock prices of Montana companies jumped after the act was passed. Last, both employees and employers suffer under the current system in which different states apply exceptions to the employment-at-will doctrine.[53] An American Good-Cause Termination Act would help balance efficiency, equity, and voice in the U.S. employment relationship.

Nonstandard Work Arrangements

Any systematic reform of U.S. public policies on work would be incomplete without addressing the vexing problem of the rise in contingent employment. As noted in Chapter 4, contingent workers—part-time employees, temps, independent contractors, and leased employees—are even worse off than regular employees when their employment standards are evaluated against the major dimensions of equity. In nonstandard employment arrangements, pay is often lower than for full-time permanent workers, benefits like health insurance are less likely to be offered, training is less likely to be provided, and employment spells are episodic. Of particular relevance for public policy reform is the fact that contingent workers fall outside of the regulatory safety net constructed for the employment relationship because of threshold requirements (such as working a minimum number of hours) or the restrictive legal tests used to determine employee status.[54] These shortcomings must be rectified through policy reform.

The most frequently used touchstone for ascertaining whether a worker is an "employee" for purposes of most U.S. employment laws is the common-law agency test. This test focuses primarily on the employer's right to control not only the "result accomplished by the work," but also the "details and means by which that result is accomplished." If such a right to control is found to exist, the worker is deemed to be an employee. In the absence of such a right to control, the worker is classified as an independent contractor and is exempt from the coverage of labor and employment regulation. A somewhat more inclusive "economic realities" test is used to determine employee status under the Fair Labor Standards Act (FLSA). This test also looks to the common-law control factors but in addition incorporates the following principle: "an employee, as distinguished from a person who is engaged as a business of his own, is one who, as a matter of economic reality follows the usual path of an employee and is dependent on the business for which he serves."[55]

During the 1970s and 1980s, many federal courts of appeal adopted a "hybrid" test for determining employee status under federal discrimination statutes that combines elements of both the common law and economic realities test. Under the hybrid approach, courts examine the economic realities of the work relationship, but with emphasis on "the employer's right to control the 'means and manner' of the worker's performance."[56] Despite the growing popularity of the hybrid test, the Supreme Court reinvigorated the common-law standard in its 1992 *Darden* decision by rejecting the use of an economic realities test to determine employee status outside the unique statutory formulation of the FLSA. The Court instead adopted a thirteen-factor formulation of the common-law test.[57] The *Darden* decision has led many courts to replace the hybrid test with the common-law test to ascertain employee status under other statutes.[58]

The restrictive *Darden* test is problematic for several reasons. For one thing, the test sets an unpredictable standard. Any formula with thirteen variables is bound to have considerable play in the joints. The *Darden* test also is prone to entrepreneurial manipulation. As the final report of President Clinton's blue-ribbon Dunlop Commission noted, the common-law test provides employers with both "a means and incentive to circumvent the employment policies of the nation."[59] The incentive, of course, is to avoid the costs and loss of flexibility associated with government regulation. The means is to structure work arrangements so that subcontractors and leased employees fall on the nonemployee side of the *Darden* divide. Finally, the restrictive common-law test is inconsistent with the fundamental objectives of contemporary employment and labor legislation. By focusing primarily on the right-to-control factor, the test denies the benefits of protective social legislation to many workers who are, in reality, subordinate to their employer. Many contract and leased workers work side-by-side with more traditional employees and, regardless of nomenclature, share an economic dependence on the business they serve. The jurisdictional boundaries of workplace laws need to be redrawn to serve their socioeconomic purposes in the contemporary contingent employment relationship.[60]

A comparative view offers the prospect for a desirable solution. The rise in contingent work is a global phenomenon, and many countries have sought legislative solutions for its accompanying problems. An approach that some countries have adopted is to recognize a third category of workers between employees and independent contractors. These "dependent contractors" are technically not employees under the traditional legal tests, but nonetheless are recognized as deserving of some employee-like legal protections by virtue of working in positions of economic dependence. Employment protection laws in Canada, Sweden, Germany, and the Netherlands, for example, treat dependent contractors like employees for some purposes, but not for others. Germany's practice with regard to this middle category of workers is the one most worthy of emulation. There, an intermediate group of "employee-like persons" are technically self-employed, yet nonetheless treated as employees for some purposes because they are "economically dependent and are in similar need of social protection." These employee-like persons are covered by statutes related to workplace health and safety, the prevention of sexual harassment, and collective bargaining. But these dependent contractors are not covered by Germany's Act on Protection Against Dismissals and the Act on Working Time. This dichotomy reflects the notion that statutory coverage should be broader where basic societal interests are at stake than where the interests in question relate more narrowly to the status of an individual worker.[61]

The United States should follow this example and extend the reach of employee protection statutes that serve core societal goals to contractors who are economically dependent on a user firm. Antidiscrimination statutes such as Title VII[62] and the Age Discrimination in Employment Act[63] clearly fall within this category. The eradication of discrimination is a well-recognized societal goal, and it will not unduly distort labor market competition to extend the antidiscrimination ban to this group of workers. The same is true for broadening the reach of the National Labor Relations Act[64] and the Occupational Health and Safety Act.[65] Reducing the number of exceptions within the body of workplace laws not only serves workers' interests, but also serves employers' interest in a more streamlined, less burdensome regulatory regime.

Achieving Equity

Equity is a public concern. And the experiences of many countries show that public policies can achieve equity in the modern employment relationship. A comparison by Dan Zuberi of Seattle hotel workers with their counterparts only 120 miles away in Vancouver, Canada, for example, clearly shows the central role of equity-related public policies. Unlike the Seattle hotel workers, those in Vancouver are not one misstep away from financial and emotional disaster. The workers in the two cities have similar demographic backgrounds and are in the same occupations and industry. The difference between their circumstances is in the strength of the social safety net established by public policies in the United States and Canada. Through provincial-level policies, Vancouver workers are entitled to more generous unemployment insurance benefits, paid statutory holidays and vacations, advance notice or compensation for dismissals not for good cause, and universal health care coverage.[66]

As brought to life by these hotel workers, equity is not about inflexible mandates that clog the economic system. Equity is about achieving the dignity and security that are the foundation of democracy and economic opportunity. The egoist model of the employment relationship emphasizes competition, but in the pluralist model the employment relationship works best for everyone when there is a balance. Equity is a critical element of this balance, as is voice. Zuberi's Vancouver hotel workers are better off than their Seattle counterparts not only because of a stronger social safety net, but also because they are more likely to be unionized.[67] These complementarities should be kept in mind as public policies for facilitating voice in the contemporary American workplace are considered in the next chapter.

CHAPTER 9

Facilitating Voice

EMPLOYEE VOICE is the ability to have input into the nature of your working life. Numerous surveys document the fact that workers want a strong voice in the workplace.[1] This desire likely reflects the fact that being involved in controlling one's destiny is an essential part of being human, that participation in decision-making is an essential part of a democratic society, and that collective voice promotes fairness by remedying power imbalances in the employment relationship. In other words, employee voice is critical for the psychological, moral, political, and economic health of individuals and society. For this reason, employee voice should be a critical concern of public policies on employment.

Public policy, however, cannot mandate voice. As illustrated by a Dilbert cartoon in which the boss forces employees to wear buttons that say, "I'm empowered," requiring employee voice contradicts the very reason for voice—giving employees some element of control over their work lives. Some might choose to remain silent or to defer to others; such decisions are legitimate uses of voice and are legitimate self-determined choices, just as more active modes of participation in decision-making are. The role of public policy is to facilitate employee voice by protecting individuals who want to exercise their voice, in whatever form, and by outlawing actions that suppress employee voice.

In Chapter 5 we outlined four key dimensions of voice in the modern employment relationship: employee free speech; individual self-determination; consultation, codetermination, and social dialogue; and countervailing collective voice. In this chapter, we revisit these four dimensions and present specific public policy ideas for facilitating each of them.

Employee Free Speech

When the 1st Amendment was adopted more than two hundred years ago, the United States was largely a rural, agrarian society.[2] The workplace was not a significant aspect of daily life and social interaction. The few private employers that existed were very small and not very powerful. But today the workplace dominates daily life, and multinational private employers rival governments in size and power. Our proposal therefore seeks to make employers subject to the same rules against violating individual liberty as governments. At the same time, public policy must balance efficiency and voice. The extension of freedom of speech to workers does not imply unlimited rights to undermine an employer's business or offend co-workers. We therefore recommend a statutory protection for employee free speech in which private and public employers are not allowed to violate any employee's freedom of speech and expression unless there is a legitimate business justification for a limitation of that right. This protection should extend beyond the workplace to include off-duty activities such as political participation, community activism, and blogging.[3]

Such free speech protection is not without precedent. In France, the Auroux Laws of 1982 include a right of employee expression. Employees are entitled to express themselves with regard to the content and organization of work and with regard to ways of improving working conditions. Although this expression is formalized through group meetings (rather than protecting spontaneous instances of free speech), the principle of enhancing the abilities of employees to provide opinions and discuss issues foreshadows our proposal.[4] In Canada, section 2(b) of the Canadian Charter endows everyone with the "fundamental freedoms . . . of thought, belief, opinion and expression" because, in the words of the Canadian Supreme Court:

> The core values which free expression promotes include self-fulfillment, participation in social and political decision-making, and the communal exchange of ideas. Free speech protects human dignity and the right to think and reflect freely on one's circumstances and condition. It allows a person to speak not only for the sake of expression itself, but also to advocate change, attempting to persuade others in the hope of improving one's life and perhaps the wider social, political, and economic environment.[5]

As a result, the Canadian Supreme Court ruled that "free expression is particularly critical in the labor context" because "the values associated with free expression relate directly to one's work. A person's employment, and the conditions of their workplace, inform one's identity, emotional health, and sense of self-worth." But at the same time, this same ruling underscores that freedom of speech rights are not absolute: "limitations are permitted, but only to the extent that this is shown to be reasonable and demonstrably necessary in a free and democratic society."[6]

In the U.S. context, Connecticut enacted a law in 1983 that makes employers liable for monetary damages for any disciplinary actions (including discharge) in response to an employee exercising his or her 1st Amendment rights, provided that the employee's actions do not "substantially or materially interfere with the employee's bona fide job performance or the working relationship between the employee and the employer."[7] However, the explicit reference to the 1st Amendment has allowed the Connecticut courts to follow the widespread public sector case law and limit employee free speech rights to issues of public concern.[8] This severely undermines the intent of a broad free speech law for workers.

Bruce Barry and Cynthia Estlund have proposed protecting employee free speech through a broader universal just- or good-cause requirement for employee discipline and discharge.[9] We agree with this approach, but in the absence of such a policy, explicit protections for speech are needed. In this vein, David Yamada has proposed a free speech law that makes it illegal for employers to "abridge [employees'] right of free speech through any type of disciplinary action" for speech in and outside of the workplace, excepting instances of disruptive speech, disloyal speech, insubordinate speech, defamatory speech, and speech that amounts to employee misconduct.[10] These categories of exceptions are largely equivalent to what we characterize as "legitimate business reasons."

Our proposal follows the well-established approach of the National Labor Relations Board (NLRB) in adjudicating unfair labor practices in which employers are accused of discriminating against an employee because of the employee's union support under section 8(a)(3) of the National Labor Relations Act (NLRA).[11] In such cases, the NLRB, pursuant to its *Wright Line* test, first determines whether an employer action interfered with the employee's NLRA rights to engage in concerted and protected activity. If the NLRB decides that such activity was a motivating factor in the employer's decision, a prima facie violation is established. In that event, an employer may avoid liability only if it proves, as an affirmative defense, that it would have taken the same employment action for a legitimate reason.[12] We envision that a similar legal analysis would be used in conjunction with a statutory protection for employee free speech. An employer's discipline or discharge of an employee who exercised his or her free speech rights will be legal if the employer can demonstrate that the employer would have taken the same disciplinary action even if the employee had not exercised his free speech rights (in other words, that a legitimate performance or business issue was the principal cause of the disciplinary action). Such an approach also is broadly consistent with existing 1st Amendment case law allowing "reasonable time, place, and manner restrictions on speech."[13] Our proposal allows employers to place similar restrictions, and in fact to go further and restrict the content of the speech when there are legitimate business reasons to do so.

In the absence of legitimate business reasons or legitimate employee performance issues, U.S. employees should be entitled to a broad freedom of speech protection. Unlike what exists today, this protection should not be limited to discussing wages and working conditions with co-workers or to issues of public concern. The effectiveness of the political process as well as respect for human dignity require that employees be able to exchange ideas, complain, and speak out over issues of either public or private concern. We believe that this can be accomplished in a straightforward fashion with statutory protections for employee free speech in which private and public employers are not allowed to violate an employee's freedom of expression either in or outside the workplace absent a legitimate business justification for a specific limitation.

Individual Self-Determination

Individual self-determination involves autonomy in one's job, such as the ability to prioritize tasks, select solutions for problems, and have input into scheduling one's work time. While legislating an absolute right to self-determination would go too far, there are important ways in which public policies can appropriately facilitate the exercise of individual self-determination without unduly impairing efficiency. Two of the most important legal supports for individual self-determination have already been discussed: good-cause dismissal and free speech protections. These protections would prevent managers from penalizing employees who exercise self-determination by making choices about their work and by speaking out, unless such behavior undermines job or business performance. Legal promotion of self-determination should not be seen as a right to be disruptive or unproductive, and this approach dovetails with our proposed good-cause dismissal and free speech protections in which discipline and discharge are acceptable for legitimate performance-related reasons. Good-cause dismissal and free speech protections, accordingly, would go a long way toward supporting the individual self-determination dimension of employee voice and balancing voice with efficiency.

Public policy can also support employee autonomy by addressing the specific dimension of determining an individual's work schedule. In the Netherlands, after one year of working for an employer, a worker can request in writing an increase or decrease in his or her work hours by specifying the desired number of weekly hours and the distribution of hours across the days of the week. Such a request can only be made every two years. The employer is required to consult with the employee and to grant the requested number of hours unless there are "serious business reasons" such as being unable to recruit another employee to work the needed hours. Germany has a similar law that grants workers the right to request specific work schedules. Even though these laws are frequently associated with enhancing workers' work-family balance, workers do not have to provide a reason for their request, which is consistent with a broad foundation in individual self-determination. The United Kingdom also has a right-to-request law, and though it applies only to parents of young or disabled children, employers must meet with the employee to discuss the request and can only deny it on "clear business grounds."[14]

The British statute is particularly intriguing because it establishes a mandatory voice mechanism in the form of an interactive dialogue between employees and employers, but does not impose any enforceable substantive standard on the outcome of those dialogues. Unlike the Dutch and German statutes, the British version does not authorize any substantive judicial review of the employer's business judgment. Nonetheless, the British approach has achieved resounding success. In 2002, the first year of the statute's operation, 75 percent of all employees submitting requests received full voluntary approval from their employers, and most employers reported no significant compliance issues.[15]

U.S. policymakers should adopt something similar to these European right-to-request policies. These policies facilitate employee voice by requiring employers to consult with individual employees, but also allow employers to reject unreasonable or unworkable requests. Such policies therefore do not create a burdensome set of unwavering standards or rigid entitlements; rather, they create a participatory framework where employees and their employers can work out mutually agreeable arrangements. In short, these statutes represent a flexible regulatory response to a work environment characterized by an increasing demand for flexibility.[16]

Another example relating to work schedules is mandatory overtime. Nearly all U.S. employees can be disciplined or discharged for refusing to work overtime, no matter how short the notice and regardless of how disruptive overtime work would be for a worker's child care arrangements or other concerns. Nearly 30 percent of full-time workers report being covered by mandatory overtime policies, and most nonunion employees could be instantly subjected to mandatory overtime requirements at their employer's discretion. This is a significant violation of individual self-determination that is easily remedied by a legislative ban on mandatory overtime. In fact, a handful of states ban mandatory overtime for nurses, such as the New Jersey provision that provides: "The acceptance by any [nurse or similar health care employee] of such work in excess of an agreed to, predetermined and regularly scheduled daily work shift, not to exceed 40 hours per week, shall be strictly voluntary and the refusal of any employee to accept such overtime work shall not be grounds for discrimination, dismissal, discharge or any other penalty or employment decision adverse to the employee."[17] With the exception of a weak statute in Maine,[18] all of the state bans pertain to nurses and similar health care employees because of the risk to patient safety that stems from overworked nurses. But we believe that the language of the New Jersey statute should be extended to all employees. This would serve employees' basic psychological need for self-determination as well as protect their physical safety and promote a better work-family balance. A similar policy reform that can promote both self-determination and physical safety is a strengthening of an employee's right to refuse to perform unsafe work tasks without penalty.[19]

Another major policy concern for protecting self-determination in the modern employment relationship pertains to monitoring and surveillance. Monitoring has long been a part of the employment relationship. In fact, the shift from the sweating system of home work to large-scale textile factories in the early 1800s was partly due to the business advantage of being able to monitor hundreds of workers at once.[20] But the development of information technologies has vastly expanded the scope of employee monitoring, from logging computer keystrokes to monitoring e-mail messages to tracking employee movements through transmitters in ID badges and cell phones. Intense monitoring can be bad for business when it reduces job satisfaction and creativity while increasing job turnover. But it becomes a public policy concern when it violates human dignity by undermining autonomy and chilling free speech. U.S. public policy should ensure that monitoring is not done secretly (except to investigate serious misconduct) and has clear business grounds.[21] Legislative proposals of this type have been introduced in Congress—such as the Privacy for Consumers and Workers Act (S. 984 in the 103rd Congress)—and are worthy of enactment. Such a policy would help ensure that employees are aware of monitoring systems and that inappropriate monitoring is not a factor in employee dismissals.

Our final recommendation for improving self-determination in the American workplace is mandatory disclosure of employment terms. Self-determination requires having accurate information. The Worker Adjustment and Retraining Notification Act requires employers to provide employees with a sixty-day advance notice of a plant closing or mass layoff. Advance notice allows workers to plan and make decisions for their future. Employers are also required to display posters outlining employee rights under the Fair Labor Standards Act, the Family and Medical Leave Act, and other laws. As noted in Chapter 5, however, employee ignorance of their rights is widespread. As such, employers should be required to provide a written description to each employee of the major terms of their employment. This should include wage and benefit information, leave policies, dismissal policies, and descriptions of their rights under the law. At-will employees, for example, should be told that they can be dismissed for any reason. Subject to relevant laws, employers would still be free to unilaterally determine and change these policies, but those changes should be transparent to employees.

This proposal for mandatory disclosure of the terms and conditions of employment has international precedents. China requires written contracts for employees that specify wages and benefits, the length of the working day, vacation policies, disciplinary policies, and methods for changing, renewing, or terminating the contract.[22] Closer to our proposal is the European Union directive "On an Employer's Obligation to Inform Employees of the Conditions Applicable to the Contract or Employment Relationship" (the Written Particulars directive), which was passed in 1991 "to avoid uncertainty and insecurity about the terms of the employment relationship and to create greater transparency." European countries therefore now have laws specifying that employers must provide written notices to employees detailing ten key elements, including wage payments, leave policies, and the expected duration of employment for temporary employees.[23]

For the United States, Richard Edwards has proposed that employers provide employees with legally binding handbooks specifying the terms of their employment. As Edwards notes, lenders are required to disclose accurate interest rates for loans, and manufacturers must reveal the ingredients of food products. Given the importance of employment to individuals, disclosure of employment terms also should be required.[24] But our proposal stops short of creating a binding contract. Disclosure would not mandate any specific terms, prevent changes, or create legally binding contracts. Rather, the central intent is to provide information. This information would be seen as the employer's unilateral statement of its view of the terms and conditions of employment. Violations would typically be remedied by monetary fines for failing to provide timely and accurate information, not by creating enforceable rights to specific terms and conditions (beyond those that already exist, such as entitlements to accrued benefits).

Consultation, Codetermination, and Social Dialogue

Turning next to collective voice, public policies on work should also support consultation, codetermination, and social dialogue—that is, industrial democracy through forms of collective voice that involve exchanges of information and views between employers and employees that stop short of formal collective bargaining. The precedent for giving workers the right to participate in shaping their destinies already exists in U.S. public policy. More specifically, at least thirteen states mandate health and safety committees such that workers must be consulted and help codetermine improved workplace safety policies.[25] Our proposals extend the logic underlying these policies to a comprehensive set of issues.

Health and safety committees are a natural starting place for improving employee access to work-related information and for facilitating greater consultation over and codetermination of work-related issues. Safer workplaces benefit not only workers but also employers and society. It is hard to argue against the right of workers to receive good information about workplace hazards, and research shows that employee involvement in safety initiatives is important for improving workplace safety. As such, the right of workers to participate in safety-related decision-making is broadly recognized in many countries. The Canadian provinces, many European countries, and even some U.S. states mandate joint labor-management health and safety committees in all workplaces of a certain size or when a minimal threshold of employee interest is satisfied. Rather than relying solely on one-size-fits-all government regulations and inspectors or on managerial goodwill, such committees can identify hazards, develop policies tailored to each workplace that fulfill the needs of both employees and employers, and monitor compliance and the need for change. While effective health and safety committees appear to require various supports (such as government-provided training) and time to develop and mature, an updated system of U.S. workplace law should extend the current patchwork of state policies to a uniform standard of mandated health and safety committees with elected employee representatives, rights to information and consultation, and protections against employer retaliation. Such reforms can contribute not only to workplace safety, but also to more effective consultation and participation for workers in critical elements of every employee's life.[26]

Works Councils

The logic of joint health and safety committees can be extended on an issue-by-issue basis to other areas such as training or workplace restructuring; but a better approach would be to avoid a proliferation of committees by promoting industrial democracy through works councils. A works council is an elected committee of workers who represent all of an organization's employees except senior executives—skilled and unskilled, blue collar and white collar, union and nonunion—in regularly communicating and dealing with management. A critical feature of works councils is that they are institutionalized by law. They are not established, defined, modified, or disbanded by management; rather, the rights and structures of works councils are defined by law and are established when employees, not employers, desire them. At the same time, works councils are not unions; they are typically restricted by law to represent only the employees of a single employer and are generally prevented from striking and from negotiating wages. Though they differ from country to country, works councils are widely found across Europe, and the relationship between management and works councils tends to be relatively cooperative and nonadversarial.[27]

The German works council system is the oldest and most well developed model, with some mandatory works councils dating back to 1905, and the contemporary system of widespread works councils dating back to 1952. Under the German Works Constitution Act, an employer who employs a minimum of five employees must establish a works council upon the request of a small number of employees. Usually, only

5 percent of the employees working at an enterprise or facility need to sign a list of candidates to trigger an election of employee representatives to a works council (or a minimum of two employees in very small establishments and a maximum of fifty in large workplaces). Significantly, the formation of a works council does not depend on obtaining the support of a majority of workers, a union, or management: "once the procedure is initiated by employees, the election of a works council is to all intents and purposes automatic."[28]

More than 90 percent of German establishments with at least 500 employees have a works council, but less than 10 percent of small establishments do; changes to the German Works Constitution Act in 2001 therefore further simplified the election process in small establishments. The size of works councils varies with the size of the workforce; for example, a 500-person establishment has an eleven-member works council, one of whom is assigned to the works council on a full-time basis. The works council must meet with an employer at least once a month, and the company pays for a works council's expenses. Companies with multiple establishments must also establish company-wide works councils. The German Works Constitution Act mandates that "the employer and the works council shall work together in a spirit of mutual trust . . . for the good of the employees and of the establishment." As noted above, German works councils cannot strike, but they can sue the relevant employer if their rights are denied.[29]

By law, German works councils have three categories of rights: information, consultation, and codetermination. Weaker rights pertain to traditional business decisions; stronger rights are granted for issues that directly affect workers' daily work lives. A works council must be given financial information regarding the firm's balance sheet, investment and marketing plans, and "any other circumstances and projects that may materially affect the interests of the employees of the company." Management must consult with the works council before introducing new technology and making changes in the nature of work, including changes in how jobs are defined. For these issues, a works council does not need to agree to the proposed changes, but management must listen to the works council's reactions and suggestions before implementing the changes. In contrast, works councils have a right of codetermination over issues directly connected to working conditions—work schedules and overtime, bonus systems, leave policies, health and safety, training, work rules and discipline, electronic employee monitoring, and methods for selecting and assigning employees. For these issues, employers must do more than consult with the works council. Codetermination rights means that a company must jointly determine any changes in cooperation with the works council; the employer cannot take action without the agreement of the works council. If agreement cannot be reached, a conciliation committee consisting of equal numbers of representatives of management and the works councils decides the matter.

In addition to various national laws supporting works councils in Europe, the European Union (EU) provides legal support at the pan-European level. The 1994 European Works Council directive requires companies with significant operations in at least two EU countries to form a transnational, company-level works council that has consultation and information rights on issues that affect workers in more than one country. More than 750 European Works Councils now exist. The European Company Statute (2001) requires companies incorporated at the European rather than the national level to provide information-sharing and consultative mechanisms for employees. And a 2002 directive on "a general framework for informing and consulting employees" requires the member countries of the EU to develop policies that will ensure that employers inform and consult with their employees. In response, the United Kingdom, for example, enacted the Information and Consultation of Employees Regulations 2004, which stipulates that if 10 percent of an employer's workers make a request, a British employer must negotiate with the employees to develop a framework for information and consultation; if no agreement can be reached, the law specifies a minimum set of information and consultation procedures that the employer must follow. Taken together, these three directives establish a continent-wide norm of collective voice through consultation with works councils and similar institutions.[30] When paired with national-level policies such as the German Works Constitution Act, it is clear that there are ample models for the United States to follow in promoting employee consultation and codetermination.

A Proposal for an American Works Councils Act

To fill the need for the employee consultation and codetermination aspect of collective employee voice, we propose an American Works Councils Act that is based on the EU's 2002 general framework directive and the German Works Constitution Act with the following features:

1. Employees have the automatic right to call for the creation of a works council in an enterprise or facility above a certain minimum size.

2. Employees are empowered to periodically elect representatives with hourly and salaried employees represented on a proportional basis.
3. The works council is entitled to receive information periodically from the employer with respect to company policies, financial conditions, and plans for future undertakings that may impact organizational performance and the organization of work.
4. The works council is entitled to consult periodically with the employer on a broad range of subjects that affect employees:
   a. terms and conditions of employment excepting those covered by sections 5 and 6 below;
   b. the manner of work performance and organization;
   c. the hiring, transfer, and termination of employees; and
   d. entrepreneurial decisions that may impact the organization of work.
5. The works council is entitled to codetermine matters of particular employee concern, including:
   a. practices and policies pertaining to employee health and safety;
   b. scheduling of working hours and breaks, policies for leaves and vacation, the allocation of overtime, and the administration of layoffs or reduced hours;
   c. procedures for resolving individual complaints including an unjust dismissal policy; and
   d. compliance with pertinent employment and labor laws and regulations.

   If the works council and the employer cannot agree on a specific issue, it will be resolved by a neutral third party such as a safety expert or arbitrator.
6. The works council does not have the right to bargain with respect to the level of employee compensation and does not have the right to strike.
7. The works council and the employer are required to seek agreements in a spirit of cooperation that serves the overall interests of employees and the employer.

This type of American works council system would effectively serve the sharp need for industrial democracy in the U.S. workplace identified in Chapter 5. Similar proposals have been made for the United States and other countries outside of Europe, such as Australia.[31]

The adoption of an American works council system would do much to close the "representation/participation gap" documented by the Worker Representation and Participation Survey (WRPS), in which 63 percent of American workers indicated that they want more influence at work. Since covered employees of the proposed American Works Council Act would have the automatic right to a participatory works council, the adoption of such a measure would mean that a majority of American employees would obtain the greater voice that they desire. Moreover, works councils resemble the type of institution that the WRPS identified as what American workers want—an independent organization that works cooperatively with management in addressing workplace issues. And works councils are consistent with what workers want to help them ensure that workplace regulations are followed in their workplaces.[32]

Although works councils are widespread in other parts of the world and mirror the type of employee involvement plan that many U.S. workers desire, we recognize that managers and union leaders frequently oppose works councils, albeit for different reasons. Some employers and commentators perceive mandatory works councils not only as a route to possible unionization, but also as costly and cumbersome. They point out that establishing and maintaining such organizations would be expensive. They fear additional costs would result from a lack of employer flexibility to adjust employment practices quickly in response to market conditions. In contrast, managers of European firms who consult with works councils "overwhelmingly . . . [report that] they have important positive effects which in general make them a net benefit to firms."[33] Even if one is skeptical of this result, most statistical analyses find little relationship between works councils and organizational performance, so it is difficult to conclude that works councils harm performance.[34] It should also be noted that many U.S. companies formed nonunion employee representation committees in the 1920s and opposed subsequent legislative efforts to restrict such initiatives.[35] And as described in Chapter 5, various agencies of the U.S. federal government already consult with unions under a provision in the Civil Service Reform Act that grants consultation rights when unions have the support of 10 to 49 percent of the workforce. We therefore see works councils as a realistic and robust option for greatly improving employee voice; at worst, they would not significantly harm efficiency, and at best they would foster less adversarial and more productive employee-employer relations.

Union supporters also find much to dislike in works councils and other employee involvement plans.[36] Not only do they believe works councils would fail to protect workers' rights in the absence of a strong labor union, dues-paying members, the right to strike, and solidarity across workplaces, but they also perceive them as sham organizations that would inherently impede true collective bargaining via employer domination and manipulation. We think this opposition to works councils is important, but misplaced. As noted by Joel Rogers, "the tension [between works councils and unions] does not amount to a convincing argument against councils. It does suggest, however, the need for some care in their potential design in the United States."[37] Employees must have support and protection against reprisals, and works councils must be designed to guard against their manipulation by employers. Preventing manipulation can be achieved by requiring employee representatives to be elected, by prohibiting works councils from dealing with compensation issues but otherwise authorizing them to set their own agendas, and by bolstering employee choice to freely choose independent union representation. Works councils, moreover, involve collective action and might very well serve as seed beds for independent unions. Workers who feel either empowered or thwarted by a works council experience may turn to independent unions to further their collective aspirations.[38]

Even if we are wrong on this last score, the argument that unions conceptually are a more desirable model of employee representation no longer provides a compelling basis for employee advocates to oppose works councils. First, we see various voice mechanisms as complements rather than substitutes. Second, union representation in the United States now stands at less than 15 percent of the workforce. The vast majority of American workers have no representation rights at all. German works councils are admittedly bolstered by strong labor unions, but under the present circumstances in the United States, some voice is better than none at all. In fact, employees report positive experiences with nonunion representation plans in Canada.[39] Nevertheless, as previously argued in Chapter 5, independent unionism is also a key dimension of employee voice, and later in this chapter we provide reform proposals that would strengthen this dimension and complement our other proposals for greater individual and collective voice in the American workplace.

Other Forms of Consultation and Social Dialogue

Works councils can and should be the centerpiece of a system of consultation and codetermination rights in the American workplace, but there are important complements to works councils that can provide collective employee voice at other levels. Returning again to the German example, in addition to workplace-level consultation rights, German employees are entitled to appoint one-third or more (depending on firm size) of the members of the supervisory board of German companies. These supervisory boards set strategic policies and appoint upper-level managers, and are therefore similar to U.S. corporate boards of directors. Employees thus have a voice when strategic decisions are being considered. U.S. unions have occasionally obtained board seats in special circumstances, but such directors confront great difficulties in the face of the strong U.S. corporate governance emphasis on maximizing shareholder wealth. To make employee representation at this level meaningful, a wholesale change is needed. In this vein, Charles Craver has proposed new legal requirements that 25 to 33 percent of corporate board members be elected by nonexecutive employees and that *all* directors have a fiduciary duty to consider both shareholder and employee interests in their deliberations and decisions.[40] The financial crisis in 2008 involving Lehman Brothers, AIG, and other financial institutions further demonstrated that more inclusive forms of corporate governance that include a variety of viewpoints are sorely needed. Including employee representatives in the corporate boardroom would not only bolster employee voice, but could also help reform corporate governance.

A voice gap would still remain at the sociopolitical level, however. To this end, U.S. government leaders should promote greater social dialogue. Recall from Chapter 5 that we define social dialogue as exchanges of information and views between representatives of employers and employees from multiple organizations that stop short of formal bargaining. Social dialogue can occur at a local, state, regional, or national level, and may also involve government representatives and other interested parties. Increasing the quantity of social dialogue does not involve legal reform per se; rather, policymakers at all levels of government should embrace an approach to policymaking that encourages representatives of employers and employees to consult with each other on policy issues. In other words, increasing social dialogue is not accomplished through new laws, but by a new approach to lawmaking. For example, policymakers could ask employer and employee groups to negotiate work-related policy proposals, could draw on these groups more heavily in the administration of work-related public policies such as government-sponsored training programs, or could seek broader input from representatives of business and workers on issues of public interest such as economic development. This call echoes Robert Drago's advocacy of inclusive processes for reshaping corporate and governmental policies on work and family.[41]

In many countries around the world, high-level social pacts or social partnership agreements have delineated aggregate wage guidelines, benefit and labor market reforms, and in some cases, additional goals for government spending, social welfare, and economic development. Such all-encompassing agreements are not feasible in the United States, but more targeted initiatives that focus on specific industries, issues, or geographic areas can be pursued. Rather than relying on one-size-fits-all legislative approaches, this social dialogue approach would help give both employers and employees a greater voice in establishing policies for their own industries or regions and in having such policies tailored to their preferences. For example, in the 1920s, the railroads and railroad unions crafted compromise legislation that became the Railway Labor Act that still governs U.S. labor relations in that industry today. Initiatives of this scale are unlikely in the near future, but there are focused areas of mutual interest that employers and employees can work on together—health care, retirement, workers' compensation, and training to name just a few. In fact, Sean Safford argues that in the wake of similar manufacturing declines, a key difference between the recovery of Allentown, Pennsylvania, and the continued economic struggles in Youngstown, Ohio, is social dialogue. Allentown, but not Youngstown, adopted a formal mechanism that brought together business leaders from diverse industries, labor leaders, urban and suburban government officials, and university officials to seek common rather than competing solutions for economic development. Social dialogue is another important element of voice and should not be overlooked by U.S. policymakers at all levels of government.[42]

Countervailing Collective Voice

Labor unions are important institutions in any modern democracy. They are a key representative of workers in the political arena, and can be effective in pursuing both equity and voice in the workplace. Solidarity among workers combined with legal independence from employers gives unions the leverage to provide checks and balances on powerful corporations. Unlike labor standards that arise from government regulations, union-negotiated labor standards embody voice and can be tailored to the needs and preferences of workers and their employers. But the definition of employee voice also includes being able to *choose* whether to be represented by a labor union. The key task for public policy is therefore to protect worker choice: individuals who wish to join and form unions should be able to do so without fear or interference. As shown in Chapter 5, U.S. labor law fails to satisfy this policy objective. Reforms are therefore warranted.

A long-standing principle of U.S. labor law is that employers are obligated to bargain with a union only after it has been certified as the representative of a group of employees. The devil is in the details, though: how to define the criteria for being certified and how to determine if the criteria have been fulfilled. Currently, a union in the U.S. private sector will be certified if it can demonstrate support of a majority of a defined group of workers through a secret ballot election supervised by the NLRB.[43] While a secret ballot election seems like a good idea in a democratic society, the unfortunate reality is that many NLRB elections turn into lengthy, bitter contests replete with delays, misinformation, accusations, intimidation, and other activities that can poison labor-management relations and interfere with employee free choice. As such, NLRB elections hardly fulfill the standards for democratic elections.

Democratic elections should be free of intimidation, but many workers are fired for trying to form unions. Freedom of speech is essential for democratic elections, but employers can limit free speech in the workplace. Democratic elections also require reasonably balanced financial resources and access to voters, but employers typically have much greater resources and access to employees. The time has come to replace these elections with a card-check certification process, similar to the Employee Free Choice Act introduced as S. 1041/H.R. 800 in the 110th Congress, in which unions are certified by presenting a sufficient number of signed cards on which employees authorize the union as their bargaining agent.[44] The U.S. House of Representatives passed the Employee Free Choice Act in March 2007, but insufficient support in the Senate and the threat of a presidential veto by George W. Bush blocked further action. Passage of the act in the 111th Congress after the 2008 elections is likely to be the labor movement's top legislative priority.

Objections to this proposal are easy to anticipate. Opponents say that card-check certification is unwise because the current election process better promotes informed decision-making through the ability of employers to provide information that counters union-provided information. They also note that the current use of secret ballots protects against undue union influence on card signers. The first objection would have more validity if election campaigns truly consisted of respectful exchanges of information. Moreover, simply by working for an employer, employees experience first-hand the employer's approaches to employment issues, so employees are already quite well informed about their employer's perspective. Last, if employers were truly concerned with having an informed electorate, they would not deny unions access to employees to present their views. The second objection, avoiding undue union influence, merits attention, but can be remedied by following the Canadian experience. More specifically, to guard against employee misunderstandings or undue union pressure, we recommend requiring signed cards to be accompanied by an individual's payment for the first month of union dues, and we also recommend setting the card-check threshold at 55 percent of a defined unit of employees. Finally, the NLRB could reserve the right to require a secret ballot election if there were concerns about misinformation, misunderstandings, or union pressure.[45]

A second key reform to U.S. labor law needs to address the fact that employers are able to prevent 25 to 30 percent of newly organized unions from successfully negotiating a first contract. A fairly straightforward remedy embodied in the proposed Employee Free Choice Act would provide for mandatory mediation when negotiations stall, and mandatory arbitration if mediation fails to produce an agreement. This would help lessen the incentive for an employer to engage in illegal labor practices that undermine the ability of a union to represent employees and help promote productive labor-management relationships. These proposals to improve both the certification process and the negotiation of first contracts should also be reinforced by improving the remedies for NLRA violations. In particular, violators of the NLRA should face punitive and compensatory damage awards, as they do for violating the Civil Rights Act.[46]

A third area of reform pertains to strike replacements. In one of its earliest decisions pertaining to the NLRA, the Supreme Court in 1938 ruled that an employer "is not bound to discharge those hired to fill the places of strikers, upon the election of the latter to resume their employment, in order to create places for them."[47] In other words, it is legal for U.S. employers to use permanent strike replacements; striking employees are entitled to get their jobs back only when positions open up, regardless of whether this is five days or five years after the strike ends. Many have argued that this rule destroys the right to strike and disrupts the balance of the U.S. labor relations system. This is most graphically illustrated by the determined employer who forces a strike through hard bargaining, hires permanent strike replacements, and rids itself of the union by engineering a decertification election.[48]

We can again look to the Canadian experience for a compromise solution. The Ontario Labour Relations Act, for example, contains the following important provision:

> 80. (1) Where an employee engaging in a lawful strike makes an unconditional application in writing to the employee's employer within six months from the commencement of the lawful strike to return to work, the employer shall . . . reinstate the employee in the employee's former employment, on such terms as the employer and employee may agree upon, and the employer in offering terms of employment shall not discriminate against the employee for exercising or have exercised any rights under this Act.[49]

Thus employers are allowed to maintain their operations during a strike by hiring replacement workers, but the hiring of *permanent* strike replacements is banned for the first six months of a lawful strike. Beyond this period, an employer is free to hire permanent strike replacements. Adopting this approach in the United States would restore the right to strike as guaranteed by the NLRA.[50] Employees could resort to a lawful strike in support of bargaining demands for up to six months without the fear of indefinite job loss or the unwanted loss of union representation. At the same time, employers could still continue their business operations by using nonstrikers, temporary replacements, and, after a specified period of time, permanent replacements. This approach also has an important political strength: amending the NLRA in this way can be framed as protecting employees' rights rather than as infringing on employers' rights.

Finally, the scope of the NLRA should be expanded so that fewer workers are excluded from its protections. Many contingent workers are not employees of the entity for whom they provide work. Thus these workers are not covered by the NLRA and are not protected against discharge or other retaliatory acts if they seek to join a union. Second, part-time and temporary workers, even though legally classified as employees, commonly are excluded from bargaining units on the grounds that they do not share a sufficient community of interests with more permanent employees. Thus they are not within the group represented even if a union is successful in obtaining exclusive representative status. Reforms are needed to bring contingent workers more squarely under the protections of the NLRA. One important step would be for the NLRB to reinstate its earlier *Sturgis* decision so as to permit contingent leased employees to obtain representation in units with other regular employees so long as the two groups share a sufficient community of interests, without requiring full employer consent.[51] Similar reforms are needed for workers who exercise independent judgment or delegate minor tasks to co-workers. Employers increasingly are trying to exclude nurses and others from coverage under the NLRA by classifying them as supervisors; such loopholes need to be closed and the definition of a supervisor considerably narrowed so that workers who are asked to think on the job are not denied the protections of U.S. labor law.[52]

None of these reforms are far-fetched. In fact, a card-check certification process, first-contract arbitration, and stiffer penalties are all included in the Employee Free Choice Act that was passed by the House of Representatives in 2007 and has garnered the support of numerous senators and representatives from both political parties. New Jersey enacted a law in 2005 in which public sector workers and private sector workers at companies too small to be covered by the NLRA can obtain recognition through a card-check procedure.[53] The United States is almost alone among industrialized countries in allowing permanent strike replacements and between 1985 and 1995, the U.S. Congress considered, but did not pass, at least four proposals to limit the use of permanent strike replacements. Minnesota bans the use of permanent strike replacements in the public sector.[54]

There are also other approaches to bolstering the NLRA. Ellen Dannin has argued that the NLRA's weaknesses are the result of decades of unfavorable court decisions that have effectively rewritten the law. In this vein, the route to strengthening the NLRA is to educate judges about labor issues and reverse these legal decisions to restore the original intent of the law.[55] Charles Morris passionately argues that the NLRA already obligates employers to bargain on a members-only basis with unions that represent less than a majority of workers, but legislative action is probably needed to make this type of reform a reality.[56] Still other reform proposals advocate loosening restrictions on secondary boycotts and expanding the scope of mandatory bargaining items.[57] Regardless of which approach is pursued, it is essential that an updated system of workplace law ensure that workers are free to form labor unions when they desire and that these labor unions have sufficient strength to act as an effective countervailing collective voice.

Facilitating Voice

A revised system of U.S. workplace law needs to support employee voice because of its impact on employees' economic, psychological, and political welfare. We have therefore outlined public policy initiatives that will promote and protect four levels of voice: employee free speech; individual self-determination; consultation, codetermination, and social dialogue; and countervailing collective voice. Other labor advocates tend to focus on specific dimensions of voice, especially works councils and labor unions, but a broader approach to public policies on voice is needed. This broader approach is consistent with the similarly broad and diverse rationales for employee voice. In other words, there is not a one-size-fits-all voice mechanism that can fulfill these diverse rationales. Also, a broader approach is consistent with what workers tell researchers: they want the workplace to contain a combination of individual and collective mechanisms, as well as a combination of consultative and bargaining mechanisms. Finally, some argue that social identities have displaced the economic identities that underlie the traditional U.S. labor law system. Thus employees with a shared identity rooted in gender, race, ethnicity, age, disability, and sexual orientation have formed employee network groups such as the Women's Association for Verizon Employees and the Shell Hispanic Employees Network.[58] Public policy therefore needs to support broader forms of voice than those rooted in traditional economic identities linked to class, industry, occupation, and employer. The employee free speech protections proposed here directly support diverse employee network groups within and across organizations.

Patricia Greenfield and Robert Pleasure have argued that true employee voice requires legitimacy (employee consent to engage in voice or be represented by others) and power (the ability to influence outcomes or decisions); otherwise, "without power and legitimacy, any individual or collective worker statement can be labeled voice, even if that voice is, in reality, muffled or inaccurate, stifled or distorted."[59] We agree. The public policies outlined in this chapter will provide both legitimacy and power to a range of voice mechanisms, from employee free speech to independent labor unions. We respectfully disagree with those on one end of the spectrum who do not see a need for supportive public policies, and with those on the other end who see independent labor unions as the only true form of employee voice. With the legal supports outlined in this chapter, both individual and collective voice can be effectively delivered in the modern employment relationship.

CHAPTER 10

Bringing Workplace Law and Public Policy into Focus and Balance

THE LAISSEZ-FAIRE, neoliberal market model currently dominates U.S. and international discourse on government regulation of the economy. Alternative models of imperfect competition are discounted, and non-economic objectives are marginalized in favor of the promotion of free markets. Critics often fail to articulate alternative models or objectives and instead focus on specific procedural deficiencies, such as weaknesses in the union organizing processes or the lack of labor standards in trade agreements. In other words, the state of this discourse is invisible hands, invisible objectives. As a consequence, workplace law and public policy are out of focus. We lack a deep understanding of this important area because we have lost sight of a key principle: the rationale for government regulation of any market-based activity is rooted in the intersection of the operation and objectives of that activity. Bringing workplace law and public policy into focus requires discussing and appreciating the full range of *explicit* models and *explicit* objectives of the employment relationship. This explicitness is the key to studying, understanding, analyzing, and reforming workplace law and public policy.

To this end, Parts One and Two developed an analytical framework of four models—the egoist, unitarist, pluralist, and critical employment relationships—and three objectives—efficiency, equity, and voice. We have shown that the four models see employment regulation in very different ways: harmful in the egoist model; largely unnecessary in the unitarist model; welfare improving in the pluralist model; and inadequate or manipulative in the critical model. And we have shown the enhanced understanding of workplace law and public policy that can result from broadly analyzing the state of efficiency, equity, and voice in the modern U.S. workplace. Some might disagree with our choice of objectives; and we welcome debate on this issue because our main goal is to increase the attention of scholars, policymakers, advocates, students, and the general public to the objectives and models of the employment relationship.

The analytical framework developed in Parts One and Two is also important as a foundation for better normative work. This is the focus of Part Three. Any system of workplace law and public policy should be comprehensive and flexible so that diverse workers and workplaces are served in ways that both match their common interests and meet their individual needs. More important, such systems must be rooted in a coherent model of the employment relationship and inspired by the fundamental objectives of this relationship. Unfortunately, as shown in Parts One and Two, the current U.S. system of employment and labor law falls short of these principles. Instead, today's system reflects one hundred years of shifting power dynamics and class interests, and is therefore a patchwork of sometimes inflexible regulations with numerous gaps built on conflicting premises with no clear objectives. *Invisible Hands, Invisible Objectives* therefore not only emphasizes the need for a comprehensive approach, but more importantly develops an analytical framework for examining work-related laws and public policies in which the core objectives are made explicit and are tied to specific models of how the employment relationship works. This approach reveals the incoherence of the current system and the necessity of grounding comprehensive reform proposals in an explicit intellectual foundation. These are fundamental lessons for anyone concerned with the employment relationship, regardless of which model one subscribes to, and irrespective of the extent to which one agrees or disagrees with our specific proposals for reform. This framework further provides the intellectual basis for analyzing and comparing the numerous reform proposals generated by academics, politicians, think tanks, and advocacy groups.

Turning to our specific proposals, at least one intellectual and two practical objections can be anticipated. Intellectually, critics might disagree with our use of the pluralist model. For several theoretical reasons, ranging from the complexities of human behavior to imperfections in the labor market, we believe that the pluralist model most effectively captures the realities of the modern workplace. Although our terminology may not be in common use, many apparently agree with the tenets of the pluralist approach. A Wall Street mentality that drives stock prices up when companies reduce benefits or when wage growth slows reflects the pluralist view that employers and employees have at least some interests that conflict. In fact, those who argue that the interests of employers and employees can always be aligned should look at DuPont's decision in 2006 to terminate its long-standing defined-benefit pension plan and scale back subsidies for retiree health insurance; regardless of what one thinks of this decision, the conflicting interests of employers and employees are clearly revealed by DuPont's calculation that these benefit cuts would increase earnings per share by 3–5 cents. Similarly, 3M reduced the generosity of its employee stock-option plan because shareholders believed that these options reduced shareholder returns.[1] This is another example that implicitly reflects the pluralist assumption that employers and employees have at least some interests that clash.

Support for a pluralist approach is found in many places beyond Wall Street. Many individuals favor some level of government-supported social safety net and therefore reject the sole reliance of the egoist and unitarist models on free markets or corporate self-interest to satisfy workers' needs. The large numbers of employees who want some form of employee voice are largely at odds with the view of the egoist model that the employment relationship is a purely economic transaction. Institutions such as the Catholic Church and the United Nations that advocate for checks and balances in the modern economy are preaching a pluralist model even if they do not use this term explicitly. Calls to replace the U.S. emphasis on a stockholder model of corporate governance with a stakeholder approach are also consistent with pluralist theory. Such widespread support notwithstanding, others will continue to adhere to an egoist, unitarist, or critical model of the employment relationship and therefore object to our use of the pluralist model. There is little we can do about this; but to counter our approach, adherents of these alternatives must explicitly root their analyses and reform proposals in their preferred model.

We also anticipate at least two practical objections to the comprehensive reforms we outline in this book. First, naysayers might pessimistically note that political gridlock prevents any reform of the U.S. employment system. Second, a common negative reaction to proposed legislative reforms is to question how to pay for new policies that are perceived as costly. In this concluding chapter we address these practical concerns.

The Difficulty of Legislative Reform

It is notoriously difficult to enact new federal legislation on employment issues in the United States. Some European countries have had paid maternity leave policies for more than a hundred years, whereas the United States did not require even unpaid leave until 1993. The Pension Protection Act in 2006 was the most significant pension reform legislation in over thirty years, and even then enacted only limited changes. The high-level Commission on the Future of Worker-Management Relations (known as the Dunlop Commission, after its chairman John Dunlop) appointed by President Clinton in 1993 failed to generate any legislative action. In fact, one needs to go back fifty years to find the last revisions to private sector labor law that affected more than a narrowly targeted set of workers. Ideological differences between political parties and a zero-sum mentality—what's good for workers or labor unions must be bad for business, and vice versa—likely underlie the lack of employment and labor law reform in the United States.[2] It often requires a dramatic event to overcome these barriers and enact major changes in U.S. labor and employment laws—such as the passage of the National Labor Relations Act (NLRA), the Fair Labor Standards Act, and the Social Security Act during the Great Depression; Title VII of the Civil Rights Act during the Civil Rights movement; and the Civil Rights Act of 1991 in the wake of the hearings on the confirmation of Clarence Thomas as a Supreme Court justice. Absent such events, workers and their advocates usually have lacked the power to enact changes favorable to their interests.

The nature of the U.S. political system adds to the difficulty of reform. Federal legislation must be passed by both the Senate and the House of Representatives. And a supramajority is effectively required in the Senate in order to defeat a filibuster. The Labor Law Reform Act of 1978 and more than one attempt to ban permanent strike replacements in the 1990s were passed by the House of Representatives but defeated by Senate filibusters. Even when legislation passes both bodies, the possibility of a presidential veto further reinforces the need for much more than simple majority support. The TEAM Act, which would have modified the company union provisions of the NLRA, was vetoed by President Clinton in 1996. And even when a law is enacted, as Ellen Dannin reminds us, the intended thrust of the statute may be blunted as a conservative judiciary exercises its power to interpret laws in ways that favor employers and the marketplace.[3]

Moreover, Jacob Hacker shows how government-supported, privately provided social benefits such as health insurance and pensions have important political ramifications that make legislative reform more difficult. Employer-provided health and retirement benefits create parties with vested interests in maintaining the status quo. Insurance companies, pension management firms, and corporate benefits managers are obvious examples of such interested parties. Employer-provided benefit plans also create "enduring societal expectations" because workers "see the workplace as the primary source of certain forms of social protection."[4] While Hacker's important insights focus on social insurance, they can be extended to the domain of employee voice as well. Like social insurance programs, employee voice is government-supported (through the NLRA) yet privately provided (through labor unions). U.S. labor law therefore creates vested interests for a number of parties and organizations such as arbitrators, mediators, anti-union consultants, human resource managers, the Society for Human Resource Management, the National Labor Relations Board, and all of the nation's labor unions. These interests limit the scope of acceptable reforms, as witnessed by the opposition among both human resource managers and union leaders to proposals for works councils and other forms of nonunion voice. Like social insurance programs, the NLRA framework has also created enduring expectations—representation through labor unions, power through strikes, and bargaining over the terms and conditions of employment but not core entrepreneurial decisions, to name just three—that make labor policy path-dependent. In other words, earlier policies affect later political dynamics and therefore limit viable policy options for reform. This is another aspect of the power dynamics that make reforming the U.S. employment system difficult.

All of these factors make reform unlikely, but not unnecessary. We believe the case for reform is strong and refuse to believe that new ideas should not be generated simply because they might be difficult to enact. Changing enduring expectations requires discourse about new expectations. Actual reform can also lag considerably behind calls for reform; a dramatic event that shifts the balance of power in favor of a long-incubating reform proposal can occur quite unexpectedly, so analyses such as ours are important. An opportune moment for reform might even be just around the corner. The credit crunch and stock market collapse of 2008 coupled with the election of Barack Obama ushered in a new reformist mood, and the time might be ripe for crafting a "renewed deal" for the American worker during the Obama administration.

On What Level? Local, State, National, and International Reforms

U.S. workplace law and public policy has been dominated by national-level legislation, and comprehensive reform needs to occur at the same level—or even internationally. But in the absence of realistic prospects for sweeping federal legislation, significant progress on creating employment with a human face can be made at the local and state levels. In the first decades of the 20th century, workers' compensation programs were developed at the state level; several decades later, equal employment opportunity policies emerged in municipalities and states (albeit after President Roosevelt's Executive Order 8802 forbidding employment discrimination by defense contractors during World War II) before resulting in federal legislation in the 1960s.[5]

A variety of recent initiatives demonstrate that local and state efforts can enhance efficiency, equity, and voice in the 21st-century American workplace without federal action; or, as the title of a conference session has put it, state and local lemonade can be made from federal lemons.[6] Common local or regional initiatives that can improve efficiency include various forms of training partnerships. Jobs With a Future, for example, was launched by Dane County in Wisconsin to help workers qualify for better jobs in the south-central part of that state. This partnership of government, business, and labor is credited with improving publicly and privately provided training in the region through better information sharing among the key parties. A number of other local training arrangements exist from coast to coast, including private industry councils and joint business-union partnerships; many are supported by government grants. With respect to equity, a major local-level example is the living-wage movement. In fact, there have been at least 140 successful living-wage campaigns that resulted in municipal or county ordinances, and a number of additional campaigns are ongoing. As another example relating to equity, in 2005 and 2006 the New York City Council overrode mayoral vetoes to pass a Health Security Act requiring grocery stores to help pay for their employees' health insurance. Interestingly, grocery chains that already provide employee health insurance supported this act as a way of leveling the playing field with other retailers. Local policy initiatives can also target employee voice, as in the case of a Milwaukee County Labor Peace ordinance that bans employers contracting with the county from making false statements to employees about unions and bars anti-union captive audience meetings. As a second voice-related example, Oakland, California, passed a card-check ordinance that requires employers having a franchise agreement with the city to recognize and bargain with a union based on signed authorization cards rather than a secret ballot election.

There is a similar variety of state-level laws and reform efforts that promote employment with a human face. Efficiency can be enhanced by streamlined regulatory enforcement reforms such as mandatory mediation and advisory arbitration to reduce crowded state court dockets. Locally focused living-wage campaigns are complemented by state-level drives to increase minimum wages. In a similar vein as the New York City ordinance, Maryland enacted the Fair Share Health Care Fund Act in 2006, which requires businesses with more than 10,000 employees to spend at least 8 percent of their payroll on health benefits or contribute to a state fund that provides health care for low-income families. California, New Jersey, and Washington have paid parental leave policies, and in 2008 bills authorizing paid sick leave were introduced in at least twelve states. Montana has a state-level good-cause dismissal law.

With respect to voice, Connecticut has had limited statutory protections for employee free speech since 1983, and a number of states have provisions for joint labor-management health and safety committees. In addition, several states have experimented with labor law reforms. In 2007, New Hampshire and Oregon passed card-check election laws; California and New York ban employers from using state funds to promote or oppose unionization; Minnesota bans permanent strike replacements. An Oregon statute filled an important gap in the law for home health care workers by making them employees (rather than independent contractors) and thus eligible to form unions, which some of these workers subsequently chose to do. Several proposed "Worker Freedom Acts" would prevent employers from firing or disciplining employees who refuse to attend employer-mandated meetings on political and religious subjects, including information sessions about joining unions or other civic associations.

These examples clearly show that progress toward employment with a human face does not need to wait for federal legislative action. In fact, as Tom Kochan and others have argued, it should be just the opposite: local and state policymakers should be encouraged to experiment.[7] Not only does this foster customization to local needs, but it also helps policymakers learn from the experiences of others. From these lessons can spring effective national policies, because ultimately federal action is required to achieve comprehensive reform. That even the definition of "employee" varies from law to law in the current patchwork system should alone be enough to demonstrate the problems with a piecemeal approach to employment and labor law. The importance of comprehensive reform is further reinforced by the fact that today's system has large gaps in some areas, such as with contingent workers; in other areas there is confusing overlap, such as when employee health issues fall under nondiscrimination, family leave, and workers' compensation policies. Comprehensive reform also means being responsive to multiple interests; workplace public policies should not pertain only to certain types of workers or specific institutional forms; rather, the interests of all employees and employers must be considered.

Comprehensive reform cannot occur at anything less than a national level; otherwise, employees and employers alike suffer from a patchwork of differing definitions and regulations. Moreover, local and state reform efforts are not infrequently stymied or at least limited by judicial rulings that invalidate local and state laws on the basis that they are preempted by federal law. The Milwaukee County Labor Peace ordinance and Maryland's Fair Share Health Care Fund Act mentioned earlier have been invalidated on this basis, as has the California prohibition on using state funds to oppose unionization. Furthermore, because of federal preemption, the state-level card-check election laws and the Minnesota permanent strike replacement ban apply only to workers not covered by the NLRA. Thus it is clear that local and state experimentation are valuable; but localities and states have different power dynamics and can only partially remedy the deficiencies of today's workplace law and public policy system.[8]

A comprehensive approach, however, does not mean that reform must be of a one-size-fits-all format. Today's employment relationship is striking for its diversity—the demographic diversity of employees, the varied skill requirements and uses of technology across occupations, sharp differences in employment arrangements across organizations and jobs, and diverse competitive conditions and human resources strategies among companies.[9] We need a broad-based approach to workplace law and public policy that embraces multiple options—different horses for different courses. Flexibility should therefore be another principle that guides the implementation of reformed laws and public policies on work. It may be difficult to prevent substandard work outcomes without some level of mandated minimum standards, but our proposals also emphasize the importance of employee voice, which allows workers and managers to tailor policies and practices to specific preferences and constraints.

Finally, the international sphere should not be overlooked. The conventions and fundamental declarations of the International Labor Organization (ILO), as well as the human rights instruments of the United Nations, highlight the importance of fulfilling equity and voice in the contemporary employment relationship. These international standards have not greatly influenced U.S. legislation and judicial rulings on employment matters, but there will likely be greater pressure to conform to international norms and laws as the global links between countries continue to strengthen. In fact, international labor standards were incorporated into U.S. policymaking when the free-trade agreement between the United States and Jordan in 2000 included a pledge to respect the core ILO labor standards; subsequent free-trade agreements including those with Australia (2005), Peru (2007), and Korea (2007) have followed this same approach. Additional efforts to strengthen the global enforcement of employment-related human rights standards are needed because transnational labor standards are becoming an essential requirement for achieving efficiency, equity, and voice. Without such standards, the race to the bottom will continue.[10]

Paying for (Im)Balance

As efficiency-related concerns such as competitiveness, productivity, and profitability have come to dominate public discourse, the idea of regulating markets, corporations, and the employment relationship to achieve other goals besides efficiency—namely, various elements of equity or voice—have come to be viewed very negatively. Corporations and others whose interests are served by a laissez-faire approach use their power and influence to maintain an anti-regulation climate, often by emphasizing the costs of new laws and public policies. In addition to the specter of political gridlock, a second anticipated practical objection to our proposals, therefore, is cost. It would be disingenuous for us to claim that enacting the policies presented in the previous chapters would be costless. However, the cost of these reforms should not be overstated, and the costs of inaction should not be understated. And in the final analysis, balancing efficiency, equity, and voice is about achieving human goals, not purely economic ones, and cost, therefore, should not be the sole metric.

In a framework of balancing efficiency, equity, and voice, improving efficiency in the American workplace is an important concern. Creating a coherent system of workplace law and public policy with a streamlined regulatory enforcement mechanism should reduce legal delays and costs. Improving training programs and increasing the portability of employee benefits should also directly enhance efficiency. And our proposals for improving equity and facilitating voice were developed with efficiency in mind. Enhanced employee consultation can improve voice and be good for business. A policy granting employees the right to request desired work schedules creates a framework for employee-supervisor dialogue, not a rigid entitlement. The proposed free speech and good-cause dismissal protections are not unlimited, but are balanced with employers' legitimate business needs. In other words, well-designed policies for equity and voice can mitigate some efficiency losses. Policies for equity and voice, however, should not be justified solely because they improve efficiency; some policies to promote equity and voice do involve real costs and will be opposed by groups that stand to lose more than they gain.

Consumers, for example, might have to pay higher prices for some goods—but this is only fair. Why should consumers benefit at the expense of the working poor, the overworked, or the voiceless worker? Goods and services should reflect their true social cost, not the economic cost produced by imperfect labor markets with limited employee bargaining power. Some of our proposals draw on European policies, and critics will likely therefore object to these proposals by associating them with Eurosclerosis—Europe's weak record on job creation and reducing unemployment. But accusations of guilt by association grossly oversimplify the issues. As noted in Chapter 3, the links between European labor policies and high unemployment rates are not as clear as critics portray. A lot of research has examined this issue, but the results are inconsistent.[11] As such, there is insufficient evidence to support a blanket claim that European labor policies increase unemployment. Critics of greater government regulation are also quick to claim that minimum wage policies increase unemployment, but the research in this regard is also ambiguous.[12] And policies that improve the balance between employers and employees might redistribute income from executives to the working poor, but such redistributive efforts do not necessarily harm efficiency.[13] With respect to international competitiveness, enacting the reforms we suggest would not result in a regulatory regime that exceeds that found in the rest of the industrialized world. None of this is to say that our proposals are costless, but the costs should not be overstated.

Our proposals are not as costly as they might initially seem because the current imbalance is costly in its own right. Employers benefit by offering low-wage jobs without health insurance coverage while society picks up the tab. Wal-Mart is frequently criticized for the large number of its employees whose low incomes and lack of health insurance require them to turn to public assistance and public hospital emergency rooms. More generally, California alone spends $10 billion annually on public assistance for families with at least one full-time worker; medical care is the single most expensive item in this social safety net for the working poor. It is estimated that these expenditures could be nearly cut in half if the working poor earned at least $8 per hour and received health insurance.[14] Excessive levels of income inequality also create numerous externalities that impose real costs on society—crime, underinvestment in education, and cynicism toward democracy, to name just a few. Income insecurity limits economic opportunity and growth.[15] Other costs of labor policy imbalances are apparent in the domain of labor relations. Poor labor-management relations are arguably partially to blame for the decline of the U.S. auto and steel industries, and research has linked the production of defective Firestone tires that were responsible for over 250 deaths to two intense periods of labor-management conflict.[16] Continuing the status quo by failing to craft a new system of workplace law and public policy is therefore costly in its own right.

Working Out a Balance

In the first few decades of the 20th century, Minneapolis was rife with labor conflict that culminated in a violent and famous strike in 1934. On the city's eastern border, St. Paul provided a stark contrast: though heavily unionized, the 1934 strike was barely noticed. As described by Mary Lethert Wingerd, Minneapolis's history of labor conflict can be traced back to social divisions—a powerful elite created a "divided city." St. Paul developed in a more egalitarian fashion—an enduring civic compact created an economically and politically inclusive city.[17] In other words, social stability, cohesiveness, and labor peace rested on a balance of power between employers and employees, and they were mediated by the important institutions of the time. Today the differences between Minneapolis and St. Paul have succumbed to national trends, but the lessons remain relevant. Research finds that countries with a balanced income distribution perform better than those with greater levels of inequality. Backlashes against globalization such as the "Battle in Seattle" protests stem from perceived power imbalances among the participants in the global economic system. In the words of an unidentified participant before the World Commission on the Social Dimension of Globalization, "A conversation between a cat and a mouse is not a conversation." From the pluralist perspective that underlies our arguments in this book then, the employment relationship works best when institutions create a balance between efficiency, equity, and voice. A balance creates fair market opportunities, promotes broadly shared prosperity, respects human dignity, and strengthens democracy.[18]

Workplace law and public policy can and should play a key role in balancing efficiency, equity, and voice. The United States only has to look to Canada for guidance on creating effective social safety nets and employee voice mechanisms through public policies on unemployment insurance benefits, paid statutory holidays and vacations, advance notice of or compensation for dismissals not for good cause, universal health care coverage, and effective labor laws.[19] Furthermore, economic insecurity and a lack of voice affect all workers. As described in the preceding three chapters, we have therefore developed a number of policy options for giving employment a human face in the United States (see Figure 10.1). Some of these policies target efficiency or equity or voice, while others promote more than one of the objectives; taken as a comprehensive package of reforms they seek to balance efficiency, equity, and voice.

Although we have focused on the American workplace, analyses of work-related laws and public policies worldwide need to be firmly grounded in the objectives of the employment relationship. Without these anchors, there are minimal foundations for understanding employment and labor law, evaluating the need for reform, and crafting new policies. The long-standing emphasis in scholarship and policy debates on how processes work must therefore be replaced by a deeper and explicit analysis of what employment should achieve in a democratic society as guided by a consistent set of intellectual principles. Although specific policies need to be tailored to the context of individual countries, in *Invisible Hands, Invisible Objectives* we offer what we believe are valuable considerations for scholars, policymakers, and students of the employment relationship from diverse perspectives in any country.

Giving employment a human face by successfully balancing efficiency, equity, and voice takes more than a reformed system of workplace law and public policy, however. It also requires overcoming long-standing power imbalances in the sociopolitical arena and creating new social norms that give workers and consumers equal importance and that give

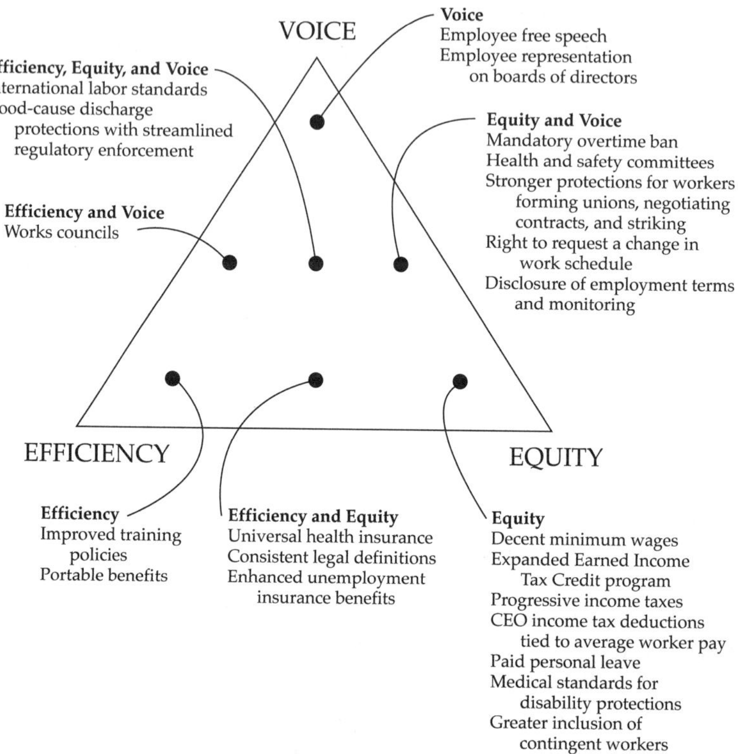

FIGURE 10.1 Public policies for employment with a human face.

people as much emphasis as profits.[20] Work has to be seen as a fully human activity rather than as a purely economic transaction. Companies that use cutting-edge human resource management practices to create efficiency while also providing equity and voice need to take a leadership role in their communities and industries in promoting such practices. Unions need to devise new strategies and structures to match the preferences of today's workforce. And the role of governments as employers should not be overlooked—new norms for the employment relationship can be fostered by public sector employers using employment practices that give employment a human face. Without intending to minimize the vexing power issues that prevent reform, we believe that all of these changes can spring from *explicit* discourse on how to work out a balance in today's employment relationship using the framework developed in this book.

We are not so bold or naive as to expect our analytical framework or reform proposals to be accepted without debate or disagreement. But if our framework promotes a deeper understanding of workplace law and public policy, and if our analyses and proposals foster long-overdue debates over U.S. and international employment policies rooted in the workings and objectives of the employment relationship, then we will have succeeded. The milieu of invisible hands and objectives should be replaced by visible hands and explicit objectives. Our understanding of employment issues and the achievement of broadly shared prosperity and security through a humane employment system demand nothing less.

Notes

NOTES TO CHAPTER 1

1. *New York Times*, June 26, 2007; October 15, 2006; March 8, 2006; April 2, 2007; March 6, 2008; May 12, 2007; March 6, 2005.

2. Jared Bernstein, *All Together Now: Common Sense for a Fair Economy* (San Francisco: Berrett-Koehler, 2006). Robert W. Drago, *Striking a Balance: Work, Family, Life* (Boston: Dollars and Sense, 2007). Steven Greenhouse, *The Big Squeeze: Tough Times for the American Worker* (New York: Knopf, 2008). Thomas A. Kochan, *Restoring the American Dream: A Working Families' Agenda for America* (Cambridge, Mass.: MIT Press, 2005). Chuck Schumer, *Positively American: Winning Back the Middle-Class Majority One Family at a Time* (Emmaus, Penn.: Rodale Books, 2007).

3. John W. Budd, *Employment with a Human Face: Balancing Efficiency, Equity, and Voice* (Ithaca, N.Y.: Cornell University Press, 2004).

4. Budd, *Employment with a Human Face*. John W. Budd and Alexander J. S. Colvin, "Improved Metrics for Workplace Dispute Resolution Procedures: Efficiency, Equity, and Voice," *Industrial Relations* 47 (July 2008): 460–79. John W. Budd, *Labor Relations: Striking a Balance*, 2nd ed. (Boston: McGraw-Hill/Irwin, 2008).

5. Charles Fried, "Individual and Collective Rights in Work Relations: Reflections on the Current State of Labor Law and Its Prospects," *University of Chicago Law Review* 51 (Fall 1984): 1012–40 at 1019–21. Paul C. Weiler, "A Principled Reshaping of Labor Law for the Twenty-First Century," *University of Pennsylvania Journal of Labor and Employment Law* 3 (Winter 2001): 177–206. Paul Osterman, *Securing Prosperity: The American Labor Market: How It Has Changed and What to Do about It* (Princeton, N.J.: Princeton University Press, 1999). Paul Osterman, Thomas A. Kochan, Richard Locke, and Michael J. Piore, *Working in America: A Blueprint for the New Labor Market* (Cambridge, Mass.: MIT Press,

2001), 10–12. Ellen Dannin, *Taking Back the Workers' Law: How to Fight the Assault on Labor Rights* (Ithaca, N.Y.: Cornell University Press, 2006).

6. John R. Commons, *Industrial Goodwill* (New York: McGraw-Hill, 1919). John T. Dunlop, *Industrial Relations Systems* (New York: Holt, 1958). Hugh Armstrong Clegg, *The Changing System of Industrial Relations in Great Britain* (Oxford: Basil Blackwell, 1979). Paul C. Weiler, *Governing the Workplace: The Future of Labor and Employment Law* (Cambridge, Mass.: Harvard University Press, 1990). Budd, *Employment with a Human Face.*

7. John W. Budd and Devasheesh Bhave, "Values, Ideologies, and Frames of Reference in Employment Relations," in Paul Blyton, Nicolas Bacon, Jack Fiorito and Edmund Heery, eds., *Sage Handbook of Industrial Relations* (London: Sage, 2008), 92–112. John W. Budd and Devasheesh Bhave, "The Employment Relationship," in Adrian Wilkinson, Tom Redman, Scott Snell, and Nick Bacon, eds., *Sage Handbook of Human Resource Management* (London: Sage, forthcoming).

8. Michael Perelman, *Railroading Economics: The Creation of the Free Market Mythology* (New York: Monthly Review Press, 2006), 25.

9. Adam Smith, *An Inquiry into the Nature and Causes of the Wealth of Nations* (1776; New York: Bantam Books, 2003), 23–24.

10. Milton Friedman and Rose Friedman, *Free to Choose: A Personal Statement* (New York: Harcourt Brace Jovanovich, 1980). Leo Troy, *Beyond Unions and Collective Bargaining* (Armonk, N.Y.: M. E. Sharpe, 1999). Martin Wolf, *Why Globalization Works* (New Haven, Conn.: Yale University Press, 2004).

11. David Harvey, *A Brief History of Neoliberalism* (Oxford: Oxford University Press, 2005). Dag Einar Thorsen and Amund Lie, "What Is Neoliberalism?" (unpublished paper, University of Oslo, 2007).

12. Bruce E. Kaufman, "Labor Markets and Employment Regulation: The View of the 'Old' Institutionalists," in Bruce E. Kaufman, ed., *Government Regulation of the Employment Relationship* (Madison, Wisc.: Industrial Relations Research Association, 1997), 11-55. Alan Manning, *Monopsony in Motion: Imperfect Competition in Labor Markets* (Princeton, N.J.: Princeton University Press, 2003). Bruce E. Kaufman, "The Social Welfare Objectives and Ethical Principles of Industrial Relations," in John W. Budd and James G. Scoville, eds., *The Ethics of Human Resources and Industrial Relations* (Champaign, Ill: Labor and Employment Relations Association, 2005), 23–59.

13. Alan Fox, *Beyond Contract: Work, Power and Trust Relations* (London: Farber and Farber, 1974). David Lewin, "IR and HR Perspectives on Workplace Conflict: What Can Each Learn from the Other?" *Human Resource Management Review* 11 (Winter 2001): 453–85.

14. Jacqueline A.-M. Coyle-Shapiro, Lynn M. Shore, M. Susan Taylor, and Lois E. Tetrick, eds., *The Employment Relationship: Examining Psychological and Contextual Perspectives* (New York: Oxford University Press, 2004).

15. Fox, *Beyond Contract*. H. A. Clegg, "Pluralism in Industrial Relations," *British Journal of Industrial Relations* 13 (November 1975): 309–16.

16. Allison Linn, "Microsoft Trimming Some Worker Benefits to Cut Costs," *Star Tribune*, May 21, 2004.

17. John W. Budd, Rafael Gomez, and Noah M. Meltz, "Why a Balance Is Best: The Pluralist Industrial Relations Paradigm of Balancing Competing Interests," in Bruce E. Kaufman, ed., *Theoretical Perspectives on Work and the Employment Relationship* (Champaign, Ill: Industrial Relations Research Association, 2004), 195–227. Dell P. Champlin and Janet T. Knoedler, eds., *The Institutionalist Tradition in Labor Economics* (Armonk, N.Y.: M. E. Sharpe, 2004).

18. Budd, *Employment with a Human Face*. Budd, Gomez, and Meltz, "Why a Balance Is Best." Kaufman, "Labor Markets and Employment Regulation." Kochan, *Restoring the American Dream*. Lewin, "IR and HR Perspectives on Workplace Conflict." Weiler, "A Principled Reshaping of Labor Law for the Twenty-First Century."

19. Paul Edwards and Judy Wajcman, *The Politics of Working Life* (Oxford: Oxford University Press, 2005). Gregor Gall, "Marxism and Industrial Relations," in Peter Ackers and Adrian Wilkinson, eds., *Understanding Work and Employment: Industrial Relations in Transition* (Oxford: Oxford University Press, 2003), 316–24. Richard Hyman, *Industrial Relations: A Marxist Introduction* (London: Macmillan, 1975). John Kelly, *Rethinking Industrial Relations: Mobilization, Collectivism and Long Waves* (London: Routledge, 1998). Paul Thompson and Kirsty Newsome, "Labor Process Theory, Work, and the Employment Relation," in Bruce E. Kaufman, ed., *Theoretical Perspectives on Work and the Employment Relationship* (Champaign, Ill.: Industrial Relations Research Association, 2004), 133–62.

20. Stanley Aronowitz, *How Class Works: Power and Social Movement* (New Haven: Yale University Press, 2003), 26. Richard Scase, *Class* (Minneapolis, University of Minnesota Press, 1992). Erik Olin Wright, ed., *Approaches to Class Analysis* (Cambridge: Cambridge University Press, 2005).

21. Paul Ryan, "Segmentation, Duality, and the Internal Labour Market," in Frank Wilkinson, ed., *The Dynamics of Labour Market Segmentation* (London: Academic Press, 1981), 3–20. Richard C. Edwards, *Contested Terrain: The Transformation of the Workplace in the Twentieth Century* (New York: Basic Books, 1979). Harry Braverman, *Labor and Monopoly Capital: The Degradation of Work in the Twentieth Century* (New York: Monthly Review Press, 1974). Karen Legge, *Human Resource Management: Rhetorics and Realities* (Basingstoke, UK: Macmillan Press, 1995). Gordon Lafer, *The Job Training Charade* (Ithaca, N.Y.: Cornell University Press, 2002).

22. Evelyn Nakano Glenn, *Unequal Freedom: How Race and Gender Shaped American Citizenship and Labor* (Cambridge, Mass.: Harvard University Press, 2002). Lynn S. Chancer and Beverly Xaviera Watkins, *Gender, Race, and Class: An Overview* (Malden, Mass.: Blackwell, 2006). Michael Zweig, ed., *What's Class Got to Do with It? American Society in the Twenty-First Century* (Ithaca, N.Y.: Cornell University Press, 2004).

23. Weiler, "A Principled Reshaping of Labor Law for the Twenty-First Century." Osterman, *Securing Prosperity*. Dannin, *Taking Back the Workers' Law*. Katherine V. W. Stone, *From Widgets to Digits: Employment Regulations for the Changing Workplace* (Cambridge: Cambridge University Press, 2004). Kochan, *Restoring the American Dream*.

24. U.S. Census Bureau, *Statistical Abstract of the United States* (Washington, D.C.: Government Printing Office, 2008). Matthew Sobek, "New Statistics on the U.S. Labor Force, 1850–1990," *Historical Methods* 34 (2001): 71–87.

25. Peter Cappelli et al., *Change at Work* (New York: Oxford University Press, 1997). Stephen A. Herzenberg, John A. Alic, and Howard Wial, *New Rules for a New Economy: Employment and Opportunity in Postindustrial America* (Ithaca, N.Y.: ILR Press, 1998). Osterman, *Securing Prosperity*. Cynthia L. Estlund, "The Ossification of American Labor Law," *Columbia Law Review* 102 (October 2002): 1527–1612. Stone, *From Widgets to Digits*. Kochan, *Restoring the American Dream*.

26. U.S. General Accounting Office, "Collective Bargaining Rights: Information on the Number of Workers with and Without Bargaining Rights," GAO-02-835 (Washington, D.C., 2002).

27. Stephen F. Befort, "Revisiting the Black Hole of Workplace Regulation: A Historical and Comparative Perspective of Contingent Work," *Berkeley Journal of Employment and Labor Law* 24 (2003): 153–78. Richard R. Carlson, "Why the Law Still Can't Tell an Employee When It Sees One and How It Ought to Stop Trying," *Berkeley Journal of Employment and Labor Law* 22 (2001): 295–368.

28. Richard Michael Fischl, "Rethinking the Tripartite Division of American Work Law," *Berkeley Journal of Employment and Labor Law* 28 (2007): 163–216.

29. Gibson Burrell, "Foucauldian and Postmodern Thought and the Analysis of Work," in Marek Korczynski, Randy Hodson, and Paul Edwards, eds., *Social Theory at Work* (Oxford: Oxford University Press, 2006), 155–81. Mark Hearn and Grant Michelson, eds., *Rethinking Work: Time, Space, and Discourse* (Melbourne: Cambridge University Press, 2006).

30. Fischl, "Rethinking the Tripartite Division of American Work Law."

31. Bruce E. Kaufman, *The Global Evolution of Industrial Relations: Events, Ideas, and the IIRA* (Geneva: International Labor Office, 2004). Commission of the European Communities, "Green Paper: Modernising Labour Law to Meet the Challenges of the 21st Century" (Brussels, 2006).

32. Bernstein, *All Together Now*. Drago, *Striking a Balance*. Greenhouse, *The Big Squeeze*. Kochan, *Restoring the American Dream*. Schumer, *Positively American*.

NOTES TO CHAPTER 2

1. Melvyn Dubofsky and Foster Rhea Dulles, *Labor in America: A History*, 7th ed. (Wheeling, Ill.: Harlan Davidson, 2004). Nelson Lichtenstein et al., *Who Built America? Working People and the Nation's Economy, Politics, Culture, and Society*, Vol. 2 (New York: Worth, 2000). Charles Perrow, *Organizing America: Wealth, Power, and the Origins of Corporate Capitalism* (Princeton, N.J.: Princeton University Press, 2002). Joseph G. Rayback, *A History of American Labor* (New York: Free Press, 1966). Christopher L. Tomlins, *Law, Labor, and Ideology in the Early American Republic* (Cambridge: Cambridge University Press, 1993).

2. Robert J. Steinfeld, *The Invention of Free Labor: The Employment Relation in English and American Law and Culture, 1350–1870* (Chapel Hill: University of North Carolina Press, 1991), 21. Robert J. Steinfeld, *Coercion, Contract, and Free*

Labor in the Nineteenth Century (Cambridge: Cambridge University Press, 2001). Tomlins, *Law, Labor, and Ideology in the Early American Republic.*

3. Jay M. Feinman, "The Development of the Employment at Will Rule," *American Journal of Legal History* 20 (April 1976): 118–35. Deborah A. Ballam, "Exploding the Original Myth Regarding Employment-at-Will: The True Origins of the Doctrine," *Berkeley Journal of Employment and Labor Law* 17 (1996): 91–130. Steinfeld, *The Invention of Free Labor*. Tomlins, *Law, Labor, and Ideology in the Early American Republic.*

4. *Payne v. Western and Atlantic R.R. Co.*, 81 Tenn. 507, 518–520 (1884), overruled on other grounds, *Hutton v. Watters*, 179 S.W. 134, 138 (Tenn. 1915).

5. *Godcharles v. Wigeman*, 113 Pa. 431, 6 A. 354 (1886). *Lochner v. New York*, 198 U.S. 45 (1905). *Adair v. U.S.*, 208 U.S. 161 (1908). *Coppage v. State of Kansas*, 236 U.S. 1 (1915). *Adkins v. Children's Hospital*, 261 U.S. 525 (1923). William E. Forbath, "The Ambiguities of Free Labor: Labor and the Law in the Gilded Age," *Wisconsin Law Review* 1985 (July/August 1985): 767–817. Michael J. Phillips, "The Progressiveness of the *Lochner* Court," *Denver University Law Review* 75 (1998): 453–505.

6. Quoted in Tomlins, *Law, Labor, and Ideology in the Early American Republic*, 291.

7. John W. Budd and James G. Scoville, "Moral Philosophy, Business Ethics, and the Employment Relationship," in John W. Budd and James G. Scoville, eds., *The Ethics of Human Resources and Industrial Relations* (Champaign, Ill.: Labor and Employment Relations Association, 2005), 1–21.

8. Jennifer Klein, *For All These Rights: Business, Labor, and the Shaping of America's Public-Private Welfare State* (Princeton, N.J.: Princeton University Press, 2003). Sanford M. Jacoby, *Employing Bureaucracy: Managers, Unions, and the Transformation of Work in American Industry, 1900–1945* (New York: Columbia University Press, 1985). Bruce E. Kaufman, *The Origins and Evolution of the Field of Industrial Relations in the United States* (Ithaca, N.Y.: ILR Press, 1993).

9. Daniel Nelson, ed., *A Mental Revolution: Scientific Management since Taylor* (Columbus: Ohio State University Press, 1992).

10. Jeremy Brecher, *Strike!* (Boston: South End Press, 1972). John W. Budd, *Labor Relations: Striking a Balance*, 2nd ed. (Boston: McGraw-Hill/Irwin, 2008). Clayton Sinyai, *Schools of Democracy: A Political History of the American Labor Movement* (Ithaca, N.Y.: Cornell University Press, 2006). Josiah Bartlett Lambert, *"If the Workers Took a Notion": The Right to Strike and American Political Development* (Ithaca, N.Y.: Cornell University Press, 2005). Stephen H. Norwood, *Strikebreaking and Intimidation: Mercenaries and Masculinity in Twentieth-Century America of the Labor Movement* (Chapel Hill: University of North Carolina Press, 2002).

11. Charles O. Gregory and Harold A. Katz, *Labor and the Law*, 3rd ed. (New York: Norton, 1979). *Commonwealth v. Hunt*, 45 Mass. 111 (Mass. 1842). Tomlins, *Law, Labor, and Ideology in the Early American Republic.*

12. William E. Forbath, *Law and the Shaping of the American Labor Movement* (Cambridge, Mass.: Harvard University Press, 1991). Felix Frankfurter and Nathan Greene, *The Labor Injunction* (New York: Macmillan, 1930). Edwin E. Witte, *The Government in Labor Disputes* (New York: McGraw-Hill, 1932).

13. Eliot Jones, *The Trust Problem in the United States* (New York: Macmillan, 1923). William Serrin, *Homestead: The Glory and Tragedy of an American Steel Town* (New York: Vintage Books, 1992).

14. *Lawlor v. Loewe*, 235 U.S. 522 (1915). Daniel R. Ernst, *Lawyers Against Labor: From Individual Rights to Corporate Liberalism* (Urbana: University of Illinois Press, 1995).

15. *American Steel Foundries v. Tri-City Central Trades Council*, 257 U.S. 184 (1921).

16. William Millikan, *A Union Against Unions: The Minneapolis Citizens Alliance and Its Fight Against Organized Labor, 1903–1947* (St. Paul: Minnesota Historical Society, 2001). Irving Bernstein, *The Lean Years: A History of the American Worker, 1920–1933* (Boston: Houghton Mifflin, 1960). Dubofsky and Dulles, *Labor in America*.

17. Matthew Josephson, *The Robber Barons: The Great American Capitalists, 1861–1901* (New York: Harcourt, Brace, 1934). Lichtenstein et al., *Who Built America?* Ezekiel H. Downey, *Workmen's Compensation* (New York: Macmillan, 1924). W. Jett Lauck and Edgar Sydenstricker, *Conditions of Labor in American Industries: A Summarization of the Results of Recent Investigations* (New York: Funk and Wagnalls, 1917). Kaufman, *The Origins and Evolution of the Field of Industrial Relations in the United States*.

18. Adam Smith, *An Inquiry into the Nature and Causes of the Wealth of Nations* (1776; New York: Bantam Books, 2003), 94.

19. Kaufman, *The Origins and Evolution of the Field of Industrial Relations in the United States*. Bruce E. Kaufman, *The Global Evolution of Industrial Relations: Events, Ideas, and the IIRA* (Geneva: International Labor Office, 2004).

20. Sidney Webb and Beatrice Webb, *Industrial Democracy* (London: Longmans, Green, 1897). Bruce E. Kaufman, "The Social Welfare Objectives and Ethical Principles of Industrial Relations," in John W. Budd and James G. Scoville, eds., *The Ethics of Human Resources and Industrial Relations* (Champaign, Ill.: Labor and Employment Relations Association, 2005), 23–59. John W. Budd, *Employment with a Human Face: Balancing Efficiency, Equity, and Voice* (Ithaca, N.Y.: Cornell University Press, 2004).

21. Kaufman, *The Global Evolution of Industrial Relations*.

22. Gregory and Katz, *Labor and the Law*.

23. Irving Bernstein, *A Caring Society: The New Deal, the Worker, and the Great Depression* (Boston: Houghton Mifflin, 1985). David M. Kennedy, *Freedom from Fear: The American People in Depression and War, 1929–1945* (New York: Oxford University Press, 1999). Cass R. Sunstein, *The Second Bill of Rights: FDR's Unfinished Revolution and Why We Need It More Than Ever* (New York: Basic Books, 2004). Budd, *Employment with a Human Face*. Kaufman, *The Global Evolution of Industrial Relations*.

24. United States Industrial Commission, *Report of the Industrial Commission on the Relations and Conditions of Capital and Labor Employed in Manufactures and General Business*, Vol. 7 (Washington, D.C.: Government Printing Office, 1901), 478.

25. Bruce E. Kaufman, "Why the Wagner Act? Reestablishing Contact with Its Original Purpose," in David Lewin, Bruce E. Kaufman, and Donna Sockell, eds., *Advances in Industrial and Labor Relations*, Vol. 7 (Greenwich, Conn.: JAI Press, 1996), 15–68.

26. Leon H. Keyserling, "Why the Wagner Act?" in Louis G. Silverberg, ed., *The Wagner Act: After Ten Years* (Washington, D.C.: Bureau of National Affairs, 1945), 5–33 at 13.

27. Patrick Hardin, ed., *The Developing Labor Law: The Board, the Courts, and the National Labor Relations Act*, 4th ed. (Washington, D.C.: BNA Books, 2001).

28. Bruce E. Kaufman, "Labor Markets and Employment Regulation: The View of the 'Old' Institutionalists," in Bruce E. Kaufman, ed., *Government Regulation of the Employment Relationship* (Madison, Wisc.: Industrial Relations Research Association, 1997), 11–55. Alvin L. Goldman, *Labor and Employment Law in the United States* (Boston: Kluwer Law International, 1996).

29. James MacGregor Burns and Stewart Burns, *A People's Charter: The Pursuit of Rights in America* (New York: Alfred A. Knopf, 1991). Sunstein, *The Second Bill of Rights*.

30. Paul Gordon Lauren, *The Evolution of International Human Rights: Visions Seen* (Philadelphia: University of Pennsylvania Press, 1998). Mary Ann Glendon, "Knowing the Universal Declaration of Human Rights," *Notre Dame Law Review* 73 (May 1998): 1153–82. James A. Gross, ed., *Workers' Rights as Human Rights* (Ithaca, N.Y.: Cornell University Press, 2003). Judy Fudge, "After Industrial Citizenship: Market Citizenship or Citizenship at Work?" *Relations Industrielles/Industrial Relations* 60 (Fall 2005): 631–53. Guy Mundlak, "Industrial Citizenship, Social Citizenship, Corporate Citizenship: I Just Want My Wages," *Theoretical Inquiries in Law* 8 (July 2007): 719–48.

31. Jacoby, *Employing Bureaucracy*. Sanford M. Jacoby, *Modern Manors: Welfare Capitalism since the New Deal* (Princeton, N.J.: Princeton University Press, 1997). Klein, *For All These Rights*. Paul Osterman, Thomas Kochan, Richard Locke, and Michael J. Piore, *Working in America: A Blueprint for the New Labor Market* (Cambridge, Mass.: MIT Press, 2001). Paul Osterman, *Securing Prosperity: The American Labor Market: How It Has Changed and What to Do about It* (Princeton, N.J.: Princeton University Press, 1999).

32. Thomas A. Kochan, Harry C. Katz, and Robert B. McKersie, *The Transformation of American Industrial Relations* (New York: Basic Books, 1986).

33. Robert Folger and Russell Cropanzano, *Organizational Justice and Human Resource Management* (Thousand Oaks, Calif.: Sage, 1998).

34. Jacob S. Hacker, *The Divided Welfare State: The Battle over Public and Private Social Benefits in the United States* (New York: Cambridge University Press, 2002). David C. Jacobs, "Prospects for National Health Insurance in the United States," in Sheldon Friedman and David C. Jacobs, eds., *The Future of the Safety Net: Social Insurance and Employee Benefits* (Champaign, Ill.: Industrial Relations Research Association, 2001), 187–200. Klein, *For All These Rights*.

35. Nancy MacLean, *Freedom Is Not Enough: The Opening of the American Workplace* (Cambridge, Mass.: Harvard University Press, 2006).

36. Alexander J. S. Colvin, "The Relationship Between Employment Arbitration and Workplace Dispute Resolution Procedures," *Ohio State Journal on Dispute Resolution* 16 (2001): 643–68. Jacoby, *Modern Manors*. Klein, *For All These Rights*. Karen Legge, *Human Resource Management: Rhetorics and Realities* (Basingstoke, UK: Macmillan Press, 1995).

37. Eileen Appelbaum and Rosemary Batt, *The New American Workplace: Transforming Work Systems in the United States* (Ithaca, N.Y.: ILR Press, 1994). Jeremy Rifkin, *The End of Work: The Decline of the Global Labor Force and the Dawn of the Post-Market Era* (New York: Putnam Books, 1995). Catherine L. Mann, "Offshore Outsourcing and the Globalization of US Services: Why Now, How Important, and What Policy Implications," in C. Fred Bergsten, ed., *The United States and the World Economy: Foreign Economic Policy for the Next Decade* (Washington, D.C.: Institute for International Economics, 2005), 281–311.

38. Sanford M. Jacoby, *The Embedded Corporation: Corporate Governance and Employment Relations in Japan and the United States* (Princeton, N.J.: Princeton University Press, 2005). Harry C. Katz and Owen Darbishire, *Converging Divergences: Worldwide Changes in Employment Systems* (Ithaca, N.Y.: ILR Press, 2000). Matthew J. Slaughter, "Globalization and Declining Unionization in the United States," *Industrial Relations* 46 (April 2007): 329–46.

39. Peter Cappelli, *The New Deal at Work: Managing the Market-Driven Workforce* (Boston: Harvard Business School Press, 1999). Osterman et al., *Working in America*. Jackie Krasas Rogers, *Temps: The Many Faces of the Changing Workplace* (Ithaca, N.Y.: Cornell University Press, 2000).

40. Douglas A. Irwin, *Free Trade under Fire* (Princeton, N.J.: Princeton University Press, 2002).

41. Marley S. Weiss, "Two Steps Forward, One Step Back—Or Vice Versa: Labor Rights under Free Trade Agreements from NAFTA, Through Jordan, via Chile, to Latin America, and Beyond," *University of San Francisco Law Review* 37 (Spring 2003): 689–755. Mario F. Bognanno and Jiangfeng Lu, "NAFTA's Labor Side Agreement: Withering as an Effective Labor Law Enforcement and MNC Compliance Strategy?" in William N. Cooke, ed., *Multinational Companies and Global Human Resource Strategies* (Westport, Conn.: Quorum Books, 2003), 369–402. Michael J. Trebilcock and Robert Howse, "Trade Policy and Labor Standards," *Minnesota Journal of Global Trade* 14 (Summer 2005): 261–300. Lori G. Kletzer and Howard Rosen, "Easing the Adjustment Burden on U.S. Workers," in C. Fred Bergsten, ed., *The United States and the World Economy: Foreign Economic Policy for the Next Decade* (Washington, D.C.: Institute for International Economics, 2005), 313–41.

42. Lizabeth Cohen, *A Consumer's Republic: The Politics of Mass Consumption in Postwar America* (New York: Alfred A. Knopf, 2003). Marek Korczynski, "Consumer Capitalism and Industrial Relations," in Peter Ackers and Adrian Wilkinson, eds., *Understanding Work and Employment: Industrial Relations in Transition* (Oxford: Oxford University Press, 2003), 265–77.

43. Gordon Lafer, *The Job Training Charade* (Ithaca, N.Y.: Cornell University Press, 2002).

44. Employment and Training Administration, "WIA Reauthorization and Reform" (Washington, D.C.: U.S. Department of Labor, no date), http://www.doleta.gov/pdf/WIA%20Reauthorization%20Summary.pdf [accessed August 15, 2005].

45. Daniel H. Pink, *Free Agent Nation: How America's New Independent Workers Are Transforming the Way We Live* (New York: Warner Books, 2001). Robert H. Frank and Philip J. Cook, *The Winner-Take-All Society: How More and More Americans Compete for Ever Fewer and Bigger Prizes, Encouraging Economic Waste, Income Inequality, and an Impoverished Cultural Life* (New York: Free Press, 1995).

46. Beverly J. Silver, *Forces of Labor: Workers' Movements and Globalization since 1870* (Cambridge: Cambridge University Press, 2003).

NOTES TO CHAPTER 3

1. Greg J. Bamber, Russell D. Lansbury, and Nick Wailes, eds., *International and Comparative Employment Relations: Globalisation and the Developed Market Economies* (London: Sage, 2004). Stephen F. Befort, "Labor and Employment Law at the Millennium: A Historical Review and Critical Assessment," *Boston College Law Review* 43 (March 2002): 351–460. Stephen F. Befort and Virginia E. Cornett, "Beyond the Rhetoric of the NAFTA Treaty Debate: A Comparative Analysis of Labor and Employment Law in Mexico and the United States," *Comparative Labor Law Journal* 17 (Winter 1996): 269–313. John W. Budd, *Labor Relations: Striking a Balance*, 2nd ed. (Boston: McGraw-Hill/Irwin, 2008).

2. Lawrence Mishel, Jared Bernstein, and Sylvia Allegretto, *The State of Working America 2006/2007* (Ithaca, N.Y.: Cornell University Press, 2007). Council of Economic Advisors, *Economic Report of the President* (Washington, D.C.: U.S. Government Printing Office, various issues). Organization for Economic Cooperation and Development, *OECD Economic Surveys: United States* (Paris, 2004). U.S. Bureau of Labor Statistics, "Comparative Civilian Labor Force Statistics, 10 Countries, 1960–2007" (Washington, D.C.: U.S. Department of Labor, 2008), http://www.bls.gov/fls/ [accessed May 18, 2008]. U.S. Bureau of Labor Statistics, "International Comparisons of Manufacturing Productivity and Unit Labor Cost Trends" (Washington, D.C.: U.S. Department of Labor, 2005), http://www.bls.gov/fls/ [accessed August 9, 2005].

3. Peter Cappelli, *The New Deal at Work: Managing the Market-Driven Workforce* (Boston: Harvard Business School Press, 1999). Douglas A. Irwin, *Free Trade under Fire* (Princeton, N.J.: Princeton University Press, 2002). Roger Blanpain, "The Changing World of Work" in Roger Blanpain and Chris Engels, eds., *Comparative Labour Law and Industrial Relations in Industrialized Market Economies*, 6th ed. (The Hague: Kluwer Law International, 1998), 23–50. Kenneth G. Dau-Schmidt, "Employment in the New Age of Trade and Technology: Implications for Labor and Employment Law," *Indiana Law Journal* 76 (Winter 2001): 1–28.

4. Kenneth F. Scheve, and Matthew J. Slaughter, *Globalization and the Perception of American Workers* (Washington, D.C.: Institute for International Economics, 2001). Irwin, *Free Trade under Fire*. World Trade Organization, *International*

Trade Statistics 2007 (Geneva, 2007). Bank for International Settlements, "Triennial Central Bank Survey: Foreign Exchange and Derivatives Market Activity in 2007" (Basel, Switzerland, 2007). United Nations, *World Investment Report 2007* (New York, 2007). United Nations, "Trends in the Total Migrant Stock: The 2005 Revision," POP/DB/MIG/Rev.2005 (New York, 2006), http://esa.un.org/migration/ [accessed May 18, 2008].

5. David Jessup and Michael E. Gordon, "Organizing in Export Processing Zones: The Bibong Experience in the Dominican Republic," in Michael E. Gordon and Lowell Turner, eds., *Transnational Cooperation Among Labor Unions* (Ithaca, N.Y.: ILR Press, 2000), 179–201.

6. Robert Bruno, *Steelworker Alley: How Class Works in Youngstown* (Ithaca, N.Y.: Cornell University Press, 1999). Steve Mellon, *After the Smoke Clears: Struggling to Get By in Rustbelt America* (Pittsburgh: University of Pittsburgh Press, 2002).

7. Barry Jones, *Sleepers Awake! Technology and the Future of Work* (Melbourne: Oxford University Press, 1995). Stephen A. Herzenberg, John A. Alic, and Howard Wial, *New Rules for a New Economy: Employment and Opportunity in Postindustrial America* (Ithaca, N.Y.: ILR Press, 1998).

8. Frank Levy and Richard J. Murnane, *The New Division of Labor: How Computers Are Creating the Next Job Market* (New York: Russell Sage Foundation, 2004). Simon Head, *The New Ruthless Economy: Work and Power in the Digital Age* (New York: Oxford University Press, 2003).

9. Maury Gittleman and Michael J. Handel, "Who Uses Computers and in What Ways: Effects on the Earnings Distribution," in Derek C. Jones, ed., *The New Economy Handbook* (Amsterdam: Elsevier, 2003), 523–44. Levy and Murnane, *The New Division of Labor*. Head, *The New Ruthless Economy*. Martin Conroy, *Sustaining the New Economy: Work, Family, and Community in the Information Age* (New York: Russell Sage Foundation, 2000).

10. Jeremy Rifkin, *The End of Work: The Decline of the Global Labor Force and the Dawn of the Post-Market Era* (New York: Putnam Books, 1995), xv.

11. Jones, *Sleepers Awake!* Levy and Murnane, *The New Division of Labor*.

12. Levy and Murnane, *The New Division of Labor*. Anthony P. Carnevale, "Enhancing Skills in the New Economy," in Ann Howard, ed., *The Changing Nature of Work* (San Francisco: Jossey-Bass, 1995), 238–51. Paul Osterman, "Skill, Training, and Work Organization in American Establishments," *Industrial Relations* 34 (April 1995): 125–46. Peter Cappelli et al., *Change at Work* (New York: Oxford University Press, 1997). Malcolm S. Cohen and Mahmood A. Zaidi, *Global Skills Shortages* (Cheltenham, UK: Edward Elgar, 2002).

13. Tony Carnevale, "The Coming Labor and Skills Shortage," *T+D* (January 2005): 37–41 at 38.

14. Cappelli et al., *Change at Work*. Gordon Lafer, *The Job Training Charade* (Ithaca, N.Y.: Cornell University Press, 2002). Morris M. Kleiner, *Licensing Occupations: Ensuring Quality or Restricting Competition?* (Kalamazoo, Mich.: Upjohn, 2005).

15. Barry Bluestone and Irving Bluestone, *Negotiating the Future: A Labor*

Perspective on American Business (New York: Basic Books, 1992). Michael J. Piore and Charles F. Sabel, *The Second Industrial Divide: Possibilities for Prosperity* (New York: Basic Books, 1984). Eileen Appelbaum and Rosemary Batt, *The New American Workplace: Transforming Work Systems in the United States* (Ithaca, N.Y.: ILR Press, 1994). Alan McKinlay, "Knowledge Management," in Stephen Ackroyd et al., eds., *The Oxford Handbook of Work and Organization* (Oxford: Oxford University Press, 2005), 242–62. Conroy, *Sustaining the New Economy.*

16. Katharine G. Abraham and Susan N. Houseman, "Does Employment Protection Inhibit Labor Market Flexibility? Lessons from Germany, France, and Belgium," in Rebecca M. Blank, ed., *Social Protection Versus Economic Flexibility: Is There a Trade-Off?* (Chicago: University of Chicago Press, 1994), 59–93. Organization for Economic Cooperation and Development, *Benefits and Wages: OECD Indicators 2004* (Paris, 2004). European Industrial Relations Observatory, "Working Time Developments—2004" (Dublin: European Foundation for the Improvement of Living and Working Conditions, 2005), http://www.eiro.eurofound.ie/2005/03/update/tn0503104u.html [accessed August 10, 2005].

17. Francine D. Blau and Lawrence M. Kahn, *At Home and Abroad: U.S. Labor-Market Performance in International Perspective* (New York: Russell Sage Foundation, 2002). Horst Siebert, "Labor Market Rigidities: At the Root of Unemployment in Europe," *Journal of Economic Perspectives* 11 (Summer 1997): 37–54.

18. Rebecca M. Blank, "The Misdiagnosis of Eurosclerosis," *American Prospect* (January–February 1997): 81–85. Abraham and Houseman, "Does Employment Protection Inhibit Labor Market Flexibility?" Dean Baker et al., "Labor Market Institutions and Unemployment: Assessment of the Cross-Country Evidence," in David R. Howell, ed., *Fighting Unemployment: The Limits of Free Market Orthodoxy* (New York: Oxford University Press, 2005), 72–118. Giuseppe Bertola, Tito Boeri, and Sandrine Cazes, "Employment Protection in Industrialized Countries: The Case for New Indicators," *International Labour Review* 139 (2000): 57–72. Stephen Nickell, "Unemployment and Labor Market Rigidities: Europe Versus North America," *Journal of Economic Perspectives* 11 (Summer 1997): 55-74. Ronald Schettkat, "Is Labor Market Regulation at the Root of European Unemployment? The Case of Germany and the Netherlands," in David R. Howell, ed., *Fighting Unemployment: The Limits of Free Market Orthodoxy* (New York: Oxford University Press, 2005), 262–83. Blau and Kahn, *At Home and Abroad.* Mishel, Bernstein, and Allegretto, *The State of Working America.*

19. Ton Wilthagen and Frank Tros, "The Concept of 'Flexicurity': A New Approach to Regulating Employment and Labour Markets," *Transfer: European Review of Labour and Research* 10 (Summer 2004): 166–86.

20. Richard S. Belous, *The Contingent Economy: The Growth of the Temporary, Part-Time and Subcontracted Workforce* (Washington, D.C.: National Planning Association, 1989). Richard N. Belous, "The Rise of the Contingent Work Force: The Key Challenges and Opportunities," *Washington and Lee Law Review* 52 (1995): 863–78. Sanford M. Jacoby, *Employing Bureaucracy: Managers, Unions, and the Transformation of Work in American Industry, 1900–1945* (New York: Columbia University Press, 1985).

21. Jennifer Middleton, "Contingent Workers in a Changing Economy: Endure, Adapt or Organize?" *New York University Review of Law and Social Change* 22 (1996): 557–621. Stephen F. Befort, "Revisiting the Black Hole of Workplace Regulation: A Historical and Comparative Perspective of Contingent Work," *Berkeley Journal of Employment and Labor Law* 24 (2003): 153–78. Commission on the Future of Worker-Management Relations, *Report and Recommendations* (Washington, D.C.: U.S. Departments of Labor and Commerce, 1994). Arne L. Kalleberg, "Evolving Employment Relations in the United States," in Ivar Berg and Arne L. Kalleberg, eds., *Sourcebook of Labor Markets: Evolving Structures and Processes* (New York: Kluwer Academic, 2001), 187–206. Sharon Cohany et al., "Counting the Workers: Results of a First Survey," in Kathleen Barker and Kathleen Christensen, eds., *Contingent Work: American Employment Relations in Transition* (Ithaca, N.Y.: ILR Press, 1998), 41–68. Belous, "The Rise of the Contingent Work Force."

22. Maria O'Brien Hylton, "The Case Against Regulating the Market for Contingent Employment," *Washington and Lee Law Review* 52 (1995): 849–62. Belous, *The Contingent Economy*. Stanley D. Nollen and Helen Axel, "Benefits and Costs to Employers," in Kathleen Barker and Kathleen Christensen, eds., *Contingent Work: American Employment Relations in Transition* (Ithaca, N.Y.: ILR Press, 1998), 126–43.

23. Frederick Winslow Taylor, *The Principles of Scientific Management* (New York: Harper and Brothers, 1911). Robert Kanigel, *The One Best Way: Frederick Winslow Taylor and the Enigma of Efficiency* (New York: Penguin, 1997). Jacoby, *Employing Bureaucracy*. Daniel Nelson, *Frederick W. Taylor and the Rise of Scientific Management* (Madison: University of Wisconsin Press, 1980).

24. Appelbaum and Batt, *The New American Workplace*.

25. Carmen DeNavas-Walt, Bernadette D. Proctor, and Jessica Smith, *Income, Poverty, and Health Insurance Coverage in the United States: 2007*, U.S. Census Bureau Current Population Reports, P60-233 (Washington, D.C.: U.S. Government Printing Office, 2007). Pamela Farley Short, "Counting and Characterizing the Uninsured," in Catherine G. McLaughlin, ed., *Health Policy and the Uninsured* (Washington, D.C.: Urban Institute Press, 2004), 1–34.

26. Kaiser Family Foundation, "Employer Health Benefits 2006 Annual Survey" (Menlo Park, Calif., 2006), http://www.kff.org/insurance/7527/ [accessed December 23, 2006]. The National Coalition on Health Care, "Health Insurance Cost" (Washington, D.C., 2006), http://www.nchc.org/facts/cost.shtml [accessed December 23, 2006]. Jason S. Lee and Laura Tollen, "How Low Can You Go? The Impact of Reduced Benefits and Increased Cost Sharing," *Health Affairs—Web Exclusive* (June 19, 2002), http://content.healthaffairs.org/cgi/content/full/hlthaff.w2.229v1/D.C.1 [accessed April 11, 2005]. Roberto Ceniceros, "Unions Fight Cost-Shifting," *Business Insurance* 37 (October 20, 2003): 1–2.

27. U.S. Bureau of Labor Statistics, "Employer Costs for Employee Compensation - December 2007" (Washington, D.C.: U.S. Department of Labor, 2008), http://www.bls.gov/ncs/ect/home.htm [accessed May 18, 2008]. Linda J. Blumberg, "Who Pays for Employer-Sponsored Health Insurance?" *Health Affairs* 18

(November/December 1999): 58–61. Brigitte Madrian, "Health Insurance and the Labor Market," in Huizhong Zhou, ed., *The Political Economy of Health Care Reform* (Kalamazoo, Mich.: W. E. Upjohn Institute for Employment Research, 2001), 87–108.

28. Jonathan Gruber and Brigitte Madrian, "Health Insurance, Labor Supply, and Job Mobility: A Critical Review of the Literature," in Catherine G. McLaughlin, ed., *Health Policy and the Uninsured* (Washington, D.C.: Urban Institute Press, 2004), 97–178. Martha Harrison Stinson, "Estimating the Relationship Between Employer-Provided Health Insurance, Worker Mobility, and Wages," Technical Paper No. TP-2002-23 (Washington, D.C.: U.S. Census Bureau, 2003).

29. Elizabeth Docteur and Howard Oxley, "Health-Care Systems: Lessons from the Reform Experience," OECD Health Working Paper No. 9 (Paris: Organization for Economic Cooperation and Development, 2003). Employment Policy Foundation, "Employer Health Insurance Costs Continue to Rise," *Employment Trends* (Washington, D.C.: August 3, 2004), 5, http://www.epf.org/pubs/newsletters/2004/et20040803.pdf [accessed April 11, 2005].

30. U.S. Bureau of Labor Statistics, "Employer Costs for Employee Compensation."

31. Ann C. Hodges, "The Limits of Multiple Rights and Remedies: A Call for Revisiting the Law of the Workplace," *Hofstra Labor and Employment Law Journal* 22 (Spring 2005): 601–26. Clyde W. Summers, "Labor Law as the Century Turns: A Changing of the Guard," *Nebraska Law Review* 67 (1988): 7–27.

32. Stephen F. Befort, "Demystifying Federal Labor and Employment Law Preemption," *Labor Lawyer* 13 (Winter/Spring 1998): 429–43. For an example of exclusive claims see *Giese v. Phoenix Co. of Chicago, Inc.*, 159 Ill.2d 507 (1994). *Ficalora v. Lockheed Corp.*, 193 Cal. App.3d 489 (1987). For examples of parallel claims see *Helmick v. Cincinnati Word Processing, Inc.*, 543 N.E.2d 1212 (Ohio 1989) and *Clay v. Advanced Computer Applications, Inc.*, 370 Pa. Super. 497, 536 A.2d 1375 (1988). For examples of a middle course see *Williams v. Marriott Corp.*, 864 F.Supp. 1168 (M.D. Fla. 1994) and *Wirig v. Kinney Shoe Corp.*, 461 N.W.2d 374 (Minn. 1990).

33. Administrative Office of the United States Courts, *Judicial Business of the United States Courts: 2007 Annual Report of the Director* (Washington, D.C.: U.S. Government Printing Office, 2008). Stuart H. Bompey, Michael Delikat, and Lisa K. McClelland, "The Attack on Arbitration and Mediation of Employment Disputes," *Labor Lawyer* 13 (Summer 1997): 21–86 at 22. James N. Dertouzos and Lynn A. Karoly, *Labor-Market Responses to Employer Liability* (Santa Monica, Calif.: Rand Institute for Civil Justice, 1992).

34. William B. Gould, *Agenda for Reform: The Future of Employment Relationships and the Law* (Cambridge, Mass.: MIT Press, 1993).

35. Susan A. FitzGibbon, "Reflections on *Gilmer* and *Cole*," *Employee Rights and Employment Policy Journal* 1 (1997): 221–62. Lewis L. Maltby, "Private Justice: Employment Arbitration and Civil Rights," *Columbia Human Rights Law Review* 30 (Fall 1998): 29–64.

36. Dertouzos and Karoly, *Labor-Market Responses to Employer Liability*. Denise V. M. Hubert, "Exactly What Is Employment ADR?," *Human Resources Professional* 11 (July–August 1998): 23–27. Howard A. Simon and Yaroslav Sochynsky, "In-House Mediation of Employment Disputes: ADR for the 1990s," *Employee Relations Law Journal* 21 (Summer 1995): 29–52.

37. Cappelli et al., *Change at Work*. Katherine V.W. Stone, "The New Psychological Contract: Implications of the Changing Workplace for Labor and Employment Law," *UCLA Law Review* 48 (February 2001): 519–661. Jacob S. Hacker, *The Great Risk Shift: The Assault on American Jobs, Families, Health Care, and Retirement—And How You Can Fight Back* (New York: Oxford University Press, 2006).

NOTES TO CHAPTER 4

1. John W. Budd, *Employment with a Human Face: Balancing Efficiency, Equity, and Voice* (Ithaca, N.Y.: Cornell University Press, 2004). Jerold Waltman, *The Case for the Living Wage* (New York: Algora, 2004).

2. Peter Cappelli et al., *Change at Work* (New York: Oxford University Press, 1997). Lawrence Mishel, Jared Bernstein, and Sylvia Allegretto, *The State of Working America 2006/2007* (Ithaca, N.Y.: Cornell University Press, 2007).

3. Jefferson Cowie, *Capital Moves: RCA's Seventy-Year Quest for Cheap Labor* (Ithaca, N.Y.: Cornell University Press, 1999). Pete Engardio et al., "Is Your Job Next?" *Business Week*, February 3, 2003, 50–60. Thomas A. Kochan, Harry C. Katz, and Robert B. McKersie, *The Transformation of American Industrial Relations* (New York: Basic Books, 1986). Kim Moody, *Workers in a Lean World: Unions in the International Economy* (London: Verso, 1998). Eileen Appelbaum, Annette Bernhardt, and Richard Murnane, eds., *Low-Wage America: How Employers Are Reshaping Opportunity in the Workplace* (New York: Russell Sage Foundation, 2003).

4. Center on Budget and Policy Priorities, "Whose Recovery? Labor Day 2006 Finds Many Americans Not Sharing in the Growing Economy" (Washington, D.C., 2006), http://www.cbpp.org/policy-points9-1-06.htm [accessed November 6, 2006]. Ellen Galinsky et al., *Overwork in America: When the Way We Work Becomes Too Much* (New York: Families and Work Institute, 2005).

5. Kenneth G. Dau-Schmidt, "Employment in the New Age of Trade and Technology: Implications for Labor and Employment Law," *Indiana Law Journal* 76 (Winter 2001): 1–28 at 25.

6. Mishel, Bernstein, and Allegretto, *The State of Working America*. Barry Bluestone and Stephen Rose, "The Enigma of Working Time Trends," in Lonnie Golden and Deborah M. Figart, eds., *Working Time: International Trends, Theory and Policy Perspectives* (London: Routledge, 2000), 21–37.

7. Fair Labor Standards Act, 29 U.S.C. §§ 201–219.

8. Jerry A. Jacobs and Kathleen Gerson, "Toward a Family-Friendly, Gender-Equitable Work Week," *University of Pennsylvania Journal of Labor and Employment Law* 1 (Fall 1998): 457–72. Juliet B. Schor, *The Overworked American: The Unexpected Decline of Leisure* (New York: Basic Books, 1991).

9. Mishel, Bernstein, and Allegretto, *The State of Working America.* U.S. Bureau of Labor Statistics, "Women in the Labor Force: A Databook," Report 985 (Washington, D.C.: U.S. Department of Labor, 2005). Jody Heymann, *The Widening Gap: Why America's Working Families Are in Jeopardy and What Can Be Done about It* (New York: Basic Books, 2000). Chinhui Juhn and Simon Potter, "Changes in Labor Force Participation in the United States," *Journal of Economic Perspectives* 20 (Summer 2006): 27–46. U.S. Bureau of Labor Statistics, "Employment Characteristics of Families in 2006" (Washington, D.C.: U.S. Department of Labor, 2007), http://www.bls.gov/news.release/famee.toc.htm [accessed May 23, 2008].

10. Stephen F. Befort, "Accommodation at Work: Lessons from the Americans with Disabilities Act and Possibilities for Alleviating the American Worker Time Crunch," *Cornell Journal of Law and Public Policy* 13 (Summer 2004): 615–36. Mishel, Bernstein, and Allegretto, *The State of Working America.* Sangheon Lee, "Working-Hour Gaps: Trends and Issues," in Jon C. Messenger, ed., *Working Time and Workers' Preferences in Industrialized Countries: Finding the Balance* (London: Routledge, 2004), 29–59. Galinsky et al., *Overwork in America.* James T. Bond et al., *The 1997 National Study of the Changing Workforce* (New York: Families and Work Institute, 1998).

11. Sylvia Ann Hewlett, *When the Bough Breaks: The Cost of Neglecting Our Children* (New York: Basic Books, 1991). Toby L. Parcel, Rebecca A. Nickoll, and Mikaela J. Dufur, "The Effects of Parental Work and Maternal Nonemployment on Children's Reading and Math Achievement," *Work and Occupations* 23 (November 1996): 461–83. Sakiko Tanaka, "Parental Leave and Child Health Across OECD Countries," *Economic Journal* 115 (February 2005): F7-F28. Lawrence M. Berger, Jennifer Hill, and Jane Waldfogel, "Maternity Leave, Early Maternal Employment and Child Health and Development in the US," *Economic Journal* 115 (February 2005): F29–F47. Heymann, *The Widening Gap.* Schor, *The Overworked American.* Robert D. Putnam, *Bowling Alone: The Collapse and Revival of American Community* (New York: Simon and Schuster, 2000). Galinsky et al., *Overwork in America.* Robert W. Drago, *Striking a Balance: Work, Family, Life* (Boston: Dollars and Sense, 2007).

12. Family and Medical Leave Act, 29 U.S.C. §§ 2601–2654.

13. David Cantor et al., *Balancing the Needs of Families and Employers: Family and Medical Leave Surveys, 2000 Update* (Washington, D.C.: U.S. Department of Labor, 2001).

14. Cal. Unemp. Ins. Code § 3300 (West Supp. 2008). Nina G. Golden, "Pregnancy and Maternity Leave: Taking Baby Steps Towards Effective Policies," *Journal of Law and Family Studies* 8 (2006): 1–38. N.J. Stat. Ann. § 34.11B-1-15 (West Supp. 2008). N.J. Stat. Ann. § 34.11B-1-15 (West Supp. 2008). Wash. Rev. Code Ann. § 49.12.360 (West Supp. 2008).

15. Jodi Grant, Taylor Hatcher, and Nirali Patel, *Expecting Better: A State-by-State Analysis of Parental Leave Programs* (Washington, D.C.: National Partnership for Women and Families, 2005). National Partnership for Women and Families, "Get Well Soon: Americans Can't Afford to Be Sick" (Washington, D.C., 2004).

Mishel, Bernstein, and Allegretto, *The State of Working America*. U.S. Bureau of Labor Statistics, "National Compensation Survey: Employee Benefits in Private Industry in the United States, March 2006," Summary 06-05 (Washington, D.C.: U.S. Department of Labor, 2006). Lonnie Golden and Helene Jorgensen, "Time after Time: Mandatory Overtime in the U.S. Economy," EPI Briefing Paper #120 (Washington, D.C.: Economic Policy Institute, 2002).

16. Budd, *Employment with a Human Face*. Waltman, *The Case for the Living Wage*. J. M. Spectar, "Pay Me Fairly, Kathie Lee! The WTO, The Right to a Living Wage, and a Proposed Protocol," *New York Law Journal of International and Comparative Law* 20 (2000): 61–92. John A. Ryan, *A Living Wage: Its Ethical and Economic Aspects* (New York: Macmillan, 1912). Norman E. Bowie, *Business Ethics: A Kantian Perspective* (Malden, Mass.: Blackwell, 1999). Joshua Cohen and Joel Rogers, *On Democracy* (New York: Penguin, 1983).

17. Waltman, *The Case for the Living Wage*. Center on Budget and Policy Priorities, "Buying Power of Minimum Wage at 51-Year Low" (Washington, D.C., 2006), http://www.epinet.org/issuebriefs/224/ib224.pdf [accessed November 10, 2006]. Mishel, Bernstein, and Allegretto, *The State of Working America*. William P. Quigley, *Ending Poverty As We Know It: Guaranteeing a Right to a Job at a Living Wage* (Philadelphia: Temple University Press, 2003). Center on Budget and Policy Priorities, "A $7.25 Minimum Wage Would Be a Useful Step in Helping Working Families Escape Poverty" (Washington, D.C., 2007), http://www.cbpp.org/1-5-07mw.htm [accessed September 23, 2007].

18. Carmen DeNavas-Walt, Bernadette D. Proctor, and Jessica Smith, *Income, Poverty, and Health Insurance Coverage in the United States: 2007*, U.S. Census Bureau Current Population Reports, P60-233 (Washington, D.C.: U.S. Government Printing Office, 2007). CPS Tabulation POV06, http://pubdb3.census.gov/macro/032007/pov/new06_000.htm [accessed May 18, 2008]. Quigley, *Ending Poverty As We Know It*. Barbara Ehrenreich, *Nickeled and Dimed: On (Not) Getting By in America* (New York: Henry Holt, 2001). Beth Shulman, *The Betrayal of Work: How Low-Wage Jobs Fail 30 Million Americans and Their Families* (New York: The New Press, 2003). David K. Shipler, *The Working Poor: Invisible in America* (New York: Alfred A. Knopf, 2004). Katherine S. Newman, *No Shame in My Game: The Working Poor in the Inner City* (New York: Alfred A. Knopf, 1999).

19. Peter Gottschalk and Sheldon Danziger, "Inequality of Wage Rates, Earnings and Family Income in the United States, 1975-2002," *Review of Income and Wealth* 51 (June 2005): 231–54. Thomas Piketty and Emmanuel Saez, "Income Inequality in The United States, 1913-1998," *Quarterly Journal of Economics* 118 (February 2003): 1–39.

20. Mishel, Bernstein, and Allegretto, *The State of Working America*. Waltman, *The Case for the Living Wage*.

21. Mishel, Bernstein, and Allegretto, *The State of Working America*. Martin J. McMahon, Jr. and Alice G. Abreu, "Winner-Take-All Markets: Easing the Case for Progressive Taxation," *Florida Tax Review* 4 (1998): 1–81. Thomas Piketty and Emmanuel Saez, "How Progressive Is the U.S. Federal Tax System? A Historical and International Perspective," *Journal of Economic Perspectives* 21 (Winter 2007):

3-24. Center on Budget and Policy Priorities, "Recent Tax and Income Trends Among High-Income Taxpayers" (Washington, D.C., 2006), http://www.cbpp.org/4-10-06tax5.htm [accessed November 12, 2006].

22. Ehrenreich, *Nickeled and Dimed*. Ray F. Marshall, ed., *Back to Shared Prosperity: The Growing Inequality of Wealth and Income in America* (Armonk, N.Y.: M. E. Sharpe, 2000). Kathryn M. Neckerman, ed., *Social Inequality* (New York: Russell Sage Foundation, 2004). Waltman, *The Case for the Living Wage*. Alan B. Krueger, "Inequality, Too Much of a Good Thing," in Benjamin M. Friedman, ed., *Inequality in America: What Role for Human Capital Policies?* (Cambridge, Mass.: MIT Press, 2003), 1–75. Pablo Fajnzylber, Daniel Lederman, and Norman Loayza, "Inequality and Violent Crime," *Journal of Law and Economics* 45 (April 2002): 1–40.

23. Robert MacCulloch, "Income Inequality and the Taste for Revolution," *Journal of Law and Economics* 48 (April 2005): 93–123.

24. Jacob S. Hacker, *The Great Risk Shift: The Assault on American Jobs, Families, Health Care, and Retirement—And How You Can Fight Back* (New York: Oxford University Press, 2006). International Labor Office, *Economic Security for a Better World* (Geneva: International Labor Organization, 2004).

25. Alan Derickson, *Health Security for All: Dreams of Universal Health Care in America* (Baltimore: Johns Hopkins University Press, 2005). Jacob S. Hacker, *The Divided Welfare State: The Battle over Public and Private Social Benefits in the United States* (New York: Cambridge University Press, 2002). Jennifer Klein, *For All These Rights: Business, Labor, and the Shaping of America's Public-Private Welfare State* (Princeton, N.J.: Princeton University Press, 2003). Greg J. Duncan and P. Lindsay Chase-Lansdale, eds., *For Better and for Worse: Welfare Reform and the Well-Being of Children and Families* (New York: Russell Sage Foundation, 2001).

26. Hacker, *The Great Risk Shift*, 31–32. Michael J. Mandel, *The High-Risk Society: Peril and Promise in the New Economy* (New York: Times Books, 1996). Peter G. Gosselin, "If America Is Richer, Why Are Its Families So Much Less Secure?" *Los Angeles Times*, October 10, 2004. Peter G. Gosselin, "The Poor Have More Things Today—Including Wild Income Swings," *Los Angeles Times*, December 12, 2004.

27. Dirk Krueger and Fabrizio Perri, "Does Income Inequality Lead to Consumption Inequality? Evidence and Theory," *Review of Economic Studies* 73 (January 2006): 163–93. Josep Pijoan-Mas, "Precautionary Savings or Working Longer Hours?" *Review of Economic Dynamics* 9 (April 2006): 326–52.

28. Christopher J. O'Leary and Stephen A. Wandner, eds., *Unemployment Insurance in the United States: Analysis of Policy Issues* (Kalamazoo, Mich.: W. E. Upjohn Institute for Employment Research, 1997). Walter Nicholson and Karen Needels, "Unemployment Insurance: Strengthening the Relationship between Theory and Policy," *Journal of Economic Perspectives* 20 (Summer 2006): 47–70. David I. Levine, *Working in the Twenty-First Century: Policies for Economic Growth Through Training, Opportunity, and Education* (Armonk, N.Y.: M. E. Sharpe, 1998).

29. Nicholson and Needels, "Unemployment Insurance."

30. Walter Corson, Karen Needels, and Walter Nicholson, "Emergency Unemployment Compensation: The 1990s Experience," Unemployment Insurance Occasional Paper No. 99-4 (Washington, D.C.: U.S. Department of Labor, 1999).

31. Michael J. Graetz and Jerry L. Mashaw, *True Security: Rethinking American Social Insurance* (New Haven: Yale University Press, 1999).

32. Demos and Center for Responsible Lending, "The Plastic Safety Net: The Reality Behind Debt in America" (New York, 2005). Tamara Draut and Javier Silva, "Borrowing to Make Ends Meet: The Growth of Credit Card Debt in the '90s" (New York: Demos, 2003). Hacker, *The Great Risk Shift*. Elisabeth Jacobs, "The Politics of Economic Insecurity," Issues in Governance Studies #10 (Washington, D.C.: Brookings Institution, 2007).

33. Board of Trustees, Federal Old-Age and Survivors Insurance and Disability Insurance Trust Funds, *2008 Annual Report* (Washington, D.C.: U.S. Government Printing Office, 2008). Peter A. Diamond and Peter R. Orszag, *Saving Social Security: A Balanced Approach* (Washington, D.C.: Brookings Institution Press, 2004). Laurence J. Kotlikoff and Scott Burns, *The Coming Generational Storm: What You Need to Know about America's Economic Future* (Cambridge, Mass.: MIT Press, 2004).

34. U.S. Government Accountability Office, "Social Security Reform: Answers to Key Questions," GAO-05-193SP (Washington, D.C., 2005). Congressional Budget Office, *Social Security: A Primer* (Washington, D.C., 2001). Social Security Administration, "Annual Statistical Supplement to the Social Security Bulletin: 2005" (Washington, D.C., 2006), http://www.ssa.gov/policy/docs/statcomps/supplement/2005 [accessed January 7, 2007]. Social Security Advisory Board, "Why Action Should Be Taken Soon" (Washington, D.C., 2005), http://www.ssab.gov/documents/WhyActionShouldbeTakenSoon.pdf [accessed January 7, 2007].

35. Pension Protection Act of 2006, Pub. L. No. 109-280, Stat. 780. Stephen F. Befort, "The Perfect Storm of Retirement Insecurity: Fixing the Three-Legged Stool of Social Security, Pensions, and Personal Savings," *Minnesota Law Review* 91 (April 2007): 938–88.

36. U.S. General Accounting Office, "Private Pensions: Issues of Coverage and Increasing Contribution Limits for Defined Contribution Plans," GAO-01-846 (Washington, D.C., 2001). Craig Copeland, "Employment-Based Retirement Plan Participation: Geographic Differences and Trends, 2005," EBRI Issue Brief No. 299 (Washington, D.C.: Employee Benefit Research Institute, 2006). Craig Copeland, "Retirement Plan Participation: Survey of Income and Program Participation (SIPP) Data," EBRI Notes No. 9 (Washington, D.C.: Employee Benefit Research Institute, 2005). Alicia H. Munnell, Annika Sundén, and Catherine Taylor, "What Determines 401(k) Participation and Contributions?" *Social Security Bulletin* 64 (2001/2002): 64–75. Brigitte C. Madrian and Dennis F. Shea, "The Power of Suggestion: Inertia in 401(k) Participation and Savings Behavior," *Quarterly Journal of Economics* 116 (November 2001): 1149–87. Hacker, *The Great Risk Shift*.

37. Marshall B. Reinsdorf, "Alternative Measures of Personal Saving," *Survey of Current Business* 87 (February 2007): 7–13. Jonathan Clements, "Forget the Rule of Thumb: Saving 10% of Your Salary Is No Longer Enough," *Wall Street Journal*, July 20, 2005. Employee Benefit Research Institute. "2006 RCS Fact Sheet: Saving For Retirement in America" (Washington, D.C., 2006), http://www.ebri.org/pdf/RCS06_FS_01_Saving_Final.pdf [accessed January 7, 2007].

38. Barbara Butrica, Howard Iams, and Karen E. Smith, "The Changing Impact of Social Security on Retirement Income in the United States," *Social Security Bulletin* 65 (2003/04): 1–13. Mark J. Warshawsky and John Ameriks, "How Prepared Are Americans for Retirement?" in Olivia S. Mitchell, P. Brett Hammond, and Anna M. Rappaport, eds., *Forecasting Retirement Needs and Retirement Wealth* (Philadelphia: University of Pennsylvania Press, 2000), 33–67. Robert Haveman et al., "Do Newly Retired Workers in the United States Have Sufficient Resources to Maintain Well-Being?" *Economic Inquiry* 44 (April 2006): 249–64.

39. Elizabeth Docteur and Howard Oxley, "Health-Care Systems: Lessons from the Reform Experience," OECD Health Working Paper No. 9 (Paris: Organization for Economic Cooperation and Development, 2003). Organization for Economic Cooperation and Development, *OECD Health Data 2006: Statistics and Indicators for 30 Countries* (Paris, 2006).

40. Graetz and Mashaw, *True Security*, 127.

41. Center on Budget and Policy Priorities, "More Americans, Including More Children, Now Lack Health Insurance" (Washington, D.C., 2007), http://www.cbpp.org/8-28-07health.htm [accessed May 23, 2008].

42. U.S. Census Bureau, "Income, Poverty, and Health Insurance Coverage in the United States." Paul Fronstin, "Sources of Health Insurance and Characteristics of the Uninsured: Analysis of the March 2007 Current Population Survey," EBRI Issue Brief No. 310 (Washington, D.C.: Employment Benefit Research Institute, 2007). Families USA, "Wrong Direction: One Out of Three Americans Are Uninsured," Families USA Publication No. 07-108 (Washington, D.C., 2007).

43. Karen Davis, "Health Care for Low-Income People," in Ray Marshall, ed., *Back to Shared Prosperity: The Growing Inequality of Wealth and Income in America* (Armonk, N.Y.: M. E. Sharpe, 2000), 311–20. Fronstin, "Sources of Health Insurance and Characteristics of the Uninsured." Jack Hadley, "Sicker and Poorer—The Consequences of Being Uninsured: A Review of the Research on the Relationship Between Health Insurance, Medical Care Use, Health, Work, and Income," *Medical Care Research and Review* 60 (June 2003): 3S–75S. Hacker, *The Great Risk Shift*.

44. U.S. Bureau of Labor Statistics, "National Compensation Survey." Families USA, "Have Health Insurance? Think You're Well Protected? Think Again!" (Washington, D.C., 2005), http://www.familiesusa.org/assets/pdfs/health-care-think-again.PDF [accessed December 3, 2006].

45. Employee Retirement Income Security Act, 29 U.S.C. §§ 1001–1461.

46. *Aetna Health, Inc. v. Davila*, 542 U.S. 200 (2004).

47. Peter J. Wiedenbeck, "ERISA's Curious Coverage," *Washington University Law Quarterly* 76 (Spring 1998): 311–50. Stephen F. Befort and Christopher J. Kopka, "The Sounds of Silence: The Libertarian Ethos of ERISA Preemption," *Florida Law Review* 52 (January 2000): 1–40. Hacker, *The Great Risk Shift*. Donald L. Barlett and James B. Steele, *Critical Condition: How Health Care in America Became Big Business—and Bad Medicine* (New York: Doubleday, 2004).

48. Päivi Hämäläinen, Jukka Takala, and Kaija Leena Saarela, "Global Estimates of Occupational Accidents," *Safety Science* 44 (February 2006): 137–56. J. Takala, "Introductory Report: Decent Work–Safe Work," XVIth World Congress on Safety and Health at Work (Vienna, May 27, 2002), http://www.ilo.org/public/english/protection/safework/wdcongrs/ilo_rep.pdf [accessed November 13, 2006]. U.S. Bureau of Labor Statistics. "Census of Fatal Occupational Injuries Summary, 2005" (Washington, D.C.: U.S. Department of Labor, 2006), http://www.bls.gov/news.release/cfoi.nro.htm [accessed November 13, 2006]. U.S. Bureau of Labor Statistics. "Workplace Injuries and Illnesses in 2005" (Washington, D.C.: U.S. Department of Labor, 2006), http://www.bls.gov/news.release/osh.nro.htm [accessed November 13, 2006]. Mark D. Brenner, David Fairris, and John Ruser, "'Flexible' Work Practices and Occupational Safety and Health: Exploring the Relationship between Cumulative Trauma Disorders and Workplace Transformation," *Industrial Relations* 43 (January 2004): 242–66.

49. Judson MacLaury, "The Job Safety Law of 1970: Its Passage Was Perilous" *Monthly Labor Review* 104 (March 1981): 18–24. Price V. Fishback and Shawn Everett Kantor, *A Prelude to the Welfare State: The Origins of Workers' Compensation* (Chicago: University of Chicago Press, 2000).

50. Occupational Safety and Health Act, 29 U.S.C. §§ 651–678.

51. MacLaury, "The Job Safety Law of 1970." Barry T. Hirsch, "Incentive Effects of Workers' Compensation," *Clinical Orthopaedics and Related Research* 336 (March 1997): 33–41. Thomas J. Kniesner and John D. Leeth, "Abolishing OSHA," *Regulation* 18 (Fall 1995): 46–56. Elizabeth A. Lambrecht Karels, "Make Employers Accountable for Workplace Safety! How the Dirty Little Secret of Workers' Compensation Puts Employees at Risk and Why Criminal Prosecution and Civil Action Will Save Lives and Money," *Hamline Journal of Public Law and Policy* 26 (Fall 2004): 111–49. Cynthia Estlund, "Rebuilding the Law of the Workplace in an Era of Self-Regulation," *Columbia Law Review* 105 (March 2005): 319–404. Daniel B. Klaff, "Evaluating Work: Enforcing Occupational Safety and Health Standards in the United States, Canada, and Sweden," *University of Pennsylvania Journal of Labor and Employment Law* 7 (Spring 2005): 613–59. AFL-CIO, *Death on the Job: The Toll of Neglect—A National and State-By-State Profile of Worker Safety and Health in the United States* (Washington, D.C., 2008). International Labor Office, "Strategies and Practice for Labour Inspection," GB.297/ESP/3 (Geneva: International Labor Organization, 2006).

52. Golden and Jorgensen, "Time after Time." Tosh Anderson, "Overwork Robs Workers' Health: Interpreting OSHA's General Duty Clause to Prohibit Long Work Hours," *New York City Law Review* 7 (Spring 2004) 85–160. Mara

Eleina Conway, "*Karoshi*: Is It Sweeping America?" *UCLA Pacific Basin Law Journal* 15 (Spring 1997): 352–80.

53. Equal Pay Act of 1963, 29 U.S.C. § 206(d). Title VII of the Civil Rights Act of 1964, 42 U.S.C. § 2000e-17. Nelson Lichtenstein, *State of the Union: A Century of American Labor* (Princeton, N.J.: Princeton University Press, 2002).

54. Age Discrimination in Employment Act of 1967, 29 U.S.C. §§ 621–634. Americans with Disabilities Act of 1990, 42 U.S.C. §§ 12101–12213. George Rutherglen, *Employment Discrimination Law: Visions of Equality in Theory and Doctrine* (New York: Foundation Press, 2001).

55. *Griggs v. Duke Power Co.*, 401 U.S. 424 (1971).

56. Rutherglen, *Employment Discrimination Law.*

57. Lewis L. Maltby, "Private Justice: Employment Arbitration and Civil Rights," *Columbia Human Rights Law Review* 30 (Fall 1998): 29–64. Christine Jolls, "The Role and Functioning of Public-Interest Legal Organizations in the Enforcement of the Employment Laws," in Richard B. Freeman, Joni Hersch, and Lawrence Mishel, eds., *Emerging Labor Market Institutions for the Twenty-First Century* (Chicago: University of Chicago Press, 2005), 141–76.

58. *Sutton v. United Air Lines, Inc.*, 527 U.S. 471 (1999). See also *Murphy v. United Parcel Serv., Inc.*, 527 U.S. 516 (1999); *Albertson's, Inc. v. Kirkingburg*, 527 U.S. 555 (1999); *Toyota Motor Mfg., Ky., Inc. v. Williams*, 534 U.S. 184 (2002).

59. Stephen F. Befort, "The Story of *Sutton v. United Airlines, Inc.*: Narrowing the Reach of the Americans with Disabilities Act," in Joel Wm. Friedman, ed., *Employment Discrimination Stories* (New York: Foundation Press, 2006), 329–62. Ruth Colker, *The Disability Pendulum: The First Decade of the Americans with Disabilities Act* (New York: New York University Press, 2005).

60. ADA Amendments Act of 2008, S. 3406, 110th Cong. (2008).

61. *Bammert v. Don's SuperValu, Inc.*, 646 N.W.2d 365 (Wisc. 2002).

62. *McConchie v. Wal-Mart Stores, Inc.*, 985 F.Supp. 273 (N.D.N.Y. 1997).

63. *Andersen v. Mid-Plains Comm.*, 394 N.W.2d 316 (Wisc. Ct. App. 1986).

64. *Payne v. Western and Atlantic R.R. Co.*, 81 Tenn. 507, 519–520 (1884).

65. Clyde W. Summers, "Individual Protection Against Unjust Dismissal: Time for a Statute," *Virginia Law Review* 62 (April 1976): 481–532. Cynthia L. Estlund, "Wrongful Discharge Protections in an At-Will World," *Texas Law Review* 74 (June 1996): 1655–92. Charles J. Muhl, "The Employment-at-Will Doctrine: Three Major Exceptions," *Monthly Labor Review* 124 (January 2001): 3–11. Robert C. Bird, "Rethinking Wrongful Discharge: A Continuum Approach," *University of Cincinnati Law Review* 73 (Winter 2004): 517–79.

66. Alexander J. S. Colvin, "Flexibility and Fairness in Liberal Market Economies: The Comparative Impact of the Legal Environment and High-Performance Work Systems," *British Journal of Industrial Relations* 26 (March 2006): 73–97.

67. *McLaughlin v. Gastrointestinal Specialists* (561 Pa. 307, 2000).

68. *Luteran v. Loral Fairchild Corp.* (455 Pa. Supp. 364, 1997).

69. Scott A. Moss, "Where There's a Will, There Are Many Ways: Redressing the Increased Incoherence of Employment-at-Will," *University of Pittsburgh Law Review* 67 (Winter 2005): 295–363.

70. Joseph E. Slater, "The 'American Rule' That Swallows the Exceptions," *Employee Rights and Employment Policy Journal* 11 (2007): 53–110 at 98.

71. Jack Stieber, "Most U.S. Workers Still May Be Fired under the Employment-at-Will Doctrine," *Monthly Labor Review* 107 (May 1984): 34–38 at 36.

72. Colvin, "Flexibility and Fairness in Liberal Market Economies." Stewart J. Schwab and Randall S. Thomas, "An Empirical Analysis of CEO Employment Contracts: What Do Top Executive Bargain For?" *Washington and Lee Law Review* 63 (Winter 2006): 231–70. Bob Hepple, "European Rules on Dismissals," *Comparative Labor Law Journal* 18 (1997): 382-407. International Labor Office, "Termination of Employment Legislation Digest" (Geneva: International Labor Organization, 2006), http://www.ilo.org/public/english/dialogue/ifpdial/info/termination/ [accessed November 24, 2006]. Ann C. McGinley, "Rethinking Civil Rights and Employment at Will: Toward a Coherent Discharge Policy," *Ohio State Law Journal* 57 (1996): 1443–1524. Slater, "The 'American Rule' That Swallows the Exceptions."

73. Cappelli et al., *Change at Work*. Katherine V. W. Stone, *From Widgets to Digits: Employment Regulation for the Changing Workplace* (Cambridge: Cambridge University Press, 2004). Thomas A. Kochan, Harry C. Katz, and Robert B. McKersie, *The Transformation of American Industrial Relations* (New York: Basic Books, 1986).

74. Slater, "The 'American Rule' That Swallows the Exceptions."

75. Richard B. Freeman and Joel Rogers, *What Workers Want*, updated ed. (Ithaca, N.Y.: Cornell University Press, 2006). Pauline T. Kim, "Bargaining with Imperfect Information: A Study of Worker Perceptions of Legal Protection in an At-Will World," *Cornell Law Review* 83 (November 1997): 105–60. Jesse Rudy, "What They Don't Know Won't Hurt Them: Defending Employment-at-Will in Light of Findings That Employees Believe They Possess Just Cause Protection," *Berkeley Journal of Employment and Labor Law* 23 (2002): 307–67. Ellen Dannin, *Taking Back the Workers' Law: How to Fight the Assault on Labor Rights* (Ithaca, N.Y.: Cornell University Press, 2006), 22.

76. Helene Jorgensen and Robert E. McGarrah, Jr., "Contingent Workers: Health and Pension Security," in Sheldon Friedman and David C. Jacobs, eds., *The Future of the Safety Net: Social Insurance and Employee Benefits* (Champaign, Ill.: Industrial Relations Research Association, 2001), 225–38. Katherine M. Forster, "Strategic Reform of Contingent Work," *Southern California Law Review* 74 (January 2001): 541–76. Jennifer Middleton, "Contingent Workers in a Changing Economy: Endure, Adapt or Organize?" *New York University Review of Law and Social Change* 22 (1996): 557–621. Kenneth G. Dau-Schmidt, "The Labor Market Transformed: Adapting Labor and Employment Law to the Rise of the Contingent Work Force," *Washington and Lee Law Review* 52 (1995): 879–88. Clyde W. Summers, "Contingent Employment in the United States," *Comparative Labor Law Journal* 18 (Summer 1997): 503–22. Kathleen Barker and Kathleen Christensen, eds., *Contingent Work: American Employment Relations in Transition* (Ithaca, N.Y.: ILR Press, 1998).

77. Anthony P. Carnevale, Lynn A. Jennings, and James M. Eisenmann,

"Contingent Workers and Employment Law," in Kathleen Barker and Kathleen Christensen, eds., *Contingent Work: American Employment Relations in Transition* (Ithaca, N.Y.: ILR Press, 1998), 281–305.

78. Stephen F. Befort, "Revisiting the Black Hole of Workplace Regulation: A Historical and Comparative Perspective of Contingent Work," *Berkeley Journal of Employment and Labor Law* 24 (2003): 153–78.

79. Annette Bernhardt et al., eds., *The Gloves-Off Economy: Workplace Standards at the Bottom of America's Labor Market* (Champaign, Ill.: Industrial Relations Research Association, 2008).

80. Dan Zuberi, *Differences That Matter: Social Policy and the Working Poor in the United States and Canada* (Ithaca, N.Y.: Cornell University Press, 2006). Mark Robert Rank, *One Nation, Underprivileged: Why American Poverty Affects Us All* (New York: Oxford University Press, 2004).

NOTES TO CHAPTER 5

1. Rick Detorie, "One Big Happy" (May 29, 2005). Richard B. Freeman and Joel Rogers, *What Workers Want*, updated ed. (Ithaca, N.Y.: Cornell University Press, 2006). Richard B. Freeman, Peter Boxall, and Peter Haynes, eds., *What Workers Say: Employee Voice in the Anglo-American World* (Ithaca, N.Y.: Cornell University Press, 2007). Debra L. Shapiro and Jeanne M. Brett, "What Is the Role of Control in Organizational Justice?" in Jerald Greenberg and Jason A. Colquit, eds., *Handbook of Organizational Justice* (Mahwah, N.J.: Erlbaum, 2005), 155–77.

2. John W. Budd, *Employment with a Human Face: Balancing Efficiency, Equity, and Voice* (Ithaca, N.Y.: Cornell University Press, 2004). Tony Dundon, Adrian Wilkinson, Mick Marchington, and Peter Ackers, "The Meanings and Purpose of Employee Voice," *International Journal of Human Resource Management* 15 (September 2004): 1149–70. Albert O. Hirschman, *Exit, Voice, and Loyalty: Responses to Decline in Firms, Organizations, and States* (Cambridge, Mass.: Harvard University Press, 1970).

3. Budd, *Employment with a Human Face*. J. A. Estey, *The Labor Problem* (New York: McGraw-Hill, 1928). James A. Gross, "A Human Rights Perspective on U.S. Labor Relations Law: A Violation of the Freedom of Association," *Employee Rights and Employment Policy Journal* 3 (1999): 65–103. Michael J. Naughton, "Participation in the Organization: An Ethical Analysis from the Papal Social Tradition," *Journal of Business Ethics* 14 (November 1995): 923–35. Norman E. Bowie, *Business Ethics: A Kantian Perspective* (Malden, Mass.: Blackwell, 1999). Lewis D. Solomon, "Perspectives on Human Nature and their Implications for Business Organizations," *Fordham Urban Law Journal* 23 (Winter 1996): 221–56. Thomas Donaldson and Lee E. Preston, "The Stakeholder Theory of the Corporation: Concepts, Evidence, and Implications," *Academy of Management Review* 20 (January 1995): 65–91. Carole Pateman, *Participation and Democratic Theory* (London: Cambridge University Press, 1970).

4. Randy Hodson, *Dignity at Work* (Cambridge: Cambridge University Press, 2001), 237.

5. Eugene Volokh, "Freedom of Speech and Workplace Harassment," *UCLA Law Review* 39 (August 1992): 1791–1872. Vicki Schultz, "The Sanitized Workplace," *Yale Law Journal* 112 (June 2003): 2061–2193.

6. Volokh, "Freedom of Speech and Workplace Harassment," 1849.

7. Bruce Barry, *Speechless: The Erosion of Free Expression in the American Workplace* (San Francisco: Berrett-Koehler, 2007). David C. Yamada, "Voices from the Cubicle: Protecting and Encouraging Private Employee Speech in the Post-Industrial Workplace," *Berkeley Journal of Employment and Labor Law* 19 (1998): 1–59. Cass R. Sunstein, *Republic.com* (Princeton, N.J.: Princeton University Press, 2001). Cynthia Estlund, *Working Together: How Workplace Bonds Strengthen a Diverse Democracy* (Oxford: Oxford University Press, 2003). Cynthia L. Estlund, "Free Speech and Due Process in the Workplace," *Indiana Law Journal* 71 (Winter 1995): 101–51. Terry Ann Halbert, "The First Amendment in the Workplace: An Analysis and Call for Reform," *Seton Hall Law Review* 17 (1987): 42–72.

8. Martin H. Redish, "The Value of Free Speech," *University of Pennsylvania Law Review* 130 (January 1982): 591–645. Thomas I. Emerson, "Colonial Intentions and Current Realities of the First Amendment," *University of Pennsylvania Law Review* 125 (April 1977): 737–60.

9. *McLaughlin v. Gastrointestinal Specialists, Inc.*, 696 A.2d 173 (Pa. Super. Ct. 1997).

10. *Prill v. NLRB*, 835 F.2d 1481 (D.C. Cir. 1987).

11. *Daley v. Aetna Life and Casualty*, 734 A.2d 112 (Conn. 1999).

12. *Monahan v. Bausch*, No. CV91 0280862 S., 1991 WL 182825 (Conn. Super. Ct. Sept. 11, 1991).

13. *Bigelow v. Bullard*, 901 P.2d 630 (Nev. 1995).

14. *Drake v. Cheyenne Newspapers, Inc.*, 891 P.2d 80 (Wyo. 1995).

15. *Cotto v. United Tech. Corp.*, 738 A.2d 623 (Conn. 1999).

16. Rafael Gely and Leonard Bierman, "Social Isolation and American Workers: Employee Blogging and Legal Reform," *Harvard Journal of Law and Technology* 20 (Spring 2007): 288–331.

17. Randy J. Kozel, "Reconceptualizing Public Employee Speech," *Northwestern University Law Review* 99 (Spring 2005): 1007–51. Marcy S. Edwards et al., *Freedom of Speech in the Public Workplace: A Legal and Practical Guide to Issues Affecting Public Employment* (Chicago: American Bar Association, 1998). Michael Kent Curtis, *Free Speech, "The People's Darling Privilege": Struggles for Freedom of Expression in American History* (Durham, N.C.: Duke University Press, 2000). *Connick v. Myers*, 461 U.S. 138 (1983). Barry, *Speechless.*

18. *Garcetti v. Ceballos*, 547 U.S. 410 (2006).

19. Daniel P. Wesman, "The Significance of the Sarbanes-Oxley Whistleblower Provision," *Labor Lawyer* 21 (Fall 2005): 141–55. Barry, *Speechless.*

20. National Labor Relations Act, 29 U.S.C. § 157. Cynthia L. Estlund, "What Do Workers Want? Employee Interests, Public Interests, and Freedom of Expression under the National Labor Relations Act," *University of Pennsylvania Law Review* 140 (January 1992): 921–1004.

21. *NLRB v. United Steelworkers*, 357 U.S. 357 (1958). *First National Bank of*

Boston v. Bellotti, 435 U.S. 765 (1978). Paul M. Secunda, "Toward the Viability of State-Based Legislation to Address Workplace Captive Audience Meetings in the United States," *Comparative Labor Law & Policy Journal* 29 (Winter 2008): 209–46. Lawrence Soley, *Censorship Inc.: The Corporate Threat to Free Speech in the United States* (New York: Monthly Review Press, 2002). Lisa B. Bingham, "Employee Free Speech in the Workplace: Using the First Amendment as Public Policy for Wrongful Discharge Actions," *Ohio State Law Journal* 55 (Spring 1994): 341–91.

22. Tom Meersman, "DNR Shifts Gears, Backs Truck Course," *Star Tribune* (Minneapolis), December 25, 2005.

23. J. Richard Hackman and Greg R. Oldham, *Work Redesign* (Reading, Mass.: Addison-Wesley, 1980), 79. Victor H. Vroom, *Work and Motivation* (New York: Wiley, 1964). Marylène Gagné and Edward L. Deci, "Self-Determination Theory and Work Motivation," *Journal of Organizational Behavior* 26 (June 2005): 331–62. Paul E. Spector et al., "Locus of Control and Well-Being at Work: How Generalizable Are Western Findings?" *Academy of Management Journal* 45 (April 2002): 453–66. Moshe Krausz, Abraham Sagie, and Yehuda Bidermann, "Actual and Preferred Work Schedules and Scheduling Control as Determinants of Job-Related Attitudes," *Journal of Vocational Behavior* 56 (February 2000): 1–11. Claus W. Langfred and Neta A. Moye, "Effects of Task Autonomy on Performance: An Extended Model Considering Motivational, Informational, and Structural Mechanisms," *Journal of Applied Psychology* 89 (December 2004): 934–45. Katherine I. Miller and Peter R. Monge, "Participation, Satisfaction, and Productivity: A Meta-Analytic Review," *Academy of Management Journal* 29 (December 1986): 727–53.

24. Richard M. Ryan and Edward L. Deci, "An Overview of Self-Determination Theory: An Organismic-Dialectical Perspective," in Edward L. Deci and Richard M. Ryan, eds., *Handbook of Self-Determination Research* (Rochester, N.Y.: University of Rochester Press, 2002), 3–33. Chris Argyris, *Personality and Organization: The Conflict Between System and the Individual* (New York: Harper and Row, 1957). Harry T. Reis et al., "Daily Well-Being: The Role of Autonomy, Competence, and Relatedness," *Personality and Social Psychology Bulletin* 26 (April 2000): 419–35. Gagné and Deci, "Self-Determination Theory and Work Motivation."

25. Spector et al., "Locus of Control and Well-Being at Work." Robert Karasek, "Control in the Workplace and Its Health-Related Aspects," in Steven L. Sauter, Joseph J. Hurrell, Jr., and Cary L. Cooper, eds., *Job Control and Worker Health* (Chichester, UK: Wiley, 1989), 129–59. David Wainwright and Michael Calnan, *Work Stress: The Making of a Modern Epidemic* (Buckingham, UK: Open University Press, 2002). L. Ala-Mursula et al., "Employee Control over Working Times: Associations with Subjective Health and Sickness Absences," *Journal of Epidemiology and Community Health* 56 (April 2002): 272–78.

26. Hodson, *Dignity at Work*. Harry Braverman, *Labor and Monopoly Capital: The Degradation of Work in the Twentieth Century* (New York: Monthly Review Press, 1974). Emma Rooksby and Natasha Cica, "Personal Autonomy and Electronic Surveillance in the Workplace," in John Weckert, ed., *Electronic Monitoring in the Workplace: Controversies and Solutions* (Hershey, Penn: Idea Group,

2005), 242–59. Norman E. Bowie, "Kantian Ethical Thought," in John W. Budd and James G. Scoville, eds., *The Ethics of Human Resources and Industrial Relations* (Champaign, Ill.: Labor and Employment Relations Association, 2005), 61–87.

27. Hackman and Oldham, *Work Redesign*, 162.

28. Robert Kanigel, *The One Best Way: Frederick Winslow Taylor and the Enigma of Efficiency* (New York: Penguin, 1997). Frederick Winslow Taylor, *The Principles of Scientific Management* (New York: Harper and Brothers, 1911). Daniel Nelson, ed., *A Mental Revolution: Scientific Management Since Taylor* (Columbus: Ohio State University Press, 1992). Eileen Appelbaum and Rosemary Batt, *The New American Workplace: Transforming Work Systems in the United States* (Ithaca, N.Y.: ILR Press, 1994).

29. European Industrial Relations Observatory, "Study Examines Workers' Freedom of Expression on Working Environment" (Dublin: European Foundation for the Improvement of Living and Working Conditions, 1999), http://www.eiro.eurofound.eu.int/1999/10/feature/se9910198f.html [accessed October 11, 2006]. Richard S. Rosenberg, "The Technological Assault on Ethics in the Modern Workplace," in John W. Budd and James G. Scoville, eds., *The Ethics of Human Resources and Industrial Relations* (Champaign, Ill.: Labor and Employment Relations Association, 2005), 141–71. John Weckert, ed., *Electronic Monitoring in the Workplace: Controversies and Solutions* (Hershey, Penn.: Idea Group, 2005). Daniel B. Klaff, "Evaluating Work: Enforcing Occupational Safety and Health Standards in the United States, Canada, and Sweden," *University of Pennsylvania Journal of Labor and Employment Law* 7 (Spring 2005): 613–59.

30. Authors' calculations from the GSS Cumulative Datafile 1972–2004, http://sda.berkeley.edu/cgi-bin/hsda?harcsda+gss04 [accessed October 9, 2006].

31. Freeman and Rogers, *What Workers Want*, 77.

32. Terence M. McMenamin, "A Time to Work: Recent Trends In Shift Work and Flexible Schedules," *Monthly Labor Review* 130 (December 2007): 3–15.

33. European Foundation for the Improvement of Living and Working Conditions, "Third European Working Conditions Survey: Data," 2000, http://www.eurofound.eu.int/working/3wc/3wcindex.htm [accessed October 9, 2006].

34. Bill Harley, "The Myth of Empowerment: Work Organisation, Hierarchy and Employee Autonomy in Contemporary Australian Workplace," *Work, Employment, and Society* (March 1999): 41–66.

35. John W. Budd and Angela Brey, "Unions and Family Leave: Early Experience under the Family and Medical Act," *Labor Studies Journal* 28 (Fall 2003): 85–105. Jane Waldfogel, "Family and Medical Leave: Evidence from the 2000 Surveys," *Monthly Labor Review* 124 (September 2001): 17–23.

36. Pauline T. Kim, "Bargaining with Imperfect Information: A Study of Worker Perceptions of Legal Protection in an At-Will World." *Cornell Law Review* 83 (November 1997): 105–60.

37. John W. Budd, "Does Employee Ignorance Undermine Shared Capitalism?" in Joseph R. Blasi, Richard B. Freeman, and Douglas Kruse, eds., *Shared Capitalism at Work: The Economic Effects of Employee Ownership, Profit Sharing, Gainsharing, and Broad-based Stock Options* (New York: Russell Sage Foundation and

National Bureau of Economic Research, forthcoming). James D. Reschovsky, J. Lee Hargraves, and Albert F. Smith, "Consumer Beliefs and Health Plan Performance: It's Not Whether You Are in an HMO but Whether You Think You Are," *Journal of Health Policy Politics and Law* 27 (June 2002): 353–77. Alan L. Gustman and Thomas L. Steinmeier, "Imperfect Knowledge of Social Security and Pensions," *Industrial Relations* 44 (April 2005): 373–95. John W. Budd and Karen Mumford, "Family-Friendly Work Practices in Britain: Availability and Perceived Accessibility," *Human Resource Management Journal* 45 (Spring 2006): 23–42.

38. Estey, *The Labor Problem*, 208.

39. Milton Derber, *The American Idea of Industrial Democracy, 1865–1965* (Urbana: University of Illinois Press, 1970). Patricia A. Greenfield and Robert J. Pleasure, "Representatives of Their Own Choosing: Finding Workers' Voice in the Legitimacy and Power of Their Unions," in Bruce E. Kaufman and Morris M. Kleiner, eds., *Employee Representation: Alternatives and Future Directions* (Madison, Wisc.: Industrial Relations Research Association, 1993), 169–96. Redish, "The Value of Free Speech." Joel Rogers and Wolfgang Streeck, eds., *Works Councils: Consultation, Representation, and Cooperation in Industrial Relations* (Chicago: University of Chicago Press, 1995).

40. Pateman, *Participation and Democratic Theory*. Estlund, *Working Together*. David Weil, "Individual Rights and Collective Agents: The Role of Old and New Workplace Institutions in the Regulation of Labor Markets," in Richard B. Freeman, Joni Hersch, and Lawrence Mishel, eds., *Emerging Labor Market Institutions for the Twenty-First Century* (Chicago: University of Chicago Press, 2005), 13–44. Joel Rogers, "United States: Lessons from Abroad and Home," in Joel Rogers and Wolfgang Streeck, eds., *Works Councils: Consultation, Representation, and Cooperation in Industrial Relations* (Chicago: University of Chicago Press, 1995), 375–410. David Weil et al., "The Effectiveness of Regulatory Disclosure Policies," *Journal of Policy Analysis and Management* 25 (Winter 2006): 155–81. Cynthia Estlund, "Rebuilding the Law of the Workplace in an Era of Self-Regulation," *Columbia Law Review* 105 (March 2005): 319–404.

41. John T. Addison, Claus Schnabel, and Joachim Wagner, "The Course of Research into the Economic Consequences of German Works Councils," *British Journal of Industrial Relations* 42 (June 2004): 255–81. Estlund, *Working Together*.

42. Freeman and Rogers, *What Workers Want*. Paul Osterman, "Work Reorganization in an Era of Restructuring: Trends in Diffusion and Effects on Employee Welfare," *Industrial and Labor Relations Review* 53 (January 2000): 179–96. Douglas Kruse, Joseph Blasi, and Rhokeun Park, "Shared Capitalism in the U.S. Economy: Prevalence, Characteristics, and Employee Views of Financial Participation in Enterprises," in Joseph R. Blasi, Richard B. Freeman, and Douglas Kruse, eds., *Shared Capitalism at Work: The Economic Effects of Employee Ownership, Profit Sharing, Gainsharing, and Broad-based Stock Options* (New York: Russell Sage Foundation and National Bureau of Economic Research, forthcoming). U.S. Bureau of Labor Statistics, "Union Members in 2007" (Washington, D.C.: U.S. Department of Labor, 2008), http://www.bls.gov/news.release/union2.nro.htm [accessed May 14, 2008]. Eric Parker and Joel Rogers, "Building the

High Road in Metro Areas: Sectoral Training and Employment Projects," in Lowell Turner, Harry C. Katz, and Richard W. Hurd, eds., *Rekindling the Movement: Labor's Quest for Relevance in the Twenty-First Century* (Ithaca, N.Y.: ILR Press, 2001), 256–74. Richard B. Freeman, "Searching for the EU Social Dialogue Model," in Nicola Acocella and Riccardo Leoni, eds., *Social Pacts, Employment, and Growth. A Reappraisal of Ezio Tarantelli's Thought* (Heidelberg: Springer-Physica Verlag, 2007), 221–38. Nelson Lichtenstein, *State of the Union: A Century of American Labor* (Princeton, N.J.: Princeton University Press, 2002).

43. Civil Service Reform Act, 5 U.S.C. §§ 7101–7135.

44. *Detroit Edison Co. v. NLRB*, 440 U.S. 301 (1979).

45. National Labor Relations Act, 29 U.S.C. § 158(a)(2).

46. *Electromation, Inc. and International Brotherhood of Teamsters, Local Union No. 1049, AFL-CIO*, 309 NLRB 990 (1992), enforced 35 F.3d 1148 (7th Cir. 1994). Robert S. Moberly, "The Story of *Electromation*: Are Employee Participation Programs a Competitive Necessity or a Wolf in Sheep's Clothing?," in Laura J. Cooper and Catherine L. Fisk, eds., *Labor Law Stories* (New York: Foundation Press, 2005), 315–51.

47. Moberly, "The Story of *Electromation*." Rochelle Gnagey Skolnick, "Control, Collaboration or Coverage: The NLRA and the St. Paul Chamber Orchestra Dilemma," *Washington University Journal of Law and Policy* 20 (2006): 403–42. Stephen F. Befort, "A New Voice for the Workplace: A Proposal for an American Works Council Act," *Missouri Law Review* 69 (Summer 2004): 607–51. Michael H. LeRoy, "Employee Participation in the New Millennium: Redefining a Labor Organization under Section 8(a)(2) of the NLRA," *Southern California Law Review* 72 (September 1999): 1651–1723.

48. Freeman and Rogers, *What Workers Want*, 180.

49. Estey, *The Labor Problem*, 114.

50. U.S. Bureau of Labor Statistics, "Union Members in 2007."

51. Gary N. Chaison and Joseph B. Rose, "The Macrodeterminants of Union Growth and Decline," in George Strauss, Daniel G. Gallagher and Jack Fiorito, eds., *The State of the Unions* (Madison, Wisc.: Industrial Relations Research Association, 1991), 3–45. Henry S. Farber and Alan B. Krueger, "Union Membership in the United States: The Decline Continues," in Bruce E. Kaufman and Morris M. Kleiner, eds., *Employee Representation: Alternatives and Future Directions* (Madison, Wisc.: Industrial Relations Research Association, 1993), 105–34. James T. Bennett and Jason E. Taylor, "Labor Unions: Victims of Their Political Success?" *Journal of Labor Research* 22 (Spring 2001): 261–73. Seymour Martin Lipset and Noah M. Meltz, with Rafael Gomez and Ivan Katchanovski, *The Paradox of American Unionism: Why Americans Like Unions More Than Canadians Do but Join Much Less* (Ithaca, N.Y.: Cornell University Press, 2004). Matthew J. Slaughter, "Globalization and Declining Unionization in the United States," *Industrial Relations* 46 (April 2007): 329–46.

52. *Oakwood Care Center*, 343 NLRB No. 76 (2004).

53. Stephen F. Befort, "Revisiting the Black Hole of Workplace Regulation: A Historical and Comparative Perspective of Contingent Work," *Berkeley Jour-*

nal of Employment and Labor Law 24 (2003): 153–78. Clyde W. Summers, "Contingent Employment in the United States," *Comparative Labor Law Journal* 18 (Summer 1997): 503–22. Danielle D. van Jaarsveld, "Overcoming Obstacles to Worker Representation: Insights from the Temporary Agency Workforce," *New York Law School Law Review* 50 (2005/2006): 355–84.

54. Stephen F. Befort, "Labor and Employment Law at the Millennium: A Historical Review and Critical Assessment," *Boston College Law Review* 43 (March 2002): 351–460. Sanford M. Jacoby, "American Exceptionalism Revisited: The Importance of Management," in Sanford M. Jacoby, ed., *Masters to Managers: Historical and Comparative Perspectives on American Employers* (New York: Columbia University Press, 1991), 173–200. Daphne Gottlieb Taras, "Collective Bargaining Regulation in Canada and the United States: Divergent Cultures, Divergent Outcomes," in Bruce E. Kaufman, ed., *Government Regulation of the Employment Relationship* (Madison, Wisc.: Industrial Relations Research Association, 1997), 295–342. Rick Fantasia and Kim Voss, *Hard Work: Remaking the American Labor Movement* (Berkeley: University of California Press, 2004). Martin Jay Levitt and Terry Conrow, *Confessions of a Union Buster* (New York: Crown, 1993). John Logan, "The Union Avoidance Industry in the United States," *British Journal of Industrial Relations* 44 (December 2006): 651–75. Paul Weiler, "Promises to Keep: Securing Workers' Rights to Self-Organization Under the NLRA," *Harvard Law Review* 96 (June 1983): 1769–1827.

55. U.S. General Accounting Office, "Collective Bargaining Rights: Information on the Number of Workers with and without Bargaining Rights," GAO-02-835 (Washington, D.C., 2002). Marley S. Weiss, "*Kentucky River* at the Intersection of Professional and Supervisory Status: Fertile Delta or Bermuda Triangle," in Laura J. Cooper and Catherine L. Fisk, eds., *Labor Law Stories* (New York: Foundation Press, 2005), 353–98.

56. John Schmitt and Ben Zipperer, "Dropping the Ax: Illegal Firings During Union Election Campaigns" (Washington, D.C.: Center for Economic and Policy Research, 2007). Robert J. LaLonde and Bernard D. Meltzer, "Hard Times for Unions: Another Look at the Significance of Employer Illegalities," *University of Chicago Law Review* 58 (Summer 1991): 953–1014. Weiler, "Promises to Keep." Paul C. Weiler, "Hard Times for Unions: Challenging Times for Scholars," *University of Chicago Law Review* 58 (Summer 1991): 1015–32. William B. Gould, *Agenda for Reform: The Future of Employment Relationships and the Law* (Cambridge, Mass.: MIT Press, 1993). Survey results from Richard B. Freeman and Joel Rogers, "Who Speaks for Us? Employee Representation in a Nonunion Labor Market," in Bruce E. Kaufman and Morris M. Kleiner, eds., *Employee Representation: Alternatives and Future Directions* (Madison, Wisc.: Industrial Relations Research Association, 1993), 13–79 at 31. Befort, "Labor and Employment Law at the Millennium."

57. *H. K. Porter Co. v. NLRB*, 397 U.S. 99 (1970). *Ex-Cello Corp.*, 185 NLRB 107 (1970), *enforced* 449 F.2d 1058 (D.C. Cir. 1971).

58. Befort, "Labor and Employment Law at the Millennium." William N. Cooke, *Union Organizing and Public Policy: Failure to Secure First Contracts*

(Kalamazoo, Mich.: W. E. Upjohn Institute for Employment Research, 1985). Kate Bronfenbrenner and Tom Juravich, "It Takes More Than House Calls: Organizing to Win with a Comprehensive Union Building Strategy," in Kate Bronfenbrenner et al., eds., *Organizing to Win: New Research on Union Strategies* (Ithaca, N.Y.: ILR Press, 1998), 19–36.

59. *NLRB v. Mackay Radio & Telegraph Co.*, 304 U.S. 333 (1938). *Laidlaw Corp.*, 171 NLRB 1366 (1968). Julius G. Getman and Thomas C. Kohler, "The Story of *NLRB v. Mackay Radio and Telegraph Co.*: The High Cost of Solidarity," in Laura J. Cooper and Catherine L. Fisk, eds., *Labor Law Stories* (New York: Foundation Press, 2005), 13–53. Josiah Bartlett Lambert, *"If the Workers Took a Notion": The Right to Strike and American Political Development* (Ithaca, N.Y.: Cornell University Press, 2005). Fantasia and Voss, *Hard Work.*

60. Freeman and Rogers, *What Workers Want*, 97. Freeman and Rogers, "Who Speaks for Us?" Lipset and Meltz, *The Paradox of American Unionism*, 95.

61. Lucius Junius Moderatus Columella, *De Re Rustica*, trans. Harrison Boyd Ash (London: William Heinemann, 1941), 93 [Book I.VIII: 15].

NOTES TO CHAPTER 6

1. Paul Osterman, Thomas Kochan, Richard Locke, and Michael J. Piore, *Working in America: A Blueprint for the New Labor Market* (Cambridge, Mass.: MIT Press, 2001). Peter D. McClelland, *The American Search for Justice* (Cambridge, Mass.: Basil Blackwell, 1990).

2. International Labor Office, *Global Employment Trends: January 2008* (Geneva: International Labor Organization, 2008).

3. Stephen A. Herzenberg, John A. Alic, and Howard Wial, *New Rules for a New Economy: Employment and Opportunity in Postindustrial America* (Ithaca, N.Y.: ILR Press, 1998). Paul Osterman, *Securing Prosperity: The American Labor Market: How It Has Changed and What to Do about It* (Princeton, N.J.: Princeton University Press, 1999). Katherine V. W. Stone, *From Widgets to Digits: Employment Regulations for the Changing Workplace* (Cambridge: Cambridge University Press, 2004).

4. Cynthia Estlund, *Working Together: How Workplace Bonds Strengthen a Diverse Democracy* (Oxford: Oxford University Press, 2003), 7.

5. John W. Budd, *Employment with a Human Face: Balancing Efficiency, Equity, and Voice* (Ithaca, N.Y.: Cornell University Press, 2004), 2. Pope John Paul II, *On Human Work: Encyclical Laborem Exercens* (Washington, D.C.: United States Catholic Conference, 1981).

6. Russell Muirhead, *Just Work* (Cambridge, Mass.: Harvard University Press, 2004). Norman E. Bowie, "Kantian Ethical Thought," in John W. Budd and James G. Scoville, eds., *The Ethics of Human Resources and Industrial Relations* (Champaign, Ill.: Labor and Employment Relations Association, 2005), 61–87. International Labor Office, *Decent Work* (Geneva: International Labor Organization, 1999).

7. Pauline T. Kim, "Bargaining with Imperfect Information: A Study of

Worker Perceptions of Legal Protection in an At-Will World," *Cornell Law Review* 83 (November 1997): 105–60.

8. *NLRB v. Mackay Radio & Telegraph Co.*, 304 U.S. 333 (1938).

9. Joseph E. Slater, "The 'American Rule' That Swallows the Exceptions," *Employee Rights and Employment Policy Journal* 11 (2007): 53–110.

10. *IBM Corp.*, 341 NLRB 1288, 1294 (2004).

11. Katherine V. W. Stone, "The Legacy of Industrial Pluralism: The Tension Between Individual Employment Rights and the New Deal Collective Bargaining System," *University of Chicago Law Review* 59 (Spring 1992): 575–644. Ann C. Hodges, "The Limits of Multiple Rights and Remedies: A Call for Revisiting the Law of the Workplace," *Hofstra Labor and Employment Law Journal* 22 (Spring 2005): 601–26. William R. Corbett, "Waiting for the Labor Law of the Twenty-First Century: Everything Old is New Again," *Berkeley Journal of Employment and Labor Law* 23 (2002): 259–306. Ellen Dannin, *Taking Back the Workers' Law: How to Fight the Assault on Labor Rights* (Ithaca, N.Y.: Cornell University Press, 2006).

12. David Weil, "Individual Rights and Collective Agents: The Role of Old and New Workplace Institutions in the Regulation of Labor Markets," in Richard B. Freeman, Joni Hersch, and Lawrence Mishel, eds., *Emerging Labor Market Institutions for the Twenty-First Century* (Chicago: University of Chicago Press, 2005), 13–44. John W. Budd and Brian P. McCall, "Unions and Unemployment Insurance Benefits Receipt: Evidence from the CPS," *Industrial Relations* 43 (April 2004): 339–55. John W. Budd and Angela M. Brey, "Unions and Family Leave: Early Experience under the Family and Medical Leave Act," *Labor Studies Journal* 28 (Fall 2003): 85–105.

13. Clyde W. Summers, "Labor Law as the Century Turns: A Changing of the Guard," *Nebraska Law Review* 67 (1988): 7–27 at 19.

14. For other calls for principled reform, see Thomas A. Kochan, "Labor Policy for the Twenty-First Century," *University of Pennsylvania Journal of Labor and Employment Law* 1 (Spring 1998): 117–31. Also, Paul C. Weiler, "A Principled Reshaping of Labor Law for the Twenty-First Century," *University of Pennsylvania Journal of Labor and Employment Law* 3 (Winter 2001): 177–206.

15. Cynthia Estlund, "Building the Law of the Workplace in an Era of Self-Regulation," *Columbia Law Review* 105 (March 2005): 319–404. Summers, "Labor Law as the Century Turns." Corbett, "Waiting for the Labor Law of the Twenty-First Century."

16. Rick Fantasia and Kim Voss, *Hard Work: Remaking the American Labor Movement* (Berkeley: University of California Press, 2004). Christopher R. Martin, *Framed! Labor and the Corporate Media* (Ithaca, N.Y.: Cornell University Press, 2004). Budd, *Employment with a Human Face.*

17. Budd, *Employment with a Human Face.* John W. Budd, Rafael Gomez, and Noah M. Meltz, "Why a Balance Is Best: The Pluralist Industrial Relations Paradigm of Balancing Competing Interests," in Bruce E. Kaufman, ed., *Theoretical Perspectives on Work and the Employment Relationship* (Champaign, Ill.: Industrial Relations Research Association, 2004), 195–227. Sidney Webb and Beatrice Webb, *Industrial Democracy* (London: Longmans, Green, 1897).

John R. Commons, *Industrial Goodwill* (New York: McGraw-Hill, 1919). Thomas A. Kochan, *Collective Bargaining and Industrial Relations: From Theory to Policy and Practice* (Homewood, Ill.: Irwin, 1980). James A. Gross, ed., *Workers Rights as Human Rights* (Ithaca, N.Y.: Cornell University Press, 2003). Bowie, "Kantian Ethical Thought."

18. Muirhead, *Just Work.*

19. Council of Economic Advisors, *Economic Report of the President* (Washington, D.C.: U.S. Government Printing Office, 2004), 149.

20. Garth Mangum and Peter Philips, eds., *Three Worlds of Labor Economics* (Armonk, N.Y.: M. E. Sharpe, 1988), 4–5.

21. Richard A. Epstein, "In Defense of the Contract at Will," *University of Chicago Law Review* 51 (Fall 1984): 947–82.

22. Sumner H. Slichter, "The Organization and Control of Economic Activity," in Rexford Guy Tugwell, ed., *The Trend of Economics* (New York: Knopf, 1924), 301–55. Richard B. Freeman and James L. Medoff, *What Do Unions Do?* (New York: Basic Books, 1984). Bruce E. Kaufman, "Labor Markets and Employment Regulation: The View of the 'Old' Institutionalists," in Bruce E. Kaufman, ed., *Government Regulation of the Employment Relationship* (Madison, Wisc.: Industrial Relations Research Association, 1997), 11–55. Mangum and Philips, *Three Worlds of Labor Economics.* Alan Manning, *Monopsony in Motion: Imperfect Competition in Labor Markets* (Princeton, N.J.: Princeton University Press, 2003). Webb and Webb, *Industrial Democracy*, 767–77. Alan B. Krueger, "Inequality, Too Much of a Good Thing," in Benjamin M. Friedman, ed., *Inequality in America: What Role for Human Capital Policies?* (Cambridge, Mass.: MIT Press, 2003), 1–75.

23. Budd, Gomez, and Meltz, "Why a Balance Is Best," 197.

24. David C. Korten, *The Post-Corporate World: Life after Capitalism* (San Francisco: Berrett-Koehler, 1999), 181.

25. Joel Bakan, *The Corporation: The Pathological Pursuit of Profit and Power* (New York: Free Press, 2004). Marjorie Kelly, *The Divine Right of Capital: Dethroning the Corporate Aristocracy* (San Francisco: Berrett-Koehler, 2001). Gordon Lafer, "The Critical Failure of Workplace Ethics," in John W. Budd and James G. Scoville, eds., *The Ethics of Human Resources and Industrial Relations* (Champaign, Ill.: Labor and Employment Relations Association, 2005), 273–97.

26. Bakan, *The Corporation.*

27. Howie Padilla, "Police Left Out of Loop about Loose Rail Car," *Star Tribune* (Minneapolis), May 26, 2005. Janet Moore, "Disclosure Defense: Guidant Says It Handled Defibrillator Flaw Properly," *Star Tribune* (Minneapolis), May 25, 2005.

28. Robert J. Steinfeld, *Coercion, Contract, and Free Labor in the Nineteenth Century* (Cambridge: Cambridge University Press, 2001). Budd, *Employment with a Human Face.* Muirhead, *Just Work.* Karl E. Klare, "Workplace Democracy and Market Reconstruction: An Agenda for Legal Reform," *Catholic University Law Review* 38 (Fall 1988): 1–68. Cass R. Sunstein, *The Second Bill of Rights: FDR's Unfinished Revolution and Why We Need It More Than Ever* (New York: Basic Books, 2004).

29. Bakan, *The Corporation.* Penny Le Couteur and Jay Burreson, *Napoleon's*

Buttons: How 17 Molecules Changed History (New York: Jeremy P. Tarcher / Putnam, 2003).

30. *Santa Clara County v. Southern Pacific Railroad Company*, 118 U.S. 394 (1886). Thom Hartmann, *Unequal Protection: The Rise of Corporate Dominance and the Theft of Human Rights* (New York: Rodale, 2002). Jack Beatty, *Age of Betrayal: The Triumph of Money in America, 1865–1900* (New York: Knopf, 2007).

31. Kelly, *The Divine Right of Capital.*

32. Sumantra Ghoshal, "Bad Management Theories Are Destroying Good Management Practices," *Academy of Management Learning and Education* 4 (March 2005): 75–91. Norman E. Bowie, *Business Ethics: A Kantian Perspective* (Malden, Mass.: Blackwell, 1999).

33. Stone, *From Widgets to Digits*. Thomas A. Kochan, *Restoring the American Dream: A Working Families' Agenda for America* (Cambridge, Mass.: MIT Press, 2005). Michael J. Piore and Sean Safford, "Changing Regimes of Workplace Governance, Shifting Axes of Social Mobilization, and the Challenge to Industrial Relations Theory," *Industrial Relations* 45 (July 2006): 299–325.

NOTES TO CHAPTER 7

1. Richard B. Freeman and James L. Medoff, *What Do Unions Do?* (New York: Basic Books, 1984). Bruce E. Kaufman, "Labor Markets and Employment Regulation: The View of the 'Old' Institutionalists," in Bruce E. Kaufman, ed., *Government Regulation of the Employment Relationship* (Madison, Wisc.: Industrial Relations Research Association, 1997), 11–55. Garth Mangum and Peter Philips, eds., *Three Worlds of Labor Economics* (Armonk, N.Y.: M. E. Sharpe, 1988). Alan Manning, *Monopsony in Motion: Imperfect Competition in Labor Markets* (Princeton, N.J.: Princeton University Press, 2003).

2. American Axle and Manufacturing, "Family Medical Leave Act: United States Senate Roundtable Discussion" (June 23, 2005): 8, http://www.nam.org/s_nam/bin.asp?CID=390&DID=235078&DOC=FILE.PDF [accessed August 26, 2006].

3. Dani Rodrik, *Has Globalization Gone Too Far?* (Washington, D.C.: Institute for International Economics, 1997). Clyde W. Summers, "The Battle in Seattle: Free Trade, Labor Rights, and Societal Values," *University of Pennsylvania Journal of International Economic Law* 22 (Spring 2001): 61–90.

4. James A. Gross, ed., *Workers' Rights as Human Rights* (Ithaca, N.Y.: Cornell University Press, 2003). Hoyt N. Wheeler, "Globalization and Business Ethics in Employment Relations," in John W. Budd and James G. Scoville, eds., *The Ethics of Human Resources and Industrial Relations* (Champaign, Ill.: Labor and Employment Relations Association, 2005), 115–40. David Weissbrodt and Muria Kruger, "Norms on the Responsibilities of Transnational Corporations and Other Business Enterprises with Regard to Human Rights," *American Journal of International Law* 97 (October 2003): 901–22.

5. Michael J. Trebilcock and Robert Howse, "Trade Policy and Labor Standards," *Minnesota Journal of Global Trade* 14 (Summer 2005): 261–300. Richard

McIntyre and Matthew M. Bodah, "The United States and ILO Conventions 87 and No. 98: The Freedom of Association and Right to Bargain Collectively," in Richard N. Block et al., eds., *Justice on the Job: Perspectives on the Erosion of Collective Bargaining in the United States* (Kalamazoo, Mich.: Upjohn, 2006), 231–47. Edward E. Potter, "A Pragmatic Assessment from the Employers' Perspective," in James A. Gross, ed., *Workers' Rights as Human Rights* (Ithaca, N.Y.: Cornell University Press, 2003), 118–35. Marley S. Weiss, "Two Steps Forward, One Step Back—Or Vice Versa: Labor Rights under Free Trade Agreements from NAFTA, Through Jordan, via Chile, to Latin America, and Beyond," *University of San Francisco Law Review* 37 (Spring 2003): 689–755. Marisa Pagnattaro, "Leveling the Playing Field: Labor Provisions in CAFTA," *Fordham International Law Journal* 29 (January 2006): 386–431.

6. Colin Crouch, "Skill Formation Systems," in Stephen Ackroyd et al., eds., *The Oxford Handbook of Work and Organization* (Oxford: Oxford University Press, 2005), 95–114.

7. Garth L. Mangum, "Manpower Policies and Worker Status since the 1930s," in Joseph P. Goldberg et al., eds., *Federal Policies and Worker Status since the Thirties* (Madison, Wisc.: Industrial Relations Research Association, 1976), 135–57 at 143.

8. Gordon Lafer, *The Job Training Charade* (Ithaca, N.Y.: Cornell University Press, 2002).

9. Harry J. Holzer and Margy Waller, "The Workforce Investment Act: Reauthorization to Address the 'Skills Gap,'" Center on Urban and Metropolitan Policy Research Brief (Washington, D.C.: Brookings Institution, 2002). W. Norton Grubb, *Learning to Work: The Case for Reintegrating Job Training and Education* (New York: Russell Sage Foundation, 1996).

10. Holzer and Waller, "The Workforce Investment Act." Ray Uhalde et al., "Toward a National Workforce Education and Training Policy" (Washington, D.C.: National Center on Education and the Economy, 2003). Stephen A. Herzenberg, John A. Alic, and Howard Wial, *New Rules for a New Economy: Employment and Opportunity in Postindustrial America* (Ithaca, N.Y.: ILR Press, 1998). Lafer, *The Job Training Charade*. Peter Cappelli et al., *Change at Work* (New York: Oxford University Press, 1997). Grubb, *Learning to Work*.

11. Crouch, "Skill Formation Systems." Mangum, "Manpower Policies and Worker Status Since the 1930s." Lafer, *The Job Training Charade*.

12. Rebecca M. Blank, ed., *Social Protection Versus Economic Flexibility: Is There a Trade-Off?* (Chicago: University of Chicago Press, 1994). David R. Howell, ed., *Fighting Unemployment: The Limits of Free Market Orthodoxy* (New York: Oxford University Press, 2005). Stephen Nickell, "Unemployment and Labor Market Rigidities: Europe versus North America," *Journal of Economic Perspectives* 11 (Summer 1997): 55–74.

13. Ton Wilthagen and Frank Tros, "The Concept of 'Flexicurity': A New Approach to Regulating Employment and Labour Markets," *Transfer: European Review of Labour and Research* 10 (Summer 2004): 166–86.

14. Sanford M. Jacoby, *Employing Bureaucracy: Managers, Unions, and the*

Transformation of Work in American Industry, 1900–1945 (New York: Columbia University Press, 1985). Jennifer Klein, *For All These Rights: Business, Labor, and the Shaping of America's Public-Private Welfare State* (Princeton, N.J.: Princeton University Press, 2003). Katherine V. W. Stone, *From Widgets to Digits: Employment Regulation for the Changing Workplace* (Cambridge, UK: Cambridge University Press, 2004).

15. Family and Medical Leave Act, 29 U.S.C. § 2611(2)(A).

16. Employee Retirement Income Security Act, 29 U.S.C. § 1053(a)(2).

17. 29 U.S.C. §§ 1052(a)(1), 1052(a)(3)(A). Virginia L. duRivage, "New Policies for the Part-time and Contingent Workforce," in Virginia L. duRivage, ed., *New Policies for Part-Time and Contingent Workers* (Armonk, N.Y.: M. E. Sharpe, 1992), 89–134. Anthony P. Carnevale, Lynn A. Jennings, and James M. Eisenmann, "Contingent Workers and Employment Law," in Kathleen Barker and Kathleen Christensen, eds., *Contingent Work: American Employment Relations in Transition* (Ithaca, N.Y.: ILR Press, 1998), 281–305.

18. Jonathan Gruber and Brigitte Madrian, "Health Insurance, Labor Supply, and Job Mobility: A Critical Review of the Literature," in Catherine G. McLaughlin, ed., *Health Policy and the Uninsured* (Washington, D.C.: Urban Institute Press, 2004), 97–178. Martha Harrison Stinson, "Estimating the Relationship Between Employer-Provided Health Insurance, Worker Mobility, and Wages," Technical Paper No. TP-2002-23 (Washington, D.C.: U.S. Census Bureau, 2003). Stone, *From Widgets to Digits*. Paul Osterman, *Securing Prosperity: The American Labor Market: How It Has Changed and What to Do about It* (Princeton, N.J.: Princeton University Press, 1999).

19. Haynes Johnson and David S. Broder, *The System: The American Way of Politics at the Breaking Point* (New York: Little Brown, 1996). David C. Jacobs, "Prospects for National Health Insurance in the United States," in Sheldon Friedman and David C. Jacobs, eds., *The Future of the Safety Net: Social Insurance and Employee Benefits* (Champaign, Ill.: Industrial Relations Research Association, 2001), 187–200. James B. Roche, "Health Care in America: Why We Need Universal Health Care and Why We Need it Now," *St. Thomas Law Review* 13 (Summer 2001): 1013–49. Matthew J. Binette, "Patients' Bill of Rights: Legislative Cure-All or Prescription for Disaster?" *North Carolina Law Review* 81 (January 2003): 653–96. Judith Feder, "Crowd-Out and the Politics of Health Reform," *Journal of Law, Medicine and Ethics* 32 (Fall 2004): 461–64. Alan Derickson, *Health Security for All: Dreams of Universal Health Care in America* (Baltimore: Johns Hopkins University Press, 2005).

20. Roche, "Health Care in America." Elizabeth Docteur and Howard Oxley, "Health-Care Systems: Lessons from the Reform Experience," OECD Health Working Paper No. 9 (Paris: Organization for Economic Cooperation and Development, 2003). Pat Armstrong, Hugh Armstrong, and Claudia Fegan, *Universal Health Care: What the United States Can Learn from the Canadian Experience* (New York: New Press, 1998). Win de Gooijer, *Trends in EU Health Care Systems* (Amsterdam: Springer, 2006). Jacob S. Hacker, *The Great Risk Shift: The Assault on American Jobs, Families, Health Care, and Retirement—And How You Can Fight*

Back (New York: Oxford University Press, 2006). Donald L. Barlett and James B. Steele, *Critical Condition: How Health Care in America Became Big Business—and Bad Medicine* (New York: Doubleday, 2004).

21. Stone, *From Widgets to Digits*. Pension and Welfare Benefits Administration, *Private Pension Plan Bulletin: Abstract of 2005 Form 5500 Annual Reports* (Washington, D.C.: U.S. Department of Labor, 2008). Employee Benefit Research Institute, *Fundamentals of Employee Benefit Programs* (Washington, D.C., 2005).

22. Consolidated Omnibus Budget Reform Act of 1985, 29 U.S.C. §§ 1161–68.

23. Health Insurance Portability and Accountability Act, 42 U.S.C. §§ 300gg-300gg-2.

24. Klein, *For All These Rights*, 14. Hacker, *The Great Risk Shift*.

25. Clyde W. Summers, "Individual Protection Against Unjust Dismissal: Time for a Statute," *Virginia Law Review* 62 (April 1976): 481–532. Theodore J. St. Antoine, "A Seed Germinates: Unjust Discharge Reform Heads to Full Flower," *Nebraska Law Review* 67 (1988): 56–81. Ann C. McGinley, "Rethinking Civil Rights and Employment at Will: Toward a Coherent National Discharge Policy," *Ohio State Law Journal* 57 (1996): 1443–1524.

26. National Conference of Commissioners on Uniform State Laws, *Uniform Law Commissioners' Model Employment Termination Act* (Chicago, 1991).

27. Theodore J. St. Antoine, "The Making of the Model Employment Termination Act," *Washington Law Review* 69 (April 1994): 361–82.

28. Wrongful Discharge from Employment Act (Montana Code §§ 32-2-901 to 2-915, 2005).

29. Paul H. Tobias, "Defects in the Model Employment Termination Act," *Labor Law Journal* 43 (August 1992): 500–3. Dawn S. Perry, "Deterring Egregious Violations of Public Policy: A Proposed Amendment to the Model Employment Termination Act," *Washington Law Review* 67 (October 1992): 915–35.

30. Stewart J. Schwab, "Life-Cycle Justice: Accommodating Just Cause and Employment at Will," *Michigan Law Review* 92 (October 1993): 8–62. Mary Jean Navaretta, "The Model Employment Termination Act—META—More Aptly the Menace to Employment Tranquility Act," *Stetson Law Review* 25 (Summer 1996): 1027–66.

31. Stephen F. Befort, "Labor and Employment Law at the Millennium: A Historical Review and Critical Assessment," *Boston College Law Review* 43 (March 2002): 351–460.

32. *McKennon v. Nashville Banner Publishing Co.*, 513 U.S. 352, 358 (1995).

33. Laura Cooper et al., *ADR in the Workplace* (St. Paul, Minn.: West Group, 2000), 500–501.

34. Samuel Estreicher, "Unjust Dismissals in Other Countries: Some Cautionary Notes," *Employee Relations Law Journal* 10 (Summer 1984): 286–302 at 296.

35. Federal Mediation and Conciliation Service, "Arbitration Statistics Fiscal Year 2007" (Washington, D.C., 2007), http://fmcs.gov/assets/

files/Arbitration/2007%20Arbitration%20Documents/Average_Days.DOC [accessed May 15, 2007]. Federal Mediation and Conciliation Service, "2007 Annual Report" (Washington, D.C., 2007), http://www.fmcs.gov/assets/files/annual%20reports/FY2007_Annual_Report.pdf [accessed May 15, 2007].

36. *Gilmer v. Interstate/Johnson Lane Corp.*, 500 U.S. 20 (1991).

37. *Circuit City Stores, Inc. v. Adams*, 532 U.S. 105 (2001).

38. *Hooters of America, Inc. v. Phillips*, 173 F.3d 933 (4th Cir. 1999) (finding arbitration agreement unenforceable where procedural rules are egregiously unfair); *Paladino v. Avnet Computer Tech. Inc.*, 134 F.3d 1054 (11th Cir. 1998) (finding arbitration agreement unenforceable where the agreement does not authorize the arbitrator to award the relief authorized by statute).

39. Joseph R. Grodin, "Arbitration of Employment Discrimination Claims: Doctrine and Policy in the Wake of *Gilmer*," *Hofstra Labor Law Journal* 1 (Fall 1996): 1–55. Alexander J. S. Colvin, "The Relationship Between Employment Arbitration and Workplace Dispute Resolution Procedures," *Ohio State Journal on Dispute Resolution* 16 (2001): 643–68. Katherine V. W. Stone, "Mandatory Arbitration of Individual Employment Rights: The Yellow Dog Contract of the 1990s," *Denver University Law Review* 73 (1996): 1017–50. Jeffrey W. Stempel, "Keeping Arbitrations from Becoming Kangaroo Courts," *Nevada Law Journal* 8 (Fall 2007): 251–70.

40. Grodin, "Arbitration of Employment Discrimination Claims." John T. Dunlop and Arnold M. Zack, *Mediation and Arbitration of Employment Disputes* (San Francisco: Jossey-Bass, 1997). American Arbitration Association, "National Rules for the Resolution of Employment Disputes" (Washington, D.C., 2005), http://www.adr.org/sp.asp?id=22075 [accessed August 27, 2006]. Richard A. Bales, "Beyond the Protocol: Recent Trends in Employment Arbitration," *Employee Rights and Employment Policy Journal* 11 (2007): 301–44.

41. Ann C. Hodges, "The Limits of Multiple Rights and Remedies: A Call for Revisiting the Law of the Workplace," *Hofstra Labor and Employment Law Journal* 22 (Spring 2005): 601–26.

NOTES TO CHAPTER 8

1. Adam Smith, *An Inquiry into the Nature and Causes of the Wealth of Nations* (1776; New York: Bantam Books, 2003), 94.

2. Sidney Webb and Beatrice Webb, *Industrial Democracy* (London: Longmans, Green, 1897). Alan B. Krueger, "Inequality, Too Much of a Good Thing," in Benjamin M. Friedman, ed., *Inequality in America: What Role for Human Capital Policies?* (Cambridge, Mass.: MIT Press, 2003), 1–75. AFL-CIO, "The Wal-Mart Tax: A Review of Studies Examining Employers' Health Care Cost-Shifting" (2005), http://www.aflcio.org/corporatewatch/walmart/upload/walmart_tax_memo.pdf [accessed November 10, 2006].

3. Roberta Rehner Iversen and Annie Laurie Armstrong, *Jobs Aren't Enough: Toward a New Economic Mobility for Low-Income Families* (Philadelphia: Temple University Press, 2006). International Labor Office, *Global Employment Trends:*

January 2008 (Geneva: International Labor Organization, 2008). National Low Income Housing Coalition. "Out of Reach 2007–2008" (Washington, D.C., 2008), http://www.nlihc.org/oor/oor2008/ [accessed May 23, 2008]. Lawrence Mishel, Jared Bernstein, and Sylvia Allegretto, *The State of Working America 2006/2007* (Ithaca, N.Y.: Cornell University Press, 2007). Peter G. Gosselin, "The Poor Have More Things Today—Including Wild Income Swings," *Los Angeles Times* (December 12, 2004).

4. Family and Medical Leave Act, 29 U.S.C. §§ 2601–2654.

5. Stephen F. Befort, "Accommodation at Work: Lessons from the Americans with Disabilities Act and Possibilities for Alleviating the American Worker Time Crunch," *Cornell Journal of Law and Public Policy* 13 (Summer 2004): 615–36.

6. Jody Heymann, Alison Earle, and Jeffrey Hayes, *The Work, Family, and Equity Index: How Does the United States Measure Up?* (Montreal: Project on Global Working Families, 2008). Mishel, Bernstein, and Allegretto, *The State of Working America*. Jodi Grant, Taylor Hatcher, and Nirali Patel, *Expecting Better: A State-by-State Analysis of Parental Leave Programs* (Washington, D.C.: National Partnership for Women and Families, 2005).

7. Jerold Waltman, *The Case for the Living Wage* (New York: Algora, 2004). David Card and Alan B. Krueger, *Myth and Measurement: The New Economics of the Minimum Wage* (Princeton, N.J.: Princeton University Press, 1995). Charles Brown, "Minimum Wages, Employment, and the Distribution of Income," in Orley Ashenfelter and David Card, eds., *Handbook of Labor Economics*, Vol. 3B (Amsterdam: Elsevier, 1999), 2101–63. David Fairris and Michael Reich, "The Impacts of Living Wage Policies: Introduction to the Special Issue," *Industrial Relations* 44 (January 2005): 1–13. Mark D. Brenner, "The Economic Impact of the Boston Living Wage Ordinance," *Industrial Relations* 44 (January 2005): 59–83.

8. William P. Quigley, *Ending Poverty as We Know It: Guaranteeing a Right to a Job at a Living Wage* (Philadelphia: Temple University Press, 2003). Mark Robert Rank, *One Nation, Underprivileged: Why American Poverty Affects Us All* (New York: Oxford University Press, 2004).

9. Katherine S. Newman, *No Shame in My Game: The Working Poor in the Inner City* (New York: Alfred A. Knopf, 1999). Rebecca M. Blank, *It Takes a Nation: A New Agenda for Fighting Poverty* (Princeton, N.J.: Princeton University Press, 1997). Quigley, *Ending Poverty as We Know It*. Rank, *One Nation, Underprivileged.* Bruce D. Meyer and Douglas Holtz-Eakin, eds., *Making Work Pay: The Earned Income Tax Credit and Its Impact on America's Families* (New York: Russell Sage Foundation, 2002).

10. David Card and John E. DiNardo, "Skill-Biased Technological Change and Rising Wage Inequality: Some Problems and Puzzles," *Journal of Labor Economics* 20 (October 2002): 753–83. Jared Bernstein and Lawrence Mishel, "Seven Reasons for Skepticism about the Technology Story of U.S. Wage Inequality," in Ivar Berg and Arne L. Kalleberg, eds., *Sourcebook of Labor Markets: Evolving Structures and Processes* (New York: Kluwer Academic, 2001), 409–27.

11. Mishel, Bernstein, and Allegretto, *The State of Working America*. Center

on Budget and Policy Priorities, "Recent Tax and Income Trends Among High-Income Taxpayers" (Washington, D.C., 2006), http://www.cbpp.org/4-10-06tax5.htm [accessed November 12, 2006]. Thomas Piketty and Emmanuel Saez, "How Progressive is the U.S. Federal Tax System? A Historical and International Perspective," *Journal of Economic Perspectives* 21 (Winter 2007): 3–24.

12. Martin J. McMahon Jr. and Alice G. Abreu, "Winner-Take-All Markets: Easing the Case for Progressive Taxation," *Florida Tax Review* 4 (1998): 1–81 at 58.

13. Robert H. Frank and Philip J. Cook, *The Winner-Take-All Society: How More and More Americans Compete for Ever Fewer and Bigger Prizes, Encouraging Economic Waste, Income Inequality, and an Impoverished Cultural Life* (New York: Free Press, 1995).

14. Melissa Lee, "Sabo Tries Again to Ease Wage Imbalance," *Star Tribune* (Minneapolis), July 13, 2005.

15. Jacob S. Hacker, *The Divided Welfare State: The Battle over Public and Private Social Benefits in the United States* (New York: Cambridge University Press, 2002). Jack Hadley, "Sicker and Poorer—The Consequences of Being Uninsured: A Review of the Research on the Relationship Between Health Insurance, Medical Care Use, Health, Work, and Income," *Medical Care Research and Review* 60 (June 2003): 3S–75S. Anne Case, Angela Fertig, and Christina Paxson, "The Lasting Impact of Childhood Health and Circumstance," *Journal of Health Economics* 24 (March 2005): 365–89.

16. Cass R. Sunstein, *The Second Bill of Rights: FDR's Unfinished Revolution and Why We Need It More Than Ever* (New York: Basic Books, 2004). Jacob S. Hacker, *The Great Risk Shift: The Assault on American Jobs, Families, Health Care, and Retirement—And How You Can Fight Back* (New York: Oxford University Press, 2006).

17. Janet L. Norwood, "Issues in Unemployment Insurance," in Peter Edelman, Dallas L. Salisbury, and Pamela J. Larson, eds., *The Future of Social Insurance: Incremental Action or Fundamental Reform?* (Washington, D.C.: National Academy of Social Insurance, 2002), 187–98 at 189.

18. Advisory Council on Unemployment Compensation, "Collected Findings and Recommendations, 1994–1996" (Washington, D.C., 1996). Michael J. Graetz and Jerry L. Mashaw, *True Security: Rethinking American Social Insurance* (New Haven, Conn.: Yale University Press, 1999). Paul Osterman, *Securing Prosperity: The American Labor Market: How It Has Changed and What to Do about It* (Princeton, N.J.: Princeton University Press, 1999). Andrew Stettner, Rebecca Smith, and Rick McHugh, "Changing Workforce, Changing Economy: State Unemployment Insurance Reforms for the 21st Century" (New York: National Employment Law Project, 2004).

19. Osterman, *Securing Prosperity*. John W. Budd and Brian P. McCall, "The Effect of Unions on the Receipt of Unemployment Insurance Benefits," *Industrial and Labor Relations Review* 50 (April 1997): 478–92. Lori G. Kletzer and Howard F. Rosen, "Reforming Unemployment Insurance for the Twenty-First Century Workforce," Hamilton Project Discussion Paper 2006-06 (2006). Hacker, *The Great Risk Shift*.

20. The White House, "Strengthening Social Security for the 21st Century" (Washington, D.C., 2005), http://www.whitehouse.gov/infocus/social-security/200501/strengthening-socialsecurity.html [accessed January 7, 2007]. Peter A. Diamond and Peter R. Orszag, *Saving Social Security: A Balanced Approach* (Washington, D.C.: Brookings Institution Press, 2004). Aaron Bernstein, Howard Gleckman, and Michael J. Mandel, "Social Security: Three New Ideas," *Business Week*, February 21, 2005.

21. Bernstein, Gleckman, and Mandel, "Three New Ideas." Diamond and Orszag, *Saving Social Security*. The White House, "Strengthening Social Security for the 21st Century."

22. Board of Trustees, Federal Old-Age and Survivors Insurance and Disability Insurance Trust Funds, *2008 Annual Report* (Washington, D.C.: U.S. Government Printing Office, 2008).

23. Stephen F. Befort, "The Perfect Storm of Retirement Insecurity: Fixing the Three-Legged Stool of Social Security, Pensions, and Personal Savings," *Minnesota Law Review* 91 (April 2007): 938–88.

24. Advisory Council on Social Security, "Report of the 1994–1996 Advisory Council on Social Security, Volume I: Findings and Recommendations" (Washington, D.C., 2007). Social Security Advisory Board, "Why Action Should Be Taken Soon" (Washington, D.C., 2005), http://www.ssab.gov/documents/WhyActionShouldbeTakenSoon.pdf [accessed January 7, 2007].

25. Bernstein, Gleckman, and Mandel, "Three New Ideas."

26. Social Security Advisory Board, "Why Action Should be Taken Soon."

27. William G. Gale, J. Mark Iwry, and Peter S. Orszag, "The Automatic 401(k): A Simple Way to Strengthen Retirement Savings," Retirement Security Project Paper No. 2005-1 (Washington, D.C.: Brookings Institution, 2005). Brigitte C. Madrian and Dennis F. Shea, "The Power of Suggestion: Inertia in 401(k) Participation and Savings Behavior," *Quarterly Journal of Economics* 116 (November 2001): 1149–87. James J. Choi et al., "Defined Contribution Pensions: Plan Rules, Participant Decisions, and the Path of Least Resistance," in James M. Poterba, ed., *Tax Policy and the Economy*, Volume 16 (Cambridge, Mass.: MIT Press, 2002), 67–113.

28. Pension Protection Act of 2006, Pub. L. No. 109-280, 120 Stat. 780.

29. Alicia H. Munnell and Annika Sundén, *Coming Up Short: The Challenge of 401(k) Plans* (Washington, D.C.: Brookings Institution, 2004). Gale, Iwry, and Orszag, "The Automatic 401(k)."

30. William G. Gale, J. Mark Iwry, and Peter S. Orszag, "The Saver's Credit: Expanding Retirement Savings for Middle- and Lower-Income Americans," Retirement Security Project Paper No. 2005-2 (Washington, D.C.: Brookings Institution, 2005).

31. Hacker, *The Great Risk Shift*, 187.

32. Alan Derickson, *Health Security for All: Dreams of Universal Health Care in America* (Baltimore: Johns Hopkins University Press, 2005).

33. 2006 Mass. Acts, Ch. 58.

34. Hacker, *The Great Risk Shift*. Families USA, "Employers Should Pay

Their Fair Share for Health Care," http://www.familiesusa.org/assets/pdfs/employer-responsibility-issue.pdf [accessed December 3, 2006]. James B. Roche, "Health Care in America: Why We Need Universal Health Care and Why We Need It Now," *St. Thomas Law Review* 13 (Summer 2001): 1013–49. The Physicians' Working Group for Single-Payer National Health Insurance, "Proposal of the Physicians' Working Group for Single-Payer National Health Insurance," *Journal of the American Medical Association* 290 (August 2003): 798–805.

35. Matthew J. Binette, "Patients' Bill of Rights: Legislative Cure-All or Prescription for Disaster?" *North Carolina Law Review* 81 (January 2003): 653–96.

36. Occupational Safety and Health Act, 29 U.S.C. §§ 651–678.

37. Thomas J. Kniesner and John D. Leeth, "Abolishing OSHA," *Regulation* 18 (Fall 1995): 46–56. Daniel B. Klaff, "Evaluating Work: Enforcing Occupational Safety and Health Standards in the United States, Canada, and Sweden," *University of Pennsylvania Journal of Labor and Employment Law* 7 (Spring 2005): 613–59.

38. David Weil, "If OSHA Is So Bad, Why Is Compliance So Good?" *RAND Journal of Economics* 27 (Autumn 1996): 618–40. Wayne B. Gray and John M. Mendeloff, "The Declining Effects of OSHA Inspections on Manufacturing Injuries, 1979–1998," *Industrial and Labor Relations Review* 58 (July 2005): 571–87. Elizabeth A. Lambrecht Karels, "Make Employers Accountable for Workplace Safety! How the Dirty Little Secret of Workers' Compensation Puts Employees at Risk and Why Criminal Prosecution and Civil Action Will Save Lives and Money," *Hamline Journal of Public Law and Policy* 26 (Fall 2004): 111–49. David Weil, "Are Mandated Health and Safety Committees Substitutes for or Supplements to Labor Unions?" *Industrial and Labor Relations Review* 52 (April 1999): 339–60.

39. Lonnie Golden and Helene Jorgensen, "Time after Time: Mandatory Overtime in the U.S. Economy," EPI Briefing Paper #120 (Washington, D.C.: Economic Policy Institute, 2002). Tosh Anderson, "Overwork Robs Workers' Health: Interpreting OSHA's General Duty Clause to Prohibit Long Work Hours," *New York City Law Review* 7 (Spring 2004) 85–160. Mara Eleina Conway, "*Karoshi*: Is It Sweeping America?" *UCLA Pacific Basin Law Journal* 15 (Spring 1997): 352–80.

40. Daniel L. Farber, "The Outmoded Debate over Affirmative Action," *California Law Review* 82 (July 1994): 893–934. Mary F. Radford, "The Affirmative Action Debate," in Bruce E. Kaufman, ed., *Government Regulation of the Employment Relationship* (Madison, Wisc.: Industrial Relations Research Association, 1997), 343–67.

41. Christine Jolls, "The Role and Functioning of Public-Interest Legal Organizations in the Enforcement of the Employment Laws," in Richard B. Freeman, Joni Hersch, and Lawrence Mishel, eds., *Emerging Labor Market Institutions for the Twenty-First Century* (Chicago: University of Chicago Press, 2005), 141–76. Janice Fine, *Worker Centers: Organizing Communities at the Edge of the Dream* (Ithaca, N.Y.: Cornell University Press, 2006). David Weil, "Individual Rights and Collective Agents: The Role of Old and New Workplace Institutions in the Regulation of Labor Markets," in Richard B. Freeman, Joni Hersch, and

Lawrence Mishel, eds., *Emerging Labor Market Institutions for the Twenty-First Century* (Chicago: University of Chicago Press, 2005), 13–44. Ann C. Hodges, "The Limits of Multiple Rights and Remedies: A Call for Revisiting the Law of the Workplace," *Hofstra Labor and Employment Law Journal* 22 (Spring 2005): 601–26.

42. Americans with Disabilities Act, 42 U.S.C. §§ 12101–12213.

43. ADA Amendments Act of 2008, S. 3406, 110th Cong. (2008).

44. Mark A. Rothstein, Serge A. Martinez, and W. Paul McKinney, "Using Established Medical Criteria to Define Disability: A Proposal to Amend the Americans with Disabilities Act," *Washington University Law Quarterly* 80 (2002): 243–97. Mary Crossley, "The Disability Kaleidoscope," *Notre Dame Law Review* 74 (March 1999): 621–716. Sharona Hoffman et al., "The Definition of Disability in the Americans with Disabilities Act: Its Successes and Shortcomings," *Employee Rights and Employment Policy Journal* 9 (2005): 473–98.

45. Adolph Koven and Susan L. Smith, *Just Cause: The Seven Tests*, 3rd ed. (Washington, D.C.: Bureau of National Affairs, 2006). Norman Brand, ed., *Discipline and Discharge in Arbitration* (Washington, D.C.: Bureau of National Affairs, 1998). Theodore J. St. Antoine, ed., *The Common Law of the Workplace: The View of Arbitrators*, 2nd ed. (Washington, D.C.: Bureau of National Affairs, 2005).

46. Wrongful Discharge from Employment Act (Montana Code §§ 32-2-901 to 2-915, 2005).

47. National Conference of Commissioners on Uniform State Laws, *Uniform Law Commissioners' Model Employment Termination Act* (Chicago, 1991).

48. Stephen F. Befort, "Labor and Employment Law at the Millennium: A Historical Review and Critical Assessment." *Boston College Law Review* 43 (March 2002): 351–460. Clyde W. Summers, "Individual Protection Against Unjust Dismissal: Time for a Statute," *Virginia Law Review* 62 (April 1976): 481–532.

49. Richard A. Epstein, "In Defense of the Contract at Will," *University of Chicago Law Review* 51 (Fall 1983): 947–82.

50. Dean Baker et al., "Labor Market Institutions and Unemployment: Assessment of the Cross-Country Evidence," in David R. Howell, ed., *Fighting Unemployment: The Limits of Free Market Orthodoxy* (Oxford: Oxford University Press, 2005), 72–118.

51. Bob Hepple, "European Rules on Dismissals," *Comparative Labor Law Journal* 18 (1997): 382-407. International Labor Office, "Termination of Employment Legislation Digest" (Geneva: International Labor Organization, 2006), http://www.ilo.org/public/english/dialogue/ifpdial/info/termination/ [accessed November 24, 2006]. Joseph E. Slater, "The 'American Rule' That Swallows the Exceptions," *Employee Rights and Employment Policy Journal* 11 (2007): 53–110.

52. Cynthia L. Estlund, "Wrongful Discharge Protections in an At-Will World," *Texas Law Review* 74 (June 1996): 1655–92. Harold S. Lewis Jr. and Elizabeth J. Norman, *Employment Discrimination Law and Practice* (St. Paul, Minn.: West Group, 2001). David Benjamin Oppenheimer, "Understanding Affirmative Action," *Hastings Constitutional Law Quarterly* 23 (Summer 1996): 921–98.

53. Steven E. Abraham, "Can a Wrongful Discharge Statute Really Benefit

Employers?" *Industrial Relations* 37 (October 1998): 499–518. Scott A. Moss, "Where There's a Will, There are Many Ways: Redressing the Increased Incoherence of Employment-at-Will," *University of Pittsburgh Law Review* 67 (Winter 2005): 295–363.

54. Stephen F. Befort, "Revisiting the Black Hole of Workplace Regulation: A Historical and Comparative Perspective of Contingent Work," *Berkeley Journal of Employment and Labor Law* 24 (2003): 153–78. Anthony P. Carnevale, Lynn A. Jennings, and James M. Eisenmann, "Contingent Workers and Employment Law," in Kathleen Barker and Kathleen Christensen, eds., *Contingent Work: American Employment Relations in Transition* (Ithaca, N.Y.: ILR Press, 1998), 281–305.

55. Lewis L. Maltby and David C. Yamada, "Beyond 'Economic Realities': The Case for Amending Federal Employment Discrimination Laws to Include Independent Contractors," *Boston College Law Review* 38 (March 1997): 239–74 at 266. Wage and Hour Opinion Letter No. 832 (Washington, D.C.: U.S. Department of Labor, June 25, 1968).

56. *Spirides v. Reinhardt*, 613 F.2d 826, 831 (D.C. Cir. 1979).

57. *Nationwide Mutual Insurance Co. v. Darden*, 503 U.S. 318 (1992).

58. Deanne M. Mosely and William C. Walter, "The Significance of the Classification of Employment Relationships in Determining Exposure to Liability," *Mississippi Law Journal* 67 (Spring 1998): 613–43 at 636.

59. Commission on the Future of Worker-Management Relations, *Report and Recommendations* (Washington, D.C.: U.S. Departments of Labor and Commerce, 1994), 38.

60. Marc Linder, "Dependent and Independent Contractors in Recent U.S. Labor Law: An Ambiguous Dichotomy Rooted in Simulated Statutory Purposelessness," *Comparative Labor Law and Policy Journal* 21 (Fall 1999): 187–230.

61. Brian A. Langille and Guy Davidov, "Beyond Employees and Independent Contractors: A View from Canada," *Comparative Labor Law and Policy Journal* 21 (Fall 1999): 7–45. Ronnie Eklund, "A Look at Contract Labor in the Nordic Countries," *Comparative Labor Law Journal* 18 (Winter 1997): 229–63. Wolfgang Daubler, "Employed or Self-Employed? The Role and Content of the Legal Distinction: Working People in Germany," *Comparative Labor Law and Policy Journal* 21 (Fall 1999): 77–98. Taco van Peijpe, "Employed or Self-Employed? The Role and Content of the Legal Distinction: Independent Contractors and Protected Workers in Dutch Law," *Comparative Labor Law and Policy Journal* 21 (Fall 1999): 141–55.

62. Title VII of the Civil Rights Act of 1964, 42 U.S.C. § 2000e-17.

63. Age Discrimination in Employment Act of 1967, 29 U.S.C. §§ 621–634.

64. National Labor Relations Act, 29 U.S.C. §§ 151–169.

65. Occupational Health and Safety Act, 29 U.S.C. §§ 651–678.

66. Dan Zuberi, *Differences That Matter: Social Policy and the Working Poor in the United States and Canada* (Ithaca, N.Y.: Cornell University Press, 2006).

67. International Labor Office, *Economic Security for a Better World* (Geneva: International Labor Organization, 2004). Hacker, *The Great Risk Shift*. John W. Budd, Rafael Gomez, and Noah M. Meltz, "Why a Balance Is Best: The Pluralist

Industrial Relations Paradigm of Balancing Competing Interests," in Bruce E. Kaufman, ed., *Theoretical Perspectives on Work and the Employment Relationship* (Champaign, Ill.: Industrial Relations Research Association, 2004), 195–227. Zuberi, *Differences That Matter*.

Notes to Chapter 9

1. Richard B. Freeman and Joel Rogers, *What Workers Want*, updated ed. (Ithaca, N.Y.: Cornell University Press, 2006). Richard B. Freeman, Peter Boxall, and Peter Haynes, eds., *What Workers Say: Employee Voice in the Anglo-American World* (Ithaca, N.Y.: Cornell University Press, 2007).

2. David C. Yamada, "Voices From the Cubicle: Protecting and Encouraging Private Employee Speech in the Post-Industrial Workplace," *Berkeley Journal of Employment and Labor Law* 19 (1998): 1–59. Lawrence Soley, *Censorship Inc.: The Corporate Threat to Free Speech in the United States* (New York: Monthly Review Press, 2002).

3. Rafael Gely and Leonard Bierman, "Social Isolation and American Workers: Employee Blogging and Legal Reform," *Harvard Journal of Law and Technology* 20 (Spring 2007): 288–331.

4. W. Rand Smith, *Crisis in the French Labour Movement: A Grassroots Perspective* (New York: St. Martin's, 1987). Alan Jenkins, *Employment Relations in France: Evolution and Innovation* (New York: Kluwer, 2000).

5. *Pepsi-Cola Canada Beverages (West) Ltd. v. R.W.D.S.U., Local 558*, 2002 S.C.C.D.J. 3164 (2002), para. 37.

6. *Ibid.*, paras. 38–42.

7. Conn. Gen. Stat. Ann. § 31–51q (West 2003).

8. Terry Ann Halbert, "The First Amendment in the Workplace: An Analysis and Call for Reform," *Seton Hall Law Review* 17 (1987): 42–72. Yamada, "Voices from the Cubicle."

9. Bruce Barry, *Speechless: The Erosion of Free Expression in the American Workplace* (San Francisco: Berrett-Koehler, 2007). Cynthia L. Estlund, "Free Speech and Due Process in the Workplace," *Indiana Law Journal* 71 (Winter 1995): 101–51.

10. Yamada, "Voices from the Cubicle."

11. National Labor Relations Act, 29 U.S.C. § 158(a)(3).

12. *Wright Line*, 251 NLRB 1083 (1980) [approved by the Supreme Court in *NLRB v. Transportation Management Corp.*, 462 U.S. 403 (1983)]. *Medeco Sec. Locks, Inc. v. NLRB*, 142 F.3d 733, 745 (4th Cir. 1998).

13. Marcy S. Edwards et al., *Freedom of Speech in the Public Workplace: A Legal and Practical Guide to Issues Affecting Public Employment* (Chicago: American Bar Association, 1998), 11.

14. Susanne D. Burri, Heike C. Opitz, and Albertine G. Veldman, "Work-Family Policies on Working Time Put into Practice: A Comparison of Dutch and German Case Law on Working Time Adjustment," *International Journal of Comparative Labour Law and Industrial Relations* 19 (September 2003): 321–46.

Department of Trade and Industry, "Flexible Working: The Right to Request and the Duty to Consider. A Guide for Employers and Employees" (London, 2004). Ariane Hegewisch, "Employers and European Flexible Working Rights: When the Floodgates Were Opened," UC Hastings Center for WorkLife Law Issue Brief (Fall 2005).

15. Employment Act, 2002, c. 22, pt. 4, § 47 (UK). Jodie Levin-Epstein, "How to Exercise Flexible Work: Take Steps with a 'Soft Touch' Law," Work-Life Balance Brief No. 3 (Washington, D.C.: Center for Law and Social Policy, 2005), http://www.clasp.org/publications/work_life3_annotated.pdf [accessed December 30, 2006]. Hegewisch, "Employers and European Flexible Working Rights."

16. Rachel Arnow-Richman, "Public Law and Private Process: Toward an Incentivized Organizational Justice Model of Equal Employment Quality for Caregivers," *Utah Law Review* 2007 (2007): 25–85.

17. N.J. Stat. Ann. § 34:11–56a34 (West Supp. 2007).

18. Me. Rev. Stat. Ann. tit.26, § 603 (West 2007).

19. Lonnie Golden and Barbara Wiens-Tuers, "Mandatory Overtime Work: Who, What and Where?" *Labor Studies Journal* 30 (Spring 2005): 1–26. Lonnie Golden and Helene Jorgensen, "Time after Time: Mandatory Overtime in the U.S. Economy," EPI Briefing Paper #120 (Washington, D.C.: Economic Policy Institute, 2002). Daniel B. Klaff, "Evaluating Work: Enforcing Occupational Safety and Health Standards in the United States, Canada, and Sweden," *University of Pennsylvania Journal of Labor and Employment Law* 7 (Spring 2005): 613–59.

20. Charles Perrow, *Organizing America: Wealth, Power, and the Origins of Corporate Capitalism* (Princeton, N.J.: Princeton University Press, 2002).

21. Richard S. Rosenberg, "The Technological Assault on Ethics in the Modern Workplace," in John W. Budd and James G. Scoville, eds., *The Ethics of Human Resources and Industrial Relations* (Champaign, Ill.: Labor and Employment Relations Association, 2005), 141–71. John Weckert, ed., *Electronic Monitoring in the Workplace: Controversies and Solutions* (Hershey, Penn.: Idea Group, 2005). Simon Head, *The New Ruthless Economy: Work and Power in the Digital Age* (New York: Oxford University Press, 2003). John Chalykoff and Thomas A. Kochan, "Computer-Aided Monitoring: Its Influence on Employee Job Satisfaction and Turnover," *Personnel Psychology* 42 (Winter 1989): 807–34. Jing Zhou, "When the Presence of Creative Coworkers Is Related to Creativity: Role of Supervisor Close Monitoring, Developmental Feedback, and Creative Personality," *Journal of Applied Psychology* 88 (May 2003): 413–22. Yamada, "Voices from the Cubicle." International Labor Office, "Protection of Workers' Personal Data: An ILO Code of Practice" (Geneva: International Labor Organization, 1997).

22. Mary Elizabeth Gallagher, *Contagious Capitalism: Globalization and the Politics of Labor in China* (Princeton, N.J.: Princeton University Press, 2005).

23. Employment, Social Affairs, and Equal Opportunities, "Report on the Implementation of Directive 91/533/EEC" (European Commission, no date), http://ec.europa.eu/employment_social/labour_law/docs/05_emplconditions_implreport_en.pdf [accessed November 14, 2006]. Jon Clark and Mark

Hall, "The Cinderella Directive? Employee Rights to Information about Conditions Applicable to Their Contract or Employment Relationship," *Industrial Law Journal* 21 (June 1992): 106–18.

24. Richard Edwards, *Rights at Work: Employment Relations in the Post-Union Era* (Washington, D.C.: Brookings Institution Press, 1993).

25. Steven L. Willborn, "Workers in Troubled Firms: When Are (Should) They Be Protected?" *University of Pennsylvania Journal of Labor and Employment Law* 7 (Fall 2004): 35–53. Matthew W. Finkin, "Employee Representation Outside the Labor Act: Thoughts on Arbitral Representation, Group Representation, and Workplace Committees," *University of Pennsylvania Journal of Labor and Employment Law* 5 (Fall 2002): 75–100.

26. Finkin, "Employee Representation Outside the Labor Act." Richard J. Butler and Yong-Seung Park, *Safety Practices, Firm Culture, and Workplace Injuries* (Kalamazoo, Mich.: Upjohn, 2005). Klaff, "Evaluating Work." Elaine Bernard, "Canada: Joint Committees on Occupational Health and Safety," in Joel Rogers and Wolfgang Streeck, eds., *Works Councils: Consultation, Representation, and Cooperation in Industrial Relations* (Chicago: University of Chicago Press, 1995), 351–74. John O'Grady, "Joint Health and Safety Committees: Finding a Balance," in Terrence Sullivan, ed., *Injury and the New World of Work* (Vancouver: UBC Press, 2000), 162–97. David Weil, "Are Mandated Health and Safety Committees Substitutes for or Supplements to Labor Unions?" *Industrial and Labor Relations Review* 52 (April 1999): 339–60. Cynthia Estlund, "Rebuilding the Law of the Workplace in an Era of Self-Regulation," *Columbia Law Review* 105 (March 2005): 319–404.

27. Joel Rogers and Wolfgang Streeck, eds., *Works Councils: Consultation, Representation, and Cooperation in Industrial Relations* (Chicago: University of Chicago Press, 1995). Roger Blanpain, ed., *Involvement of Employees in the European Union: Works Councils, Company Statute, Information and Consultation Rights* (The Hague: Kluwer Law International, 2002).

28. Walther Müller-Jentsch, "Germany: From Collective Voice to Co-Management," in Joel Rogers and Wolfgang Streeck, eds., *Works Councils: Consultation, Representation, and Cooperation in Industrial Relations* (Chicago: University of Chicago Press, 1995), 53–78. John T. Addison et al., "The Reform of the German Works Constitution Act: A Critical Assessment," *Industrial Relations* 43 (April 2004): 392–420 at 398.

29. Müller-Jentsch, "Germany." Addison et al., "The Reform of the German Works Constitution Act."

30. Peter Kerckhofs, *European Works Councils—Facts and Figures 2006* (Brussels: European Trade Union Institute, 2006). Wolfgang Lecher et al., *European Works Councils: Developments, Types, and Networking* (Aldershot, Hampshire, UK: Gower, 2001). Manfred Weiss, "Workers' Involvement in the European Company," in Marco Biagi, ed., *Quality of Work and Employee Involvement in Europe* (The Hague: Kluwer Law International, 2002), 63–79. Berndt Keller, "The European Company Statute: Employee Involvement—And Beyond," *Industrial Relations Journal* 33 (December 2002): 424–45. Alan C. Neal, "Information and Consultation for Employees—Still Seeking the Philosopher's Stone?"

in Marco Biagi, ed., *Quality of Work and Employee Involvement in Europe* (The Hague: Kluwer Law International, 2002), 83–99. Mark Hall, "Assessing the Information and Consultation of Employees Regulations," *Industrial Law Journal* 34 (June 2005): 103–26.

31. Stephen F. Befort, "A New Voice for the Workplace: A Proposal for an American Works Council Act," *Missouri Law Review* 69 (Summer 2004): 607–51. Paul C. Weiler, *Governing the Workplace: The Future of Labor and Employment Law* (Cambridge, Mass.: Harvard University Press, 1990). Charles B. Craver, "Mandatory Worker Participation Is Required in a Declining Union Environment to Provide Employees with Meaningful Industrial Democracy," *George Washington Law Review* 66 (November 1997): 135–71. David Fairris, *Shopfloor Matters: Labor-Management Relations in Twentieth-Century American Manufacturing* (London: Routledge, 1997). Paul J. Gollan, Ray Markey, and Iain Ross, eds., *Works Councils in Australia: Future Prospects and Possibilities* (Sydney: Federation Press, 2002).

32. Freeman and Rogers, *What Workers Want.*

33. Richard B. Freeman and Joel Rogers, "Who Speaks for Us? Employee Representation in a Nonunion Labor Market," in Bruce E. Kaufman and Morris M. Kleiner, eds., *Employee Representation: Alternatives and Future Directions* (Madison, Wisc.: Industrial Relations Research Association, 1993), 13–79 at 51. Bruce E. Kaufman, "The Employee Participation/Representation Gap: An Assessment and Proposed Solution," *University of Pennsylvania Journal of Labor and Employment Law* 3 (Spring 2001): 491–550. Carol D. Rasnic, "Germany's Statutory Works Councils and Employee Codetermination: A Model for the United States?" *Loyola of Los Angeles International and Comparative Law Journal* 14 (February 1992): 275–300.

34. John T. Addison, Claus Schnabel, and Joachim Wagner, "The Course of Research into the Economic Consequences of German Works Councils," *British Journal of Industrial Relations* 42 (June 2004): 255-81.

35. Bruce E. Kaufman, "Accomplishments and Shortcomings of Nonunion Employee Representation in the Pre–Wagner Act Years: A Reassessment," in Bruce E. Kaufman and Daphne Gottlieb Taras, eds., *Nonunion Employee Representation: History, Contemporary Practice, and Policy* (Armonk, N.Y.: M. E. Sharpe, 2000), 21–60.

36. Michael C. Harper, "A Framework for the Rejuvenation of the American Labor Movement," *Indiana Law Journal* 76 (Winter 2001): 103–33. Jonathan Hiatt and Lawrence Gold, "Employer-Employee Committees: A Union Perspective," in Bruce E. Kaufman and Daphne Gottlieb Taras, eds., *Nonunion Employee Representation: History, Contemporary Practice, and Policy* (Armonk, N.Y.: M. E. Sharpe, 2000), 498–511.

37. Joel Rogers, "United States: Lessons from Abroad and Home," in Joel Rogers and Wolfgang Streeck, eds., *Works Councils: Consultation, Representation, and Cooperation in Industrial Relations* (Chicago: University of Chicago Press, 1995), 375–410 at 400.

38. Alvin L. Goldman, "Potential Refinements of Employment Relations Law in the 21st Century," *Employee Rights and Employment Policy Journal* 3 (1999):

269–303. George Strauss, "Is the New Deal System Collapsing? With What May It Be Replaced?" *Industrial Relations* 34 (July 1995): 329–49.

39. Strauss, "Is the New Deal System Collapsing?" Bruce E. Kaufman and Daphne Gottlieb Taras, eds., *Nonunion Employee Representation: History, Contemporary Practice, and Policy* (Armonk, N.Y.: M. E. Sharpe, 2000). Befort, "A New Voice for the Workplace."

40. James C. Furlong, *Labor in the Boardroom: The Peaceful Revolution* (Princeton, N.J.: Dow Jones Books, 1977). Kirsten S. Wever, *Negotiating Competitiveness: Employment Relations and Organizational Innovation in Germany and the United States* (Boston: Harvard Business School Press, 1995). Larry W. Hunter, "Can Strategic Participation be Institutionalized? Union Representation on American Corporate Boards," *Industrial and Labor Relations Review* 51 (July 1998): 557–78. Craver, "Mandatory Worker Participation Is Required."

41. Robert W. Drago, *Striking a Balance: Work, Family, Life* (Boston: Dollars and Sense, 2007).

42. Tayo Fashoyin, "Tripartite Cooperation, Social Dialogue and National Development," *International Labour Review* 143 (2004): 341–72. Paul Marginson and Keith Sisson, *European Integration and Industrial Relations: Multi-Level Governance in the Making* (London: Palgrave/Macmillan, 2004). Harry C. Katz, Wonduck Lee, and Joohee Lee, eds., *The New Structure of Labor Relations: Tripartism and Decentralization* (Ithaca, N.Y.: Cornell University Press, 2004). Directorate-General for Employment and Social Affairs, "Promoting Social Dialogue in an Enlarged Europe" (Brussels: European Commission, 2004). Sean C. Safford, *Why the Garden Club Couldn't Save Youngstown: The Transformation of the Rust Belt* (Cambridge, Mass.: Harvard University Press, 2009).

43. 29 U.S.C. § 159(c)(1).

44. Clyde W. Summers, "Questioning the Unquestioned in Collective Labor Law," *Catholic University Law Review* 47 (Spring 1998): 791–823. Stephen F. Befort, "Labor and Employment Law at the Millennium: A Historical Review and Critical Assessment," *Boston College Law Review* 43 (March 2002): 351–460. David L. Cingranelli, "International Election Standards and NLRB Representation Elections," in Richard N. Block et al., eds., *Justice on the Job: Perspectives on the Erosion of Collective Bargaining in the United States* (Kalamazoo, Mich.: Upjohn, 2006), 41–56.

45. Befort, "Labor and Employment Law at the Millennium." Sheila Murphy, "A Comparison of the Selection of Bargaining Representatives in the United States and Canada: *Linden Lumber, Gissel,* and the Right to Challenge Majority Status," *Comparative Labor Law Journal* 10 (Fall 1988): 65–97. James J. Brudney, "Neutrality Agreements and Card Check Recognition: Prospects for Changing Paradigms," *Iowa Law Review* 90 (March 2005): 819–85.

46. Befort, "Labor and Employment Law at the Millennium." Commission on the Future of Worker-Management Relations, *Report and Recommendations* (Washington, D.C.: U.S. Departments of Labor and Commerce, 1994). Charles B. Craver, *Can Unions Survive? The Rejuvenation of the American Labor Movement* (New York: New York University Press, 1993).

47. *NLRB v. Mackay Radio and Telegraph Co.*, 304 U.S. 333, 346 (1938).

48. Samuel Estreicher, "Collective Bargaining Or 'Collective Begging'? Reflections On Antistrikebreaker Legislation," *Michigan Law Review* 93 (December 1994): 577–608. Matthew W. Finkin, "Labor Policy and the Enervation of the Economic Strike," *University of Illinois Law Review* 1990 (1990): 547–74. Paul Weiler, "Striking a New Balance: Freedom of Contract and the Prospects for Union Representation," *Harvard Law Review* 98 (December 1984): 351–420. Rick Fantasia and Kim Voss, *Hard Work: Remaking the American Labor Movement* (Berkeley: University of California Press, 2004). Josiah Bartlett Lambert, *"If the Workers Took a Notion": The Right to Strike and American Political Development* (Ithaca, N.Y.: Cornell University Press, 2005).

49. Labour Relations Act, 1995, S.O. 1995, c. 1, Sch. A.

50. Befort, "Labor and Employment Law at the Millennium."

51. *M.B. Sturgis, Inc.*, 331 NLRB 1298 (2000), overruled by *Oakwood Care Center*, 343 NLRB No. 76 (2004).

52. Clyde W. Summers, "Contingent Employment in the United States," *Comparative Labor Law and Policy Journal* 18 (Summer 1997): 503–22. Stephen F. Befort, "Revisiting the Black Hole of Workplace Regulation: A Historical and Comparative Perspective of Contingent Work," *Berkeley Journal of Employment and Labor Law* 24 (2003): 153–78. Virginia L. duRivage, François Carré, and Chris Tilly, "Making Labor Law Work for Part-Time and Contingent Workers," in Kathleen Barker and Kathleen Christensen, eds., *Contingent Work: American Employment Relations in Transition* (Ithaca, N.Y.: ILR Press, 1998), 263–80. Jeff Vockrodt, "Realizing the Need for and Logic of an Equal Pay Act for Temporary Workers," *Berkeley Journal of Employment and Labor Law* 14 (2005), 583–605. Marley S. Weiss, "*Kentucky River* at the Intersection of Professional and Supervisory Status: Fertile Delta or Bermuda Triangle," in Laura J. Cooper and Catherine L. Fisk, eds., *Labor Law Stories* (New York: Foundation Press, 2005), 353–98.

53. N.J. Stat. Ann. § 34:13A-5.1 (West Supp. 2008).

54. Minn. Stat. § 179A.13, Subd. 2(12) (2006).

55. Ellen Dannin, *Taking Back the Workers' Law: How to Fight the Assault on Labor Rights* (Ithaca, N.Y.: Cornell University Press, 2006).

56. Charles J. Morris, *The Blue Eagle at Work: Reclaiming Democratic Rights in the American Workplace* (Ithaca, N.Y.: Cornell University Press, 2005).

57. Craver, *Can Unions Survive?* Katherine V. W. Stone, *From Widgets to Digits: Employment Regulation for the Changing Workplace* (Cambridge: Cambridge University Press, 2004).

58. Michael J. Piore and Sean Safford, "Changing Regimes of Workplace Governance, Shifting Axes of Social Mobilization, and the Challenge to Industrial Relations Theory," *Industrial Relations* 45 (July 2006): 299–325. Raymond A. Friedman and Kellina M. Craig, "Predicting Joining and Participating in Minority Employee Network Groups," *Industrial Relations* 43 (October 2004): 793–816.

59. Patricia A. Greenfield and Robert J. Pleasure, "Representatives of Their Own Choosing: Finding Workers' Voice in the Legitimacy and Power of Their

Unions," in Bruce E. Kaufman and Morris M. Kleiner, eds., *Employee Representation: Alternatives and Future Directions* (Madison, Wisc.: Industrial Relations Research Association, 1993), 169–96 at 194.

NOTES TO CHAPTER 10

1. Bob Fernandez, "DuPont to Close Pension, Put in Two-Thirds Less," *Philadelphia Inquirer*, August 28, 2006. Dee DePass, "Cuts in Incentives Upset 3M Supervisors," *Star Tribune* (Minneapolis), December 16, 2006.

2. Richard N. Block, "Rethinking the National Labor Relations Act and Zero-Sum Labor Law: An Industrial Relations View," *Berkeley Journal of Employment and Labor Law* 18 (1997): 30–55. Cynthia L. Estlund, "The Ossification of American Labor Law," *Columbia Law Review* 102 (October 2002): 1527–1612.

3. Jacob S. Hacker, *The Divided Welfare State: The Battle over Public and Private Social Benefits in the United States* (New York: Cambridge University Press, 2002). Estlund, "The Ossification of American Labor Law." Ellen Dannin, *Taking Back the Workers' Law: How to Fight the Assault on Labor Rights* (Ithaca, N.Y.: Cornell University Press, 2006).

4. Hacker, *The Divided Welfare State*, 56.

5. Price V. Fishback and Shawn Everett Kantor, *A Prelude to the Welfare State: The Origins of Workers' Compensation* (Chicago: University of Chicago Press, 2000). Paul D. Moreno, *From Direct Action to Affirmative Action: Fair Employment Law and Policy in America, 1933–1972* (Baton Rouge: Louisiana State University Press, 1997). Timothy N. Thurber, *The Politics of Equality: Hubert Humphrey and the African American Freedom Struggle, 1945–1978* (New York: Columbia University Press, 1999).

6. Thomas A. Kochan, *Restoring the American Dream: A Working Families' Agenda for America* (Cambridge, Mass.: MIT Press, 2005). Maurice Emsellem, "Innovative State Reforms Shape New National Economic Security Plan for the 21st Century" (New York: National Employment Law Project, 2006). "Making State and Local Lemonade from Federal Lemons," Labor and Employment Relations Association 59th Annual Meeting (Chicago, January 5, 2007).

7. Kochan, *Restoring the American Dream*. Paul Osterman, Thomas A. Kochan, Richard Locke, and Michael J. Piore, *Working in America: A Blueprint for the New Labor Market* (Cambridge, Mass.: MIT Press, 2001).

8. *Chamber of Commerce v. Brown*, 128 S.Ct. 2408 (U.S. 2008). Osterman et al., *Working in America*. Emsellem, "Innovative State Reforms Shape New National Economic Security Plan for the 21st Century." Stephen F. Befort and Bryan N. Smith, "At the Cutting Edge of Labor Law Preemption: A Critique of *Chamber of Commerce v. Lockyer*," *Labor Lawyer* 20 (Summer 2004): 107–36. Paul M. Secunda, "Toward the Viability of State-Based Legislation to Address Workplace Captive Audience Meetings in the United States," *Comparative Labor Law and Policy Journal* 29 (Winter 2008): 209–46.

9. Harry C. Katz and Owen Darbishire, *Converging Divergences: Worldwide Changes in Employment Systems* (Ithaca, N.Y.: ILR Press, 2000). Thomas A.

Kochan, "On the Paradigm Guiding Industrial Relations Theory and Research: Comment on John Godard and John T. Delaney, "Reflections on the 'High Performance' Paradigm's Implications for Industrial Relations as a Field,'" *Industrial and Labor Relations Review* 53 (July 2000): 704–11. Dharam Ghai, "Decent Work: Universality and Diversity," Education and Outreach Programme Discussion Paper 159 (Geneva: International Institute for Labour Studies, 2005).

10. John W. Budd, *Employment with a Human Face: Balancing Efficiency, Equity, and Voice* (Ithaca, N.Y.: Cornell University Press, 2004). Richard McIntyre and Matthew M. Bodah, "The United States and ILO Conventions 87 and No. 98: The Freedom of Association and Right to Bargain Collectively," in Richard N. Block et al., eds., *Justice on the Job: Perspectives on the Erosion of Collective Bargaining in the United States* (Kalamazoo, Mich.: Upjohn, 2006), 231–47. Marley S. Weiss, "Two Steps Forward, One Step Back—Or Vice Versa: Labor Rights under Free Trade Agreements from NAFTA, Through Jordan, via Chile, to Latin America, and Beyond," *University of San Francisco Law Review* 37 (Spring 2003): 689–755.

11. Dean Baker et al., "Labor Market Institutions and Unemployment: Assessment of the Cross-Country Evidence," in David R. Howell, ed., *Fighting Unemployment: The Limits of Free Market Orthodoxy* (New York: Oxford University Press, 2005), 72–118. Stephen Nickell, "Unemployment and Labor Market Rigidities: Europe versus North America," *Journal of Economic Perspectives* 11 (Summer 1997): 55–74.

12. David Card and Alan B. Krueger, *Myth and Measurement: The New Economics of the Minimum Wage* (Princeton, N.J.: Princeton University Press, 1995).

13. Richard B. Freeman, "Labor Market Institutions Around the World," in Paul Blyton, Nicolas Bacon, Jack Fiorito and Edmund Heery, eds., *Sage Handbook of Industrial Relations* (London: Sage, 2008), 640–58.

14. Carol Zabin, Arindrajit Dube, and Ken Jacobs, "The Hidden Public Costs of Low-Wage Jobs in California," *The State of California Labor* 4 (2004): 3–44. Beth Shulman, *The Betrayal of Work: How Low-Wage Jobs Fail 30 Million Americans and Their Families* (New York: The New Press, 2003).

15. Alan B. Krueger, "Inequality, Too Much of a Good Thing," in Benjamin M. Friedman, ed., *Inequality in America: What Role for Human Capital Policies?* (Cambridge, Mass.: MIT Press, 2003), 1–75. Kathryn M. Neckerman, ed., *Social Inequality* (New York: Russell Sage Foundation, 2004). Jacob S. Hacker, *The Great Risk Shift: The Assault on American Jobs, Families, Health Care, and Retirement—And How You Can Fight Back* (New York: Oxford University Press, 2006).

16. Alan B. Krueger and Alexandre Mas, "Strikes, Scabs and Tread Separations: Labor Strife and the Production of Defective Bridgestone/Firestone Tires," *Journal of Political Economy* 112 (April 2004): 253–89.

17. Mary Lethert Wingerd, *Claiming the City: Politics, Faith, and the Power of Place in St. Paul* (Ithaca, N.Y.: Cornell University Press, 2001), 4.

18. World Commission on the Social Dimension of Globalization, *A Fair Globalization: Creating Opportunities for All* (Geneva, 2004), 22. John W. Budd, Rafael Gomez, and Noah M. Meltz, "Why a Balance Is Best: The Pluralist Industrial

Relations Paradigm of Balancing Competing Interests," in Bruce E. Kaufman, ed., *Theoretical Perspectives on Work and the Employment Relationship* (Champaign, Ill.: Industrial Relations Research Association, 2004), 195–227.

19. Rebecca M. Blank and Maria J. Hanratty, "Responding to Need: A Comparison of Social Safety Nets in Canada and the United States," in David Card and Richard B. Freeman, eds., *Small Differences That Matter: Labor Markets and Income Maintenance in Canada and the United States* (Chicago: University of Chicago Press, 1993), 191–231. Daphne Gottlieb Taras, "Collective Bargaining Regulation in Canada and the United States: Divergent Cultures, Divergent Outcomes," in Bruce E. Kaufman, ed., *Government Regulation of the Employment Relationship* (Madison, Wisc.: Industrial Relations Research Association, 1997), 295–342. Dan Zuberi, *Differences That Matter: Social Policy and the Working Poor in the United States and Canada* (Ithaca, N.Y.: Cornell University Press, 2006).

20. Budd, *Employment with a Human Face*. Robert W. Drago, *Striking a Balance: Work, Family, Life* (Boston: Dollars and Sense, 2007).

Bibliography

Abraham, Katharine G., and Susan N. Houseman. "Does Employment Protection Inhibit Labor Market Flexibility? Lessons from Germany, France, and Belgium." In Rebecca M. Blank, ed., *Social Protection Versus Economic Flexibility: Is There a Trade-Off?*, 59–93. Chicago: University of Chicago Press, 1994.

Abraham, Steven E. "Can a Wrongful Discharge Statute Really Benefit Employers?" *Industrial Relations* 37 (October 1998): 499–518.

Addison, John T., et al. "The Reform of the German Works Constitution Act: A Critical Assessment." *Industrial Relations* 43 (April 2004): 392–420.

Addison, John T., Claus Schnabel, and Joachim Wagner. "The Course of Research into the Economic Consequences of German Works Councils." *British Journal of Industrial Relations* 42 (June 2004): 255–81.

Administrative Office of the United States Courts. *Judicial Business of the United States Courts: 2007 Annual Report of the Director*. Washington, D.C.: U.S. Government Printing Office, 2008.

Advisory Council on Social Security. *Report of the 1994–1996 Advisory Council on Social Security. Vol. I: Findings and Recommendations*. Washington, D.C., 2007.

Advisory Council on Unemployment Compensation. "Collected Findings and Recommendations, 1994–1996." Washington, D.C., 1996.

AFL-CIO. *Death on the Job: The Toll of Neglect—A National and State-by-State Profile of Worker Safety and Health in the United States*. Washington, D.C., 2008.

———. "The Wal-Mart Tax: A Review of Studies Examining Employers' Health Care Cost-Shifting." Washington, D.C., 2005. http://www.aflcio.org/corporatewatch/walmart/upload/walmart_tax_memo.pdf [accessed November 10, 2006].

Ala-Mursula, L., et al. "Employee Control over Working Times: Associations with Subjective Health and Sickness Absences." *Journal of Epidemiology and Community Health* 56 (April 2002): 272–78.

American Arbitration Association. "National Rules for the Resolution of Employment Disputes." Washington, D.C., 2005. http://www.adr.org/sp.asp?id=22075 [accessed August 27, 2006].

American Axle and Manufacturing. "Family Medical Leave Act: United States Senate Roundtable Discussion" (June 23, 2005). http://www.nam.org/s_nam/bin.asp?CID=390&DID=235078&DOC=FILE.PDF [accessed August 26, 2006].

Anderson, Tosh. "Overwork Robs Workers' Health: Interpreting OSHA's General Duty Clause to Prohibit Long Work Hours." *New York City Law Review* 7 (Spring 2004): 85–160.

Appelbaum, Eileen, and Rosemary Batt. *The New American Workplace: Transforming Work Systems in the United States*. Ithaca, N.Y.: ILR Press, 1994.

Appelbaum, Eileen, Annette Bernhardt, and Richard Murnane, eds. *Low-Wage America: How Employers Are Reshaping Opportunity in the Workplace*. New York: Russell Sage Foundation, 2003.

Argyris, Chris. *Personality and Organization: The Conflict Between System and the Individual*. New York: Harper and Row, 1957.

Armstrong, Pat, Hugh Armstrong, and Claudia Fegan. *Universal Health Care: What the United States Can Learn from the Canadian Experience*. New York: New Press, 1998.

Arnow-Richman, Rachel. "Public Law and Private Process: Toward an Incentivized Organizational Justice Model of Equal Employment Quality for Caregivers." *Utah Law Review* 2007 (2007): 25–85.

Aronowitz, Stanley. *How Class Works: Power and Social Movement*. New Haven, Conn.: Yale University Press, 2003.

Bakan, Joel. *The Corporation: The Pathological Pursuit of Profit and Power*. New York: Free Press, 2004.

Baker, Dean, et al. "Labor Market Institutions and Unemployment: Assessment of the Cross-Country Evidence." In David R. Howell, ed., *Fighting Unemployment: The Limits of Free Market Orthodoxy*, 72–118. Oxford: Oxford University Press, 2005.

Bales, Richard A. "Beyond the Protocol: Recent Trends in Employment Arbitration." *Employee Rights and Employment Policy Journal* 11 (2007): 301–44.

Ballam, Deborah A. "Exploding the Original Myth Regarding Employment-at-Will: The True Origins of the Doctrine." *Berkeley Journal of Employment and Labor Law* 17 (1996): 91–130.

Bamber, Greg J. Russell D. Lansbury, and Nick Wailes, eds. *International and Comparative Employment Relations: Globalisation and the Developed Market Economies*. London: Sage, 2004.

Bank for International Settlements. "Triennial Central Bank Survey: Foreign Exchange and Derivatives Market Activity in 2007." Basel, Switzerland, 2007.

Barker, Kathleen, and Kathleen Christensen, eds. *Contingent Work: American Employment Relations in Transition*. Ithaca, N.Y.: ILR Press, 1998.

Barlett, Donald L., and James B. Steele. *Critical Condition: How Health Care in America Became Big Business—and Bad Medicine*. New York: Doubleday, 2004.

Barry, Bruce. *Speechless: The Erosion of Free Expression in the American Workplace.* San Francisco: Berrett-Koehler, 2007.

Beatty, Jack. *Age of Betrayal: The Triumph of Money in America, 1865–1900.* New York: Knopf, 2007.

Befort, Stephen F. "Accommodation at Work: Lessons from the Americans with Disabilities Act and Possibilities for Alleviating the American Worker Time Crunch." *Cornell Journal of Law and Public Policy* 13 (Summer 2004): 615–36.

———. "Demystifying Federal Labor and Employment Law Preemption." *Labor Lawyer* 13 (Winter/Spring 1998): 429–43.

———. "Labor and Employment Law at the Millennium: A Historical Review and Critical Assessment." *Boston College Law Review* 43 (March 2002): 351–460.

———. "A New Voice for the Workplace: A Proposal for an American Works Council Act." *Missouri Law Review* 69 (Summer 2004): 607–51.

———. "The Perfect Storm of Retirement Insecurity: Fixing the Three-Legged Stool of Social Security, Pensions, and Personal Savings." *Minnesota Law Review* 91 (April 2007): 938–88.

———. "Revisiting the Black Hole of Workplace Regulation: A Historical and Comparative Perspective of Contingent Work." *Berkeley Journal of Employment and Labor Law* 24 (2003): 153–78.

———. "The Story of *Sutton v. United Airlines, Inc.*: Narrowing the Reach of the Americans with Disabilities Act." In Joel Wm. Friedman, ed., *Employment Discrimination Stories*, 329–62. New York: Foundation Press, 2006.

Befort, Stephen F., and Virginia E. Cornett. "Beyond the Rhetoric of the NAFTA Treaty Debate: A Comparative Analysis of Labor and Employment Law in Mexico and the United States." *Comparative Labor Law Journal* 17 (Winter 1996): 269–313.

Befort, Stephen F., and Christopher J. Kopka. "The Sounds of Silence: The Libertarian Ethos of ERISA Preemption." *Florida Law Review* 52 (January 2000): 1–40.

Befort, Stephen F., and Bryan N. Smith. "At the Cutting Edge of Labor Law Preemption: A Critique of *Chamber of Commerce v. Lockyer*." *Labor Lawyer* 20 (Summer 2004): 107–36.

Belous, Richard S. *The Contingent Economy: The Growth of the Temporary, Part-Time and Subcontracted Workforce.* Washington, D.C.: National Planning Association, 1989.

———. "The Rise of the Contingent Work Force: The Key Challenges and Opportunities." *Washington and Lee Law Review* 52 (1995): 863–78.

Bennett, James T., and Jason E. Taylor. "Labor Unions: Victims of Their Political Success?" *Journal of Labor Research* 22 (Spring 2001): 261–73.

Berger, Lawrence M., Jennifer Hill, and Jane Waldfogel. "Maternity Leave, Early Maternal Employment and Child Health and Development in the U.S." *Economic Journal* 115 (February 2005): F29–F47.

Bernard, Elaine. "Canada: Joint Committees on Occupational Health and Safety." In Joel Rogers and Wolfgang Streeck, eds., *Works Councils: Consultation, Representation, and Cooperation in Industrial Relations*, 351–74. Chicago: University of Chicago Press, 1995.

Bernhardt, Annette, et al., eds. *The Gloves-Off Economy: Workplace Standards at the Bottom of America's Labor Market*. Champaign, Ill.: Industrial Relations Research Association, 2008.

Bernstein, Aaron, Howard Gleckman, and Michael J. Mandel. "Social Security: Three New Ideas." *Business Week*, February 21, 2005.

Bernstein, Irving. *A Caring Society: The New Deal, the Worker, and the Great Depression*. Boston: Houghton Mifflin, 1985.

———. *The Lean Years: A History of the American Worker, 1920–1933*. Boston: Houghton Mifflin, 1960.

Bernstein, Jared. *All Together Now: Common Sense for a Fair Economy*. San Francisco: Berrett-Koehler, 2006.

Bernstein, Jared, and Lawrence Mishel. "Seven Reasons for Skepticism about the Technology Story of U.S. Wage Inequality." In Ivar Berg and Arne L. Kalleberg, eds., *Sourcebook of Labor Markets: Evolving Structures and* Processes, 409–27. New York: Kluwer Academic, 2001.

Bertola, Giuseppe, Tito Boeri, and Sandrine Cazes. "Employment Protection in Industrialized Countries: The Case for New Indicators." *International Labour Review* 139 (2000): 57–72.

Binette, Matthew J. "Patients' Bill of Rights: Legislative Cure-all or Prescription for Disaster?" *North Carolina Law Review* 81 (January 2003): 653–96.

Bingham, Lisa B. "Employee Free Speech in the Workplace: Using the First Amendment as Public Policy for Wrongful Discharge Actions." *Ohio State Law Journal* 55 (Spring 1994): 341–91.

Bird, Robert C. "Rethinking Wrongful Discharge: A Continuum Approach." *University of Cincinnati Law Review* 73 (Winter 2004): 517–79.

Blank, Rebecca M. *It Takes a Nation: A New Agenda for Fighting Poverty*. Princeton, N.J.: Princeton University Press, 1997.

———. "The Misdiagnosis of Eurosclerosis." *American Prospect* (January–February 1997): 81–85.

———, ed. *Social Protection Versus Economic Flexibility: Is There a Trade-Off?* Chicago: University of Chicago Press, 1994.

Blank, Rebecca M., and Maria J. Hanratty. "Responding to Need: A Comparison of Social Safety Nets in Canada and the United States." In David Card and Richard B. Freeman, eds., *Small Differences That Matter: Labor Markets and Income Maintenance in Canada and the United States*, 191–231. Chicago: University of Chicago Press, 1993.

Blanpain, Roger. "The Changing World of Work." In Roger Blanpain and Chris Engels, eds., *Comparative Labour Law and Industrial Relations in Industrialized Market Economies*, 6th ed., 23–50. The Hague: Kluwer Law International, 1998.

———, ed. *Involvement of Employees in the European Union: Works Councils, Company Statute, Information and Consultation Rights*. The Hague: Kluwer Law International, 2002.

Blau, Francine D., and Lawrence M. Kahn. *At Home and Abroad: U.S. Labor-Market Performance in International Perspective*. New York: Russell Sage Foundation, 2002.

Block, Richard N. "Rethinking the National Labor Relations Act and Zero-Sum Labor Law: An Industrial Relations View." *Berkeley Journal of Employment and Labor Law* 18 (1997): 30–55.

Bluestone, Barry, and Irving Bluestone. *Negotiating the Future: A Labor Perspective on American Business.* New York: Basic Books, 1992.

Bluestone, Barry, and Stephen Rose. "The Enigma of Working Time Trends." In Lonnie Golden and Deborah M. Figart, eds., *Working Time: International Trends, Theory and Policy Perspectives*, 21–37. London: Routledge, 2000.

Blumberg, Linda J. "Who Pays for Employer-Sponsored Health Insurance?" *Health Affairs* 18 (November/December 1999): 58–61.

Board of Trustees, Federal Old-Age and Survivors Insurance and Disability Insurance Trust Funds. *2008 Annual Report.* Washington, D.C.: U.S. Government Printing Office, 2008.

Bognanno, Mario F., and Jiangfeng Lu. "NAFTA's Labor Side Agreement: Withering as an Effective Labor Law Enforcement and MNC Compliance Strategy?" In William N. Cooke, ed., *Multinational Companies and Global Human Resource Strategies*, 369–402. Westport, Conn.: Quorum Books, 2003.

Bompey, Stuart H., Michael Delikat, and Lisa K. McClelland. "The Attack on Arbitration and Mediation of Employment Disputes." *Labor Lawyer* 13 (Summer 1997): 21–86.

Bond, James T., et al. *The 1997 National Study of the Changing Workforce.* New York: Families and Work Institute, 1998.

Bowie, Norman E. *Business Ethics: A Kantian Perspective.* Malden, Mass.: Blackwell, 1999.

———. "Kantian Ethical Thought." In John W. Budd and James G. Scoville, eds., *The Ethics of Human Resources and Industrial Relations*, 61–87. Champaign, Ill.: Labor and Employment Relations Association, 2005.

Brand, Norman, ed. *Discipline and Discharge in Arbitration.* Washington, D.C.: Bureau of National Affairs, 1998.

Braverman, Harry. *Labor and Monopoly Capital: The Degradation of Work in the Twentieth Century.* New York: Monthly Review Press, 1974.

Brecher, Jeremy. *Strike!* Boston: South End Press, 1972.

Brenner, Mark D. "The Economic Impact of the Boston Living Wage Ordinance." *Industrial Relations* 44 (January 2005): 59–83.

Brenner, Mark D., David Fairris, and John Ruser. "'Flexible' Work Practices and Occupational Safety and Health: Exploring the Relationship Between Cumulative Trauma Disorders and Workplace Transformation." *Industrial Relations* 43 (January 2004): 242–66.

Bronfenbrenner, Kate, and Tom Juravich. "It Takes More Than House Calls: Organizing to Win with a Comprehensive Union Building Strategy." In Kate Bronfenbrenner et al., eds., *Organizing to Win: New Research on Union Strategies*, 19–36. Ithaca, N.Y.: ILR Press, 1998.

Brown, Charles. "Minimum Wages, Employment, and the Distribution of Income." In Orley Ashenfelter and David Card, eds., *Handbook of Labor Economics.* Volume 3B, 2101–63. Amsterdam: Elsevier, 1999.

Brudney, James J. "Neutrality Agreements and Card Check Recognition: Prospects for Changing Paradigms." *Iowa Law Review* 90 (March 2005): 819–85.

Bruno, Robert. *Steelworker Alley: How Class Works in Youngstown.* Ithaca, N.Y.: Cornell University Press, 1999).

Budd, John W. "Does Employee Ignorance Undermine Shared Capitalism?" In Joseph R. Blasi, Richard B. Freeman, and Douglas Kruse, eds., *Shared Capitalism at Work: The Economic Effects of Employee Ownership, Profit Sharing, Gainsharing, and Broad-based Stock Options.* New York: Russell Sage Foundation and National Bureau of Economic Research, forthcoming.

———. *Employment with a Human Face: Balancing Efficiency, Equity, and Voice.* Ithaca, N.Y.: Cornell University Press, 2004.

———. *Labor Relations: Striking a Balance*, 2nd ed. Boston: McGraw-Hill/Irwin, 2008.

Budd, John W., and Devasheesh Bhave. "The Employment Relationship." In Adrian Wilkinson, Tom Redman, Scott Snell, and Nick Bacon, eds., *Sage Handbook of Human Resource Management.* London: Sage, forthcoming.

———. "Values, Ideologies, and Frames of Reference in Employment Relations." In Paul Blyton, Nicolas Bacon, Jack Fiorito and Edmund Heery, eds., *Sage Handbook of Industrial Relations*, 92–112. London: Sage, 2008.

Budd, John W., and Angela Brey. "Unions and Family Leave: Early Experience under the Family and Medical Act." *Labor Studies Journal* 28 (Fall 2003): 85–105.

Budd, John W., and Alexander J. S. Colvin. "Improved Metrics for Workplace Dispute Resolution Procedures: Efficiency, Equity, and Voice." *Industrial Relations* 47 (July 2008): 460–79.

Budd, John W., and Brian P. McCall. "The Effect of Unions on the Receipt of Unemployment Insurance Benefits." *Industrial and Labor Relations Review* 50 (April 1997): 478–92.

———. "Unions and Unemployment Insurance Benefits Receipt: Evidence from the CPS." *Industrial Relations* 43 (April 2004): 339–55.

Budd, John W., and Karen Mumford. "Family-Friendly Work Practices in Britain: Availability and Perceived Accessibility." *Human Resource Management Journal* 45 (Spring 2006): 23–42.

Budd, John W., and James G. Scoville. "Moral Philosophy, Business Ethics, and the Employment Relationship." In John W. Budd and James G. Scoville, eds., *The Ethics of Human Resources and Industrial Relations*, 1–21. Champaign, Ill.: Labor and Employment Relations Association, 2005.

Budd, John W., Rafael Gomez, and Noah M. Meltz. "Why a Balance Is Best: The Pluralist Industrial Relations Paradigm of Balancing Competing Interests." In Bruce E. Kaufman, ed., *Theoretical Perspectives on Work and the Employment Relationship*, 195–227. Champaign, Ill.: Industrial Relations Research Association, 2004.

Burns, James MacGregor, and Stewart Burns. *A People's Charter: The Pursuit of Rights in America.* New York: Alfred A. Knopf, 1991.

Burrell, Gibson. "Foucauldian and Postmodern Thought and the Analysis of

Work." In Marek Korczynski, Randy Hodson, and Paul Edwards, eds., *Social Theory at Work*, 155–81. Oxford: Oxford University Press, 2006.

Burri, Susanne D., Heike C. Opitz, and Albertine G. Veldman. "Work-Family Policies on Working Time Put into Practice: A Comparison of Dutch and German Case Law on Working Time Adjustment." *International Journal of Comparative Labour Law and Industrial Relations* 19 (September 2003): 321–46.

Butler, Richard J., and Yong-Seung Park. *Safety Practices, Firm Culture, and Workplace Injuries*. Kalamazoo, Mich.: Upjohn, 2005.

Butrica, Barbara, Howard Iams, and Karen E. Smith. "The Changing Impact of Social Security on Retirement Income in the United States." *Social Security Bulletin* 65 (2003/04): 1–13.

Cantor, David, et al. *Balancing the Needs of Families and Employers: Family and Medical Leave Surveys, 2000 Update*. Washington, D.C.: U.S. Department of Labor, 2001.

Cappelli, Peter. *The New Deal at Work: Managing the Market-Driven Workforce*. Boston: Harvard Business School Press, 1999.

Cappelli, Peter, et al. *Change at Work*. New York: Oxford University Press, 1997.

Card, David, and John E. DiNardo. "Skill-Biased Technological Change and Rising Wage Inequality: Some Problems and Puzzles." *Journal of Labor Economics* 20 (October 2002): 753–83.

Card, David, and Alan B. Krueger. *Myth and Measurement: The New Economics of the Minimum Wage*. Princeton, N.J.: Princeton University Press, 1995.

Carlson, Richard R. "Why the Law Still Can't Tell an Employee When It Sees One and How It Ought to Stop Trying." *Berkeley Journal of Employment and Labor Law* 22 (2001): 295–368.

Carnevale, Anthony P. "The Coming Labor and Skills Shortage." *T+D* (January 2005): 37–41.

———. "Enhancing Skills in the New Economy." In Ann Howard, ed., *The Changing Nature of Work*, 238–51. San Francisco: Jossey-Bass, 1995.

Carnevale, Anthony P., Lynn A. Jennings, and James M. Eisenmann. "Contingent Workers and Employment Law." In Kathleen Barker and Kathleen Christensen, eds., *Contingent Work: American Employment Relations in Transition*, 281–305. Ithaca, N.Y.: ILR Press, 1998.

Case, Anne, Angela Fertig, and Christina Paxson. "The Lasting Impact of Childhood Health and Circumstance." *Journal of Health Economics* 24 (March 2005): 365–89.

Ceniceros, Roberto. "Unions Fight Cost-Shifting." *Business Insurance* 37 (October 20, 2003): 1–2.

Center on Budget and Policy Priorities. "Buying Power of Minimum Wage at 51–Year Low." Washington, D.C., 2006. http://www.epinet.org/issuebriefs/224/ib224.pdf [accessed November 10, 2006].

———. "More Americans, Including More Children, Now Lack Health Insurance." Washington, D.C., 2007. http://www.cbpp.org/8-28-07health.htm [accessed May 23, 2008].

———. "Recent Tax and Income Trends among High-Income Taxpayers." Washington, D.C., 2006. http://www.cbpp.org/4-10-06tax5.htm [accessed November 12, 2006].

———. "A $7.25 Minimum Wage Would Be a Useful Step in Helping Working Families Escape Poverty." Washington, D.C., 2007. http://www.cbpp.org/1-5-07mw.htm [accessed September 23, 2007].

———. "Whose Recovery? Labor Day 2006 Finds Many Americans Not Sharing in the Growing Economy." Washington, D.C., 2006. http://www.cbpp.org/policy-points9-1-06.htm [accessed November 6, 2006].

Chaison, Gary N., and Joseph B. Rose. "The Macrodeterminants of Union Growth and Decline." In George Strauss, Daniel G. Gallagher, and Jack Fiorito, eds., *The State of the Unions*, 3–45. Madison, Wisc.: Industrial Relations Research Association, 1991.

Chalykoff, John, and Thomas A. Kochan. "Computer-Aided Monitoring: Its Influence on Employee Job Satisfaction and Turnover." *Personnel Psychology* 42 (Winter 1989): 807–34.

Champlin, Dell P., and Janet T. Knoedler, eds. *The Institutionalist Tradition in Labor Economics*. Armonk, N.Y.: M. E. Sharpe, 2004.

Chancer, Lynn S., and Beverly Xaviera Watkins. *Gender, Race, and Class: An Overview*. Malden, Mass.: Blackwell, 2006.

Choi, James J., et al. "Defined Contribution Pensions: Plan Rules, Participant Decisions, and the Path of Least Resistance." In James M. Poterba, ed., *Tax Policy and the Economy*, Volume 16, 67–113. Cambridge, Mass.: MIT Press, 2002).

Cingranelli, David L. "International Election Standards and NLRB Representation Elections." In Richard N. Block et al., eds., *Justice on the Job: Perspectives on the Erosion of Collective Bargaining in the United States*, 41–56. Kalamazoo, Mich.: Upjohn, 2006.

Clark, Jon, and Mark Hall. "The Cinderella Directive? Employee Rights to Information about Conditions Applicable to their Contract or Employment Relationship." *Industrial Law Journal* 21 (June 1992): 106–18.

Clegg, H. A. *The Changing System of Industrial Relations in Great Britain*. Oxford: Basil Blackwell, 1979.

———. "Pluralism in Industrial Relations." *British Journal of Industrial Relations* 13 (November 1975): 309–16.

Clements, Jonathan. "Forget the Rule of Thumb: Saving 10% of Your Salary Is No Longer Enough." *Wall Street Journal*, July 20, 2005.

Cohany, Sharon, et al. "Counting the Workers: Results of a First Survey." In Kathleen Barker and Kathleen Christensen, eds., *Contingent Work: American Employment Relations in* Transition, 41–68. Ithaca, N.Y.: ILR Press, 1998.

Cohen, Joshua, and Joel Rogers. *On Democracy*. New York: Penguin, 1983.

Cohen, Lizabeth. *A Consumer's Republic: The Politics of Mass Consumption in Postwar America*. New York: Alfred A. Knopf, 2003.

Cohen, Malcolm S., and Mahmood A. Zaidi. *Global Skills Shortages*. Cheltenham, UK: Edward Elgar, 2002.

Colker, Ruth. *The Disability Pendulum: The First Decade of the Americans with Disabilities Act*. New York: New York University Press, 2005.

Columella, Lucius Junius Moderatus. *De Re Rustica*. Trans. Harrison Boyd Ash. London: William Heinemann, 1941.

Colvin, Alexander J. S. "The Relationship Between Employment Arbitration and Workplace Dispute Resolution Procedures." *Ohio State Journal on Dispute Resolution* 16 (2001): 643–68.

Colvin, Alexander J. S. "Flexibility and Fairness in Liberal Market Economies: The Comparative Impact of the Legal Environment and High-Performance Work Systems." *British Journal of Industrial Relations* 26 (March 2006): 73–97.

Commission of the European Communities. "Green Paper: Modernising Labour Law to Meet the Challenges of the 21st Century." Brussels, 2006.

Commission on the Future of Worker-Management Relations. *Report and Recommendations*. Washington, D.C.: U.S. Departments of Labor and Commerce, 1994.

Commons, John R. *Industrial Goodwill*. New York: McGraw-Hill, 1919.

Congressional Budget Office. *Social Security: A Primer*. Washington, D.C., 2001.

Conroy, Martin. *Sustaining the New Economy: Work, Family, and Community in the Information Age*. New York: Russell Sage Foundation, 2000.

Conway, Mara Eleina. "*Karoshi*: Is It Sweeping America?" *UCLA Pacific Basin Law Journal* 15 (Spring 1997): 352–80.

Cooke, William N. *Union Organizing and Public Policy: Failure to Secure First Contracts*. Kalamazoo, Mich.: W. E. Upjohn Institute for Employment Research, 1985.

Cooper, Laura, et al. *ADR in the Workplace*. St. Paul, Minn.: West Group, 2000.

Copeland, Craig. "Employment-Based Retirement Plan Participation: Geographic Differences and Trends, 2005." EBRI Issue Brief No. 299. Washington, D.C.: Employee Benefit Research Institute, 2006.

———. "Retirement Plan Participation: Survey of Income and Program Participation (SIPP) Data." EBRI Notes No. 9. Washington, D.C.: Employee Benefit Research Institute, 2005.

Corbett, William R. "Waiting for the Labor Law of the Twenty-First Century: Everything Old Is New Again." *Berkeley Journal of Employment and Labor Law* 23 (2002): 259–306.

Corson, Walter, Karen Needels, and Walter Nicholson. "Emergency Unemployment Compensation: The 1990s Experience." Unemployment Insurance Occasional Paper No. 99-4. Washington, D.C.: U.S. Department of Labor, 1999.

Council of Economic Advisors. *Economic Report of the President*. Washington, D.C.: U.S. Government Printing Office, various issues.

Cowie, Jefferson. *Capital Moves: RCA's Seventy-Year Quest for Cheap Labor*. Ithaca, N.Y.: Cornell University Press, 1999.

Coyle-Shapiro, Jacqueline A.-M., Lynn M. Shore, M. Susan Taylor, and Lois E. Tetrick, eds. *The Employment Relationship: Examining Psychological and Contextual Perspectives*. New York: Oxford University Press, 2004.

Craver, Charles B. *Can Unions Survive? The Rejuvenation of the American Labor Movement*. New York: New York University Press, 1993.

———. "Mandatory Worker Participation Is Required in a Declining Union Environment to Provide Employees with Meaningful Industrial Democracy." *George Washington Law Review* 66 (November 1997): 135–71.

Crossley, Mary. "The Disability Kaleidoscope." *Notre Dame Law Review* 74 (March 1999): 621–716.

Crouch, Colin. "Skill Formation Systems." In Stephen Ackroyd et al., eds., *The Oxford Handbook of Work and Organization*, 95–114. Oxford: Oxford University Press, 2005.

Curtis, Michael Kent. *Free Speech, "The People's Darling Privilege": Struggles for Freedom of Expression in American History*. Durham, N.C.: Duke University Press, 2000.

Dannin, Ellen. *Taking Back the Workers' Law: How to Fight the Assault on Labor Rights*. Ithaca, N.Y.: Cornell University Press, 2006.

Daubler, Wolfgang. "Employed or Self-Employed? The Role and Content of the Legal Distinction: Working People in Germany." *Comparative Labor Law and Policy Journal* 21 (Fall 1999): 77–98.

Dau-Schmidt, Kenneth G. "Employment in the New Age of Trade and Technology: Implications for Labor and Employment Law." *Indiana Law Journal* 76 (Winter 2001): 1–28.

———. "The Labor Market Transformed: Adapting Labor and Employment Law to the Rise of the Contingent Work Force." *Washington and Lee Law Review* 52 (1995): 879–88.

Davis, Karen. "Health Care for Low-Income People." In Ray Marshall, ed., *Back to Shared Prosperity: The Growing Inequality of Wealth and Income in America*, 311–20. Armonk, N.Y.: M. E. Sharpe, 2000.

de Gooijer, Win. *Trends in EU Health Care Systems*. Amsterdam: Springer, 2006.

Demos and Center for Responsible Lending. "The Plastic Safety Net: The Reality Behind Debt in America." New York, 2005.

DeNavas-Walt, Carmen, Bernadette D. Proctor, and Jessica Smith. *Income, Poverty, and Health Insurance Coverage in the United States: 2007*. U.S. Census Bureau Current Population Reports, P60–233. Washington, D.C.: U.S. Government Printing Office, 2007.

Department of Trade and Industry. "Flexible Working: The Right to Request and the Duty to Consider. A Guide for Employers and Employees." London, 2004.

DePass, Dee. "Cuts in Incentives Upset 3M Supervisors." *Star Tribune* (Minneapolis), December 16, 2006.

Derber, Milton. *The American Idea of Industrial Democracy, 1865–1965*. Urbana: University of Illinois Press, 1970.

Derickson, Alan. *Health Security for All: Dreams of Universal Health Care in America*. Baltimore: Johns Hopkins University Press, 2005.

Dertouzos, James N., and Lynn A. Karoly. *Labor-Market Responses to Employer Liability*. Santa Monica, Calif.: Rand Institute for Civil Justice, 1992.

Diamond, Peter A., and Peter R. Orszag. *Saving Social Security: A Balanced Approach.* Washington, D.C.: Brookings Institution Press, 2004.

Directorate-General for Employment and Social Affairs. "Promoting Social Dialogue in an Enlarged Europe." Brussels: European Commission, 2004.

Docteur, Elizabeth, and Howard Oxley. "Health-Care Systems: Lessons from the Reform Experience." OECD Health Working Paper No. 9. Paris: Organization for Economic Cooperation and Development, 2003.

Donaldson, Thomas, and Lee E. Preston. "The Stakeholder Theory of the Corporation: Concepts, Evidence, and Implications." *Academy of Management Review* 20 (January 1995): 65–91.

Downey, Ezekiel H. *Workmen's Compensation.* New York: Macmillan, 1924.

Drago, Robert W. *Striking a Balance: Work, Family, Life.* Boston: Dollars and Sense, 2007.

Draut, Tamara, and Javier Silva. "Borrowing to Make Ends Meet: The Growth of Credit Card Debt in the '90s." New York: Demos, 2003.

Dubofsky, Melvyn, and Foster Rhea Dulles. *Labor in America: A History,* 7th ed. Wheeling, Ill.: Harlan Davidson, 2004.

Duncan, Greg J., and P. Lindsay Chase-Lansdale, eds. *For Better and for Worse: Welfare Reform and the Well-Being of Children and Families.* New York: Russell Sage Foundation, 2001.

Dundon, Tony, Adrian Wilkinson, Mick Marchington, and Peter Ackers. "The Meanings and Purpose of Employee Voice." *International Journal of Human Resource Management* 15 (September 2004): 1149–70.

Dunlop, John T. *Industrial Relations Systems.* New York: Holt, 1958.

Dunlop, John T., and Arnold M. Zack. *Mediation and Arbitration of Employment Disputes.* San Francisco: Jossey-Bass, 1997.

duRivage, Virginia L. "New Policies for the Part-Time and Contingent Workforce." In Virginia L. duRivage, ed., *New Policies for Part-Time and Contingent Workers,* 89–134. Armonk, N.Y.: M. E. Sharpe, 1992.

duRivage, Virginia L., François Carré, and Chris Tilly. "Making Labor Law Work for Part-Time and Contingent Workers. In Kathleen Barker and Kathleen Christensen, eds., *Contingent Work: American Employment Relations in Transition,* 263–80. Ithaca, N.Y.: ILR Press, 1998.

Edwards, Marcy S., et al. *Freedom of Speech in the Public Workplace: A Legal and Practical Guide to Issues Affecting Public Employment.* Chicago: American Bar Association, 1998.

Edwards, Paul, and Judy Wajcman. *The Politics of Working Life.* Oxford: Oxford University Press, 2005.

Edwards, Richard. *Contested Terrain: The Transformation of the Workplace in the Twentieth Century.* New York: Basic Books, 1979.

———. *Rights at Work: Employment Relations in the Post-Union Era.* Washington, D.C.: Brookings Institution, 1993.

Ehrenreich, Barbara. *Nickeled and Dimed: On (Not) Getting By in America.* New York: Henry Holt, 2001.

Eklund, Ronnie. "A Look at Contract Labor in the Nordic Countries." *Comparative Labor Law Journal* 18 (Winter 1997): 229–63.

Emerson, Thomas I. "Colonial Intentions and Current Realities of the First Amendment." *University of Pennsylvania Law Review* 125 (April 1977): 737–60.

Employment and Training Administration. "WIA Reauthorization and Reform." Washington, D.C.: U.S. Department of Labor, no date. http://www.doleta.gov/pdf/WIA%20Reauthorization%20Summary.pdf [accessed August 15, 2005].

Employee Benefit Research Institute. *Fundamentals of Employee Benefit Programs*. Washington, D.C., 2005.

———. "2006 RCS Fact Sheet: Saving for Retirement in America." Washington, D.C., 2006. http://www.ebri.org/pdf/RCS06_FS_01_Saving_Final.pdf [accessed January 7, 2007].

Employment Policy Foundation. "Employer Health Insurance Costs Continue to Rise." *Employment Trends*. Washington, D.C.: August 3, 2004. http://www.epf.org/pubs/newsletters/2004/et20040803.pdf [accessed April 11, 2005].

Employment, Social Affairs, and Equal Opportunities. "Report on the Implementation of Directive 91/533/EEC." European Commission, no date. http://ec.europa.eu/employment_social/labour_law/docs/05_emplconditions_implreport_en.pdf [accessed November 14, 2006].

Emsellem, Maurice. "Innovative State Reforms Shape New National Economic Security Plan for the 21st Century." New York: National Employment Law Project, 2006.

Engardio, Pete, et al. "Is Your Job Next?" *Business Week*, February 3, 2003.

Epstein, Richard A. "In Defense of the Contract at Will." *University of Chicago Law Review* 51 (Fall 1983): 947–82.

Ernst, Daniel R. *Lawyers Against Labor: From Individual Rights to Corporate Liberalism*. Urbana: University of Illinois Press, 1995.

Estey, J. A. *The Labor Problem*. New York: McGraw-Hill, 1928.

Estlund, Cynthia L. "Free Speech and Due Process in the Workplace." *Indiana Law Journal* 71 (Winter 1995): 101–51.

———. "The Ossification of American Labor Law." *Columbia Law Review* 102 (October 2002): 1527–1612.

———. "Rebuilding the Law of the Workplace in an Era of Self-Regulation." *Columbia Law Review* 105 (March 2005): 319–404.

———. "What Do Workers Want? Employee Interests, Public Interests, and Freedom of Expression under the National Labor Relations Act." *University of Pennsylvania Law Review* 140 (January 1992): 921–1004.

———. *Working Together: How Workplace Bonds Strengthen a Diverse Democracy*. Oxford: Oxford University Press, 2003.

———. "Wrongful Discharge Protections in an At-Will World." *Texas Law Review* 74 (June 1996): 1655–92.

Estreicher, Samuel. "Collective Bargaining Or 'Collective Begging'? Reflections on Antistrikebreaker Legislation." *Michigan Law Review* 93 (December 1994): 577–608.

———. "Unjust Dismissals in Other Countries: Some Cautionary Notes." *Employee Relations Law Journal* 10 (Summer 1984): 286–302.

European Foundation for the Improvement of Living and Working Conditions. "Third European Working Conditions Survey: Data." http://www.eurofound.eu.int/working/3wc/3wcindex.htm [accessed October 9, 2006].

European Industrial Relations Observatory. "Study Examines Workers' Freedom of Expression on Working Environment." Dublin: European Foundation for the Improvement of Living and Working Conditions, 1999. http://www.eiro.eurofound.eu.int/1999/10/feature/se9910198f.html [accessed October 11, 2006].

———. "Working Time Developments—2004." Dublin: European Foundation for the Improvement of Living and Working Conditions, 2005. http://www.eiro.eurofound.ie/2005/03/update/tn0503104u.html [accessed August 10, 2005].

Fairris, David. *Shopfloor Matters: Labor-Management Relations in Twentieth-Century American Manufacturing*. London: Routledge, 1997.

Fairris, David, and Michael Reich. "The Impacts of Living Wage Policies: Introduction to the Special Issue." *Industrial Relations* 44 (January 2005): 1–13.

Fajnzylber, Pablo, Daniel Lederman, and Norman Loayza. "Inequality and Violent Crime." *Journal of Law and Economics* 45 (April 2002): 1–40.

Families USA. "Employers Should Pay Their Fair Share for Health Care." Washington, D.C., 2006. http://www.familiesusa.org/assets/pdfs/employer-responsibility-issue.pdf [accessed December 3, 2006].

———. "Have Health Insurance? Think You're Well Protected? Think Again!" Washington, D.C., 2005. http://www.familiesusa.org/assets/pdfs/health-care-think-again.PDF [accessed December 3, 2006].

———. "Wrong Direction: One out of Three Americans Are Uninsured." Families USA Publication No. 07–108. Washington, D.C., 2007.

Fantasia, Rick, and Kim Voss. *Hard Work: Remaking the American Labor Movement*. Berkeley: University of California Press, 2004.

Farber, Daniel L. "The Outmoded Debate over Affirmative Action." *California Law Review* 82 (July 1994): 893–934.

Farber, Henry S., and Alan B. Krueger. "Union Membership in the United States: The Decline Continues." In Bruce E. Kaufman and Morris M. Kleiner, eds., *Employee Representation: Alternatives and Future Directions*, 105–34. Madison, Wisc.: Industrial Relations Research Association, 1993.

Fashoyin, Tayo. "Tripartite Cooperation, Social Dialogue and National Development." *International Labour Review* 143 (2004): 341–72.

Feder, Judith. "Crowd-Out and the Politics of Health Reform." *Journal of Law, Medicine and Ethics* 32 (Fall 2004): 461–64.

Federal Mediation and Conciliation Service. "Arbitration Statistics Fiscal Year 2007." Washington, D.C., 2007. http://fmcs.gov/assets/files/Arbitration/2007%20Arbitration%20Documents/Average_Days.DOC [accessed May 15, 2007].

———. "2007 Annual Report." Washington, D.C., 2007. http://www.fmcs.gov/assets/files/annual%20reports/FY2007_Annual_Report.pdf [accessed May 15, 2007].

Feinman, Jay M. "The Development of the Employment at Will Rule." *American Journal of Legal History* 20 (April 1976): 118–35.

Fernandez, Bob. "DuPont to Close Pension, Put in Two-Thirds Less." *Philadelphia Inquirer*, August 28, 2006.

Fine, Janice. *Worker Centers: Organizing Communities at the Edge of the Dream.* Ithaca, N.Y.: Cornell University Press, 2006.

Finkin, Matthew W. "Employee Representation Outside the Labor Act: Thoughts on Arbitral Representation, Group Representation, and Workplace Committees." *University of Pennsylvania Journal of Labor and Employment Law* 5 (Fall 2002): 75–100.

———. "Labor Policy and the Enervation of the Economic Strike." *University of Illinois Law Review* 1990 (1990): 547–74.

Fischl, Richard Michael. "Rethinking the Tripartite Division of American Work Law." *Berkeley Journal of Employment and Labor Law* 28 (2007): 163–216.

Fishback, Price V., and Shawn Everett Kantor. *A Prelude to the Welfare State: The Origins of Workers' Compensation.* Chicago: University of Chicago Press, 2000.

FitzGibbon, Susan A. "Reflections on *Gilmer* and *Cole.*" *Employee Rights and Employment Policy Journal* 1 (1997): 221–62.

Folger, Robert, and Russell Cropanzano. *Organizational Justice and Human Resource Management.* Thousand Oaks, Calif.: Sage, 1998.

Forbath, William E. "The Ambiguities of Free Labor: Labor and the Law in the Gilded Age." *Wisconsin Law Review* 1985 (July/August 1985): 767–817.

———. *Law and the Shaping of the American Labor Movement.* Cambridge, Mass.: Harvard University Press, 1991.

Forster, Katherine M. "Strategic Reform of Contingent Work." *Southern California Law Review* 74 (January 2001): 541–76.

Fox, Alan. *Beyond Contract: Work, Power and Trust Relations.* London: Farber and Farber, 1974.

Frank, Robert H., and Philip J. Cook. *The Winner-Take-All Society: How More and More Americans Compete for Ever Fewer and Bigger Prizes, Encouraging Economic Waste, Income Inequality, and an Impoverished Cultural Life.* New York: Free Press, 1995.

Frankfurter, Felix, and Nathan Greene. *The Labor Injunction.* New York: Macmillan, 1930.

Freeman, Richard B. "Labor Market Institutions Around the World." In Paul Blyton, Nicolas Bacon, Jack Fiorito, and Edmund Heery, eds., *Sage Handbook of Industrial Relations*, 640–58. London: Sage, 2008.

———. "Searching for the EU Social Dialogue Model." In Nicola Acocella and Riccardo Leoni, eds., *Social Pacts, Employment, and Growth. A Reappraisal of Ezio Tarantelli's Thought*, 221–38. Heidelberg: Springer-Physica Verlag, 2007.

Freeman, Richard B., Peter Boxall, and Peter Haynes, eds. *What Workers Say: Employee Voice in the Anglo-American World.* Ithaca, N.Y.: Cornell University Press, 2007.

Freeman, Richard B., and James L. Medoff. *What Do Unions Do?* New York: Basic Books, 1984.

Freeman, Richard B., and Joel Rogers. *What Workers Want*. Updated ed. Ithaca, N.Y.: Cornell University Press, 2006.

———. "Who Speaks for Us? Employee Representation in a Nonunion Labor Market." In Bruce E. Kaufman and Morris M. Kleiner, eds., *Employee Representation: Alternatives and Future Directions*, 13–79. Madison, Wisc.: Industrial Relations Research Association, 1993.

Fried, Charles. "Individual and Collective Rights in Work Relations: Reflections on the Current State of Labor Law and Its Prospects." *University of Chicago Law Review* 51 (Fall 1984): 1012–40.

Friedman, Milton, and Rose Friedman. *Free to Choose: A Personal Statement* (New York: Harcourt Brace Jovanovich, 1980).

Friedman, Raymond A., and Kellina M. Craig. "Predicting Joining and Participating in Minority Employee Network Groups." *Industrial Relations* 43 (October 2004): 793–816.

Fronstin, Paul. "Sources of Health Insurance and Characteristics of the Uninsured: Analysis of the March 2007 Current Population Survey." EBRI Issue Brief No. 310. Washington, D.C.: Employment Benefit Research Institute, 2007.

Fudge, Judy. "After Industrial Citizenship: Market Citizenship or Citizenship at Work?" *Relations Industrielles/Industrial Relations* 60 (Fall 2005): 631–53.

Furlong, James C. *Labor in the Boardroom: The Peaceful Revolution*. Princeton, N.J.: Dow Jones Books, 1977.

Gagné, Marylène, and Edward L. Deci. "Self-Determination Theory and Work Motivation." *Journal of Organizational Behavior* 26 (June 2005): 331–62.

Gale, William G., J. Mark Iwry, and Peter S. Orszag. "The Automatic 401(k): A Simple Way to Strengthen Retirement Savings." Retirement Security Project Paper No. 2005–1. Washington, D.C.: Brookings Institution, 2005.

———. "The Saver's Credit: Expanding Retirement Savings for Middle- and Lower-Income Americans." Retirement Security Project Paper No. 2005–2. Washington, D.C.: Brookings Institution, 2005.

Galinsky, Ellen, et al. *Overwork in America: When the Way We Work Becomes Too Much*. New York: Families and Work Institute, 2005.

Gall, Gregor. "Marxism and Industrial Relations." In Peter Ackers and Adrian Wilkinson, eds., *Understanding Work and Employment: Industrial Relations in Transition*, 316–24. Oxford: Oxford University Press, 2003.

Gallagher, Mary Elizabeth. *Contagious Capitalism: Globalization and the Politics of Labor in China*. Princeton, N.J.: Princeton University Press, 2005.

Gely, Rafael, and Leonard Bierman. "Social Isolation and American Workers: Employee Blogging and Legal Reform." *Harvard Journal of Law and Technology* 20 (Spring 2007): 288–331.

Getman, Julius G., and Thomas C. Kohler. "The Story of *NLRB v. Mackay Radio and Telegraph Co.*: The High Cost of Solidarity." In Laura J. Cooper and Catherine L. Fisk, eds., *Labor Law Stories*, 13–53. New York: Foundation Press, 2005.

Ghai, Dharam. "Decent Work: Universality and Diversity." Education and Outreach Programme Discussion Paper 159. Geneva: International Institute for Labour Studies, 2005.

Ghoshal, Sumantra. "Bad Management Theories Are Destroying Good Management Practices." *Academy of Management Learning and Education* 4 (March 2005): 75–91.

Gittleman, Maury, and Michael J. Handel. "Who Uses Computers and in What Ways: Effects on the Earnings Distribution." In Derek C. Jones, ed., *The New Economy Handbook*, 523–44. Amsterdam: Elsevier, 2003.

Glendon, Mary Ann. "Knowing the Universal Declaration of Human Rights." *Notre Dame Law Review* 73 (May 1998): 1153–82.

Glenn, Evelyn Nakano. *Unequal Freedom: How Race and Gender Shaped American Citizenship and Labor*. Cambridge, Mass.: Harvard University Press, 2002.

Golden, Lonnie, and Helene Jorgensen. "Time after Time: Mandatory Overtime in the U.S. Economy." EPI Briefing Paper No. 120. Washington, D.C.: Economic Policy Institute, 2002.

Golden, Lonnie, and Barbara Wiens-Tuers. "Mandatory Overtime Work: Who, What and Where?" *Labor Studies Journal* 30 (Spring 2005): 1–26.

Golden, Nina G. "Pregnancy and Maternity Leave: Taking Baby Steps Towards Effective Policies." *Journal of Law and Family Studies* 8 (2006): 1–38.

Goldman, Alvin L. *Labor and Employment Law in the United States*. Boston: Kluwer Law International, 1996.

———. "Potential Refinements of Employment Relations Law in the 21st Century." *Employee Rights and Employment Policy Journal* 3 (1999): 269–303.

Gollan, Paul J., Ray Markey, and Iain Ross, eds. *Works Councils in Australia: Future Prospects and Possibilities*. Sydney: Federation Press, 2002.

Gosselin, Peter G. "If America Is Richer, Why Are Its Families So Much Less Secure?" *Los Angeles Times*, October 10, 2004.

———. "The Poor Have More Things Today—Including Wild Income Swings." *Los Angeles Times*, December 12, 2004.

Gottschalk, Peter, and Sheldon Danziger. "Inequality of Wage Rates, Earnings and Family Income in the United States, 1975-2002." *Review of Income and Wealth* 51 (June 2005): 231–54.

Gould, William B. *Agenda for Reform: The Future of Employment Relationships and the Law*. Cambridge, Mass.: MIT Press, 1993.

Graetz, Michael J., and Jerry L. Mashaw. *True Security: Rethinking American Social Insurance*. New Haven, Conn.: Yale University Press, 1999.

Grant, Jodi, Taylor Hatcher, and Nirali Patel. *Expecting Better: A State-by-State Analysis of Parental Leave Programs*. Washington, D.C.: National Partnership for Women and Families, 2005.

Gray, Wayne B., and John M. Mendeloff. "The Declining Effects of OSHA Inspections on Manufacturing Injuries, 1979–1998." *Industrial and Labor Relations Review* 58 (July 2005): 571–87.

Greenfield, Patricia A., and Robert J. Pleasure. "Representatives of Their Own Choosing: Finding Workers' Voice in the Legitimacy and Power of Their

Unions." In Bruce E. Kaufman and Morris M. Kleiner, eds., *Employee Representation: Alternatives and Future Directions*, 169–96. Madison, Wisc.: Industrial Relations Research Association, 1993.

Greenhouse, Steven. *The Big Squeeze: Tough Times for the American Worker*. New York: Knopf, 2008.

Gregory, Charles O., and Harold A. Katz. *Labor and the Law*. 3rd ed. New York: Norton, 1979.

Grodin, Joseph R. "Arbitration of Employment Discrimination Claims: Doctrine and Policy in the Wake of *Gilmer*." *Hofstra Labor Law Journal* 1 (Fall 1996): 1–55.

Gross, James A. "A Human Rights Perspective on U.S. Labor Relations Law: A Violation of the Freedom of Association." *Employee Rights and Employment Policy Journal* 3 (1999): 65–103.

———, ed. *Workers' Rights as Human Rights*. Ithaca, N.Y.: Cornell University Press, 2003.

Grubb, W. Norton. *Learning to Work: The Case for Reintegrating Job Training and Education*. New York: Russell Sage Foundation, 1996.

Gruber, Jonathan, and Brigitte Madrian. "Health Insurance, Labor Supply, and Job Mobility: A Critical Review of the Literature." In Catherine G. McLaughlin, ed., *Health Policy and the Uninsured*, 97–178. Washington, D.C.: Urban Institute Press, 2004.

Gustman, Alan L., and Thomas L. Steinmeier. "Imperfect Knowledge of Social Security and Pensions." *Industrial Relations* 44 (April 2005): 373–95.

Hacker, Jacob S. *The Divided Welfare State: The Battle over Public and Private Social Benefits in the United States*. New York: Cambridge University Press, 2002.

———. *The Great Risk Shift: The Assault on American Jobs, Families, Health Care, and Retirement—And How You Can Fight Back*. New York: Oxford University Press, 2006.

Hackman, J. Richard, and Greg R. Oldham. *Work Redesign*. Reading, Mass.: Addison-Wesley, 1980.

Hadley, Jack. "Sicker and Poorer—The Consequences of Being Uninsured: A Review of the Research on the Relationship Between Health Insurance, Medical Care Use, Health, Work, and Income." *Medical Care Research and Review* 60 (June 2003): 3S–75S.

Halbert, Terry Ann. "The First Amendment in the Workplace: An Analysis and Call for Reform." *Seton Hall Law Review* 17 (1987): 42–72.

Hall, Mark. "Assessing the Information and Consultation of Employees Regulations." *Industrial Law Journal* 34 (June 2005): 103–26.

Hämäläinen, Päivi, Jukka Takala, and Kaija Leena Saarela. "Global Estimates of Occupational Accidents." *Safety Science* 44 (February 2006): 137–56.

Hardin, Patrick, ed. *The Developing Labor Law: The Board, the Courts, and the National Labor Relations Act*. 4th ed. Washington, D.C.: BNA Books, 2001.

Harley, Bill. "The Myth of Empowerment: Work Organisation, Hierarchy and Employee Autonomy in Contemporary Australian Workplace." *Work, Employment, and Society* (March 1999): 41–66.

Harper, Michael C. "A Framework for the Rejuvenation of the American Labor Movement." *Indiana Law Journal* 76 (Winter 2001): 103–33.

Hartmann, Thom. *Unequal Protection: The Rise of Corporate Dominance and the Theft of Human Rights*. New York: Rodale, 2002.

Harvey, David. *A Brief History of Neoliberalism*. Oxford: Oxford University Press, 2005.

Haveman, Robert, et al. "Do Newly Retired Workers in the United States Have Sufficient Resources to Maintain Well-Being?" *Economic Inquiry* 44 (April 2006): 249–64.

Head, Simon. *The New Ruthless Economy: Work and Power in the Digital Age*. New York: Oxford University Press, 2003.

Hearn, Mark, and Grant Michelson, eds. *Rethinking Work: Time, Space, and Discourse*. Melbourne: Cambridge University Press, 2006.

Hegewisch, Ariane. "Employers and European Flexible Working Rights: When the Floodgates Were Opened." UC Hastings Center for WorkLife Law Issue Brief (Fall 2005).

Hepple, Bob. "European Rules on Dismissals." *Comparative Labor Law Journal* 18 (1997): 382-407.

Herzenberg, Stephen A., John A. Alic, and Howard Wial. *New Rules for a New Economy: Employment and Opportunity in Postindustrial America*. Ithaca, N.Y.: ILR Press, 1998.

Hewlett, Sylvia Ann. *When the Bough Breaks: The Cost of Neglecting Our Children*. New York: Basic Books, 1991.

Heymann, Jody. *The Widening Gap: Why America's Working Families Are in Jeopardy and What Can Be Done about It*. New York: Basic Books, 2000.

Heymann, Jody, Alison Earle, and Jeffrey Hayes. *The Work, Family, and Equity Index: How Does the United States Measure Up?* Montreal: Project on Global Working Families, 2008.

Hiatt, Jonathan, and Lawrence Gold. "Employer-Employee Committees: A Union Perspective." In Bruce E. Kaufman and Daphne Gottlieb Taras, eds., *Nonunion Employee Representation: History, Contemporary Practice, and Policy*, 498–511. Armonk, N.Y.: M. E. Sharpe, 2000.

Hirsch, Barry T. "Incentive Effects of Workers' Compensation." *Clinical Orthopaedics and Related Research* 336 (March 1997): 33–41.

Hirschman, Albert O. *Exit, Voice, and Loyalty: Responses to Decline in Firms, Organizations, and States*. Cambridge, Mass.: Harvard University Press, 1970.

Hodges, Ann C. "The Limits of Multiple Rights and Remedies: A Call for Revisiting the Law of the Workplace." *Hofstra Labor and Employment Law Journal* 22 (Spring 2005): 601–26.

Hodson, Randy. *Dignity at Work*. Cambridge: Cambridge University Press, 2001.

Hoffman, Sharona, et al. "The Definition of Disability in the Americans with Disabilities Act: Its Successes and Shortcomings." *Employee Rights and Employment Policy Journal* 9 (2005): 473–98.

Holzer, Harry J., and Margy Waller. "The Workforce Investment Act: Reauthorization to Address the 'Skills Gap.'" Center on Urban and Metropolitan

Policy Research Brief. Washington, D.C.: Brookings Institution, 2002.

Howell, David R., ed. *Fighting Unemployment: The Limits of Free Market Orthodoxy*. New York: Oxford University Press, 2005.

Hubert, Denise V. M. "Exactly What Is Employment ADR?" *Human Resources Professional* 11 (July–August 1998): 23–27.

Hunter, Larry W. "Can Strategic Participation be Institutionalized? Union Representation on American Corporate Boards." *Industrial and Labor Relations Review* 51 (July 1998): 557–78.

Hylton, Maria O'Brien. "The Case Against Regulating the Market for Contingent Employment." *Washington and Lee Law Review* 52 (1995): 849–62.

Hyman, Richard. *Industrial Relations: A Marxist Introduction*. London: Macmillan, 1975.

International Labor Office. *Decent Work*. Geneva: International Labor Organization, 1999.

———. *Economic Security for a Better World*. Geneva: International Labor Organization, 2004.

———. *Global Employment Trends: January 2008*. Geneva: International Labor Organization, 2008.

———. "Protection of Workers' Personal Data: An ILO Code of Practice." Geneva: International Labor Organization, 1997.

———. "Strategies and Practice for Labour Inspection." GB.297/ESP/3. Geneva: International Labor Organization, 2006.

———. "Termination of Employment Legislation Digest." Geneva: International Labor Organization, 2006. http://www.ilo.org/public/english/dialogue/ifpdial/info/termination/ [accessed November 24, 2006].

Irwin, Douglas A. *Free Trade under Fire*. Princeton, N.J.: Princeton University Press, 2002.

Iversen, Roberta Rehner, and Annie Laurie Armstrong. *Jobs Aren't Enough: Toward a New Economic Mobility for Low-Income Families*. Philadelphia: Temple University Press, 2006.

Jacobs, David C. "Prospects for National Health Insurance in the United States." In Sheldon Friedman and David C. Jacobs, eds., *The Future of the Safety Net: Social Insurance and Employee Benefits*, 187–200. Champaign, Ill.: Industrial Relations Research Association, 2001.

Jacobs, Elisabeth. "The Politics of Economic Insecurity." Issues in Governance Studies No. 10. Washington, D.C.: Brookings Institution, 2007.

Jacobs, Jerry A., and Kathleen Gerson. "Toward a Family-Friendly, Gender-Equitable Work Week." *University of Pennsylvania Journal of Labor and Employment Law* 1 (Fall 1998): 457–72.

Jacoby, Sanford M. "American Exceptionalism Revisited: The Importance of Management." In Sanford M. Jacoby, ed., *Masters to Managers: Historical and Comparative Perspectives on American Employers*, 174–200. New York: Columbia University Press, 1991.

———. *The Embedded Corporation: Corporate Governance and Employment Relations in Japan and the United States*. Princeton, N.J.: Princeton University Press, 2005.

———. *Employing Bureaucracy: Managers, Unions, and the Transformation of Work in American Industry, 1900–1945*. New York: Columbia University Press, 1985.

———. *Modern Manors: Welfare Capitalism since the New Deal*. Princeton, N.J.: Princeton University Press, 1997.

Jenkins, Alan. *Employment Relations in France: Evolution and Innovation*. New York: Kluwer, 2000.

Jessup, David, and Michael E. Gordon. "Organizing in Export Processing Zones: The Bibong Experience in the Dominican Republic." In Michael E. Gordon and Lowell Turner, eds., *Transnational Cooperation among Labor Unions*, 179–201. Ithaca, N.Y.: ILR Press, 2000.

Johnson, Haynes, and David S. Broder. *The System: The American Way of Politics at the Breaking Point*. New York: Little Brown, 1996.

Jolls, Christine. "The Role and Functioning of Public-Interest Legal Organizations in the Enforcement of the Employment Laws." In Richard B. Freeman, Joni Hersch, and Lawrence Mishel, eds., *Emerging Labor Market Institutions for the Twenty-First Century*, 141–76. Chicago: University of Chicago Press, 2005.

Jones, Barry. *Sleepers Awake! Technology and the Future of Work*. Melbourne: Oxford University Press, 1995.

Jones, Eliot. *The Trust Problem in the United States*. New York: Macmillan, 1923.

Jorgensen, Helene, and Robert E. McGarrah, Jr. "Contingent Workers: Health and Pension Security." In Sheldon Friedman and David C. Jacobs, eds., *The Future of the Safety Net: Social Insurance and Employee Benefits*, 225–38. Champaign, Ill.: Industrial Relations Research Association, 2001.

Josephson, Matthew. *The Robber Barons: The Great American Capitalists, 1861–1901*. New York: Harcourt, Brace, 1934.

Juhn, Chinhui, and Simon Potter. "Changes in Labor Force Participation in the United States," *Journal of Economic Perspectives* 20 (Summer 2006): 27–46.

Kaiser Family Foundation. "Employer Health Benefits 2006 Annual Survey." Menlo Park, Calif., 2006. http://www.kff.org/insurance/7527/ [accessed December 23, 2006].

Kalleberg, Arne L. "Evolving Employment Relations in the United States." In Ivar Berg and Arne L. Kalleberg, eds., *Sourcebook of Labor Markets: Evolving Structures and Processes*, 187–206. New York: Kluwer Academic, 2001.

Kanigel, Robert. *The One Best Way: Frederick Winslow Taylor and the Enigma of Efficiency*. New York: Penguin, 1997.

Karasek, Robert. "Control in the Workplace and Its Health-Related Aspects." In Steven L. Sauter, Joseph J. Hurrell, Jr., and Cary L. Cooper, eds., *Job Control and Worker Health*, 129–59. Chichester, UK: Wiley, 1989.

Karels, Elizabeth A. Lambrecht. "Make Employers Accountable for Workplace Safety! How the Dirty Little Secret of Workers' Compensation Puts Employees at Risk and Why Criminal Prosecution and Civil Action Will Save Lives and Money." *Hamline Journal of Public Law and Policy* 26 (Fall 2004): 111–49.

Katz, Harry C., and Owen Darbishire. *Converging Divergences: Worldwide Changes in Employment Systems*. Ithaca, N.Y.: ILR Press, 2000.

Katz, Harry C., Wonduck Lee, and Joohee Lee, eds. *The New Structure of Labor*

Relations: Tripartism and Decentralization. Ithaca, N.Y.: Cornell University Press, 2004.

Kaufman, Bruce E. "Accomplishments and Shortcomings of Nonunion Employee Representation in the Pre–Wagner Act Years: A Reassessment." In Bruce E. Kaufman and Daphne Gottlieb Taras, eds., *Nonunion Employee Representation: History, Contemporary Practice, and Policy*, 21–60. Armonk, N.Y.: M. E. Sharpe, 2000.

———. "The Employee Participation/Representation Gap: An Assessment and Proposed Solution." *University of Pennsylvania Journal of Labor and Employment Law* 3 (Spring 2001): 491–550.

———. *The Global Evolution of Industrial Relations: Events, Ideas, and the IIRA.* Geneva: International Labor Office, 2004.

———. "Labor Markets and Employment Regulation: The View of the 'Old' Institutionalists." In Bruce E. Kaufman, ed., *Government Regulation of the Employment Relationship*, 11–55. Madison, Wisc.: Industrial Relations Research Association, 1997.

———. *The Origins and Evolution of the Field of Industrial Relations in the United States.* Ithaca, N.Y.: ILR Press, 1993.

———. "The Social Welfare Objectives and Ethical Principles of Industrial Relations." In John W. Budd and James G. Scoville, eds., *The Ethics of Human Resources and Industrial Relations*, 23–59. Champaign, Ill.: Labor and Employment Relations Association, 2005.

———. "Why the Wagner Act? Reestablishing Contact with Its Original Purpose." In David Lewin, Bruce E. Kaufman, and Donna Sockell, eds., *Advances in Industrial and Labor Relations*, Vol. 7, 15–68. Greenwich, Conn.: JAI Press, 1996.

Kaufman, Bruce E., and Daphne Gottlieb Taras, eds. *Nonunion Employee Representation: History, Contemporary Practice, and Policy.* Armonk, N.Y.: M. E. Sharpe, 2000.

Keller, Berndt. "The European Company Statute: Employee Involvement—And Beyond." *Industrial Relations Journal* 33 (December 2002): 424–45.

Kelly, John. *Rethinking Industrial Relations: Mobilization, Collectivism and Long Waves.* London: Routledge, 1998.

Kelly, Marjorie. *The Divine Right of Capital: Dethroning the Corporate Aristocracy.* San Francisco: Berrett-Koehler, 2001.

Kennedy, David M. *Freedom from Fear: The American People in Depression and War, 1929–1945.* New York: Oxford University Press, 1999.

Kerckhofs, Peter. *European Works Councils—Facts and Figures 2006.* Brussels: European Trade Union Institute, 2006.

Keyserling, Leon H. "Why the Wagner Act?" In Louis G. Silverberg, ed., *The Wagner Act: After Ten Years*, 5–33. Washington, D.C.: Bureau of National Affairs, 1945.

Kim, Pauline T. "Bargaining with Imperfect Information: A Study of Worker Perceptions of Legal Protection in an At-Will World." *Cornell Law Review* 83 (November 1997): 105–60.

Klaff, Daniel B. "Evaluating Work: Enforcing Occupational Safety and Health Standards in the United States, Canada, and Sweden." *University of Pennsylvania Journal of Labor and Employment Law* 7 (Spring 2005): 613–59.

Klare, Karl E. "Workplace Democracy and Market Reconstruction: An Agenda for Legal Reform." *Catholic University Law Review* 38 (Fall 1988): 1–68.

Klein, Jennifer. *For All These Rights: Business, Labor, and the Shaping of America's Public-Private Welfare State*. Princeton, N.J.: Princeton University Press, 2003.

Kleiner, Morris M. *Licensing Occupations: Ensuring Quality Or Restricting Competition?* Kalamazoo, Mich.: Upjohn, 2005.

Kletzer, Lori G., and Howard Rosen. "Easing the Adjustment Burden on U.S. Workers." In C. Fred Bergsten, ed., *The United States and the World Economy: Foreign Economic Policy for the Next Decade*, 313–41. Washington, D.C.: Institute for International Economics, 2005.

———. "Reforming Unemployment Insurance for the Twenty-First Century Workforce." Hamilton Project Discussion Paper 2006-06, 2006.

Kniesner, Thomas J., and John D. Leeth. "Abolishing OSHA." *Regulation* 18 (Fall 1995): 46–56.

Kochan, Thomas A. *Collective Bargaining and Industrial Relations: From Theory to Policy and Practice*. Homewood, Ill.: Irwin, 1980.

———. "Labor Policy for the Twenty-First Century." *University of Pennsylvania Journal of Labor and Employment Law* 1 (Spring 1998): 117–31.

———. "On the Paradigm Guiding Industrial Relations Theory and Research: Comment on John Godard and John T. Delaney, 'Reflections on the 'High Performance' Paradigm's Implications for Industrial Relations as a Field.'" *Industrial and Labor Relations Review* 53 (July 2000): 704–11.

———. *Restoring the American Dream: A Working Families' Agenda for America*. Cambridge, Mass.: MIT Press, 2005.

Kochan, Thomas A., Harry C. Katz, and Robert B. McKersie. *The Transformation of American Industrial Relations*. New York: Basic Books, 1986.

Korczynski, Marek. "Consumer Capitalism and Industrial Relations." In Peter Ackers and Adrian Wilkinson, eds., *Understanding Work and Employment: Industrial Relations in Transition*, 265–77. Oxford: Oxford University Press, 2003.

Korten, David C. *The Post-Corporate World: Life after Capitalism*. San Francisco: Berrett-Koehler, 1999.

Kotlikoff, Laurence J., and Scott Burns. *The Coming Generational Storm: What You Need to Know about America's Economic Future*. Cambridge, Mass.: MIT Press, 2004.

Koven, Adolph, and Susan L. Smith. *Just Cause: The Seven Tests*. 3rd ed. Washington, D.C.: Bureau of National Affairs, 2006.

Kozel, Randy J. "Reconceptualizing Public Employee Speech." *Northwestern University Law Review* 99 (Spring 2005): 1007–51.

Krausz, Moshe, Abraham Sagie, and Yehuda Bidermann. "Actual and Preferred Work Schedules and Scheduling Control as Determinants of Job-Related Attitudes." *Journal of Vocational Behavior* 56 (February 2000): 1–11.

Krueger, Alan B. "Inequality, Too Much of a Good Thing." In Benjamin M.

Friedman, ed., *Inequality in America: What Role for Human Capital Policies?*, 1–75. Cambridge, Mass.: MIT Press, 2003.

Krueger, Alan B., and Alexandre Mas. "Strikes, Scabs and Tread Separations: Labor Strife and the Production of Defective Bridgestone/Firestone Tires." *Journal of Political Economy* 112 (April 2004): 253–89.

Krueger, Dirk, and Fabrizio Perri. "Does Income Inequality Lead to Consumption Inequality? Evidence and Theory." *Review of Economic Studies* 73 (January 2006): 163–93.

Kruse, Douglas, Joseph Blasi, and Rhokeun Park. "Shared Capitalism in the U.S. Economy: Prevalence, Characteristics, and Employee Views of Financial Participation in Enterprises." In Joseph R. Blasi, Richard B. Freeman, and Douglas Kruse, eds., *Shared Capitalism at Work: The Economic Effects of Employee Ownership, Profit Sharing, Gainsharing, and Broad-based Stock Options.* New York: Russell Sage Foundation and National Bureau of Economic Research, forthcoming.

Lafer, Gordon. "The Critical Failure of Workplace Ethics." In John W. Budd and James G. Scoville, eds., *The Ethics of Human Resources and Industrial Relations*, 273–97. Champaign, Ill.: Labor and Employment Relations Association, 2005.

———. *The Job Training Charade*. Ithaca, N.Y.: Cornell University Press, 2002.

LaLonde, Robert J., and Bernard D. Meltzer. "Hard Times for Unions: Another Look at the Significance of Employer Illegalities." *University of Chicago Law Review* 58 (Summer 1991): 953–1014.

Lambert, Josiah Bartlett. *"If the Workers Took a Notion": The Right to Strike and American Political Development*. Ithaca, N.Y.: Cornell University Press, 2005.

Langfred, Claus W., and Neta A. Moye. "Effects of Task Autonomy on Performance: An Extended Model Considering Motivational, Informational, and Structural Mechanisms." *Journal of Applied Psychology* 89 (December 2004): 934–45.

Langille, Brian A., and Guy Davidov. "Beyond Employees and Independent Contractors: A View from Canada." *Comparative Labor Law and Policy Journal* 21 (Fall 1999): 7–45.

Lauck, W. Jett, and Edgar Sydenstricker. *Conditions of Labor in American Industries: A Summarization of the Results of Recent Investigations*. New York: Funk and Wagnalls, 1917.

Lauren, Paul Gordon. *The Evolution of International Human Rights: Visions Seen*. Philadelphia: University of Pennsylvania Press, 1998.

Le Couteur, Penny, and Jay Burreson. *Napoleon's Buttons: How 17 Molecules Changed History*. New York: Jeremy P. Tarcher / Putnam, 2003.

Lecher, Wolfgang, et al. *European Works Councils: Developments, Types, and Networking*. Aldershot, UK: Gower, 2001.

Lee, Jason S., and Laura Tollen. "How Low Can You Go? The Impact of Reduced Benefits and Increased Cost Sharing." *Health Affairs—Web Exclusive*, June 19, 2002. http://content.healthaffairs.org/cgi/content/full/hlthaff.w2.229v1/D.C.1 [accessed April 11, 2005].

Lee, Melissa. "Sabo Tries Again to Ease Wage Imbalance." *Star Tribune* (Minneapolis), July 13, 2005.

Lee, Sangheon. "Working-Hour Gaps: Trends and Issues." In Jon C. Messenger, ed., *Working Time and Workers' Preferences in Industrialized Countries: Finding the Balance*, 29–59. London: Routledge, 2004.

Legge, Karen. *Human Resource Management: Rhetorics and Realities*. Basingstoke, UK: Macmillan, 1995.

LeRoy, Michael H. "Employee Participation in the New Millennium: Redefining a Labor Organization under Section 8(a)(2) of the NLRA." *Southern California Law Review* 72 (September 1999): 1651–1723.

Levine, David I. *Working in the Twenty-First Century: Policies for Economic Growth Through Training, Opportunity, and Education*. Armonk, N.Y.: M. E. Sharpe, 1998.

Levin-Epstein, Jodie. "How to Exercise Flexible Work: Take Steps with a 'Soft Touch' Law." Work-Life Balance Brief No. 3. Washington, D.C.: Center for Law and Social Policy, 2005. http://www.clasp.org/publications/work_life3_annotated.pdf [accessed December 30, 2006].

Levitt, Martin Jay, and Terry Conrow. *Confessions of a Union Buster*. New York: Crown, 1993.

Levy, Frank, and Richard J. Murnane. *The New Division of Labor: How Computers Are Creating the Next Job Market*. New York: Russell Sage Foundation, 2004.

Lewin, David. "IR and HR Perspectives on Workplace Conflict: What Can Each Learn from the Other?" *Human Resource Management Review* 11 (Winter 2001): 453–85.

Lewis, Jr., Harold S., and Elizabeth J. Norman. *Employment Discrimination Law and Practice*. St. Paul, Minn.: West Group, 2001.

Lichtenstein, Nelson. *State of the Union: A Century of American Labor*. Princeton, N.J.: Princeton University Press, 2002.

Lichtenstein, Nelson, et al. *Who Built America? Working People and the Nation's Economy, Politics, Culture, and Society*, Vol. 2. New York: Worth, 2000.

Linder, Marc. "Dependent and Independent Contractors in Recent U.S. Labor Law: An Ambiguous Dichotomy Rooted in Simulated Statutory Purposelessness." *Comparative Labor Law and Policy Journal* 21 (Fall 1999): 187–230.

Linn, Allison. "Microsoft Trimming Some Worker Benefits to Cut Costs." *Star Tribune* (Minneapolis), May 21, 2004.

Lipset, Seymour Martin, and Noah M. Meltz, with Rafael Gomez and Ivan Katchanovski. *The Paradox of American Unionism: Why Americans Like Unions More Than Canadians Do but Join Much Less*. Ithaca, N.Y.: Cornell University Press, 2004.

Logan, John. "The Union Avoidance Industry in the United States." *British Journal of Industrial Relations* 44 (December 2006): 651–75.

MacCulloch, Robert. "Income Inequality and the Taste for Revolution." *Journal of Law and Economics* 48 (April 2005): 93–123.

MacLaury, Judson. "The Job Safety Law of 1970: Its Passage Was Perilous." *Monthly Labor Review* 104 (March 1981): 18–24.

MacLean, Nancy. *Freedom Is Not Enough: The Opening of the American Workplace*. Cambridge, Mass.: Harvard University Press, 2006.

Madrian, Brigitte. "Health Insurance and the Labor Market." In Huizhong Zhou, ed., *The Political Economy of Health Care Reform*, 87–108. Kalamazoo, Mich.: W. E. Upjohn Institute for Employment Research, 2001.

Madrian, Brigitte C., and Dennis F. Shea. "The Power of Suggestion: Inertia in 401(k) Participation and Savings Behavior." *Quarterly Journal of Economics* 116 (November 2001): 1149–87.

Maltby, Lewis L. "Private Justice: Employment Arbitration and Civil Rights." *Columbia Human Rights Law Review* 30 (Fall 1998): 29–64.

Maltby, Lewis L., and David C. Yamada. "Beyond 'Economic Realities': The Case for Amending Federal Employment Discrimination Laws to Include Independent Contractors." *Boston College Law Review* 38 (March 1997): 239–74.

Mandel, Michael J. *The High-Risk Society: Peril and Promise in the New Economy*. New York: Times Books, 1996.

Mangum, Garth L. "Manpower Policies and Worker Status since the 1930s." In Joseph P. Goldberg et al., eds., *Federal Policies and Worker Status Since the Thirties*, 1135–57. Madison, Wisc.: Industrial Relations Research Association, 1976.

Mangum, Garth, and Peter Philips, eds. *Three Worlds of Labor Economics*. Armonk, N.Y.: M. E. Sharpe, 1988.

Mann, Catherine L. "Offshore Outsourcing and the Globalization of U.S. Services: Why Now, How Important, and What Policy Implications." In C. Fred Bergsten, ed., *The United States and the World Economy: Foreign Economic Policy for the Next Decade*, 281–311. Washington, D.C.: Institute for International Economics, 2005.

Manning, Alan. *Monopsony in Motion: Imperfect Competition in Labor Markets*. Princeton, N.J.: Princeton University Press, 2003.

Marginson, Paul, and Keith Sisson. *European Integration and Industrial Relations: Multi-Level Governance in the Making*. London: Palgrave/Macmillan, 2004.

Marshall, Ray F. ed. *Back to Shared Prosperity: The Growing Inequality of Wealth and Income in America*. Armonk, N.Y.: M. E. Sharpe, 2000.

Martin, Christopher R. *Framed! Labor and the Corporate Media*. Ithaca, N.Y.: Cornell University Press, 2004.

McClelland, Peter D. *The American Search for Justice*. Cambridge, Mass.: Basil Blackwell, 1990.

McGinley, Ann C. "Rethinking Civil Rights and Employment at Will: Toward a Coherent Discharge Policy." *Ohio State Law Journal* 57 (1996): 1443–1524.

McIntyre, Richard, and Matthew M. Bodah. "The United States and ILO Conventions 87 and No. 98: The Freedom of Association and Right to Bargain Collectively." In Richard N. Block et al., eds., *Justice on the Job: Perspectives on the Erosion of Collective Bargaining in the United States*, 231–47. Kalamazoo, Mich.: Upjohn, 2006.

McKinlay, Alan. "Knowledge Management." In Stephen Ackroyd et al., eds., *The Oxford Handbook of Work and Organization*, 242–62. Oxford: Oxford University Press, 2005.

McMahon, Martin J., Jr., and Alice G. Abreu. "Winner-Take-All Markets: Easing the Case for Progressive Taxation." *Florida Tax Review* 4 (1998): 1–81.

Meersman, Tom. "DNR Shifts Gears, Backs Truck Course." *Star Tribune* (Minneapolis), December 25, 2005.

Mellon, Steve. *After the Smoke Clears: Struggling to Get By in Rustbelt America.* Pittsburgh: University of Pittsburgh Press, 2002.

Meyer, Bruce D., and Douglas Holtz-Eakin, eds. *Making Work Pay: The Earned Income Tax Credit and Its Impact on America's Families.* New York: Russell Sage Foundation, 2002.

Middleton, Jennifer. "Contingent Workers in a Changing Economy: Endure, Adapt or Organize?" *New York University Review of Law and Social Change* 22 (1996): 557–621.

Miller, Katherine I., and Peter R. Monge. "Participation, Satisfaction, and Productivity: A Meta-Analytic Review." *Academy of Management Journal* 29 (December 1986): 727–53.

Millikan, William. *A Union Against Unions: The Minneapolis Citizens Alliance and Its Fight Against Organized Labor, 1903–1947.* St. Paul: Minnesota Historical Society, 2001.

Mishel, Lawrence, Jared Bernstein, and Sylvia Allegretto. *The State of Working America 2006/2007.* Ithaca, N.Y.: Cornell University Press, 2007.

Moberly, Robert S. "The Story of *Electromation*: Are Employee Participation Programs a Competitive Necessity or a Wolf in Sheep's Clothing?" In Laura J. Cooper and Catherine L. Fisk, eds., *Labor Law Stories,* 315–51. New York: Foundation Press, 2005.

Moody, Kim. *Workers in a Lean World: Unions in the International Economy.* London: Verso, 1998.

Moore, Janet. "Disclosure Defense: Guidant Says It Handled Defibrillator Flaw Properly, " *Star Tribune* (Minneapolis), May 25, 2005.

Moreno, Paul D. *From Direct Action to Affirmative Action: Fair Employment Law and Policy in America, 1933–1972.* Baton Rouge: Louisiana State University Press, 1997.

Morris, Charles J. *The Blue Eagle at Work: Reclaiming Democratic Rights in the American Workplace.* Ithaca, N.Y.: Cornell University Press, 2005.

Mosely, Deanne M., and William C. Walter. "The Significance of the Classification of Employment Relationships in Determining Exposure to Liability." *Mississippi Law Journal* 67 (Spring 1998): 613–43.

Moss, Scott A. "Where There's a Will, There Are Many Ways: Redressing the Increased Incoherence of Employment-at-Will." *University of Pittsburgh Law Review* 67 (Winter 2005): 295–363.

Muhl, Charles J. "The Employment-at-Will Doctrine: Three Major Exceptions." *Monthly Labor Review* 124 (January 2001): 3–11.

Muirhead, Russell. *Just Work.* Cambridge, Mass.: Harvard University Press, 2004.

Müller-Jentsch, Walther. "Germany: From Collective Voice to Co-Management." In Joel Rogers and Wolfgang Streeck, eds., *Works Councils: Consultation, Rep-*

resentation, and Cooperation in Industrial Relations, 52–78. Chicago: University of Chicago Press, 1995.

Mundlak, Guy. "Industrial Citizenship, Social Citizenship, Corporate Citizenship: I Just Want My Wages." *Theoretical Inquiries in Law* 8 (July 2007): 719–48.

Munnell, Alicia H., and Annika Sundén. *Coming Up Short: The Challenge of 401(k) Plans*. Washington, D.C.: Brookings Institution, 2004.

Munnell, Alicia H., Annika Sundén, and Catherine Taylor. "What Determines 401(k) Participation and Contributions?" *Social Security Bulletin* 64 (2001/2002): 64–75.

Murphy, Sheila. "A Comparison of the Selection of Bargaining Representatives in the United States and Canada: *Linden Lumber, Gissel*, and the Right to Challenge Majority Status." *Comparative Labor Law Journal* 10 (Fall 1988): 65–97.

National Coalition on Health Care. "Health Insurance Cost." Washington, D.C., 2006. http://www.nchc.org/facts/cost.shtml [accessed December 23, 2006].

National Conference of Commissioners on Uniform State Laws. *Uniform Law Commissioners' Model Employment Termination Act*. Chicago, 1991.

National Low Income Housing Coalition. "Out of Reach 2007–2008." Washington, D.C., 2008. http://www.nlihc.org/oor/oor2008/ [accessed May 23, 2008].

National Partnership for Women and Families. "Get Well Soon: Americans Can't Afford to Be Sick." Washington, D.C., 2004.

Naughton, Michael J. "Participation in the Organization: An Ethical Analysis from the Papal Social Tradition." *Journal of Business Ethics* 14 (November 1995): 923–35.

Navaretta, Mary Jean. "The Model Employment Termination Act—META—More Aptly the Menace to Employment Tranquility Act." *Stetson Law Review* 25 (Summer 1996): 1027–66.

Neal, Alan C. "Information and Consultation for Employees—Still Seeking the Philosopher's Stone?" In Marco Biagi, ed., *Quality of Work and Employee Involvement in Europe*, 83–99. The Hague: Kluwer Law International, 2002.

Neckerman, Kathryn M., ed. *Social Inequality*. New York: Russell Sage Foundation, 2004.

Nelson, Daniel. *Frederick W. Taylor and the Rise of Scientific Management*. Madison: University of Wisconsin Press, 1980.

———, ed. *A Mental Revolution: Scientific Management Since Taylor*. Columbus: Ohio State University Press, 1992.

Newman, Katherine S. *No Shame in My Game: The Working Poor in the Inner City*. New York: Alfred A. Knopf, 1999.

Nicholson, Walter, and Karen Needels. "Unemployment Insurance: Strengthening the Relationship Between Theory and Policy." *Journal of Economic Perspectives* 20 (Summer 2006): 47–70.

Nickell, Stephen. "Unemployment and Labor Market Rigidities: Europe Versus North America." *Journal of Economic Perspectives* 11 (Summer 1997): 55-74.

Nollen, Stanley D., and Helen Axel. "Benefits and Costs to Employers." In Kathleen Barker and Kathleen Christensen, eds., *Contingent Work: American Employment Relations in Transition*, 126–43. Ithaca, N.Y.: ILR Press, 1998.

Norwood, Janet L. "Issues in Unemployment Insurance." In Peter Edelman, Dallas L. Salisbury, and Pamela J. Larson, eds., *The Future of Social Insurance: Incremental Action or Fundamental Reform?*, 187–98. Washington, D.C.: National Academy of Social Insurance, 2002.

Norwood, Stephen H. *Strikebreaking and Intimidation: Mercenaries and Masculinity in Twentieth-Century America*. Chapel Hill: University of North Carolina Press, 2002.

O'Grady, John. "Joint Health and Safety Committees: Finding a Balance." In Terrence Sullivan, ed., *Injury and the New World of Work*, 162–97. Vancouver: University of British Columbia Press, 2000.

O'Leary, Christopher J., and Stephen A. Wandner, eds. *Unemployment Insurance in the United States: Analysis of Policy Issues*. Kalamazoo, Mich.: W. E. Upjohn Institute for Employment Research, 1997.

Oppenheimer, David Benjamin. "Understanding Affirmative Action." *Hastings Constitutional Law Quarterly* 23 (Summer 1996): 921–98.

Organization for Economic Cooperation and Development. *Benefits and Wages: OECD Indicators 2004*. Paris, 2004.

———. *OECD Economic Surveys: United States*. Paris, 2004.

———. *OECD Health Data 2006: Statistics and Indicators for 30 Countries*. Paris, 2006.

Osterman, Paul. *Securing Prosperity: The American Labor Market: How It Has Changed and What to Do about It*. Princeton, N.J.: Princeton University Press, 1999.

———. "Skill, Training, and Work Organization in American Establishments." *Industrial Relations* 34 (April 1995): 125–46.

———. "Work Reorganization in an Era of Restructuring: Trends in Diffusion and Effects on Employee Welfare." *Industrial and Labor Relations Review* 53 (January 2000): 179–96.

Osterman, Paul, Thomas A. Kochan, Richard Locke, and Michael J. Piore. *Working in America: A Blueprint for the New Labor Market*. Cambridge, Mass.: MIT Press, 2001.

Padilla, Howie. "Police Left out of Loop about Loose Rail Car." *Star Tribune* (Minneapolis), May 26, 2005.

Pagnattaro, Marisa. "Leveling the Playing Field: Labor Provisions in CAFTA." *Fordham International Law Journal* 29 (January 2006): 386–431.

Parcel, Toby L., Rebecca A. Nickoll, and Mikaela J. Dufur. "The Effects of Parental Work and Maternal Nonemployment on Children's Reading and Math Achievement." *Work and Occupations* 23 (November 1996): 461–83.

Parker, Eric, and Joel Rogers. "Building the High Road in Metro Areas: Sectoral Training and Employment Projects." In Lowell Turner, Harry C. Katz, and Richard W. Hurd, eds., *Rekindling the Movement: Labor's Quest for Relevance in the Twenty-First Century*, 256–74. Ithaca, N.Y.: ILR Press, 2001.

Pateman, Carole. *Participation and Democratic Theory*. London: Cambridge University Press, 1970.

Pension and Welfare Benefits Administration. *Private Pension Plan Bulletin: Abstract of 2005 Form 5500 Annual Reports*. Washington, D.C.: U.S. Department of Labor, 2008.

Perelman, Michael. *Railroading Economics: The Creation of the Free Market Mythology*. New York: Monthly Review Press, 2006.

Perrow, Charles. *Organizing America: Wealth, Power, and the Origins of Corporate Capitalism*. Princeton, N.J.: Princeton University Press, 2002.

Perry, Dawn S. "Deterring Egregious Violations of Public Policy: A Proposed Amendment to the Model Employment Termination Act." *Washington Law Review* 67 (October 1992): 915–35.

Phillips, Michael J. "The Progressiveness of the *Lochner* Court." *Denver University Law Review* 75 (1998): 453–505.

Physicians' Working Group for Single-Payer National Health Insurance. "Proposal of the Physicians' Working Group for Single-Payer National Health Insurance." *Journal of the American Medical Association* 290 (August 2003): 798–805.

Pijoan-Mas, Josep. "Precautionary Savings or Working Longer Hours?" *Review of Economic Dynamics* 9 (April 2006): 326–52.

Piketty, Thomas, and Emmanuel Saez. "How Progressive Is the U.S. Federal Tax System? A Historical and International Perspective." *Journal of Economic Perspectives* 21 (Winter 2007): 3–24.

———. "Income Inequality in the United States, 1913-1998." *Quarterly Journal of Economics* 118 (February 2003): 1–39.

Pink, Daniel H. *Free Agent Nation: How America's New Independent Workers Are Transforming the Way We Live*. New York: Warner Books, 2001.

Piore, Michael J., and Charles F. Sabel. *The Second Industrial Divide: Possibilities for Prosperity*. New York: Basic Books, 1984.

Piore, Michael J., and Sean Safford. "Changing Regimes of Workplace Governance, Shifting Axes of Social Mobilization, and the Challenge to Industrial Relations Theory." *Industrial Relations* 45 (July 2006): 299–325.

Pope John Paul II. *On Human Work: Encyclical Laborem Exercens*. Washington, D.C.: United States Catholic Conference, 1981.

Potter, Edward E. "A Pragmatic Assessment from the Employers' Perspective." In James A. Gross, ed., *Workers' Rights as Human Rights*, 118–35. Ithaca, N.Y.: Cornell University Press, 2003.

Putnam, Robert D. *Bowling Alone: The Collapse and Revival of American Community*. New York: Simon and Schuster, 2000.

Quigley, William P. *Ending Poverty As We Know It: Guaranteeing a Right to a Job at a Living Wage*. Philadelphia: Temple University Press, 2003.

Radford, Mary F. "The Affirmative Action Debate." In Bruce E. Kaufman, ed., *Government Regulation of the Employment Relationship*, 343–67. Madison, Wisc.: Industrial Relations Research Association, 1997.

Rank, Mark Robert. *One Nation, Underprivileged: Why American Poverty Affects Us All*. New York: Oxford University Press, 2004.

Rasnic, Carol D. "Germany's Statutory Works Councils and Employee Codetermination: A Model for the United States?" *Loyola of Los Angeles International and Comparative Law Journal* 14 (February 1992): 275–300.

Rayback, Joseph G. *A History of American Labor*. New York: Free Press, 1966.

Redish, Martin H. "The Value of Free Speech." *University of Pennsylvania Law Review* 130 (January 1982): 591–645.

Reinsdorf, Marshall B. "Alternative Measures of Personal Saving." *Survey of Current Business* 87 (February 2007): 7–13.

Reis, Harry T., et al. "Daily Well-Being: The Role of Autonomy, Competence, and Relatedness." *Personality and Social Psychology Bulletin* 26 (April 2000): 419–35.

Reschovsky, James D., J. Lee Hargraves, and Albert F. Smith. "Consumer Beliefs and Health Plan Performance: It's Not Whether You Are in an HMO but Whether You Think You Are." *Journal of Health Policy Politics and Law* 27 (June 2002): 353–77.

Rifkin, Jeremy. *The End of Work: The Decline of the Global Labor Force and the Dawn of the Post-Market Era*. New York: Putnam Books, 1995.

Roche, James B. "Health Care in America: Why We Need Universal Health Care and Why We Need It Now." *St. Thomas Law Review* 13 (Summer 2001): 1013–49.

Rodrik, Dani. *Has Globalization Gone Too Far?* Washington, D.C.: Institute for International Economics, 1997.

Rogers, Jackie Krasas. *Temps: The Many Faces of the Changing Workplace*. Ithaca, N.Y.: Cornell University Press, 2000.

Rogers, Joel. "United States: Lessons from Abroad and Home." In Joel Rogers and Wolfgang Streeck, eds., *Works Councils: Consultation, Representation, and Cooperation in Industrial Relations*, 375–410. Chicago: University of Chicago Press, 1995.

Rogers, Joel, and Wolfgang Streeck, eds. *Works Councils: Consultation, Representation, and Cooperation in Industrial Relations*. Chicago: University of Chicago Press, 1995.

Rooksby, Emma, and Natasha Cica. "Personal Autonomy and Electronic Surveillance in the Workplace." In John Weckert, ed., *Electronic Monitoring in the Workplace: Controversies and Solutions*, 242–59. Hershey, Penn.: Idea Group, 2005.

Rosenberg, Richard S. "The Technological Assault on Ethics in the Modern Workplace." In John W. Budd and James G. Scoville, eds., *The Ethics of Human Resources and Industrial Relations*, 141–71. Champaign, Ill.: Labor and Employment Relations Association, 2005.

Rothstein, Mark A., Serge A. Martinez, and W. Paul McKinney. "Using Established Medical Criteria to Define Disability: A Proposal to Amend the Americans with Disabilities Act." *Washington University Law Quarterly* 80 (2002): 243–97.

Rudy, Jesse. "What They Don't Know Won't Hurt Them: Defending Employment-at-Will in Light of Findings That Employees Believe They Possess Just

Cause Protection." *Berkeley Journal of Employment and Labor Law* 23 (2002): 307–67.

Rutherglen, George. *Employment Discrimination Law: Visions of Equality in Theory and Doctrine*. New York: Foundation Press, 2001.

Ryan, John A. *A Living Wage: Its Ethical and Economic Aspects*. New York: Macmillan, 1912.

Ryan, Paul. "Segmentation, Duality, and the Internal Labour Market." In Frank Wilkinson, ed., *The Dynamics of Labour Market Segmentation*, 3–20. London: Academic Press, 1981.

Ryan, Richard M., and Edward L. Deci. "An Overview of Self-Determination Theory: An Organismic-Dialectical Perspective." In Edward L. Deci and Richard M. Ryan, eds., *Handbook of Self-Determination Research*, 3–33. Rochester, N.Y.: University of Rochester Press, 2002.

Safford, Sean C. *Why the Garden Club Couldn't Save Youngstown: The Transformation of the Rust Belt*. Cambridge, Mass.: Harvard University Press, 2009.

Scase, Richard. *Class*. Minneapolis, University of Minnesota Press, 1992.

Schettkat, Ronald. "Is Labor Market Regulation at the Root of European Unemployment? The Case of Germany and the Netherlands." In David R. Howell, ed., *Fighting Unemployment: The Limits of Free Market Orthodoxy*, 262–83. New York: Oxford University Press, 2005.

Scheve, Kenneth F., and Matthew J. Slaughter. *Globalization and the Perception of American Workers*. Washington, D.C.: Institute for International Economics, 2001.

Schmitt, John, and Ben Zipperer. "Dropping the Ax: Illegal Firings During Union Election Campaigns." Washington, D.C.: Center for Economic and Policy Research, 2007.

Schor, Juliet B. *The Overworked American: The Unexpected Decline of Leisure*. New York: Basic Books, 1991.

Schultz, Vicki. "The Sanitized Workplace." *Yale Law Journal* 112 (June 2003): 2061–2193.

Schumer, Chuck. *Positively American: Winning Back the Middle-Class Majority One Family at a Time*. Emmaus, Penn.: Rodale Books, 2007.

Schwab, Stewart J. "Life-Cycle Justice: Accommodating Just Cause and Employment at Will." *Michigan Law Review* 92 (October 1993): 8–62.

Schwab, Stewart J., and Randall S. Thomas. "An Empirical Analysis of CEO Employment Contracts: What Do Top Executives Bargain For?" *Washington and Lee Law Review* 63 (Winter 2006): 231–70.

Secunda, Paul M. "Toward the Viability of State-Based Legislation to Address Workplace Captive Audience Meetings in the United States." *Comparative Labor Law and Policy Journal* 29 (Winter 2008): 209–46.

Serrin, William. *Homestead: The Glory and Tragedy of an American Steel Town*. New York: Vintage Books, 1992.

Shapiro, Debra L., and Jeanne M. Brett. "What Is the Role of Control in Organizational Justice?" In Jerald Greenberg and Jason A. Colquit, eds., *Handbook of Organizational Justice*, 155–77. Mahwah, N.J.: Erlbaum, 2005.

Shipler, David K. *The Working Poor: Invisible in America*. New York: Alfred A. Knopf, 2004.

Short, Pamela Farley. "Counting and Characterizing the Uninsured." In Catherine G. McLaughlin, ed., *Health Policy and the Uninsured*, 1–34. Washington, D.C.: Urban Institute Press, 2004.

Shulman, Beth. *The Betrayal of Work: How Low-Wage Jobs Fail 30 Million Americans and Their Families*. New York: The New Press, 2003.

Siebert, Horst. "Labor Market Rigidities: At the Root of Unemployment in Europe." *Journal of Economic Perspectives* 11 (Summer 1997): 37-54.

Silver, Beverly J. *Forces of Labor: Workers' Movements and Globalization since 1870*. Cambridge: Cambridge University Press, 2003.

Simon, Howard A., and Yaroslav Sochynsky. "In-House Mediation of Employment Disputes: ADR for the 1990s." *Employee Relations Law Journal* 21 (Summer 1995): 29–52.

Sinyai, Clayton. *Schools of Democracy: A Political History of the American Labor Movement*. Ithaca, N.Y.: Cornell University Press, 2006.

Skolnick, Rochelle Gnagey. "Control, Collaboration or Coverage: The NLRA and the St. Paul Chamber Orchestra Dilemma." *Washington University Journal of Law and Policy* 20 (2006): 403–42.

Slater, Joseph E. "The 'American Rule' That Swallows the Exceptions." *Employee Rights and Employment Policy Journal* 11 (2007): 53–110.

Slaughter, Matthew J. "Globalization and Declining Unionization in the United States." *Industrial Relations* 46 (April 2007), 329–46.

Slichter, Sumner H. "The Organization and Control of Economic Activity." In Rexford Guy Tugwell, ed., *The Trend of Economics*, 301–55. New York: Knopf, 1924.

Smith, Adam. *An Inquiry into the Nature and Causes of the Wealth of Nations*. 1776. New York: Bantam Books, 2003.

Smith, W. Rand. *Crisis in the French Labour Movement: A Grassroots Perspective*. New York: St. Martin's Press, 1987.

Sobek, Matthew. "New Statistics on the U.S. Labor Force, 1850-1990." *Historical Methods* 34 (2001): 71-87.

Social Security Administration, "Annual Statistical Supplement to the Social Security Bulletin: 2005." Washington, D.C., 2006. http://www.ssa.gov/policy/docs/statcomps/supplement/2005 [accessed January 7, 2007].

Social Security Advisory Board. "Why Action Should Be Taken Soon." Washington, D.C., 2005. http://www.ssab.gov/documents/WhyActionShouldbe TakenSoon.pdf [accessed January 7, 2007].

Soley, Lawrence. *Censorship Inc.: The Corporate Threat to Free Speech in the United States*. New York: Monthly Review Press, 2002.

Solomon, Lewis D. "Perspectives on Human Nature and Their Implications for Business Organizations." *Fordham Urban Law Journal* 23 (Winter 1996): 221–56.

Spectar, J. M. "Pay Me Fairly, Kathie Lee! The WTO, The Right to a Living Wage, and a Proposed Protocol." *New York Law Journal of International and Comparative Law* 20 (2000): 61–92.

Spector, Paul E., et al. "Locus of Control and Well-Being at Work: How Generalizable Are Western Findings?" *Academy of Management Journal* 45 (April 2002): 453–66.

St. Antoine, Theodore J., "The Making of the Model Employment Termination Act." *Washington Law Review* 69 (April 1994): 361–82.

———. "A Seed Germinates: Unjust Discharge Reform Heads to Full Flower." *Nebraska Law Review* 67 (1988): 56–81.

———, ed. *The Common Law of the Workplace: The View of Arbitrators*. 2nd ed. Washington, D.C.: Bureau of National Affairs, 2005.

Steinfeld, Robert J. *Coercion, Contract, and Free Labor in the Nineteenth Century*. Cambridge: Cambridge University Press, 2001.

———. *The Invention of Free Labor: The Employment Relation in English and American Law and Culture, 1350–1870*. Chapel Hill: University of North Carolina Press, 1991.

Stempel, Jeffrey W. "Keeping Arbitrations from Becoming Kangaroo Courts." *Nevada Law Journal* 8 (Fall 2007): 251–70.

Stettner, Andrew, Rebecca Smith, and Rick McHugh. "Changing Workforce, Changing Economy: State Unemployment Insurance Reforms for the 21st Century." New York: National Employment Law Project, 2004.

Stieber, Jack. "Most U.S. Workers Still May Be Fired under the Employment-at-Will Doctrine." *Monthly Labor Review* 107 (May 1984): 34–38.

Stinson, Martha Harrison. "Estimating the Relationship Between Employer-Provided Health Insurance, Worker Mobility, and Wages." Technical Paper No. TP-2002-23. Washington, D.C.: U.S. Census Bureau, 2003.

Stone, Katherine Van Wezel. *From Widgets to Digits: Employment Regulation for the Changing Workplace*. Cambridge: Cambridge University Press, 2004.

———. "The Legacy of Industrial Pluralism: The Tension Between Individual Employment Rights and the New Deal Collective Bargaining System." *University of Chicago Law Review* 59 (Spring 1992): 575–644.

———. "Mandatory Arbitration of Individual Employment Rights: The Yellow Dog Contract of the 1990s." *Denver University Law Review* 73 (1996): 1017–50.

———. "The New Psychological Contract: Implications of the Changing Workplace for Labor and Employment Law." *UCLA Law Review* 48 (February 2001): 519–661.

Strauss, George. "Is the New Deal System Collapsing? With What May It Be Replaced?" *Industrial Relations* 34 (July 1995): 329–49.

Summers, Clyde W. "The Battle in Seattle: Free Trade, Labor Rights, and Societal Values." *University of Pennsylvania Journal of International Economic Law* 22 (Spring 2001): 61–90.

———. "Contingent Employment in the United States." *Comparative Labor Law and Policy Journal* 18 (Summer 1997): 503–22.

———. "Individual Protection Against Unjust Dismissal: Time for a Statute." *Virginia Law Review* 62 (April 1976): 481–532.

———. "Labor Law as the Century Turns: A Changing of the Guard." *Nebraska Law Review* 67 (1988): 7–27.

———. "Questioning the Unquestioned in Collective Labor Law." *Catholic University Law Review* 47 (Spring 1998): 791–823.

Sunstein, Cass R. *Republic.com*. Princeton, N.J.: Princeton University Press, 2001.

———. *The Second Bill of Rights: FDR's Unfinished Revolution and Why We Need It More Than Ever*. New York: Basic Books, 2004.

Takala, J. "Introductory Report: Decent Work–Safe Work," XVIth World Congress on Safety and Health at Work. Vienna, May 27, 2002. http://www.ilo.org/public/english/protection/safework/wD.C.ongrs/ilo_rep.pdf [accessed November 13, 2006].

Tanaka, Sakiko. "Parental Leave and Child Health Across OECD Countries." *Economic Journal* 115 (February 2005): F7-F28.

Taras, Daphne Gottlieb. "Collective Bargaining Regulation in Canada and the United States: Divergent Cultures, Divergent Outcomes." In Bruce E. Kaufman, ed., *Government Regulation of the Employment Relationship*, 295–342. Madison, Wisc.: Industrial Relations Research Association, 1997.

Taylor, Frederick Winslow. *The Principles of Scientific Management*. New York: Harper and Brothers, 1911.

Thompson, Paul, and Kirsty Newsome. "Labor Process Theory, Work, and the Employment Relation." In Bruce E. Kaufman, ed., *Theoretical Perspectives on Work and the Employment Relationship*, 133–62. Champaign, Ill.: Industrial Relations Research Association, 2004.

Thorsen, Dag Einar, and Amund Lie. "What Is Neoliberalism?" Unpublished paper, University of Oslo, 2007.

Thurber, Timothy N. *The Politics of Equality: Hubert Humphrey and the African American Freedom Struggle, 1945–1978*. New York: Columbia University Press, 1999.

Tobias, Paul H. "Defects in the Model Employment Termination Act." *Labor Law Journal* 43 (August 1992): 500–503.

Tomlins, Christopher L. *Law, Labor, and Ideology in the Early American Republic*. Cambridge: Cambridge University Press, 1993.

Trebilcock, Michael J., and Robert Howse. "Trade Policy and Labor Standards." *Minnesota Journal of Global Trade* 14 (Summer 2005): 261–300.

Troy, Leo. *Beyond Unions and Collective Bargaining*. Armonk, N.Y.: M. E. Sharpe, 1999.

Uhalde, Ray, et al. "Toward a National Workforce Education and Training Policy." Washington, D.C.: National Center on Education and the Economy, 2003.

United Nations. "Trends in the Total Migrant Stock: The 2005 Revision." POP/DB/MIG/Rev.2005. New York: 2006. http://esa.un.org/migration/ [accessed May 18, 2008].

———. *World Investment Report 2007*. New York, 2007.

United States Industrial Commission. *Report of the Industrial Commission on the Relations and Conditions of Capital and Labor Employed in Manufactures and General Business*. Vol. 7. Washington, D.C.: Government Printing Office, 1901.

U.S. Bureau of Labor Statistics. "Census of Fatal Occupational Injuries Summary, 2005." Washington, D.C.: U.S. Department of Labor, 2006. http://www.bls.gov/news.release/cfoi.nro.htm [accessed November 13, 2006].

———. "Comparative Civilian Labor Force Statistics, 10 Countries, 1960–2007." Washington, D.C.: U.S. Department of Labor, 2008. http://www.bls.gov/fls/ [accessed May 18, 2008].

———. "Employment Characteristics of Families in 2006." Washington, D.C.: U.S. Department of Labor, 2007. http://www.bls.gov/news.release/famee.toc.htm [accessed May 23, 2008].

———. "Employer Costs for Employee Compensation—December 2007." Washington, D.C.: U.S. Department of Labor, 2008. http://www.bls.gov/ncs/ect/home.htm [accessed May 18, 2008].

———. "International Comparisons of Manufacturing Productivity and Unit Labor Cost Trends." Washington, D.C.: U.S. Department of Labor, 2005. http://www.bls.gov/fls/ [accessed August 9, 2005].

———. "National Compensation Survey: Employee Benefits in Private Industry in the United States, March 2006." Summary 06–05. Washington, D.C.: U.S. Department of Labor, 2006.

———. "Union Members in 2007." Washington, D.C.: U.S. Department of Labor, 2008. http://www.bls.gov/news.release/union2.nro.htm [accessed May 14, 2008].

———. "Women in the Labor Force: A Databook." Report 985. Washington, D.C.: U.S. Department of Labor, 2005.

———. "Workers on Flexible and Shift Schedules in May 2004." Washington, D.C.: U.S. Department of Labor, 2005. http://www.bls.gov/news.release/flex.nro.htm [accessed May 27, 2008].

———. "Workplace Injuries and Illnesses in 2005." Washington, D.C.: U.S. Department of Labor, 2006. http://www.bls.gov/news.release/osh.nro.htm [accessed November 13, 2006].

U.S. Census Bureau. *Statistical Abstract of the United States*. Washington, D.C.: Government Printing Office, 2008.

U.S. General Accounting Office. "Collective Bargaining Rights: Information on the Number of Workers with and Without Bargaining Rights." GAO-02-835. Washington, D.C., 2002.

———. "Private Pensions: Issues of Coverage and Increasing Contribution Limits for Defined Contribution Plans." GAO-01-846. Washington, D.C., 2001.

U.S. Government Accountability Office. "Social Security Reform: Answers to Key Questions." GAO-05-193SP. Washington, D.C., 2005.

van Jaarsveld, Danielle D. "Overcoming Obstacles to Worker Representation: Insights from the Temporary Agency Workforce." *New York Law School Law Review* 50 (2005/2006): 355–84.

van Peijpe, Taco. "Employed or Self-Employed? The Role and Content of the Legal Distinction: Independent Contractors and Protected Workers in Dutch Law." *Comparative Labor Law and Policy Journal* 21 (Fall 1999): 141–55.

Vockrodt, Jeff. "Realizing the Need for and Logic of an Equal Pay Act for Temporary Workers." *Berkeley Journal of Employment and Labor Law* 14 (2005): 583–605.

Volokh, Eugene. "Freedom of Speech and Workplace Harassment." *UCLA Law Review* 39 (August 1992): 1791–872.

Vroom, Victor H. *Work and Motivation*. New York: Wiley, 1964.

Wainwright, David, and Michael Calnan. *Work Stress: The Making of a Modern Epidemic*. Buckingham, UK: Open University Press, 2002.

Waldfogel, Jane. "Family and Medical Leave: Evidence from the 2000 Surveys." *Monthly Labor Review* 124 (September 2001): 17–23.

Waltman, Jerold. *The Case for the Living Wage*. New York: Algora, 2004.

Warshawsky, Mark J., and John Ameriks. "How Prepared Are Americans for Retirement?" In Olivia S. Mitchell, P. Brett Hammond, and Anna M. Rappaport, eds., *Forecasting Retirement Needs and Retirement Wealth*, 33–67. Philadelphia: University of Pennsylvania Press, 2000.

Webb, Sidney, and Beatrice Webb. *Industrial Democracy*. London: Longmans, Green, 1897.

Weckert, John, ed. *Electronic Monitoring in the Workplace: Controversies and Solutions*. Hershey, Penn.: Idea Group, 2005.

Weil, David. "Are Mandated Health and Safety Committees Substitutes for or Supplements to Labor Unions?" *Industrial and Labor Relations Review* 52 (April 1999): 339–60.

———. "If OSHA Is So Bad, Why Is Compliance So Good?" *RAND Journal of Economics* 27 (Autumn 1996): 618–40.

———. "Individual Rights and Collective Agents: The Role of Old and New Workplace Institutions in the Regulation of Labor Markets." In Richard B. Freeman, Joni Hersch, and Lawrence Mishel, eds., *Emerging Labor Market Institutions for the Twenty-First Century*, 13–44. Chicago: University of Chicago Press, 2005.

Weil, David, et al. "The Effectiveness of Regulatory Disclosure Policies." *Journal of Policy Analysis and Management* 25 (Winter 2006): 155–81.

Weiler, Paul C. *Governing the Workplace: The Future of Labor and Employment Law*. Cambridge, Mass.: Harvard University Press, 1990.

———. "Hard Times for Unions: Challenging Times for Scholars." *University of Chicago Law Review* 58 (Summer 1991): 1015–32.

———. "A Principled Reshaping of Labor Law for the Twenty-First Century." *University of Pennsylvania Journal of Labor and Employment Law* 3 (Winter 2001): 177–206.

———. "Promises to Keep: Securing Workers' Rights to Self-Organization under the NLRA." *Harvard Law Review* 96 (June 1983): 1769–1827.

———. "Striking a New Balance: Freedom of Contract and the Prospects for Union Representation." *Harvard Law Review* 98 (December 1984): 351–420.

Weiss, Manfred. "Workers' Involvement in the European Company." In Marco

Biagi, ed., *Quality of Work and Employee Involvement in Europe*, 63–79. The Hague: Kluwer Law International, 2002.

Weiss, Marley S. "*Kentucky River* at the Intersection of Professional and Supervisory Status: Fertile Delta or Bermuda Triangle." In Laura J. Cooper and Catherine L. Fisk, eds., *Labor Law Stories*, 353–98. New York: Foundation Press, 2005.

———. "Two Steps Forward, One Step Back—Or Vice Versa: Labor Rights under Free Trade Agreements from NAFTA, Through Jordan, via Chile, to Latin America, and Beyond." *University of San Francisco Law Review* 37 (Spring 2003): 689–755.

Weissbrodt, David, and Muria Kruger. "Norms on the Responsibilities of Transnational Corporations and Other Business Enterprises with Regard to Human Rights." *American Journal of International Law* 97 (October 2003): 901–22.

Wesman, Daniel P. "The Significance of the Sarbanes-Oxley Whistleblower Provision." *Labor Lawyer* 21 (Fall 2005): 141–55.

Wever, Kirsten S. *Negotiating Competitiveness: Employment Relations and Organizational Innovation in Germany and the United States*. Boston: Harvard Business School Press, 1995.

Wheeler, Hoyt N. "Globalization and Business Ethics in Employment Relations." In John W. Budd and James G. Scoville, eds., *The Ethics of Human Resources and Industrial Relations*, 115–40. Champaign, Ill.: Labor and Employment Relations Association, 2005.

White House. "Strengthening Social Security for the 21st Century." Washington, D.C., 2005. http://www.whitehouse.gov/infocus/social-security/200501/strengthening-socialsecurity.html [accessed January 7, 2007].

Wiedenbeck, Peter J. "ERISA's Curious Coverage." *Washington University Law Quarterly* 76 (Spring 1998): 311–50.

Willborn, Steven L. "Workers in Troubled Firms: When Are (Should) They Be Protected?" *University of Pennsylvania Journal of Labor and Employment Law* 7 (Fall 2004): 35–53.

Wilthagen, Ton, and Frank Tros. "The Concept of 'Flexicurity': A New Approach to Regulating Employment and Labour Markets." *Transfer: European Review of Labour and Research* 10 (Summer 2004): 166–86.

Wingerd, Mary Lethert. *Claiming the City: Politics, Faith, and the Power of Place in St. Paul*. Ithaca, N.Y.: Cornell University Press, 2001.

Witte, Edwin E. *The Government in Labor Disputes*. New York: McGraw-Hill, 1932.

Wolf, Martin. *Why Globalization Works*. New Haven, Conn.: Yale University Press, 2004.

World Commission on the Social Dimension of Globalization. *A Fair Globalization: Creating Opportunities for All*. Geneva, 2004.

World Trade Organization. *International Trade Statistics 2007*. Geneva, 2007.

Wright, Erik Olin, ed., *Approaches to Class Analysis*. Cambridge: Cambridge University Press, 2005.

Yamada, David C. "Voices from the Cubicle: Protecting and Encouraging Private Employee Speech in the Post-Industrial Workplace." *Berkeley Journal of Employment and Labor Law* 19 (1998): 1–59.

Zabin, Carol, Arindrajit Dube, and Ken Jacobs. "The Hidden Public Costs of Low-Wage Jobs in California." *The State of California Labor* 4 (2004): 3–44.

Zhou, Jing. "When the Presence of Creative Coworkers Is Related to Creativity: Role of Supervisor Close Monitoring, Developmental Feedback, and Creative Personality." *Journal of Applied Psychology* 88 (May 2003): 413-22.

Zuberi, Dan. *Differences That Matter: Social Policy and the Working Poor in the United States and Canada*. Ithaca, N.Y.: Cornell University Press, 2006.

Zweig, Michael, ed. *What's Class Got to Do with It? American Society in the Twenty-First Century*. Ithaca, N.Y.: Cornell University Press, 2004.

About the Authors

STEPHEN F. BEFORT is the Gray, Plant, Mooty, Mooty, and Bennett Professor of Law at the University of Minnesota Law School. He holds a JD degree from the University of Minnesota and is the author of *Employment Law and Practice* (West Group) and more than sixty articles on labor and employment subjects, including more than thirty articles in leading law reviews and journals. He served as co-editor of the annually published *Proceedings of the National Academy of Arbitrators* (Bureau of National Affairs) from 2005 to 2008. He is a past secretary of the Labor and Employment Section of the American Bar Association, a member of the National Academy of Arbitrators, a member of the Labor Law Group, and a member of the Executive Board of the International Society for Labor Law and Social Security. Professor Befort practiced law in the labor and employment field extensively before joining the University of Minnesota Law School faculty in 1982, and he continues to serve as a frequent arbitrator of labor and employment disputes.

JOHN W. BUDD holds the Industrial Relations Land Grant Chair at the University of Minnesota's Carlson School of Management. He has a PhD in economics from Princeton University and is the author of the award-winning *Employment with a Human Face: Balancing Efficiency, Equity, and Voice* (Cornell University Press) and the award-winning *Labor Relations: Striking a Balance* (McGraw-Hill / Irwin). He has published over forty refereed journal articles and book chapters on employment-related topics in *Industrial and Labor Relations Review*, *Industrial Relations*, the *Journal of Labor Economics*, the *Review of Economics and Statistics*, the *British*

Journal of Industrial Relations, and other journals and edited volumes. He is on the editorial boards of the *British Journal of Industrial Relations*, *Industrial and Labor Relations Review*, and *WorkingUSA*. From 1998 to 2008, Professor Budd was also director of graduate studies for the University of Minnesota's graduate programs in Human Resources and Industrial Relations.

Index